PUZZLES

SHARPER BRAIN

BRIGHTER FUTURE

KALMAN TOTH M.A. M.PHIL.

Brain Puzzles

ISBN: 9781731194909

FASCINATING LANGUAGE, WORD, PICTURE, MATH & LOGIC PUZZLES, QUIZZES, BRAIN TEASERS & HOLLYWOOD TRIVIA TO IMPROVE VOCABULARY, VISUAL QUICKNESS, SHORT-TERM MEMORY, MULTI-TASKING, TIME MANAGEMENT & INTELLIGENCE (IQ).

CONTENTS AT A GLANCE

KEEPING THE BRAIN FIT 1

TV SHOWS WORD SEARCH PUZZLES 6

FUN BRAIN TEASERS 32

U.S. CITIZENSHIP QUIZZES 131

MINI CROSSWORD SQUARES 142

HOLLYWOOD STARS MOVIES SEARCH 180

DIAGONAL WORD SQUARE PUZZLES 208

HOLLYWOOD MOVIE TRIVIA QUIZZES 234

MATH DRILLS TO KEEP YOUR BRAIN SPINNING 262

SUDOKU LOGIC PUZZLES 292

SHOPPING MATH PUZZLES 330

AIRLINE TRAVEL MATH PUZZLES 346

MINI CROSSWORD SQUARE SOLUTIONS 358

DIAGONAL WORD SQUARE PUZZLE SOLUTIONS 370

SUDOKU LOGIC PUZZLE SOLUTIONS 379

PICTURE PUZZLE SOLUTIONS 387

MARTIAN "LANDING" SITE MARKER

It is real! Where is it located?

ANSWER: YESREJ WEN ,NOITCNUJ NOTECNIRP

Find & Circle 1 BULL or 1 BEAR in Each Quadrant

U	L	L	L	B	L	L	U	A	A	R	E	R	R	R	R	U	B	L	U	B	L	L	L
B	L	U	U	B	L	U	L	R	B	E	B	R	E	E	B	B	L	L	U	L	B	U	B
U	L	L	L	U	L	L	L	B	E	E	B	B	B	R	A	B	B	L	U	B	L	U	L
U	L	L	L	B	L	L	B	A	E	A	B	E	E	E	R	L	L	L	L	L	L	L	U
L	U	B	L	L	L	L	U	B	B	E	R	B	R	B	B	L	U	B	U	U	L	U	L
L	L	B	L	B	U	U	B	B	R	B	E	B	B	E	A	L	U	L	U	L	L	B	L
L	B	L	L	L	U	L	L	R	A	A	R	A	E	R	E	L	U	L	U	U	B	B	B
B	L	U	B	L	L	B	L	R	R	A	B	E	E	B	E	U	L	L	U	L	U	L	L
E	A	E	R	B	B	B	B									R	E	R	E	E	E	R	B
R	R	B	A	E	B	B	R									R	E	E	R	A	R	R	R
R	B	B	R	B	A	A	B									E	R	R	A	B	B	B	A
R	R	R	R	R	A	A	B									B	R	A	B	R	R	A	A
R	B	B	B	R	R	E	B									R	B	B	E	R	R	B	A
A	B	A	R	R	A	E	R									B	B	B	R	B	R	E	R
A	E	R	R	E	A	E	E									A	A	A	E	A	R	R	E
A	R	B	B	A	A	A	B									E	E	E	R	E	B	E	B
B	B	L	U	L	B	U	L									U	L	L	L	L	U	U	L
B	U	B	B	L	L	U	L									B	B	U	L	U	L	U	L
L	L	B	B	B	L	B	L									L	L	L	L	U	L	B	L
B	U	U	L	L	L	L	U									L	L	B	B	U	B	B	L
L	B	B	L	L	L	L	L									B	L	U	L	B	L	L	B
B	L	L	B	L	L	B	L									U	L	B	L	L	L	B	U
U	L	L	L	B	U	L	B									U	U	L	L	L	L	L	L
U	U	L	B	L	L	B	B									U	L	U	B	B	B	U	B
A	B	R	R	R	R	A	B	L	B	B	B	U	B	L	U	R	E	R	R	E	A	E	A
E	E	B	B	E	R	R	R	B	U	U	L	L	L	L	L	B	B	B	B	R	R	B	B
A	R	E	R	E	E	A	E	B	B	L	U	U	L	L	L	R	B	E	B	E	A	E	E
B	B	R	E	R	A	R	R	L	L	B	L	U	B	L	B	A	A	B	E	E	R	B	A
A	A	A	E	E	B	R	R	L	U	B	B	L	U	B	U	R	A	A	E	R	B	E	B
A	A	E	R	A	A	B	E	L	L	U	L	L	L	B	U	R	R	B	E	E	R	B	A
E	B	A	E	E	B	E	A	U	B	U	U	U	U	L	L	R	E	B	A	B	E	B	R
R	E	E	A	B	B	B	B	L	U	L	L	U	L	L	L	E	A	A	B	R	E	E	R

Quizzes on the Lighter Side

Find the answer by thinking or looking on the web

1. Martians from the Red Planet landed and invaded Princeton Junction, NJ. The US Army is mobilized to confront the aliens. How can American soldiers tell who is Earthling or Martian?

____

2. A few golden eagles fly toward the salmon rush feast on the Yukon River in Alaska. Aerial fight breaks out for the few trees on the river bank. One eagle has no tree left to settle on. If two eagles settle on each tree, one tree would be left free. How many eagles & how many trees?

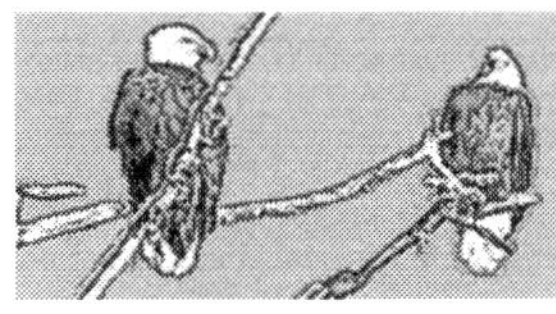

____

3. When the castle tower clock struck midnight, Cinderella ran down the stairs at the prince's palace and lost what?

____

4. Zip-a-dee-doo-dah, zip-a-dee-ay; My, oh, my, what a ___ day; Plenty of ___ headin' my way; Zip-a-dee-doo-dah, zip-a-dee-ay! What are the missing 2 words?

____

5. What is the name of Snowman in Disney's "Frozen" which was inspired by Hans Christian Andersen's fairy tale "The Snow Queen"?

____

6. Disney's computer-animated feature "Tangled", based on the fairy tale "Rapunzel" by Brothers Grimm, stars a character with exceptionally long what?

____

7. What were the names of the characters in the original "The Three Stooges", an American vaudeville and comedy team?

____

8. "Davy, Davy Crockett, King of the Wild Frontier", who died heroically at the Alamo, wore a famous hat with a tail, made out of the fur of this animal?

____

9. The "Little Engine That Could", in a children's locomotive story, said this as he tried to go up on a steep railroad incline. Hint: Not "I am out of steam".

____

10. The Fort at Niagara Falls, the oldest continuously occupied military site in North America, was originally built by this nation in 1678.

____

11. Pippi Longstocking, the main superhumanly strong character in a series of children's books by the Swedish author Astrid Lindgren, like Peter Pan did not want to do this.

____

12. When the US landed 2 astronauts on the Moon in 1969, Neil Armstrong said: "One small step for man, one giant leap for mankind." Was the American flag waving in the wind?

____

ANSWERS: 1. sesnecil gnivird der evah snaitraM 2. seert eerht dna selgae ruoF 3.)eohs(reppils ssalG 4. enihsnus ,lufrednoW 5. falO 6. riah lacigaM 7. ylruC & yrraL ,eoM 8. nooccaR 9. nac I kniht I 10. hcnerF 11. pu worG 12. dniw on dna erehpsomta on sah nooM eht ,oN

ALL THAT GLITTERS IS NOT ____.

Name the items based on the pictures. They all start with the same metal.

1.

____

5.

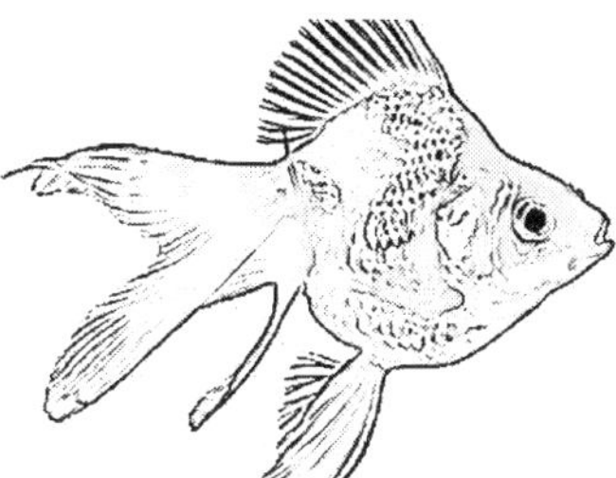

____

2.

____

6.

____

3.

____

7.

____

4.

____

8.

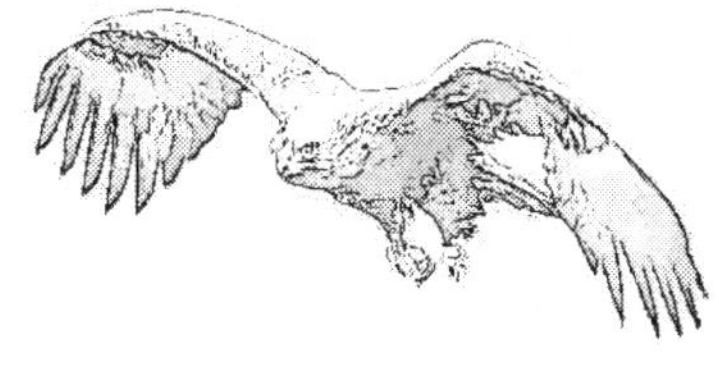

____

ANSWERS. 1. NOILLUB DLOG 2. HSUR DLOG 3. LADEM DLOG 4. NIOC DLOG 5. HSIFDLOG 6. REGGID DLOG 7. ENIM DLOG 8. ELGAE NEDLOG

USA & WYOMING ROAD WELCOME SIGNS

IS THE USA WELCOME LOCATED ON THE MEXICAN OR CANADIAN BORDER?
WHAT FAMOUS NATIONAL PARK IS LOCATED IN WYOMING?

ANSWERS: REDROB NAIDANAC; ENOTSWOLLEY

Musical Magic Quizzes

All the questions related to famous musicals.

1. The Lord above gave man an arm of iron / But, with a little bit of luck, with a little bit of luck / Someone else will do the blinkin' work?

____

2. In this life, one thing counts / In the bank, large amounts / I'm afraid these don't grow on trees, / You've got to pick-a-pocket or two?

____

3. I wanted to marry her when I saw the moonlight shining on the barrel of her father's shotgun?

____

4. Before a cat will condescend / To treat you as a trusted friend / Some little token of esteem / Is needed, like a dish of cream?

____

5. I have my own washing machine / What will you have not to keep clean / Skyscrapers bloom in America / Cadillacs zoom in America / Industry boom in America?

____

6. Typical isn't it? You wait 20 years for a dad and then three come along at once?

____

7. It's just life, so keep dancing through... It's time to trust my instincts, close my eyes, and leap?

____

8. And you, Scarecrow, have the affrontery to ask for a brain, you billowing bale of bovine fodder?

____

9. Wendy, one girl is more use than twenty boys?

____

10. I'm your Hairy Dogfather... Oh! I mean, your Fairy Godmother?

____

11. It doesn't matter if you win or lose, it's what you do with your dancin' shoes?

____

12. Give 'em the old razzle dazzle / Razzle Dazzle 'em / Give 'em an act with lots of flash in it / And the reaction will be passionate?

____

ANSWERS: 1. YDAL RIAF YM 2. !REVILO 3. !AMOHALKO 4. STAC 5. YROTS EDIS TSEW 6. !AIM AMMAM 7. DEKCIW 8. ZO FO DRAZIW 9. .NAP RETEP 10. ALLEREDNIC 11. ESAERG 12. OGACIHC

4x4 Mini Crossword Squares

Fill-in the missing letters

Puzzle 1. WILD WEST COWBOYS

			G
		N	
	A		
P			

Row 1: A piece of metal used as a step in a ladder.
Row 2: Pigs do it.
Row 3: Product label has it.
Row 4: A large tasty freshwater fish.
Diagonal: To be carried on a horse.
Left Column: To play roughly.

Puzzle 2. SEMI JACKKNIFE

			E
		E	
	E		
S			

Row 1: To view at with side glances.
Row 2: Tractor trailer has a lot.
Row 3: Columbus dreaded it.
Row 4: An overzealous celebrity fan.
Diagonal: Bulls and cows.
Left Column: Used to propel boats.

Puzzle 3. QUEEN MARY 2

Row 1: Revise a document.
Row 2: A very large group of soldiers.
Row 3: A very large boat that crosses the seas.
Row 4: Other; one beside.
Diagonal: One of the Great Lakes.
Left Column: Freedom from worry.

Puzzle 4. DOG & CAT

			Y
		T	
	I		
D			

Row 1: A flat piece of plastic to carry food.
Row 2: Healthy cereal.
Row 3: He points his gun toward the hyenas.
Row 4: Dreadful; terrible.
Diagonal: Able to live with human beings.
Left Column: Looks like a frog.

1. RUNG, OINK, MADE, PIKE 2. OGLE, AXES, REEF, STAN 3. EDIT, ARMY, SHIP, ELSE 4. TRAY, OATS, AIMS, DIRE

KEEPING THE BRAIN FIT

Millions of people go to gyms, fitness centers and parks or participate in sports everyday to keep their body & soul fit. Millions of people diet to get rid of excess fat. Yet the same millions may not be paying attention to their brain, which is the greatest and most essential asset we have. While a neglected body shows visually, a neglected brain is hidden inside the skull. An agile brain is necessary for learning, performing at work and making the right business decisions. A higher intelligence and sharper mind may also help us to succeed in inter-personal relationships.

God gave the average man or woman an IQ of 150. Yet in practice most people's IQ level is around 120. Some may be as low as 100. A chimpanzee's IQ is 80, equivalent to the IQ of a four 4 year old child. Some of us are very fortunate to have professions or life interests that require the use of brainpower, but for most of us extra exercises are necessary to keep our minds sharp. The human brain is similar to other organs in one respect: you use it or lose it. Daily life forces to use a certain minimal amount of brain function. We know from our school years, that the human brain is capable of much more than the minimal requirements of everyday life.

The goal of this mixed puzzles book is to provide brain fitness exercises for adults and seniors. The human brain is a very complex instrument and must be challenged in many ways. It is anticipated that the readers' IQ may advance from 120 to 140 by working through to the end of this book. How about the final 10 points necessary to climb to God-given IQ of 150? For that you may need to do brain challenging activities beyond this book: reading, studying science & engineering, programming computers, crossword puzzles, watching movies & TV trivia shows and learning new skills. It is very important to try all different kinds of puzzles to motivate every area of our brains. Some puzzles use only certain areas of the brain, for example, finding missing letters in words requires a dictionary search in our brain. We can be pretty organized about it, like a computer, trying all 26 letters of the alphabet.

This puzzle book is designed to keeping your brain active in an entertaining and often humorous way. Recent scientific research has shown that keeping the brain active with a mixture puzzles of various types can lead to a longer, more fulfilling life and reduce the chances of Alzheimer's Disease, Parkinson's Disease, memory loss & dementia associated with advanced age. In the case of a stroke, daily puzzle solving can be instrumental in recovering some of the brain's normal functions quickly.

The left side of brain is the analytical side, responsible for logic, science and mathematics. Interestingly enough, it also controls the right side of the body. The right side of the brain is in charge of creativity and the arts. It also controls the left side of the body.

Both types of thinking are required in order to solve picture puzzles, crossword & word search puzzles. Thus using both sides of the brain at the same time, we create connections between the left and right brain hemispheres. These connections are important requirements for learning, discovering and remembering. During puzzle solving the production of dopamine increases. This element is essential for the proper functioning of brain cells. (In Parkinson's disease dopamine levels drop.)

The major puzzle groups in this book are: language, math, logic, picture puzzles, quizzes and brain teasers. Puzzles with grids and graphics are especially good for improving short-term visual memory. Puzzles help us develop brain skills to solve problems quickly and innovatively and to communicate clearheaded ideas. These skills are greatly valued intellectual assets in the job marketplace. Trial & error, alternative approaches, creating theories, testing hypotheses, learning from experience, performing calculations and changing our point of views are required brain processes whether solving a word search puzzle or even perhaps designing a mission to Mars!

Enjoy the puzzles while boosting your brainpower – I'll look for you on Mars!!

ELEPHANT SANCTUARY PINNAWALA, SRI LANKA (CEYLON)

What is the meaning of two young elephants locking trunks?

ANSWER: GNITEERG & NOITCEFFA

PICTURE PUZZLE 1. GEORGE WASHINGTON BRIDGE ON 4TH OF JULY

PICTURE PUZZLE 1. FIND & CIRCLE THE TEN DIFFERENCES

TV SHOWS WORD SEARCH PUZZLES

How to Solve Word Search Puzzles

Brain health benefits of word search puzzle solving

Your IQ may be 150 (brilliant thinker), but you will never know it if you don't exercise your brain. You may be operating your brain at the 110 IQ level (understand prices & discounts in a supermarket). Word search puzzle solving is one kind of cognitive therapy work out which is good for the brain. Word searches are fun & educational once you get the hang of how to solve them. They also bring a number of direct & indirect benefits you may not realize. Puzzle solving can play an important role in keeping you mentally fit for business, work, family and social life. Don't let anyone tell you that puzzles - word searches, word scrambles, diagonal word squares, missing letters, crosswords, Sudokus - are nothing more than mechanical amusement. Scientific studies have shown that word search puzzle solving can help improve short term memory, attention, pattern recognition, vocabulary, and overall mental sharpness. Solving word puzzles has immeasurable benefits for everyday life, and those benefits extend well beyond the following list.

Benefits of Solving Word Search Puzzles

- A fun way to keep you mentally active and fit
- Improved word power and vocabulary
- Effortless educational spelling exercise
- A great way to expand the vocabulary; learn words and spelling in English

- An enjoyable & challenging word game puzzle for people with dyslexia
- Apply puzzle solving methods to solve real life problems
- Word search puzzle solving accentuates pattern recognition, a key cognitive function of the brain to create meaning, order & rules from often confusing data around us
- Enhanced pattern recognition skills are useful in driving an automobile, analyzing stock market data, dealing with information overload and many other areas of daily life
- Smartphone Charging Stations or expensive batteries are not required
- A fun activity which can be done by a couple or two family members to solve the word search puzzle together
- Group competition for fastest solution can be setup by duplicating a page or cutting out pages from the book for each person in the game
- Easy on the pocket, portable -airline travel, cruise ship, beach, camping, waiting room - entertainment
- Our brains reward us with a surge of dopamine (specialized brain cell - reward molecule) when we find a word which in turn will keep us motivated in other areas of our everyday lives
- The AARP, the Alzheimer's Association & American Parkinson Disease Association recommend that puzzle solving should be part of a brain healthy lifestyle

Strategy One: Scan in each row, column & diagonal

This method is well-organized and guarantees finding all words in the puzzle. You don't leave anything to chance; you cover each row, column & diagonal methodically. If a word list is not provided with the puzzle, this is the only method to find the words. You may use a finger, smart phone/smart tablet stylus pen, a retracted ball-point pen or the non-writing end of regular pen or pencil to help guide your search. You may also use a ruler to focus on the current row, column or diagonal. When you find a word, circle it or mark it with a highlighter pen. Also checkmark the word found on the provided word list if any. Here is the full scanning method:

- Start at the top row of the grid, and look from left to right in each row
- Do it again from the bottom right to top row, finding words placed backwards horizontally
- Start at the left column, and look from top to bottom in each column
- Do it again from the right column, finding words bottom to top placed backwards vertically
- Start looking for diagonally placed words from top left corner(\), first looking from top to bottom in each upper-left to lower-right diagonal, then bottom to top finding words placed backwards diagonally
- Finally go through looking for diagonally placed words in the same manner from top right corner(/), first looking from top to bottom in each top right to bottom left diagonal, then bottom to top finding words placed backwards diagonally

Strategy Two: Search word by word

You may enjoy the casual searching strategy more if you find the methodical grid scan above boring. The word by word search strategy however is typically slower than the full puzzle grid scan. You select a word from the list and scan the puzzle to find the word left to right, right to left, top down, down up, and on the diagonals forward and backward. Occasionally, you may get stuck and cannot find a word, then you can be methodical and start from top left of the puzzle grid and look for every occurrence of the first letter of that word in the grid, then move out from that letter in all directions – left, right, up, down, diagonally up & down (eight surrounding letters) - until you discover the letter that is part of that word.

Helpful word find tips:

- Search for less-frequent letters in the English language, such as W, Y, B, V, K, X, J, Q, or Z
- Search the puzzle grid for double letters in a list word, such as LL, SS, EE, FF, OO, MM, TT, ZZ, NN, II, RR, DD, GG, or BB
- Start with the longer words, they are easier to spot
- Look for round & easy to spot letters, especially O, D, Q, U, X, and Z
- If you don't find a word forward, try the reverse e.g. NODNOL for LONDON
- Checkmark the words on the provided word list as you find them

This book has wide inner margins for easier readability. You may cut out a page for convenient puzzle solving on a flat surface.
Have fun, get smarter, be successful and achieve your God-given IQ potential!

The following page displays an example for word search puzzle solution.

WORD SEARCH SOLUTION EXAMPLE

TV Show Puzzle 11 Solution: Keeping Up Appearances

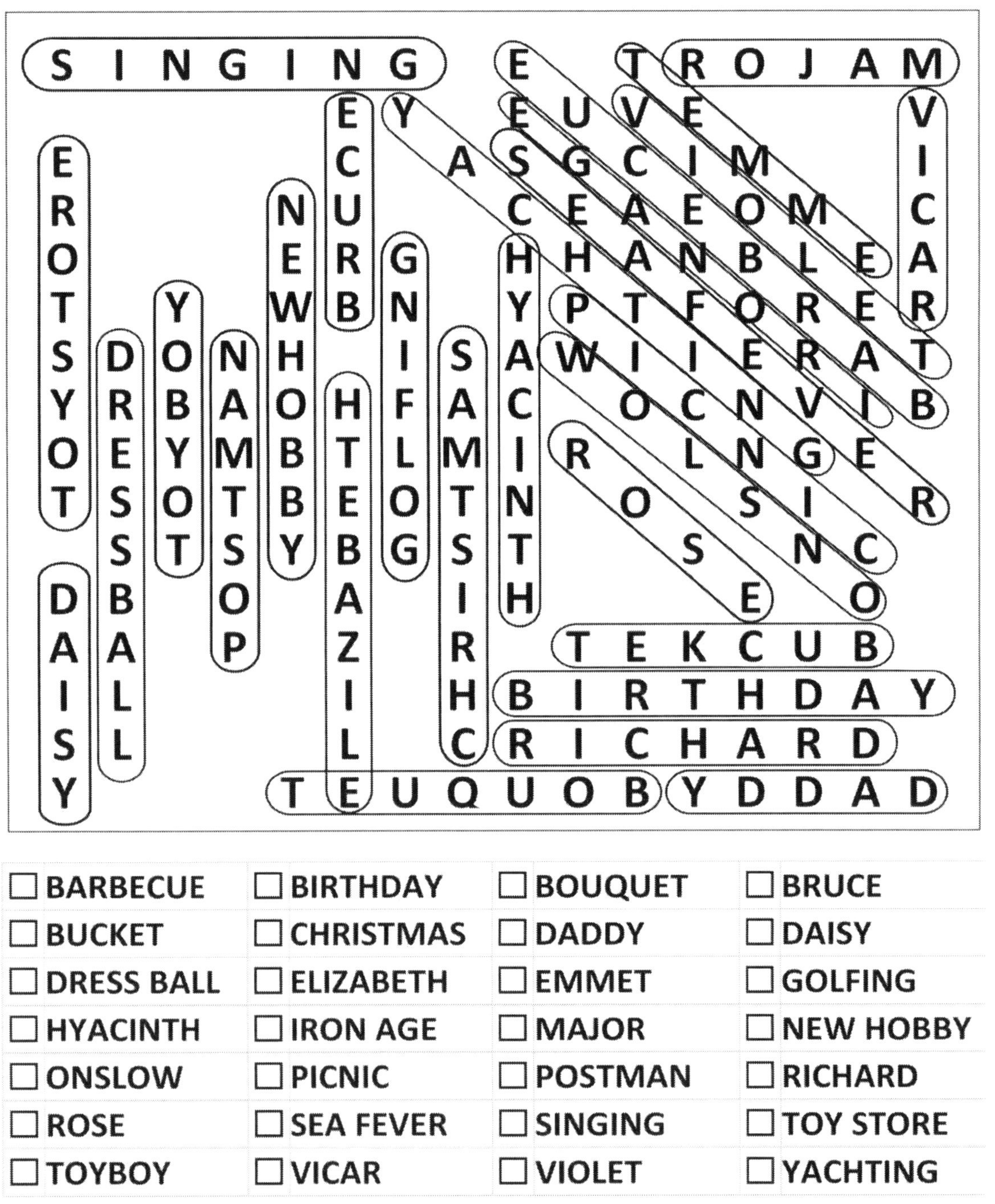

☐ BARBECUE	☐ BIRTHDAY	☐ BOUQUET	☐ BRUCE
☐ BUCKET	☐ CHRISTMAS	☐ DADDY	☐ DAISY
☐ DRESS BALL	☐ ELIZABETH	☐ EMMET	☐ GOLFING
☐ HYACINTH	☐ IRON AGE	☐ MAJOR	☐ NEW HOBBY
☐ ONSLOW	☐ PICNIC	☐ POSTMAN	☐ RICHARD
☐ ROSE	☐ SEA FEVER	☐ SINGING	☐ TOY STORE
☐ TOYBOY	☐ VICAR	☐ VIOLET	☐ YACHTING

Fun Puzzle 1 : Cheers

TED DANSON
SHELLY LONG

E	H	R	C	Q	N	A	C	C	E	B	E	R	Y	X	J
I	R	A	E	O	C	C	E	S	E	V	W	A	O	M	W
H	E	O	R	N	O	E	R	Y	W	Y	D	S	N	A	N
T	D	M	C	A	W	E	U	B	K	Y	D	O	R	S	A
I	F	S	C	S	B	O	Y	M	A	E	T	A	R	L	V
L	S	H	S	M	G	E	M	M	R	S	B	A	R	Z	M
I	K	J	A	E	N	I	V	D	O	A	L	A	T	A	Z
L	B	H	E	O	R	I	B	B	I	U	C	L	L	N	S
E	C	A	M	L	Y	T	F	R	G	A	I	O	F	I	U
D	S	H	R	P	O	E	I	E	E	A	N	A	W	C	Q
K	Y	R	C	T	I	T	R	A	T	E	P	E	E	K	L
U	D	R	I	L	E	T	H	K	W	F	U	P	G	N	P
Z	O	U	E	A	L	N	C	A	R	E	F	S	Z	A	Z
T	O	R	U	K	F	O	D	H	R	A	V	I	N	M	A
V	W	F	M	T	C	F	A	E	E	I	I	O	L	E	Z
M	C	H	E	Z	P	H	A	A	R	R	O	V	L	C	V

☐ AFFAIRS	☐ BAR	☐ BARTENDER	☐ BIG SCORE
☐ BOSTON	☐ CARLA	☐ CHAMBERS	☐ CLIFF
☐ COACH	☐ COCKTAIL	☐ DIANE	☐ LILITH
☐ LOTHARIO	☐ LOVE	☐ MALONE	☐ MAYDAY
☐ MONEY	☐ NICKNAME	☐ NORM	☐ OWNER
☐ PITCHER	☐ REBECCA	☐ RED SOX	☐ REGULAR
☐ RELIEF	☐ SAM	☐ WAITRESS	☐ WOODY

Fun Puzzle 2 : I Love Lucy

LUCILLE BALL

S	L	O	P	L	O	V	E	Z	R	E	L	N	W	H	L
N	A	I	V	I	V	T	Y	E	E	W	Z	V	Y	E	V
C	K	C	F	V	H	N	T	G	L	A	P	E	N	V	V
R	I	R	A	E	A	H	A	U	N	W	L	N	A	T	T
V	E	N	L	B	G	I	C	R	R	W	E	U	R	W	R
D	C	I	U	U	R	I	A	E	A	I	D	Z	I	I	O
E	T	C	A	R	L	Q	D	R	D	E	I	L	C	E	P
I	N	L	A	L	H	A	F	E	V	B	L	A	D	Z	I
I	E	M	E	W	E	R	M	I	W	I	R	N	L	B	C
M	M	Q	K	L	Y	O	L	O	A	D	O	L	I	N	A
N	T	V	D	C	C	L	H	M	O	L	A	E	S	E	N
M	R	N	U	G	E	S	V	T	B	B	Z	Y	E	W	A
I	A	L	M	E	M	M	Y	A	W	A	R	D	D	Y	Z
B	P	P	D	A	E	H	D	E	R	D	Q	E	D	O	S
B	A	J	V	G	C	Y	M	Z	L	E	D	O	M	R	P
K	N	V	Y	K	C	I	R	T	K	S	F	W	J	K	V

☐ APARTMENT	☐ ARNAZ	☐ BALL	☐ BANDLEADER
☐ BLONDE	☐ COMEDIENNE	☐ CUBAN	☐ DESI
☐ EMMY AWARD	☐ ETHEL	☐ FRAWLEY	☐ FRED
☐ LAUGHTER	☐ LOVE	☐ LUCILLE	☐ LUCY
☐ MARRIAGE	☐ MODEL	☐ NEW YORK	☐ REDHEAD
☐ RICARDO	☐ RICKY	☐ SHOWBIZ	☐ TROPICANA
☐ VANCE	☐ VAUDEVILLE	☐ VIVIAN	☐ WILLIAM

Fun Puzzle 3 : M*A*S*H

ALAN ALDA

M	I	L	I	T	A	R	Y	C	D	Y	S	H	C	H	U
H	G	S	Q	W	R	U	B	U	O	O	D	T	S	Y	C
A	O	B	S	A	I	H	C	O	K	L	C	E	N	A	Y
H	P	T	D	E	L	N	E	A	T	L	O	T	M	E	M
A	L	A	L	R	S	N	C	L	L	T	I	N	O	O	T
W	R	E	L	I	A	R	Y	H	I	A	O	N	E	R	C
K	W	G	R	M	P	M	U	M	E	C	N	M	G	L	S
E	N	R	R	K	O	S	A	N	E	S	O	A	S	E	C
Y	M	E	N	I	A	C	O	V	O	N	T	P	L	U	R
E	H	I	Z	M	D	Y	E	O	D	F	E	E	T	D	P
S	H	D	K	O	R	E	A	N	W	A	R	U	R	E	A
N	V	K	I	E	S	L	A	T	I	P	S	O	H	D	R
J	V	S	G	A	Y	V	V	L	A	C	I	D	E	M	T
T	Y	R	I	W	M	Y	O	P	E	R	A	T	I	O	N
Z	U	B	I	G	M	A	C	J	S	J	M	A	J	O	R
S	Q	J	G	U	E	M	S	E	L	R	A	H	C	F	N

☐ ALAN ALDA	☐ BIG MAC	☐ BOTTOMS UP	☐ CHARLES
☐ COLONEL	☐ COMEDY	☐ DOCTORS	☐ DRAMA
☐ EMMYS	☐ ENEMY	☐ HAWK EYE	☐ HELICOPTER
☐ HOSPITAL	☐ HOT LIPS	☐ KLINGER	☐ KOREAN WAR
☐ MAJOR	☐ MASH	☐ MEDICAL	☐ MILITARY
☐ NOVOCAINE	☐ NURSES	☐ OPERATION	☐ RADAR
☐ SHERMAN	☐ SURGERY	☐ TENTS	☐ WINCHESTER

Fun Puzzle 4 : Friends

E G L Y U L M M F R I P J O E Y
H S R N N P A L A L E B L A N C
E G U E S N A S L N Y L V S W K
O I H O E S U R T E H Z L Q B E
O E O Z H N S F T N H A B E K Q
R Y D B J L T C C I I C T L G I
I W A I N E L N R H E G A T C Y
S C N J V A A O E E A S H R A H
K S S O M M C L D M A N G T M N
Y E F R T Y O I O G T M D N B O
A I R O E S E R N U N R E L I K
F L I S J D I A P O S I A R E B
F L E S O K S N O O M Y D P O R
U U N F O O T B A L L A U D A D
B B D F A K E P A R T Y J C E N
V Y S O V T R I B B I A N I N W

☐ ANISTON	☐ APARTMENT	☐ BING	☐ BUFFAY
☐ BULLIES	☐ CHANDLER	☐ DOLLHOUSE	☐ FAKE PARTY
☐ FLASHBACK	☐ FOOTBALL	☐ FRIENDS	☐ FUNNY
☐ GELLER	☐ GREEN	☐ JEALOUSY	☐ JOEY
☐ LASAGNAS	☐ LAST NIGHT	☐ LEBLANC	☐ MANHATTAN
☐ MONICA	☐ PARTIES	☐ PROM VIDEO	☐ RACHEL
☐ ROSS	☐ SCREAMER	☐ TRIBBIANI	☐ WEDDING

Fun Puzzle 5 : The Big Bang Theory

L	A	N	Z	N	Y	T	T	I	K	T	F	O	S	B	H
Y	G	P	L	A	I	V	Y	B	E	S	R	F	D	E	A
G	S	N	F	I	Z	E	L	L	S	C	T	W	H	M	R
N	H	P	I	N	F	Z	T	Z	O	C	N	U	N	L	R
A	E	D	P	K	E	E	Y	S	T	V	I	E	A	L	A
B	L	L	U	P	W	D	T	B	N	I	E	S	I	R	F
G	D	R	E	O	S	A	R	T	E	I	W	C	Y	C	T
I	O	N	Y	O	E	E	H	A	E	T	E	O	A	H	S
B	N	M	O	J	N	G	T	P	G	D	A	Z	L	R	P
H	H	Y	V	T	I	A	B	A	A	B	A	T	Y	O	H
A	O	C	N	N	A	R	R	A	M	S	R	N	E	M	W
V	U	W	E	N	C	E	E	D	Z	M	A	E	R	S	A
R	M	T	A	T	E	I	H	L	F	I	O	D	H	E	T
Z	A	I	B	R	L	P	M	W	W	D	N	O	E	G	B
D	E	R	E	T	D	A	T	S	F	O	H	G	R	N	Y
C	O	O	P	E	R	Z	C	G	I	C	F	R	A	B	A

☐ AMY	☐ BAZINGA	☐ BERNADETTE	☐ BETA TEST
☐ BIG BANG	☐ CALTECH	☐ COOPER	☐ DATE NIGHT
☐ EINSTEIN	☐ FARRAH	☐ FOWLER	☐ HAWKING
☐ HERB GARDEN	☐ HOFSTADTER	☐ HOWARD	☐ LEONARD
☐ LOVE CAR	☐ PASADENA	☐ PENNY	☐ PHYSICS
☐ ROOMMATES	☐ SCIENCE	☐ SHELDON	☐ SOFT KITTY
☐ STUART	☐ WHEATON	☐ WOLOWITZ	☐ ZAZZY

Fun Puzzle 6 : As Time Goes By

JUDI DENCH

Z	V	L	S	J	A	I	A	B	Q	S	E	Y	C	P	Y
S	T	E	U	V	R	D	T	L	A	S	S	C	R	D	L
U	A	T	Q	Z	R	E	R	L	I	O	V	O	M	I	Y
C	I	T	N	A	M	O	R	R	N	S	P	V	O	U	C
R	T	E	I	V	C	E	P	O	L	O	T	N	V	I	N
R	M	R	V	K	S	R	O	C	S	G	E	A	F	E	E
I	M	A	O	I	U	T	N	A	D	L	G	V	I	C	G
L	I	N	U	S	J	A	L	N	B	B	W	F	Y	R	A
O	Z	R	O	U	E	Z	E	O	R	E	N	O	S	I	B
V	C	M	D	J	S	Y	Y	I	D	E	C	L	I	A	E
E	Z	I	R	A	P	F	T	D	W	E	I	D	T	F	S
R	P	O	N	P	R	I	I	H	A	K	N	F	C	F	R
S	O	D	A	I	S	N	O	E	E	A	C	L	O	A	U
P	Y	H	E	H	G	B	R	N	E	Y	I	A	M	Z	N
C	E	N	Q	C	B	O	Y	J	O	O	P	M	C	A	L
Z	D	R	I	Y	K	A	S	T	A	L	K	E	R	S	O

☐ AFFAIR	☐ AGENCY	☐ ALISTAIR	☐ BOYFRIEND
☐ BRITISH	☐ CRUISE	☐ HAPPY END	☐ JEAN
☐ JUDI	☐ KENYA	☐ KOREA	☐ LETTER
☐ LIONEL	☐ LOVERS	☐ NEW HOBBY	☐ NURSE
☐ OLD FLAME	☐ PICNIC	☐ POOR JEAN	☐ PROPOSAL
☐ ROCK ON	☐ ROMANTIC	☐ SANDY	☐ SITCOM
☐ STALKER	☐ SURPRISE	☐ TOO NOSY	☐ WEDDING

Fun Puzzle 7 : Two and a Half Men

CHARLIE SHEEN

O	C	M	B	R	O	E	K	A	J	A	S	S	P	H	A
R	O	A	C	H	A	R	L	I	E	R	L	E	G	K	F
O	N	S	L	O	M	B	B	B	J	N	Z	A	N	Q	G
S	A	H	M	I	M	Y	E	G	R	Q	O	I	N	O	G
E	I	E	T	R	F	P	Q	A	C	O	D	T	S	N	J
I	P	E	B	E	E	O	O	V	C	Y	T	C	H	S	Z
Q	G	N	A	J	A	Y	R	S	K	H	H	H	U	S	C
K	U	T	C	H	E	R	R	N	E	M	F	G	E	I	A
K	K	Y	H	G	W	K	I	C	I	R	N	R	T	R	Q
O	N	B	E	A	U	W	C	D	N	A	B	S	O	U	Z
U	W	I	L	N	W	P	T	H	J	O	I	E	E	N	R
T	B	D	O	Z	T	I	T	U	E	N	J	L	R	E	T
V	E	I	R	D	B	R	D	I	O	L	G	F	P	T	A
N	M	Z	L	S	C	I	U	D	G	N	S	R	H	P	A
K	L	R	N	A	T	T	E	O	I	H	A	E	K	A	Z
Q	C	S	J	H	M	H	T	J	C	H	T	P	A	I	F

☐ ALAN	☐ ANGUS	☐ ASHTON	☐ BACHELOR
☐ BEACHFRONT	☐ BERTA	☐ BROTHER	☐ CALIFORNIA
☐ CHARLIE	☐ CHELSEA	☐ COMPOSER	☐ COURTNEY
☐ HARPER	☐ HEDONISTIC	☐ JAKE	☐ JINGLE
☐ JON CRYER	☐ JONES	☐ JUDITH	☐ KUTCHER
☐ MALIBU	☐ PIANO	☐ ROSE	☐ SCHMIDT
☐ SHEEN	☐ UPTIGHT	☐ WALDEN	☐ WINKY-DINK

Fun Puzzle 8 : The Honeymooners

JACKIE GLEASON

I	P	F	O	Z	Y	V	U	R	S	L	M	N	H	O	S
T	R	C	N	N	Y	J	A	E	A	E	U	L	C	H	E
G	X	E	F	O	Y	D	U	C	I	L	D	Z	K	B	L
N	B	A	L	J	S	L	E	H	A	K	P	A	R	T	K
I	M	E	R	E	G	A	K	M	O	T	C	H	L	S	C
V	E	O	A	K	W	N	E	O	O	M	I	A	N	B	I
I	U	I	S	S	C	E	I	L	O	C	E	O	J	T	P
R	G	H	X	U	T	B	J	L	G	R	O	R	N	A	A
D	E	B	C	I	O	E	A	N	W	C	B	O	U	U	U
I	D	I	P	T	R	L	R	S	C	O	N	S	N	N	S
W	W	R	R	B	E	T	A	A	E	O	B	E	U	D	H
O	A	T	O	U	V	K	R	E	R	B	D	D	R	B	U
R	R	H	W	H	R	M	S	T	J	M	A	I	L	B	M
B	D	D	L	D	P	G	O	N	A	N	V	L	T	V	J
K	O	A	E	T	R	N	Q	R	C	E	C	I	L	A	Y
V	B	Y	R	U	L	Z	K	E	R	P	U	E	E	L	K

☐ ALICE	☐ BASEBALL	☐ BIRTHDAY	☐ BLADES
☐ BOWLING	☐ BROOKLYN	☐ BUS	☐ COMEDY
☐ DANCE	☐ DRIVER	☐ DRIVING	☐ EASTER
☐ EDWARD	☐ GLEASON	☐ HOME RUN	☐ JACKIE
☐ JEALOUS	☐ JEWELER	☐ KRAMDEN	☐ KRAX
☐ NORTON	☐ PICKLES	☐ PROWLER	☐ RACCOONS
☐ RALPH	☐ SKETCH	☐ TRIXIE	☐ VACATION

Fun Puzzle 9 : Keeping Up Appearances

R	O	S	E	S	O	N	S	L	O	W	E	C	U	R	B
C	Z	F	A	E	O	G	N	I	F	L	O	G	A	K	J
N	I	R	Z	A	W	F	Y	O	B	Y	O	T	O	Z	C
E	A	O	K	F	O	E	U	C	E	B	R	A	B	Y	Y
W	O	J	B	E	I	S	A	M	T	S	I	R	H	C	V
H	Y	A	E	V	T	S	N	T	H	Y	S	I	A	D	Y
O	Y	M	S	E	H	P	Y	T	E	U	Q	U	O	B	A
B	S	A	L	R	G	Y	E	I	O	K	A	Y	I	B	C
B	S	O	D	L	I	B	A	P	R	Y	C	D	O	Z	H
Y	I	I	Y	H	A	R	M	C	I	O	S	U	J	Y	T
V	T	O	N	Z	T	B	I	I	I	C	N	T	B	A	I
V	C	E	I	G	D	R	S	C	L	N	N	A	O	F	N
J	K	L	M	I	I	A	I	S	H	K	T	I	G	R	G
V	E	Y	W	M	N	N	D	B	E	A	M	H	C	E	E
A	L	D	C	E	E	K	G	D	W	R	R	A	Y	Q	Y
B	P	O	S	T	M	A	N	A	Y	W	D	D	N	Z	R

☐ BARBECUE	☐ BIRTHDAY	☐ BOUQUET	☐ BRUCE
☐ BUCKET	☐ CHRISTMAS	☐ DADDY	☐ DAISY
☐ DRESS BALL	☐ ELIZABETH	☐ EMMET	☐ GOLFING
☐ HYACINTH	☐ IRON AGE	☐ MAJOR	☐ MILKMAN
☐ NEW HOBBY	☐ ONSLOW	☐ PICNIC	☐ POSTMAN
☐ RICHARD	☐ ROSE	☐ SEA FEVER	☐ SINGING
☐ TOY STORE	☐ TOYBOY	☐ VIOLET	☐ YACHTING

Fun Puzzle 10 : Doc Martin

MARTIN CLUNES

S	E	M	A	J	P	N	D	N	H	S	I	N	R	O	C
Z	H	W	W	C	E	A	N	Y	E	C	V	A	P	L	O
S	V	S	B	B	O	L	T	E	C	E	W	H	D	O	S
Y	U	E	U	Q	N	R	L	I	W	A	D	G	K	U	C
M	R	R	T	O	P	I	N	I	E	T	M	L	H	I	H
T	M	Y	G	H	I	H	T	W	N	N	R	R	E	S	O
S	N	P	T	E	G	C	T	R	A	G	T	O	A	A	O
D	C	E	F	O	R	I	A	E	A	L	H	S	P	H	L
H	E	E	D	I	U	Y	N	N	A	M	L	A	T	B	P
Y	A	A	C	I	S	R	G	G	G	C	C	M	M	L	F
T	R	R	D	N	C	H	I	L	A	U	H	O	V	O	H
R	R	U	B	P	A	C	I	S	A	T	P	E	D	O	B
H	Y	O	J	O	A	M	A	N	T	S	S	F	R	D	I
H	W	V	P	N	U	N	O	H	G	R	S	J	E	T	B
A	B	K	G	U	I	R	S	R	B	Y	L	O	T	A	O
W	G	R	O	U	C	H	Y	N	R	O	U	J	N	Y	R

☐ ACCIDENT	☐ BERT	☐ BLOOD	☐ CORNISH
☐ CORNWALL	☐ DEADPAN	☐ DOC MARTIN	☐ ELLINGHAM
☐ FEAR	☐ FISHING	☐ GLASSON	☐ GROUCHY
☐ HARBOUR	☐ INJURY	☐ JAMES	☐ LOUISA
☐ NEEDLE	☐ PATIENTS	☐ PHARMACY	☐ PORT
☐ PORTWENN	☐ PUGNACIOUS	☐ ROMANCE	☐ SCHOOL
☐ STAG NIGHT	☐ SURGERY	☐ TEACHER	☐ TOURIST

Fun Puzzle 11 : All in the Family

CARROLL O'CONNOR

S	Y	D	F	N	H	Y	R	E	I	N	E	R	V	C	C
F	R	I	A	T	A	E	D	H	M	N	W	P	M	I	T
S	P	E	I	N	L	W	S	E	E	E	L	K	H	V	U
L	N	D	H	I	I	N	C	I	M	K	H	A	P	I	N
Z	E	O	G	T	E	E	N	G	E	O	M	Z	A	T	Z
V	D	I	S	E	U	A	L	D	Y	P	C	M	Z	S	M
R	O	B	U	R	H	R	A	L	H	S	C	I	F	T	A
N	E	Q	A	P	E	E	T	C	E	T	O	C	Q	A	N
O	Q	T	E	I	H	F	R	S	A	U	R	H	S	P	T
J	C	T	H	T	R	A	F	N	R	O	O	A	A	L	E
E	S	O	A	G	I	O	A	E	A	L	N	E	L	E	I
A	R	E	N	R	U	R	L	R	J	M	A	L	L	T	V
N	M	O	T	N	E	A	C	G	I	Q	Z	D	Y	O	K
S	D	A	B	T	O	H	L	L	M	Q	L	F	C	N	V
U	P	K	E	Z	I	R	L	Y	N	E	W	Y	O	R	K
I	N	V	F	E	L	S	U	R	E	K	N	U	B	B	V

☐ ARCHIE	☐ BUNKER	☐ COMEDY	☐ CORONA
☐ DANIELLE	☐ EDITH	☐ GLORIA	☐ JEAN
☐ JEFFERSONS	☐ LAUGHTER	☐ MEATHEAD	☐ MICHAEL
☐ MILLS	☐ NEW YORK	☐ O'CONNOR	☐ OUTSPOKEN
☐ PATRIARCH	☐ QUEENS	☐ REINER	☐ RELIGION
☐ ROB	☐ SALLY	☐ STAPLETON	☐ STEPHANIE
☐ STIVIC	☐ STRUTHERS	☐ VETERAN	☐ VIETNAM

Fun Puzzle 12 : The Simpsons

HOMER SIMPSON

S	T	I	S	E	L	M	A	M	Y	Q	S	M	Q	W	U
A	R	N	A	H	C	A	B	N	T	M	A	T	S	O	P
N	E	S	H	G	S	S	O	B	I	R	C	P	Y	I	A
T	P	P	J	I	M	T	A	T	G	H	R	U	N	A	N
A	L	E	L	Z	T	R	H	E	R	I	G	S	J	N	A
S	E	C	A	A	N	E	D	I	N	Y	N	R	M	I	I
F	H	T	F	E	R	O	S	G	L	O	E	A	M	M	D
T	Z	O	Y	S	C	T	F	I	S	M	T	E	L	A	N
U	U	R	Q	L	M	I	M	P	O	R	L	L	L	T	I
G	T	M	R	A	E	A	M	H	I	I	Y	C	A	E	N
I	R	I	S	L	F	I	Z	A	T	T	D	U	B	D	C
T	G	A	D	I	S	I	R	T	T	I	B	N	W	I	H
M	R	E	M	H	V	C	L	A	S	W	Z	D	O	W	F
W	R	A	O	P	H	E	P	C	Y	B	R	V	N	G	V
N	F	Z	B	M	A	M	O	S	I	E	E	B	S	T	F
M	D	R	O	Y	A	M	G	V	M	M	B	U	R	N	S

☐ ANIMATED	☐ BARNEY	☐ BART	☐ BURNS
☐ CHRISTMAS	☐ DISCO	☐ FAMILY GUY	☐ FAT TONY
☐ GIRL CODE	☐ GRAMPA	☐ HELPER	☐ HOMER
☐ INDIAN APU	☐ INSPECTOR	☐ LISA	☐ LITTLE
☐ MARGE	☐ MATRIARCH	☐ MAYOR	☐ MOE
☐ NUCLEAR	☐ PATTY	☐ SANTAS	☐ SELMA
☐ SIMPSONS	☐ SMITHERS	☐ SNOWBALL	☐ SPRINGFIELD

Fun Puzzle 13 : Game Of Thrones

I	Z	P	O	S	R	A	W	W	Z	Y	E	B	N	D	E
S	T	H	G	I	F	D	A	O	Z	Q	E	B	Y	C	D
M	R	O	W	Y	E	R	G	N	H	I	N	W	L	A	D
D	Y	T	F	W	B	M	F	S	O	C	N	S	E	R	A
K	K	R	E	T	S	I	N	N	A	L	E	B	T	Y	R
T	R	K	F	W	L	O	Z	O	D	D	I	R	A	A	D
Y	A	A	T	A	G	I	S	J	A	N	R	A	C	I	P
A	T	F	T	A	N	Y	A	G	O	O	B	N	E	K	O
S	S	B	R	S	R	T	E	R	P	E	J	S	R	A	J
M	A	D	A	E	B	N	A	E	S	H	F	T	D	R	O
A	S	O	N	T	E	B	T	S	O	T	O	A	N	H	F
R	N	E	I	R	T	Y	O	D	Y	N	Z	R	U	T	F
T	A	I	A	R	R	L	O	R	M	A	C	K	M	O	R
D	S	H	S	P	A	R	E	I	A	R	J	Z	R	D	E
M	E	D	I	E	V	A	L	S	S	A	U	L	O	B	Y
E	N	A	G	E	L	C	D	I	U	B	I	K	T	O	H

☐ ARYA	☐ BARANTHEON	☐ BATTLES	☐ BRAN STARK
☐ BRIENNE	☐ CATELYN	☐ CLEGANE	☐ DAARIO
☐ DAENERYS	☐ DOTHRAKI	☐ DRAGONS	☐ EDDARD
☐ FANTASY	☐ FIGHTS	☐ GREY WORM	☐ HODOR
☐ JOFFREY	☐ JON SNOW	☐ LANNISTER	☐ LIARS
☐ MEDIEVAL	☐ PETYR	☐ RAMSAY	☐ RENEGADES
☐ ROBB STARK	☐ SANSA STARK	☐ TORMUND	☐ WARS

Fun Puzzle 14 : The Twilight Zone

ROD SERLING

E	C	O	V	D	R	G	J	E	N	I	L	R	I	A	P
B	O	O	K	I	E	E	Y	S	M	J	T	L	B	A	N
W	J	C	Q	Z	W	S	D	G	Z	O	K	E	S	E	N
U	U	N	G	K	A	J	M	I	O	M	I	S	R	E	Q
S	N	A	I	T	R	A	M	N	L	L	A	V	E	N	E
Z	S	N	N	J	C	N	A	P	M	G	O	U	R	N	Z
C	C	A	K	A	S	C	O	D	E	U	Q	H	O	G	E
S	F	T	B	L	I	C	O	I	S	Z	K	Z	T	L	N
C	U	R	W	R	L	O	I	G	T	I	L	B	I	N	J
E	E	S	E	I	M	A	N	E	N	C	P	N	G	Z	A
M	I	M	P	S	L	I	B	G	N	I	I	B	W	S	N
M	A	N	D	E	X	I	R	E	A	C	L	F	E	A	N
V	A	A	E	O	N	A	G	N	S	Z	E	R	D	S	E
G	Y	R	B	G	V	S	O	H	P	A	I	N	E	O	P
Y	C	I	S	E	M	Z	E	Z	T	E	B	A	H	S	R
S	M	O	T	N	A	H	P	L	S	Z	Z	Y	O	N	U

☐ AIRLINE	☐ AMERICAN	☐ ANTHOLOGY	☐ BASEBALL
☐ BOOKIE	☐ BOXING	☐ DOOMSDAY	☐ FANTASY
☐ FICTION	☐ GENIE	☐ GLIDER	☐ GRAVE
☐ MACABRE	☐ MARS	☐ MARTIANS	☐ NERVOUS
☐ NILE	☐ PASSAGE	☐ PHANTOMS	☐ PIANO
☐ QUEEN	☐ ROD	☐ SCIENCE	☐ SERIES
☐ SERLING	☐ SUSPENSE	☐ TWILIGHT	☐ ZONE

Fun Puzzle 15 : Star Trek

WILLIAM SHATNER

N	K	R	I	K	K	C	O	P	S	Z	E	R	R	M	J
M	O	I	Q	M	R	E	T	R	O	P	S	N	A	R	T
N	T	I	V	Z	U	C	T	E	E	L	F	R	A	T	S
H	A	U	T	H	D	K	R	T	Q	S	P	A	C	E	I
E	Y	R	U	A	L	E	G	E	O	U	G	Q	P	C	G
I	B	R	A	I	R	I	E	J	I	P	F	E	O	P	S
N	A	U	N	D	V	E	Y	P	J	T	S	R	D	C	T
J	E	G	C	U	A	O	D	E	S	I	N	A	O	Z	A
C	O	B	L	G	C	M	L	E	R	P	R	O	D	W	R
N	B	C	P	C	R	L	N	P	F	K	A	R	R	R	T
N	A	U	M	L	Y	O	R	I	N	O	A	C	E	F	R
N	T	Z	R	F	A	E	B	E	A	C	I	G	E	Y	E
D	G	P	I	N	T	N	S	Z	I	T	A	Z	N	P	K
G	S	S	M	N	I	S	E	P	W	Y	P	B	R	H	A
H	H	P	E	H	S	N	Z	T	O	Y	L	A	S	E	R
N	Q	U	A	R	K	D	E	V	S	S	W	G	C	M	W

☐ BORG CUBE	☐ CAPTAIN	☐ DARKNESS	☐ DEEP SPACE
☐ ENTERPRISE	☐ FEDERATION	☐ FRONTIER	☐ JELLYFISH
☐ KIRK	☐ KLINGON	☐ LASER	☐ MCCOY
☐ NARADA	☐ NINE	☐ PICARD	☐ PLANETS
☐ QUARK	☐ SPACE	☐ SPOCK	☐ SPOT
☐ STAR TREK	☐ STARFLEET	☐ TRANSPORTER	☐ UHURA
☐ VOYAGER	☐ VULCAN	☐ WARP	☐ WORF

Fun Puzzle 16: Seinfeld

JERRY SEINFELD

K	K	A	P	A	N	A	Z	H	Z	E	B	Q	Y	E	C
C	R	P	O	S	A	B	H	M	B	N	O	S	A	I	P
R	A	O	L	M	O	S	Z	J	O	O	Y	H	D	Z	E
A	M	L	L	E	R	T	G	U	J	R	F	A	A	A	T
Z	E	O	E	L	R	I	E	N	E	E	R	M	Y	N	E
Y	R	G	H	L	A	N	O	K	S	P	I	P	A	P	R
J	A	Y	S	Y	Z	E	R	M	O	A	E	T	D	U	M
O	I	C	S	C	I	N	G	A	N	H	N	O	A	O	A
E	N	I	I	A	B	C	E	I	L	C	D	N	H	S	N
E	C	R	K	R	Q	E	Z	L	I	O	M	S	O	C	Y
N	O	T	Y	V	B	U	B	B	L	E	B	O	Y	U	R
I	A	N	F	I	I	L	A	B	E	L	M	A	K	E	R
A	T	E	D	L	E	F	N	I	E	S	H	Y	B	P	E
L	S	C	B	C	Z	N	Y	U	G	L	O	O	P	Z	J
E	V	C	P	Z	L	S	S	O	U	L	M	A	T	E	E
Q	N	E	W	M	A	N	A	Z	N	A	T	S	O	C	D

☐ ABSTINENCE	☐ APOLOGY	☐ BIZARRO	☐ BOYFRIEND
☐ BUBBLE BOY	☐ CHAPERONE	☐ COSMO	☐ COSTANZA
☐ CRAZY JOE	☐ ECCENTRIC	☐ ELAINE	☐ GEORGE
☐ HAMPTONS	☐ JERRY	☐ JUNK MAIL	☐ KISS HELLO
☐ KRAMER	☐ LABELMAKER	☐ NEWMAN	☐ NOSE JOB
☐ PETERMAN	☐ POOL GUY	☐ RAINCOATS	☐ SEINFELD
☐ SMELLY CAR	☐ SOUL MATE	☐ SOUP NAZI	☐ YADA YADA

Fun Puzzle 17: Get Smart

DON ADAMS

D	V	C	G	O	C	S	U	C	A	T	R	A	M	S	D
E	V	I	A	N	U	E	Y	Y	D	E	M	O	C	U	Z
E	J	N	O	I	T	C	A	B	H	E	Q	P	Y	G	Q
E	N	O	H	P	E	O	H	S	A	D	W	G	A	A	R
D	M	R	Q	T	Q	S	K	U	M	B	G	D	S	A	S
E	G	P	R	F	E	Y	E	M	O	U	N	M	D	W	U
Y	W	U	H	C	R	R	A	P	B	A	A	V	I	C	S
V	T	K	R	E	I	X	E	Z	H	R	E	T	O	E	L
H	G	E	T	T	A	R	V	N	T	N	C	N	F	K	A
W	T	S	A	S	A	S	O	M	T	H	T	F	U	G	Y
R	Y	S	O	T	R	R	A	U	W	R	A	Y	E	K	M
M	S	A	I	W	I	X	R	N	O	G	S	N	C	E	M
N	K	O	I	C	W	E	Y	L	T	M	T	U	R	U	Z
N	N	D	D	E	Z	L	N	A	U	L	L	N	R	W	P
O	O	H	L	F	K	F	V	L	J	Y	E	E	G	H	S
W	Q	L	W	M	U	O	C	N	N	G	S	O	Z	Q	L

☐ ACTION	☐ ADVENTURE	☐ AGENT	☐ BABY
☐ BUGGY	☐ CLUMSY	☐ COMEDY	☐ CONTROL
☐ GAFFES	☐ GENRE	☐ IRONHAND	☐ KAOS
☐ LUCKY	☐ MAX	☐ MAXWELL	☐ MYSTERY
☐ NAIVE	☐ OPERATION	☐ PHEASANT	☐ SATIRE
☐ SECRET	☐ SERUM	☐ SHOEPHONE	☐ SMART
☐ SMARTACUS	☐ SWITCH	☐ TRUTH	☐ WIDOW

Fun Puzzle 18: The Andy Griffith Show

M	L	R	H	G	D	L	E	S	S	O	N	Y	M	I	G
D	F	K	E	O	N	Y	S	Z	Z	G	N	E	Y	D	R
N	N	I	L	B	B	I	F	K	N	B	X	T	I	O	U
E	H	L	S	D	O	F	D	O	Y	I	U	N	R	E	T
I	Y	M	O	H	I	O	I	D	C	P	N	U	E	G	F
R	G	O	I	R	I	T	G	O	E	E	J	E	L	N	U
F	G	F	E	W	A	N	S	D	R	W	B	U	O	I	I
L	R	H	M	U	A	I	G	L	A	T	S	O	N	T	I
R	S	A	T	A	Y	J	T	Z	N	O	Z	K	Z	N	K
I	P	I	L	E	Y	E	E	U	P	Z	M	T	K	U	E
G	S	I	N	E	B	B	A	I	P	V	M	E	L	H	F
Z	L	R	A	D	I	Z	E	L	I	C	N	U	O	C	C
Z	A	A	O	N	B	G	K	R	G	R	O	T	C	O	D
B	P	O	O	N	O	R	H	T	R	R	B	E	A	R	D
W	G	A	N	I	L	O	R	A	C	Y	K	A	T	W	W
S	S	T	A	T	U	E	C	O	M	E	D	Y	A	Y	F

☐ AUNT BEE	☐ BARNEY	☐ BEARD	☐ CAROLINA
☐ COMEDY	☐ COUNCIL	☐ DEPUTY	☐ DINNER
☐ DOCTOR	☐ DOLLY	☐ FISHING	☐ GIRLFRIEND
☐ GOOBER	☐ GOOD BET	☐ GOODBYE	☐ HUNTING
☐ JUROR	☐ LESSON	☐ MAYBERRY	☐ MEXICO
☐ NOSTALGIA	☐ OPIE	☐ PIANO	☐ RALEIGH
☐ SHERIFF	☐ SITUATION	☐ STATUE	☐ WEDDING

Country Ice Cream Stand

Circle each flavor you have enjoyed in the past. In the next 90 days try all the other flavors.

PICTURE PUZZLE 2. ST MARTEEN ISLAND AIRPLANE LANDING OVER BEACH

PICTURE PUZZLE 2. CIRCLE THE TEN DIFFERENCES

FUN BRAIN TEASERS

Brain Teaser Word Find Puzzle

Find & circle all occurrences of DOG(6), CAT(5), PIG(3), COW(4), FOX(4), ELK(1)

D	G	G	G	G	O				A	A	C	T	A	A	A
O	O	D	G	G	G				T	C	C	C	C	T	A
O	G	G	G	O	O				T	A	A	T	T	T	C
D	O	O	O	O	O	D	G	T	C	C	C	A	A	C	T
O	O	G	O	O	D	G	D	A	A	A	T	A	T	T	T
O	G	G	G	D	D	O	D	T	A	A	T	A	A	T	A
D	O	O	O	D	G	G	D	T	C	C	C	A	A	A	A
G	G	G	O	O	D	G	G	T	T	A	A	A	A	T	A
I	P	I	I	G	P	P	G	O	C	O	C	W	W	O	W
I	I	I	G	G	G	I	G	C	O	C	C	C	O	C	O
I	I	I	I	G	I	I	G	O	C	O	O	O	O	W	W
P	I	I	I	I	G	P	G	O	C	C	O	C	W	W	C
P	P	G	G	G	G	G	G	W	C	W	O	O	C	O	C
G	P	I	I	P	I	P	G	W	W	O	O	O	W	W	W
P	G	I	G	G	G	I	G	W	O	W	O	O	C	C	C
I	I	G	I	I	I	I	G	W	W	W	C	C	C	O	O
X	X	X	X	X	O	X	O	K	K	E	E	K	K	L	L
X	X	F	F	F	X	F	O	K	E	K					E
O	X	X	X	O	X	X	X	K	K	E					L
X	F	X	F	F	X	X	X	L	L	E					L
F	X	F	F	O	O	X	O	K	L	L					K
O	F	X	X	O	X	O	O	E	L	E					E
O	F	F	X	X	X	X	F	L	E	L					K
O	X	O	O	O	O	O	F	L	E	L	L	E	L	L	E

Wild Wild West - Yeehaw!

Find the missing information for each cowboy question.

1. The Loony Tunes gun-slinging cartoon cowboy, __________ is constantly outwitted by his archenemy Bugs Bunny.

____

2. Lucas McCain aka The Rifleman, played by Chuck Connors, was raising his son __________ while battling dangerous bad guys – desperados - in New Mexico.

____

3. What is it called when a herd of cattle is startled and suddenly runs off in a panic?

____

4. The cartoon character Sheriff QUICK DRAW MCGRAW had a sidekick deputy named BABA LOOEY. What kind of animals were Quick Draw and Baba?

____

5. Ben, the patriarch of the Cartwright all-male Nevada ranching family of the TV series Bonanza, had 3 sons: Adam, Hoss, and ________. The adventuresome family owned & defended the Ponderosa Ranch near Virginia City, Nevada Territory.

____

6. The original 1960 Western film, The Magnificent Seven, starred Yul Brynner, Steve McQueen, Charles Bronson, James Coburn, and others. Who starred in the 2016 remake of the movie?

____

7. "The Gun that Won the West" was this type of rifle which was a lever-action repeating weapon that could fire 16 times before reloading. The revolver can fire 6 times.

____

8. In Rooster Cogburn starring John Wayne, a one-eyed aging marshal, helps a bible-toting spinster find the outlaws who killed her father. What famous actress played the spinster?

____

9. Did cowboys make coffee from whole beans over cattle drive campfire in the latter half of the 1800s?

____

10. In the 1880s , what was the most common drink and food ordered by cowboys in a Saloon?

____

11. GUNSMOKE's marshal Matt Dillon, played by James Arness, lived in what Kansas town?

____

12. This 1969 Western movie is about a pair of outlaws, starring Paul Newman & Robert Redford, who were on the run after a failed train robbery picking a bizarre destination - Bolivia.

____

ANSWERS: 1. maS etimesoY 2. kraM 3. edepmatS 4. orrub nacixeM ,esroH 5. eoJ elttiL 6. srehto dna ekwaH nahtE ,tterP sirhC ,notgnihsaW lezneD 7. retsehcniW 8. nrubpeH enirahtaK 9. desu saw eeffoc "elkcubrA" dnuorg yllausu ,oN 10. ilihc & yeksihW 11. ytiC egdoD 12. diK ecnadnuS eht dna ydissaC hctuB

RUDOLF THE ___NOSED REINDEER

Name the items based on the pictures. They all start with the same color.

1.

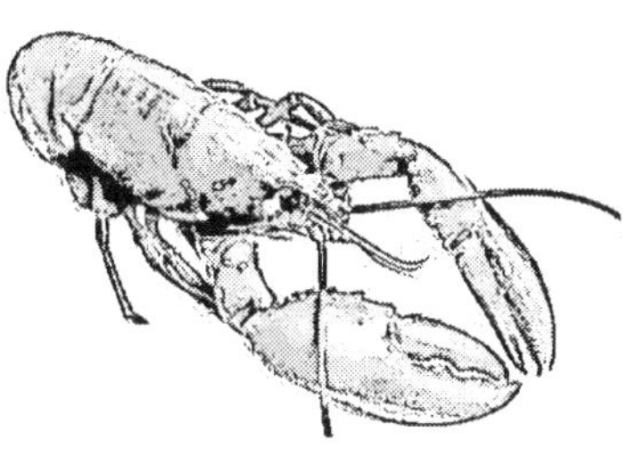

5.

2.

6.

3.

7.

4.

8.

ANSWERS. 1. RETSBOL DER 2. ELAS GAT DER 3. SREPPEP DER 4. XOBDER 5. XOS DER 6. XOF DER 7. YMRA DER 8. THGILF EYE DER

African Safari Quiz

All the questions related to African wild animals.

1. How can a giraffe infant survive the 7 foot drop to the ground upon birth?

___

2. How can two zebra friends find each other in a large herd since all look the same?

___

3. A crocodile and a lion fighting over a baby water buffalo at a river bank. What can the water buffalo mom do?

___

4. Lions likes to eat lots of other animals. What animal likes to eat lion meat?

___

5. How can an elephant escape becoming a meal with 2 lions on its back and one hanging on its tail?

___

6. Can an angry elephant bull throw an adult water buffalo up in the air?

___

7. How much time after birth does an antelope baby have to learn to run and to keep up with the herd (or be left behind)?

___

8. How large is an ostrich egg?

___

9. Can a polar bear mate with a grizzly bear?

___

10. The largest African vulture weighs 15 LBS with a wingspan of 9 ft. What is its favorite food?

___

11. What is the best strategy for a tiger when facing a lion?

___

12. Can a peaceful gorilla fight off a lion?

___

ANSWERS: 1. .YARP DNA SEYE EHT ESOLC 2. .TXET RO PPA ENOHPTRAMS A ESU 3. .ELIDOCORC EHT NO TI WORHT DNA NOIL EHT EROG 4. .SANEYH & SERUTLUV 5. .NUR DNA PLEH ROF TEPMURT 6. .SBL 002,1 OLAFFUB RETAW A ,SBL 000,51 HGIEW NAC TNAHPELE LLUB A .SEY 7. .SYAD OWT YLNO 8. .EPUOLATNAC LLAMS A FO EZIS 9. .RAEB RALORG :GNIRPSFFO .RAEB RALOP ELAMEF A HTIW SETAM YLZZIRG ELAM A YLLANOISACCO .SEY 10. .STNAHPELE GNIDULCNI SLAMINA EMAG GIB FO SESSACRAC 11. .YAWA NUR 12. .TSRIF PU DELIR EB OT SAH EH TUB SEY

Name That City in 5 Minutes!

Find at least 3 American or World Cities for each letter (if any).

1. A-B

2. C-D

3. E-F

4. G-H

5. I-J

6. K-L

7. M-N

8. O-P

9. Q-R

10. S-T

11. U-V-W

12. X-Y-Z

ANSWERS: 1. TSEPADUB ,NOTSOB ,NILREB ,EROMITLAB ,ATNALTA ,NOTGNILRA ,EGAROHCNA ,MADRETSMA 2. IABUD ,TIORTED ,IHLED ,SALLAD ,ITANNICNIC ,OGACIHC ,ACNALBASAC ,ORIAC 3. TRUFKNARF ,HTROW TROF ,ELADREDUAL TROF ,ECNEROLF ,SKNABRIAF ,HCAEB AWE ,OSAP LE ,HGRUBNIDE 4. IKNISLEH ,ANAVAH ,DROFTRAH ,GRUBMAH ,UOHZGNAUG ,HCIWNEERG ,ADANARG ,WOGSALG 5. UAENUJ ,GRUBSENNAHOJ ,MELASUREJ ,HADDEJ ,ATRAKAJ ,ELLIVNOSKCAJ ,LUBMATSI ,KSTUKRI ,SILOPANAIDNI 6. SELEGNA SOL ,NOBSIL ,AMIL ,SAGEV SAL ,OTOYK ,RUPMUL ALAUK ,WOKARK ,VEIK ,IHCARAK ,YTIC SASNAK 7. GREBNRUN ,YTIC KROY WEN ,SNAELRO WEN ,SELPAN ,WOCSOM ,LAERTNOM ,SILOPAENNIM ,YTIC OCIXEM ,NATTAHNAM ,DIRDAM 8. EUGARP ,XINEOHP ,AIHPLEDALIHP ,GNIKEP ,SIRAP ,DROFXO ,OLSO ,ODNALRO ,AHAMO ,YTIC AMOHALKO 9. EMOR ,RETSEHCOR ,HDAYIR ,ORIENAJ ED OIR ,AGIR ,YTIC NOZEUQ ,SNEEUQ ,OADGNIQ 10. NOSCUT ,OTNOROT ,OYKOT ,NARHET ,GRUBSRETEP .TS ,IAHGNAHS ,OLUAP OAS ,OCSICNARF NAS ,OGEID NAS 11. ATIHCIW ,NOTGNIHSAW ,WASRAW ,ECINEV ,NACITAV ,REVUOCNAV ,DROFSELTTU ,MLU ,ENIDU 12. AZOGARAZ ,EYHZOROPAZ ,ELLIVSENAZ ,BERGAZ ,AMAHOKOY ,EVALSORAY ,NOGNAY ,NAIX ,NEMAIX ,REIVAX

Hilarious Fruitcake Quiz

Before you give it as a gift, answer all questions.

1. You buy Indian plum cake in nice tin can for $10. You are on a diet. How can you enjoy the fruitcake?

2. Can you keep a fruitcake till next Christmas and still enjoy it?

3. When Princess Diana married Prince Charles, she served fruitcake so their marriage would last forever & ever. Why did their marriage fail?

4. How many recent films are titled "Fruitcake"?

5. Name the missing fruitcake ingredient: flour, eggs, sugar, spices, cherries, citron, ginger, vanilla, raisins, walnuts, whiskey, canned Hawaiian pineapple.

6. What happened to the fruitcake that travelled to the Moon with Apollo 11 in 1969?

7. Which TV personality said: "There is only one fruitcake in the entire world, and people keep sending it to each other".

8. Is there such a thing as a great fruitcake toss competition?

9. Why was fruitcake popular at weddings in Victorian England?

10. Can you give fruitcake as a Christmas gift to your husband?

11. Why don't they serve fruitcake in jails?

12. What kind of cake was served at the wedding of Queen Elizabeth & Prince Philip in 1947?

ANSWERS: 1. .SLERRIUQS & SDRIB OT TSER EHT EVIG DNA ETIB ENO EVAH 2. .REVE TI YOJNE LLIW UOY TAHT YLEKILNU SAMTSIRHC TSAL TI YOJNE TON DID UOY ECNIS 3. .TI NI NOMEL DEIDNAC HCUM OOT DAH EKACTIURF EHT ESUACEB 4. 6102 ,4102 ,3002 :SRAEY ;EERHT 5. RETTUB 6. ..C.D NOTGNIHSAW ,MUESUM ECAPS & RIA NAINOSHTIMS EHT NI DETIBIHXE SI TI 7. 5891 WOHS THGINOT FO TSOH ,NOSRAC YNNHOJ 8. YRAUNAJ YREVE SSOT EKACTIURF ;ODAROLOC ,SGNIRPS UOTINAM .SEY 9. .GNIDDEW TXEN EHT LLIT DETSAL EKACTIURF EHT DNA ROTAREGIRFER ON SAW EREHT ESUACEB 10. .SAMTSIRHC TXEN DEPPARW YLECIN KCAB TI EVIECER TNAW UOY FI YLNO 11. .NOPAEW A SA DESU EB NAC TI ESUACEB 12. GNICI LAYOR & REYAL NAPIZRAM HTIW EKACTIURF GNIDDEW DNUOP-005 ,DEREIT-RUOF

Double in Middle Words in 10 Minutes

All the words have double letters exactly in the middle.

1. The act of hating intensely.; Approachable.

____

2. Allowed evidence in court.; Permission to enter the theater.

____

3. Diplomatic representative sent by one country to another.; A plant that grows leaves & roots the first year, and flowers & fruits the second.

____

4. A person who boasts vainly.; To arrange in classes on the basis of resemblance.

____

5. The department of an army charged with providing food.; An untrained shallow amateur.

____

6. To fail to fulfill high expectation.; To view with fault.

____

7. Possession of eminently superior qualities.; Discharge of blood from a ruptured blood-vessel.

____

8. That cannot be passed through.; Blameless, faultless.

____

9. Not able to be done.; Illness in some part of the body characterized by heat, swelling, & pain.

____

10. A small decorative article.; A happening.

____

11. Exclusion on purpose or by mistake.; Possessing great power.

____

12. Smooth surface so that you slip, as on ice.; Showing strong-willed determination.

____

ANSWERS: 1. ELBISSECCA ;ECNERROHBA 2. ECNATTIMDA ;ELBISSIMDA 3. LAINNEIB ;RODASSABMA 4. YFISSALC ;TRAGGARB 5. ETNATTELID ;TAIRASSIMMOC 6. EVORPPASID ;TNIOPPASID 7. EGAHRROMEH ;ECNELLECXE 8. ELBACCEPMI ;ELBASSAPMI 9. NOITAMMALFNI ;ELBISSOPMI 10. ECNERRUCCO ;KCANKKCINK 11. TNASSIUP ;NOISSIMO 12. NROBBUTS ;YREPPILS

Dinosaur Fantasy Quiz

All the questions related to dinosaurs which went extinct 65 million years ago.

1. How big was the egg of a tyrannosaurus rex (T-REX)?

____

2. What was the name of the Flintstones pet dinosaur?

____

3. The "Age of Dinosaurs" spanned from 250 million years ago to 65 million years ago. What was the size of the population?

____

4. What did the largest dinosaurs (Brachiosaurus and Apatosaurus) eat for lunch?

____

5. What was the most dangerous dinosaurs in the original Jurassic Park movie?

____

6. Were the dinosaurs the heaviest animals ever? (100 tons)

____

7. Did dinosaurs and humans live at the same time?

____

8. What are the largest dinosaur descendant today?

____

9. There are 15 types of 3-horned triceratops. Did they live in North America?

____

10. What dinosaur from the Jurassic Park movie actually lived in the Jurassic Period?

____

11. What did the T-REX eat for breakfast?

____

12. Where can you see civil war soldiers fighting against dinosaurs?

____

ANSWERS: 1. DAERB HCNERF TAF A FO EPAHS DNA EZIS 2. ONID 3. SENO LLAMS NOILLIM 005 DNA SRUASONID EGRAL NOILLIM 02 ETAMITSE 4. NAIRATEGEV EREW YEHT ,STNALP 5. SROTPARICOLEV 6. .SNOT 002 EB NAC ELAHW EULB EHT .ON 7. .ETAD RETAL A TA SRAM EHT MORF EMAC SNAMUH ESUACEB ,ON 8. HCIRTSO DNA ELIDOCORC 9. .HATU NI ,SEY 10.)DNELIAT OT HTEET MORF TEEF 001(SURUASOIHCARB 11. SEKALF MLAP DETSORF 12. .AINIGRIV NI KRAP TNEMESUMA MODGNIK RUASONID EHT TA

One Way Trip To Mars Quiz

All the questions related to the dreamed, unrealistic (pricetag: $50 billion) one-way trip to Mars.

1. Why not establish a colony on the Moon before going to Mars? Or in the 14,000 ft extremely dry Atacama Desert of Chile which looks like the desolate red Martian landscape at several places?

____

2. What do colonizers do during the 7 months of travel to Mars?

____

3. After the colonizers land, they are very weak. How do they get out of the spacecraft?

____

4. How do you say in Martian: Hello!; Good Morning!; How are you? I am from Earth. I need water & potato.

____

5. What is the most popular outside recreational activity on Mars?

____

6. What is the best survival strategy for the colonizers?

____

7. One of the colonizers discovers an area with large gold nuggets. He tells the Martian King. What is the king's response?

____

8. What should colonizers do to make reality TV broadcasts to Earth interesting?

____

9. A Martian red sand storm blocked the entrance to the living quarters tunnel. What to do?

____

10. One male colonizer passed away after falling into a red sand sinkhole leaving 9 men and 10 women. What are they supposed to do?

____

11. The internet connection to Earth is lost. Colonizers cannot watch their favorite TV channels. What should they do?

____

12. Your oxygen supply is running low. You know this is the end of the one-way trip. What is your last message to earthlings?

____

ANSWERS: 1. BECAUSE THE EARTH LOOKS LIKE A GIANT BLUE MOON FROM THE MOON, TOO CLOSE FOR AN ADVENTURE! 2. THEY STUDY THE HISTORY OF MARTIAN CIVILIZATION. 3. MARTIANS WILL HELP THEM OUT. 4. MELLO!; MOOD MORNING! MOW ARE YOU? ME BLUE PLANET. ME H2O AND MOTATO. 5. LOOKING FOR A GOLF BALL WHICH FLIES VERY FAR IN MARTIAN GRAVITY. 6. MARRY THE MARTIAN KING'S AND MARTIAN NOBLEMEN'S DAUGHTERS. 7. WE DON'T LIKE YELLOW GOLD, WE ONLY LIKE RED GOLD. 8. DANCE WITH MARTIAN GIRLS. 9. RADIO EARTH FOR NEW COLONIZERS TO DIG THEM OUT. 10. MARRY OFF THE WIDOW TO A MARTIAN PRINCE. 11. JOG AROUND THE TUNNEL AND SING. 12. DON'T COME HERE! BUILD YELLOW SAND COLONY IN SAHARA FOR ADVENTURE!

Five Words with a 4 Letter Suffix in 5 Minutes

Find words ending with the given 4 letters.

1. Suffix AWAY

___

2. Suffix BAND

___

3. Suffix BONE

___

4. Suffix DOWN

___

5. Suffix HAND

___

6. Suffix LION

___

7. Suffix LOCK

___

8. Suffix PINE

___

9. Suffix PORT

___

10. Suffix RENT

___

11. Suffix WELL

___

12. Suffix WOOD

___

ANSWERS: 1. YAWAWORHT ,YAWANUR ,YAWARAF ,YAWATSAC ,YAWARAC 2. DNABREBBUR ,DNABSUH MDNABSID ,DNABARTNOC ,DNABDAORB ,DNABMRA 3. ENOBHSIW ,ENOBMORT ,ENOBED ,ENOBKEEHC ,ENOBKCAB 4. NWODHCUOT ,NWODWOLS ,NWODEKAHS ,NWODKCARC ,NWODEMOC ,NWODKAERB 5. DNAHEGATS ,DNAHTROHS ,DNAHDNOCES ,DNAHFFO ,DNAHWOC ,DNAHKCAB 6. NOILLIRT ,NOILLEBER ,NOILLIM ,NOILLADEM ,NOILEDNAD ,NOILLIB ,NOILATTAB 7. KCOLDEW ,KCOLBDAOR ,KCOLMEH ,KCOLDIRG ,KCOLDAED ,KCOLC ,KCOLB 8. ENIPS ,ENIPAR ,ENIPUCROP ,ENIPPILIHP ,ENIPLA 9. TROPS ,TROPAES ,TROPSSAP ,TROPMI ,TROPXE ,TROPED ,TROPRIA 10. TNERROT ,TNERAP ,TNEREFFID ,TNERRUC ,TNEREGILLEB ,TNERAPPA 11. LLEWRIATS ,LLEWKNI ,LLEWSDNUORG ,LLEWERAF ,LLEWD 12. DOOWYLP ,DOOWYLLOH ,DOOWERIF ,DOOWGOD ,DOOWDAED

THE QUINTESSENTIAL LETTER Q CHALLENGE

Funny fact: "Queueing" has 5 consecutive vowels. Name the objects based on the pictures. They all start with "Q".

1. 

5. 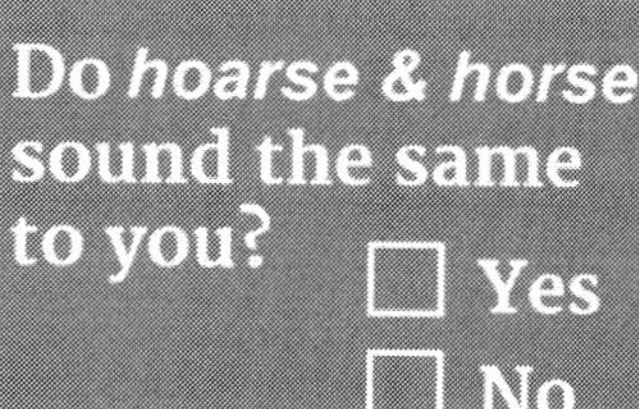

2. 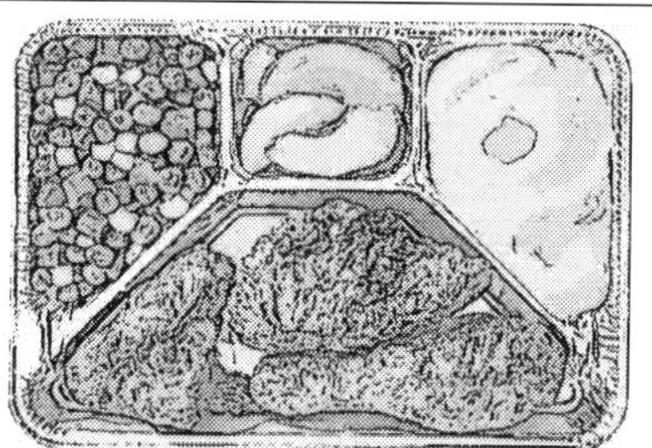

6. 

3. 

7. 

4. 

8. 

ANSWERS: 1. HTEBAZILE NEEUQ 2. RENNID VT KCIUQ 3. LIAUQ 4. WARD KCIUQ 5. NOITSEUQ ZIUQ 6. TETRAUQ 7. TIURF ECNIUQ 8. RODAUCE FO LATIPAC - OTIUQ

5x5 Mini Crossword Squares

Fill-in the missing letters

Puzzle 1. FLYING SLEIGH

<table>
<tr><td></td><td></td><td></td><td></td><td>A</td></tr>
<tr><td></td><td></td><td></td><td>I</td><td></td></tr>
<tr><td></td><td></td><td>N</td><td></td><td></td></tr>
<tr><td></td><td>S</td><td></td><td></td><td></td></tr>
<tr><td>T</td><td></td><td></td><td></td><td></td></tr>
</table>

Row 1: He comes at Christmas time on a flying sled.
Row 2: A person who is taught by a teacher.
Row 3: Humorous version of language.
Row 4: An outstanding problem.
Row 5: A group of soldiers.
Diagonal: Sunrise.
Left Column: Cut something into two long pieces.

Puzzle 2. STONE HOUSE

<table>
<tr><td></td><td></td><td></td><td></td><td>E</td></tr>
<tr><td></td><td></td><td></td><td>L</td><td></td></tr>
<tr><td></td><td></td><td>O</td><td></td><td></td></tr>
<tr><td></td><td>N</td><td></td><td></td><td></td></tr>
<tr><td>D</td><td></td><td></td><td></td><td></td></tr>
</table>

Row 1: A kind of stone used for roofs.
Row 2: To lay, place or adjust.
Row 3: The possessive case of who.
Row 4: To endow with some quality, gift, or ability.
Row 5: A thin turf used for covering cottages.
Diagonal: A small tube through which liquid is poured.
Left Column: A shortened shotgun.

Puzzle 3. CAR WITH 16 SPEAKERS

<table>
<tr><td></td><td></td><td></td><td></td><td>E</td></tr>
<tr><td></td><td></td><td></td><td>W</td><td></td></tr>
<tr><td></td><td></td><td>D</td><td></td><td></td></tr>
<tr><td></td><td>H</td><td></td><td></td><td></td></tr>
<tr><td>H</td><td></td><td></td><td></td><td></td></tr>
</table>

Row 1: Living, not dead.
Row 2: Physical strength, powerful muscle.
Row 3: Sound as used in electronics.
Row 4: The past tense of shake.
Row 5: High estimation, respect.
Diagonal: Intensity of passion.
Left Column: To destroy the self-confidence.

Puzzle 4. LIBRARY OF ALEXANDRIA

<table>
<tr><td></td><td></td><td></td><td></td><td>N</td></tr>
<tr><td></td><td></td><td></td><td>B</td><td></td></tr>
<tr><td></td><td></td><td>I</td><td></td><td></td></tr>
<tr><td></td><td>R</td><td></td><td></td><td></td></tr>
<tr><td>S</td><td></td><td></td><td></td><td></td></tr>
</table>

Row 1: Straighten its feathers with its beak.
Row 2: Middle Eastern people.
Row 3: To crush something into a powder.
Row 4: A mistake.
Row 5: More secure.
Diagonal: Preceding in the order of time.
Left Column: Book has them.

ANSWERS: 1. SANTA, PUPIL, LINGO, ISSUE, TROOP, SUNUP, SPLIT 2. SLATE, APPLY, WHOSE, ENDUE, DIVOT, SPOUT, SAWED 3. ALIVE, BRAWN, AUDIO, SHOOK, HONOR, ARDOR, ABASH 4. PREEN, ARABS, GRIND, ERROR, SAFER, PRIOR, PAGES

Smiling Math Quiz

Enjoy math without calculus homework questions.

1. When you enter Germany from the Czech Republic on a superhighway, you see a circle traffic sign with 120 crossed over. What does that mean?

---

2. When it is 40 degrees Celsius by The Great Pyramid of Giza (1/2 mile from Cairo outskirts), is it very hot?

---

3. In the Egyptian Museum of Cairo one can see a beautiful golden chariot. What was the battle speed of the chariots?

---

4. The Taj Mahal (Agra, India) was built by 20,000 workers for 20 years. If each worker ate 2 pounds of flat bread (wheat or chickpea) a day, how many tons of bread needed for the construction?

---

5. A European bison weighs 600 kg. An American buffalo weighs 635 kg. What is the difference in pounds?

---

6. The distance between the Canary Islands and Hispaniola (Dominican Republic/Haiti) is 5,700 km. Columbus's ships, Santa Maria, Nina, Pinta, were pushed by westerly trade wind from September 6, 1492 to October 12 same year. What was the average speed of the sailships?

---

7. Columbus was an expert trade winds sailor. He could estimate the ship's speed just by looking at the sails. To measure actual speed, he threw a buoy on a loose rope into the water and said "QUEEN ISABELLA" 5 times. He retrieved the buoy and the rope measured 27m. What was the speed of Santa Maria (flagship)?

---

8. Columbus underestimated the distance from Spain to India as 5,000 km (about 3,100 miles). He provisioned the ships with sufficient food & water for a long month trip. How much is the actual distance? Hint: Lisbon-Panama, Panama City-Jakarta, Jakarta-Calcutta

---

9. On a scale of 1 to 10, my girlfriend is the square root of 81. Is she pretty?

---

10. If I have 4 children, same for my children and my grandchildren and their children. How many great great grand children am I going to have?

---

11. You plan to put a multi-color Happy Birthday ribbon around a 9" blueberry pie. How long ribbon you need? (Hint: PI is 3.14)

---

12. 1999 in Roman numerals is MCMXCIX { 1000+(-100+1000)+(-10+100)+(-1+10) }. What is 2040 in Roman numerals?

ANSWERS: 1. .)HPM 57 = HPK 021(S-NHABOTUA NAMREG NO DEEPS DETIMILNU 2. .TIEHNERHAF NI RUOF DERDNUH ENO ,SEY 3.)HPM 21(HPK YTNEWT 4. .SNOT SU SDNASUOHT YTFIF DERDNUH ENO TUOBA 5. .SDNUOP NEVES-YTNEVES 6. .)HPM RUOF(HPK NEVES 7. .)HPM XIS(HPK NET DEEPS .SDNOCES NET EMIT 8. .)SELIM DNASUOHT NEETRUOF(MK DNASUOHT OWT-YTNEWT 9. .ENIN A SI EHS .SEY 10. .XIS-YTFIF DERDNUH OWT .REWOP HTRUOF OT RUOF 11. .SEHCNI THGIE-YTNEWT TUOBA 12. .LXMM

VIDEO POKER JACKPOT PAYOUT QUIZ

Royal Flush with Maximum Bet is Top Prize

ROYAL FLUSH	250	500	750	1000	4000
STRAIGHT FLUSH	50	100	150	200	250
FOUR OF A KIND	25	50	75	100	125
FULL HOUSE	9	18	27	36	45
FLUSH	6	12	18	24	30
STRAIGHT	4	8	12	16	20
THREE OF A KIND	3	6	9	12	15
TWO PAIRS	2	4	6	8	10
JACKS OR BETTER	1	2	3	4	5

1. If the denomination is $.25 (quarter), how much is the Royal Flush jackpot when betting 5 ($1.25)?
2. If the denomination is $.50 (half dollar), how much is the Royal Flush jackpot when betting 5 ($2.50)?
3 If the denomination is $1, how much is the Royal Flush jackpot when betting 5 ($5)?
4. If the denomination is $2, how much is the Royal Flush jackpot when betting 5 ($10)?
5. If the denomination is $5, how much is the Royal Flush jackpot when betting 5 ($25)?
6. If the denomination is $10, how much is the Royal Flush jackpot when betting 5 ($50)?
7. If the denomination is $25, how much is the Royal Flush jackpot when betting 5 ($125)?
8. If the denomination is $100, how much is the Royal Flush jackpot when betting 5 ($500)?

ANSWERS: 1. SRALLOD DNASUOHT ENO 2. SRALLOD DNASUOHT OWT 3. SRALLOD DNASUOHT RUOF 4. SRALLOD DNASUOHT THGIE 5. SRALLOD DNASUOHT YTNEWT 6. SRALLOD DNASUOHT YTROF 7. SRALLOD DNASUOHT DERDNUH ENO 8. SRALLOD DNASUOHT DERDNUH RUOF

Smiling Physics Quiz

Enjoy physics without nuclear science homework questions.

1. Can Artificial Intelligence help us to overcome gravitation so we can hop like astronauts on the Moon?

____

2. Can AI help us to clone great physicist like Newton who would be amazed to see how the world changed?

____

3. Can we humans go to the Mars in the near future?

____

4. What was the profession of Einstein's first wife?

____

5. How many horsepower did Tarzan have?

____

6. Can humans fly like birds with giant wings?

____

7. How many horsepower engine needed for a motor-assisted glider?

____

8. Why isn't an aircraft with flapping wings like birds?

____

9. Why don't airliners have a giant parachute to increase safety?

____

10. Can airliners fly without pilots?

____

11. How can the relatively small wings lift the heavy airliner?

____

12. The dual World Trade Center towers had 110 floors each. The Dubai tower has 156 floors. The Saudi Jeddah tower will have over 200 floors. Can a tower be constructed with 300 floors?

____

ANSWERS: 1. NO. GRAVITATION IS A BASIC PROPERTY OF MATTER. 2. THAT WILL BE POSSIBLE ONE DAY. 3. ONLY IN THE MOVIES. WHILE TECHNOLOGICALLY FEASIBLE, THE COST OF MARS ROUNDTRIP TRAVEL (LIKE $100 BILLION) IS PROHIBITIVE. 4. MILENA MARIC WAS ALSO A BRILLIANT PHYSICIST. 5. BRIEFLY 3 HP. SUSTAINABLY 0.4 HP. 6. HUMANS CAN GLIDE LIKE A BIRD; NOT STRONG ENOUGH TO FLAP. 7. AT LEAST 50 HP. LESS FOR ULTRALIGHT AIRCRAFT. 8. EXPERIMENTAL ORNITHOPTER EXISTS. NOT YET PRACTICAL DUE TO THE COMPLEXITY OF FLAPPING WINGS. 9. COST WOULD BE TOO HIGH WITH LIMITED BENEFITS. WOULD NOT HAVE HELPED ON 9/11 SINCE THE PILOTS WERE KILLED. 10. ALREADY CAN FLY ON AUTOPILOT. IN THE NEAR FUTURE COMPUTERS CAN FLY AIRPLANES FROM TAKEOFF TO LANDING. 11. TRY TO OPEN A CAR DOOR (SAFELY!) AT 70 MPH. YOU WILL FEEL THE TREMENDOUS POWER OF RUSHING AIR. 12. PROBABLY. CHINA NEXT? WOULD YOU LIKE WORK ON THE 295TH FLOOR?

AIRPLANES FROM AVIATION HISTORY

Name the airplanes based on the pictures.

1. 

2. 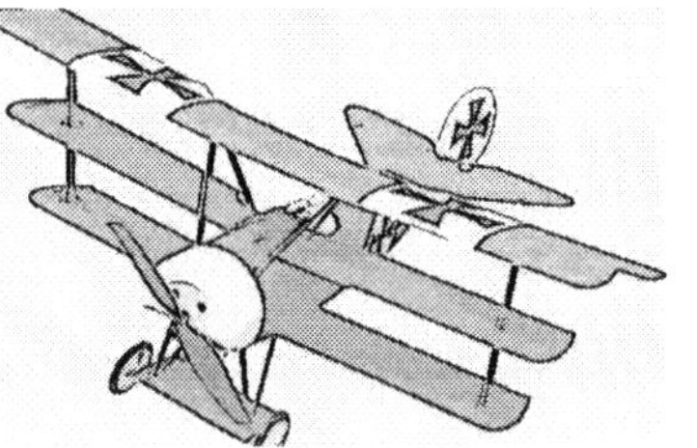

3. 

4. 

5. 

6. 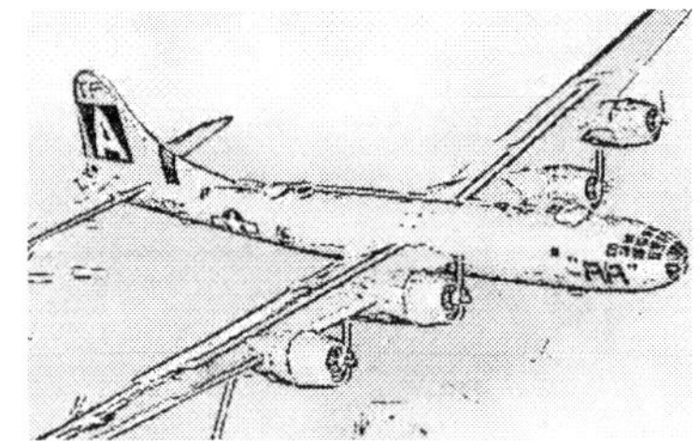

7. 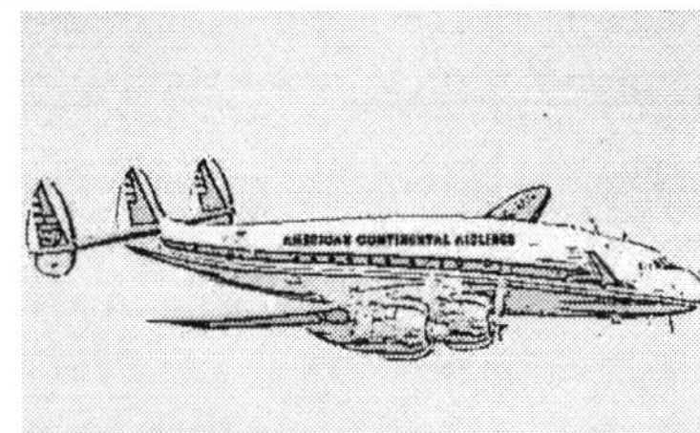

8. 

ANSWERS. 1. REYLF THGIRW 2. REKKOF 1WW NAMREG - ENALPIRT 3. NAMRAETS NACIREMA - ENALPIB 4. KCUD NAMMURG NACIREMA - ENALPORDYH 5. GNATSUM 2WW NACIREMA - RETHGIF 6. SSERTROFREPUS 92-B 2WW NACIREMA - REBMOB 7. S0591 NOITALLETSNOC DEEHKCOL - RENILRIA REGNESSAP 8. OBMUJ 747 GNIEOB - RENILRIA TEJ

Find & Circle the First Part of a Ball Game in Each Quadrant

B	E	S	A	S	A	B	E	E	B	T	A	B	K	B	S	O	R	R	R	O	B	R	M
E	A	E	A	B	A	A	E	A	T	S	A	B	A	S	S	O	O	R	O	B	M	O	O
S	E	S	S	A	S	E	B	T	T	S	B	E	E	T	E	R	O	R	B	R	O	O	O
B	A	E	E	B	B	B	S	K	E	S	K	S	T	E	E	M	O	O	R	R	M	O	M
E	B	B	S	S	B	A	B	K	A	K	T	E	A	S	B	O	O	B	B	B	R	O	R
A	A	A	B	S	S	B	A	E	T	B	S	B	B	T	T	R	M	M	B	B	O	R	R
S	S	B	S	A	S	E	S	E	T	S	A	A	S	E	A	R	B	M	R	R	O	M	O
B	A	E	E	S	S	B	A	T	K	A	T	T	B	S	E	B	O	O	R	O	O	B	B
E	O	E	D	D	D	G	D									F	F	O	O	O	O	F	T
G	D	D	G	O	G	G	G									T	O	O	O	O	T	F	T
G	G	D	D	G	D	E	G									T	F	O	O	O	O	T	T
O	E	G	E	D	D	D	D									O	T	T	T	O	F	O	F
G	D	D	E	G	O	E	D									F	T	F	O	T	T	F	T
D	G	D	D	D	D	E	O									O	F	O	T	F	T	O	O
G	D	O	E	E	D	O	D									O	O	T	O	O	O	F	T
G	D	D	O	O	O	O	D									F	F	O	F	O	O	O	O
N	N	A	N	H	N	A	H									I	K	K	K	I	C	I	I
D	D	A	A	D	N	H	N									K	K	K	I	C	C	K	K
A	H	D	N	D	N	A	N									K	I	I	I	C	I	C	K
H	N	A	A	A	H	H	N									C	I	K	K	K	I	K	K
N	A	A	H	H	A	N	A									C	K	K	K	K	K	K	K
N	D	D	H	N	N	N	N									I	I	K	K	C	K	C	I
D	A	N	D	N	A	N	N									K	K	I	K	I	K	K	K
H	H	D	N	N	A	A	H									C	I	K	C	C	I	K	I
N	E	E	E	E	N	E	E	T	F	F	F	S	S	F	T	L	L	L	O	L	O	L	Y
N	N	T	T	N	E	E	N	T	S	F	F	T	S	T	F	E	E	Y	L	Y	E	V	V
E	N	N	N	E	N	N	E	F	T	O	O	O	T	S	S	Y	O	Y	E	O	E	L	O
E	N	T	T	E	T	E	E	O	T	O	F	O	O	S	F	O	L	O	V	L	L	V	L
N	N	N	T	E	E	E	E	T	T	O	S	T	F	S	S	E	Y	L	L	E	L	L	V
E	E	N	E	N	T	E	E	S	O	O	T	O	F	T	S	O	O	O	E	O	L	O	Y
E	E	N	T	N	T	T	T	T	T	F	S	O	F	O	F	Y	V	Y	O	Y	O	Y	V
E	N	T	T	N	N	N	E	S	F	F	F	T	T	S	O	L	Y	E	L	Y	O	E	L

UTAH & ROSWELL WELCOME SIGNS

What is Utah's state dinosaur? When did aliens "land" in Roswell?

SEE DINOSAURS

ANSWERS: SURUASOLLA; NEVES-YTROF NEETENIN

Five Words with a 5 Letter Suffix in 5 Minutes

Find words ending with the given 5 letters.

1. Suffix ANGLE

---

2. Suffix DANCE

---

3. Suffix FIELD

---

4. Suffix LANCE

---

5. Suffix LOWER

---

6. Suffix MAKER

---

7. Suffix NANCE

---

8. Suffix OLDER

---

9. Suffix PHONE

---

10. Suffix POINT

---

11. Suffix TRESS

---

12. Suffix WATER

ANSWERS: 1. ELGNARW ,ELGNARTS ,ELGNATCER ,ELGNAM ,ELGNATNE ,ELGNAD 2. ECNADNUDER ,ECNADEPMI ,ECNADIUG ,ECNADNETTA ,ECNADNUBA 3. DLEIFTUO ,DLEIFLIO ,DLEIFENIM ,DLEIFDIM ,DLEIFELTTAB ,DLEIFRIA 4. ECNALIGIV ,ECNALLIEVRUS ,ECNALBMESER ,ECNALRAP ,ECNALEERF ,ECNALAB ,ECNALUBMA 5. REWOLLEY ,REWOLS ,REWOLLAHS ,REWOLLEM ,REWOLG ,REWOLLOF ,REWOLB 6. REKAMELBUORT ,REKAMECAEP ,REKAMHCTAM ,REKAMEMOH ,REKAMEEFFOC ,REKAMKOOB 7. ECNANOSER ,ECNANIDRO ,ECNANIF ,ECNANIMOD ,ECNANOSNOC 8. REDLOS ,REDLOMS ,REDLOP ,REDLOF ,REDLOC ,REDLOB 9. ENOHPOLYX ,ENOHPOXAS ,ENOHPORCIM ,ENOHPOCNARF ,ENOHPATCID ,ENOHPLLEC 10. TNIOPWEIV ,TNIOPNIP ,TNIOPNUG ,TNIOPKCEHC ,TNIOPLLAB ,TNIOPPA 11. SSERTIAW ,SSERTSMAES ,SSERTSIM ,SSERTTAM ,SSERTROF ,SSERTSID ,SSERTTUB ,SSERTCA 12. RETAWETSAW ,RETAWAES ,RETAWDNUORG ,RETAWDOOLF ,RETAWHSID ,RETAWHTAB

LEARN TO MEMORIZE LICENSE PLATES TO FIGHT CRIME

Best Picture Oscar Winners Word Search Puzzle 

I	R	R	C	W	I	N	G	S	N	A	M	N	I	A	R
H	E	J	T	I	T	A	N	I	C	I	S	A	W	A	S
D	B	Q	Y	R	A	O	M	G	B	U	G	G	R	P	Z
N	E	G	E	Q	S	C	H	O	E	M	R	I	O	G	M
A	C	N	T	T	C	S	N	D	G	A	A	T	G	T	O
G	C	I	F	O	A	A	A	A	N	A	L	R	R	W	W
L	A	T	M	R	M	M	V	D	L	I	C	A	T	N	L
A	T	S	C	A	A	J	H	A	G	B	E	I	O	Y	L
D	H	E	E	Z	R	O	O	H	L	H	A	T	H	K	A
I	G	H	N	G	T	R	T	N	E	C	T	S	U	C	H
A	I	T	B	E	Q	G	O	V	E	A	A	O	A	W	E
T	L	J	L	A	E	Z	A	N	P	S	K	D	B	C	I
O	N	T	H	E	A	R	T	I	S	T	Z	P	E	R	N
R	O	L	J	D	B	U	N	F	O	R	G	I	V	E	N
H	O	Y	K	C	O	R	K	N	A	M	D	R	I	B	A
M	M	C	E	P	L	A	T	O	O	N	O	Y	C	L	E

☐ AMADEUS	☐ ANNIE HALL	☐ ARGO	☐ BIRDMAN
☐ BRAVEHEART	☐ CASABLANCA	☐ CAVALCADE	☐ CHICAGO
☐ CIMARRON	☐ CRASH	☐ GANDHI	☐ GIGI
☐ GLADIATOR	☐ GRAND HOTEL	☐ MARTY	☐ MOONLIGHT
☐ PATTON	☐ PLATOON	☐ RAIN MAN	☐ REBECCA
☐ ROCKY	☐ SPOTLIGHT	☐ THE ARTIST	☐ THE STING
☐ TITANIC	☐ TOM JONES	☐ UNFORGIVEN	☐ WINGS

ZODIAC CONSTELLATIONS

Zodiac constellations are bright star constellations that lie along the plane of the annual path of the Sun. The word zodiac derived from a Greek word, meaning the circle of animals. Your zodiac sign - based on your birthdate - is a strong tool for understanding yourself & your relationships. Write the names of 12 signs of the zodiac - Aquarius, Pisces, Aries, Taurus, Gemini, Cancer, Leo, Virgo, Libra, Scorpio, Sagittarius, & Capricorn - into the box under the corresponding image.

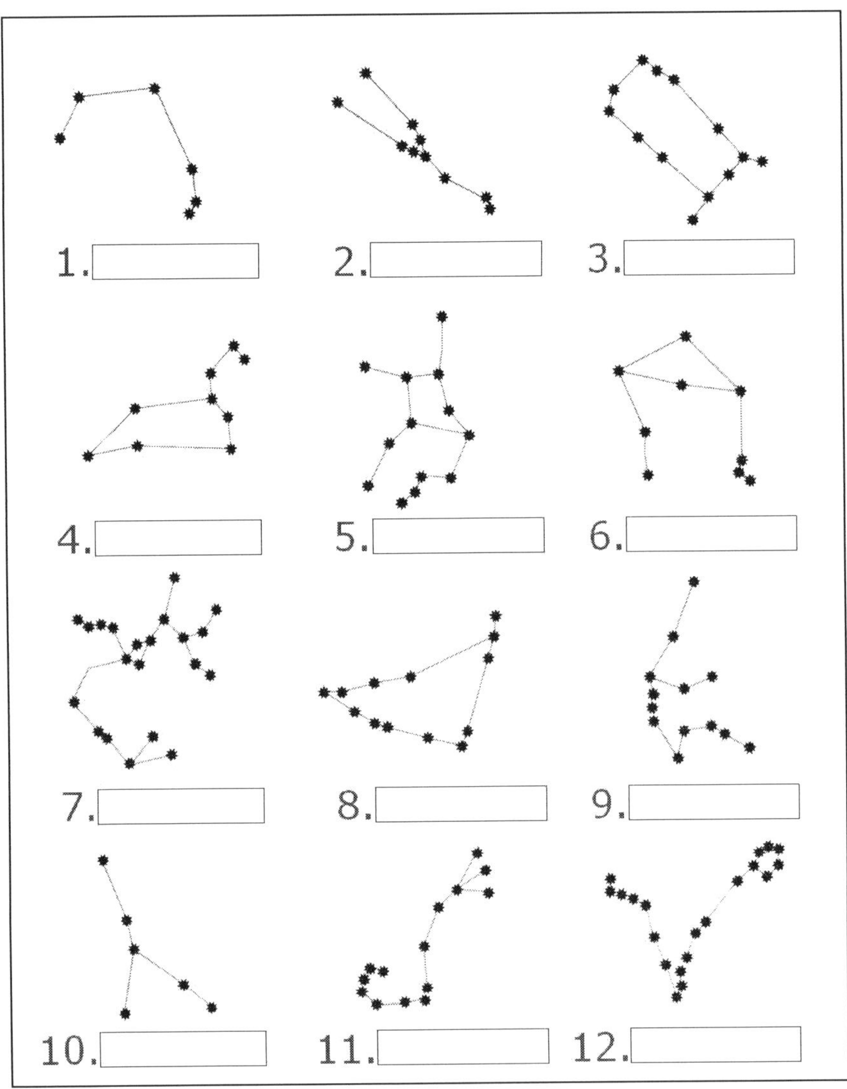

ANSWERS: SECSIP .21 OIPROCS .11 RECNAC .01 SUIRAUQA .9 NROCIRPAC .8 SUIRATTIGAS .7 ARBIL .6 OGRIV .5 OEL .4 INIMEG .3 SURUAT .2 SEIRA .1

Find & Circle 1 Animal in Each Quadrant

S	S	S	E	R	E	S	O	T	E	E	I	T	I	E	G	A	K	A	N	S	N	N	K
E	H	O	H	O	R	H	E	E	R	R	G	E	I	T	T	S	S	A	K	S	S	E	K
R	R	S	R	S	O	O	H	T	E	T	G	G	I	T	E	N	S	K	N	E	K	N	K
H	O	E	S	R	R	R	H	I	R	E	G	G	I	G	E	K	A	N	K	A	S	S	A
H	S	E	S	S	O	H	O	E	I	E	E	R	E	I	T	S	S	A	N	K	E	E	N
E	S	E	H	R	R	O	E	G	T	G	G	R	R	I	I	A	E	S	S	E	K	S	A
R	E	O	O	O	E	S	R	T	R	G	G	I	E	T	T	E	N	E	E	A	K	K	S
O	H	O	S	O	R	R	H	G	T	I	E	I	T	E	G	A	E	E	S	N	K	A	A
N	P	A	A	A	N	A	A									B	Z	E	A	B	R	E	B
A	P	A	D	D	D	A	A									Z	Z	B	E	Z	A	A	B
A	P	P	P	P	P	N	A									A	E	E	B	R	B	E	Z
A	A	A	N	A	N	P	D									B	A	A	B	R	B	A	B
A	D	N	D	A	A	A	N									E	E	E	Z	B	B	R	E
P	A	N	A	A	N	N	N									E	Z	B	Z	Z	E	A	A
D	A	A	D	D	A	N	A									E	Z	E	R	A	A	R	R
P	A	A	P	P	A	A	P									A	E	R	B	R	R	R	R
A	L	O	A	A	A	L	K									M	S	O	U	O	S	S	S
K	K	A	L	O	A	O	A									E	S	O	U	U	U	O	E
A	A	O	O	A	L	K	A									O	O	O	O	S	O	O	U
A	O	O	K	K	O	L	O									S	M	E	E	U	U	U	S
A	L	A	O	O	L	A	L									E	S	O	O	M	E	O	M
L	L	A	L	A	A	K	A									S	O	O	U	E	O	U	S
A	A	A	A	A	A	L	K									O	O	E	U	S	E	S	M
A	K	L	A	K	A	A	A									E	U	U	E	S	E	U	M
P	E	S	E	S	S	H	S	L	L	E	L	H	W	E	A	M	H	I	M	P	M	C	I
P	E	P	E	E	E	E	E	E	E	E	H	E	W	L	H	M	I	M	I	I	C	P	I
E	E	E	H	H	E	E	H	H	W	E	H	A	A	W	L	M	H	M	H	C	C	I	C
H	P	E	S	E	E	P	P	H	H	H	L	L	A	H	A	M	M	M	C	M	H	I	P
S	E	H	S	H	P	E	H	W	A	L	W	A	W	L	A	P	P	H	C	H	I	I	M
E	E	P	E	S	E	E	E	H	E	H	W	L	H	L	L	P	I	H	P	C	I	P	M
P	E	E	E	H	H	E	P	E	W	L	A	W	E	W	H	M	I	P	P	M	H	M	P
H	H	P	H	E	S	P	P	H	A	A	A	E	H	A	E	H	I	C	I	H	I	I	P

Five Words with a 6 Letter Suffix in 5 Minutes

Find words ending with the given 6 letters.

1. Suffix ACTIVE

---

2. Suffix CEMENT

---

3. Suffix DINESS

---

4. Suffix HOLDER

---

5. Suffix LARITY

---

6. Suffix MATICS

---

7. Suffix METRIC

---

8. Suffix PHILIA

---

9. Suffix SCENCE

---

10. Suffix SPHERE

---

11. Suffix TATIVE

---

12. Suffix UALITY

ANSWERS: 1. EVITCAORTER ,EVITCAOIDAR ,EVITCAORP ,EVITCANI ,EVITCAREPYH ,EVITCARTTA 2. TNEMECROFNIER ,TNEMECALP ,TNEMECITNE ,TNEMECNAHNE ,TNEMECNEMMOC ,TNEMECNUONNA 3. SSENIDRAT ,SSENIDAER ,SSENIDEERG ,SSENIDDIG ,SSENIDRAHLOOF ,SSENIDUOLC 4. REDLOHEKATS ,REDLOHERAHS ,REDLOHYCILOP ,REDLOHESAEL ,REDLOHEERF 5. YTIRALUGNIS ,YTIRALUPOP ,YTIRALOP ,YTIRALUGERRI ,YTIRALUNARG ,YTIRALC 6. SCITAMEHCS ,SCITAMSIMUN ,SCITAMEHTAM ,SCITAMROFNI ,SCITAMOLPID 7. CIRTEMONOGIRT ,CIRTEMMYS ,CIRTEMOEG ,CIRTEMOIB ,CIRTEMMYSA 8. AILIHPOOZ ,AILIHPONEX ,AILIHPOMEAH ,AILIHPONAC ,AILIHPOLGNA 9. ECNECSINIMER ,ECNECSEROHPSOHP ,ECNECSELOSBO ,ECNECSEROULF ,ECNECSELODA 10. EREHPSOPORT ,EREHPSOTARTS ,EREHPSIMEH ,EREHPSOEG ,EREHPSOIB ,EREHPSOMTA 11. EVITATEGEV ,EVITATNET ,EVITATUP ,EVITATIMI ,EVITATIOLPXE ,EVITATNEMUGRA 12. YTILAUTIRIPS ,YTILAUXES ,YTILAUQ ,YTILAUTCNUP ,YTILAUQENI ,YTILAUQE ,YTILAUD

"GONE WITH THE WIND"

CLARK GABLE & VIVIEN LEIGH HISTORIC MARKERS

OHIO HISTORICAL MARKER

CLARK GABLE, "THE KING OF ________"

Born in Cadiz, ____, on February 1, 1901, William Clark Gable lived and a______ school in Hopedale from 1903 to 1917. After several years as a stage actor he ______ Hollywood, where he made sixty-seven ______ in remarkable career that spanned four ______. Gable won an Academy Award for It H______ One Night in 1934 but is best known for ______ as Rhett Butler in the 1939 classic Gone with the Wind. Gable joined the U.S. Army A______ during World War II and fought in E____. He died in Los Angeles in 1960. His b______ home is located 1/4 mile south on Mill street.

THE OHIO BICENTENNIAL COMMISSION
THE LONGABERGER COMPANY
THE VILLAGE OF HOPEDALE
THE OHIO HISTORICAL SOCIETY
2000

2~34

ANSWERS: DOOHYOB ,EPORUE ,SPROC RIA ,ELOR SIH ,DENEPPAH ,SEDACED ,SEIVOM ,OT TNEW ,DEDNETTA ,OIHO ,DOOWYLLOH

Words Starting with SW

What is the SW word based on the meaning?

1. Popular sauce & soup in Chinese cooking made with sugar & vinegar.

____

2. A small country in the Alps with lots of chocolate & ski slopes. Also popular place with the rich to hide their money.

____

3. A place to jump into water and paddle with your arms & legs.

____

4. A landlocked kingdom in southern Africa with fascinating wild life reserves featuring rhinoceroses.

____

5. A highly aerial small bird similar to swallow. Also an international bank wire transfer system.

____

6. A big game fish (sadly overfished) with a unicorn nose. Frequently confused with marlin, a large billfish which was featured in Hemingway's Old Man and the Sea.

____

7. A part of your body is painfully larger & rounder than usual, as a result of insect bite or other causes.

____

8. No longer popular practice of wrapping infants in narrow bands of cloth

____

9. Popular dry or wet sweeping, mopping, & dusting device for every home surface.

____

10. A pig. Also a contemptible, arrogant, disgusting person.

____

11. To enter the Paris subway & rail system you have to do this with your transit card.

____

12. A European country with reindeer, Volvo automobile & IKEA factories.

____

ANSWERS: 1. RUOS & TEEWS 2. DNALREZTIWS 3. LOOP GNIMMIWS 4. DNALIZAWS 5. TFIWS 6. HSIFDROWS 7. NELLOWS 8. GNILDDAWS 9. REFFIWS 10. ENIWS 11. EPIWS 12. NEDEWS

The Ultimate Amusing Gardening Quiz

Do you have a green thumb?

1. What is absolutely the best place to buy deer-proof flowers?

2. What is the best advertised product to chase away burrowing moles?

3. Other than Jack's Magic Beanstalk what evergreen plant can grow 35" in one day?

4. What flower bulbs were more valuable than gold in Holland during the 1600s?

5. What on Earth (or Mars) are Brussels Sprouts anyhow? (Hint: very popular in Brussels, Belgium)

6. Is Spanish paella yellow from Saffron or common substitutes like turmeric?

7. Why is ananas (Latin name) named pineapple by European explorers in America?

8. What is the famous pink colored sweet & sour pie made of the mix of a fruit & a vegetable?

9. Why do blueberries sink in water while cranberries float & bounce when dropped? (The bog is flooded when the cranberries are to be harvested.)

10. How many square feet of garden can you cover, 2 inches thick, with 1 cubic yard of mulch?

11. Will fencing your garden keep the groundhogs (woodchuck/marmota monax) away? (Groundhog Day, February 2, ceremony held at Punxsutawney in western Pennsylvania centering on a semi-mythical rodant named Phil. Also a movie.)

12. How many ears of corn can grow on each stalk? How many kernels on a cob of corn? How high can a corn stalk grow?

ANSWERS: 1. .SRAM NO NOITCELES EROM TUB ,NOOM EHT YRT NAC UOY 2. .SREHTO EHT EKIL TSUJ KROW TON SEOD & PAEHC SI TI ESUACEB PARTESUOM A YUB OT TSEB 3. OOBMAB 4. AINAMOILUT DELLAC SAW EZARC EHT ;SBLUB PILUT 5. SNEZOD EHT YB KLATS NO WORG TAHT SEGABBAC ERUTAINIM 6. SETUTITSBUS ESU STNARUATSER RALUGER ;NEEUQ & GNIK HSINAPS EHT ROF DEVRES NEHW YLNO DESU NORFFAS 7. .ELPPA FO ETSAT DNA SENOCENIP FO MEHT DEDNIMER TI 8. EIP BRABUHR YRREBWARTS 9. .TAOLF MEHT EKAM HCIHW STEKCOP RIA EVAH SEIRREBNARC 10. TEEF ERAUQS OWT YTXIS DERDNUH ENO 11. .TI REVO BMILC RO ECNEF EHT REDNU OG LLIW GOHDNUORG 12. TEEF NEETFIF ;SLENREK DERDNUH EVLEWT OT DERDNUH EVIF ;OWT RO ENO YLTSOM

The ______ Rose Of Cairo (Woody Allen movie)

Name the items based on the pictures. They all start with the same color.

1. ______________________

2. ______________________

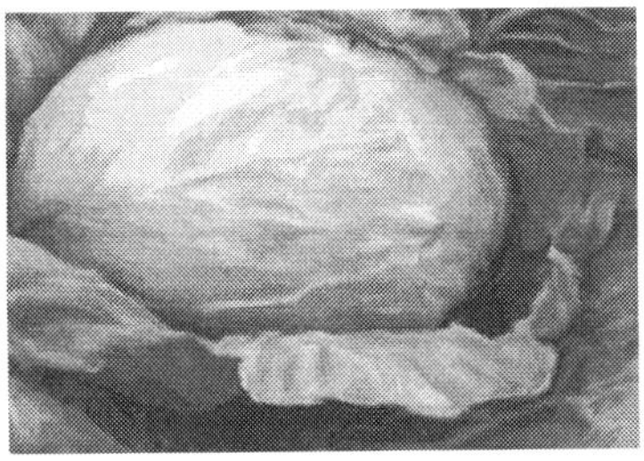

3. ______________________

4. ______________________

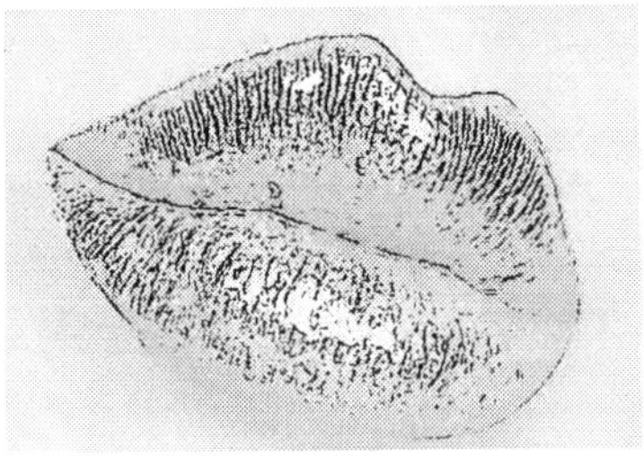

5. ______________________

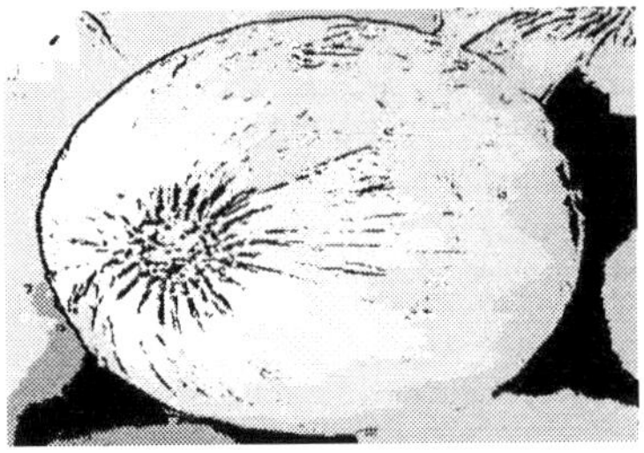

6. ______________________

7. ______________________

8. ______________________

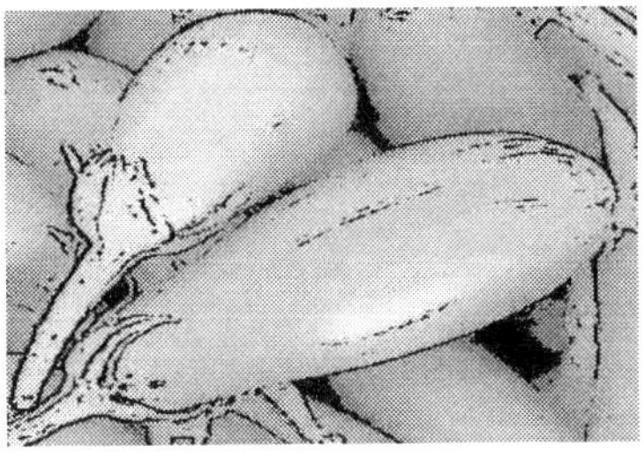

ANSWERS: 1. TRAEH ELPRUP 2. EGABBAC ELPRUP 3. ONOMIK ELPRUP 4. SPIL ELPRUP 5. NOINO)ADUMREB(ELPRUP 6. ECNIRP YB NIAR ELPRUP 7. SIRAP FO SEERT GNIREWOLF ELPRUP 8. TNALPGGE ELPRUP

The Ford Mustang Brain Booster

All questions related to the iconic American car.

1. The fast & macho sport car, Mustang, was introduced to the public at the 1964 World Fair in this city? Some of the fair structures, like the Globe, still standing.

____

2. How much horse power did the Mustang have in 1964? 2018?

____

3. What 007 James Bond movie involving a gold mining magnate featured the Mustang whereby Volpe(Luciana Paluzzi), a female beauty (likely triple agent 7770), drives 007 to the Bahamas hotel at 100 miles per hour?

____

4. How many Mustangs were manufactured from 1964 to 2018?

____

5. In this movie Steve McQueen takes the Mustang for a spin, chasing the bad guys on the sloped streets of San Francisco, frequently becoming airborne?

____

6. Superstar Kevin Costner, in a baseball player role, roams the streets of the NC town in a Mustang convertible, occasionally with co-star Susan Sarandon?

____

7. In this 007 movie, James Bond (Sean Connery) & Tiffany Case (Jill St. John), a pretty diamond-smuggler, drive around Las Vegas in a red Ford Mustang while he breaks up a diamond-smuggling ring.

____

8. A 1966 Shelby GT 350 H driven by Tom Cruise, in the role of a longshoreman, in this 2005 movie about an alien invasion in NYC.

____

9. In this TV hit show, Farrah Fawcett plays a hot angel woman with a hot white & blue-striped 1976 Mustang Cobra II.

____

10. Sylvester Stallone, as an incarcerated skilled mechanic from Hoboken, New Jersey (birthplace of Frank Sinatra) refurbishes a Ford Mustang in the prison shop with the help of other inmates.

____

11. Incredibly it takes only seconds for Oscar winning actor Nicolas Cage to steal a 1967 Mustang Shelby GT 500 named "Eleanor" in this movie.

____

12. In this 1999 remake of the Steve McQueen classic, Pierce Brosnan royally drives an off-road dark green 1968 Shelby Mustang GT500 convertible complete with raised suspension, and huge tires.

____

ANSWERS: 1. YTIC KROY WEN ,SNEEUQ 2. NET DERDNUH EERHT ;EVIF DERDNUH ENO 3. REGNIFDLOG 4. SNOILLIM NET 5. TTILLUB 6. MAHRUD LLUB 7. REVEROF ERA SDNOMAID 8. SDLROW EHT FO RAW 9. SLEGNA S'EILRAHC 10. PU KCOL 11. SDNOCES 06 NI ENOG 12. RIAFFA NWORC SAMOHT

Popcorn & Peanuts - A Crackerjack Quiz

All the questions related to the iconic American snack foods.

1. What is Cracker Jack snackfood, featuring a prize in the package, made of?

2. How many cups of popcorn are in a large bucket (tub) that we buy in a movie theatre?

3. Is plain popcorn a healthy food with whole grain, vitamins & minerals and anti-oxidants? Is it appropriate for a one-way Mars trip?

4. How many quarts of popcorn are consumed by Americans (world leader) each year per person?

5. What are the popular references for unpopped popcorn kernels that remain after popping?

6. Why does a popcorn pop? Should popcorn be stored in a refrigerator before popping?

7. Are peanuts (earthnuts, groundnuts and goobers) technically nuts or legumes?

8. Can you pick peanuts off a tree like hazelnuts or walnuts?

9. Can you use popcorn, instead of plastic peanuts, as a packing material?

10. Which American president was a peanut farmer?

11. The botanist George Washington Carver (1860-1943) devised over 300 uses for peanuts. Did he invent peanut butter?

12. What cartoon features Charlie Brown, Linus, Lucy, and Snoopy?

ANSWERS: 1. STUNAEP DNA NROCPOP ,LEMARAC ,SESSALOM 2. YTNEWT DNA NEETFIF NEEWTEB 3. PIRT SRAM A ROF LAEDI ;SEVITIDDA TUOHTIW SEY 4.)SDNUOP NOILLIB 2.1 :ASU LATOT(STRAUQ OWT YTROF 5. SDIAM DLO ,SRETSNIPS 6. DRAOBPUC LOOC A NI RENIATNOC DELAES NI TI EROTS ,ON ;SEDOLPXE DNA MAETS OTNI SNRUT HCIHW ERUTSIOM SNIATNOC NROCPOP 7. YOS DNA SLITNEL ,SNAEB EKIL SEMUGEL 8. DNUORGREDNU WORG YEHT ,ON 9. MEHT TAE DLUOW ECIM DNA STAR ESUACEB ,ON 10. RETRAC YMMIJ TNEDISERP 11. .OCIXEM NI RETTUB TUNAEP ETA SCETZA TNEICNA EHT .ON 12. STUNAEP

THE SECRET OF LONG LIFE

Circle each item necessary for long life and cross out all harmful items.

string beans	almond milk yoghurt	soft chewy cookies	raw onion spinach	zucchini celery
potato chips	leafy greens	sweet/boiled potato	swimming	cherries/figs
brussels/bean sprouts	french fries	eggplant	candy chocolate	canned tuna olive oil
nonfat sour cream	salmon/cod	broccoli/beets	alcohol	chili nachos
intimacy 10 sit ups a day	dancing zumba yoga	cakes/tortes	eggs/egg white	1 foot hot dog
gym/biking				raw garlic asparagus
lean meats				white bread
sugary drinks				tofu/soups
apples/pears				diet sodas
daily long walk				sardines mackarel
tomatoes peppers	green salad steamed veggies	blue cheese dressing	nonfat cottage cheese	avocados
drugs smoking	lo-cal dressing	macaroni salad	chicken breast	lentils/beans
bacon cheeseburger	walnuts almonds	ice cream	peas & carrots	fried foods
skim milk fat free ricotta	triple cheese pizza	sausages salamis	coconut milk	berries bananas
cauliflower	red wine	pumpkin	mango/peach	junk food

3 New Words with Same Letters in 5 min

Find other words based on all letters in the given word.

1. TEAM

___

2. EAST

___

3. DIET

___

4. TIME

___

5. POST

___

6. SCARE

___

7. REACT

___

8. STEAK

___

9. NEPAL

___

10. STEAL

___

11. LISTEN

___

12. STAPLE

___

ANSWERS: 1. EMAT ,TAEM ,ETAM 2. TAES ,ETAS ,STAE 3. DEIT ,EDIT ,TIDE 4. ETIM ,METI ,TIME 5. SPOT ,POTS ,TOPS ,STOP 6. SECAR ,SERAC ,SERCA 7. ECART ,ETARC ,RETAC ,TERAC 8. SEKAT ,EKATS ,ETAKS 9. ENALP ,LANEP ,LENAP 10. SELAT ,ELATS ,ETALS ,TSAEL 11. LESNIT ,TNELIS ,STELNI ,TSILNE 12. STAELP ,SETALP ,SLATEP ,LETSAP ,TSELAP

4x4 Mini Crossword Squares

Fill-in the missing letters

Puzzle 1. ROCKY MOUNTAINS

			A
		C	
	N		
P			

Row 1: Capital of Fiji.
Row 2: You need a key for it.
Row 3: Pre-Columbus Empire in the Americas.
Row 4: Top of a mountain.
Diagonal: Something you put on your feet.
Left Column: To slide accidentally.

Puzzle 2. SOLAR SYSTEM

			E
		R	
	A		
M			

Row 1: A large freshwater fish.
Row 2: That belongs to us!
Row 3: He bites the banana.
Row 4: The red planet next to us.
Diagonal: He placed the glass down.
Left Column: Edgar Allan Poe wrote many.

Puzzle 3. TIMES SQUARE

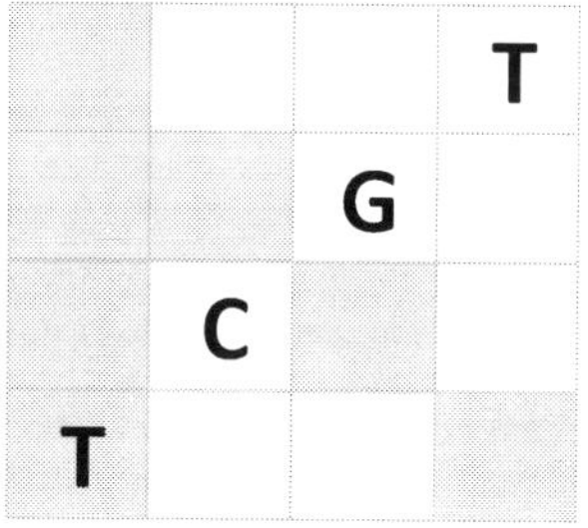

Row 1: When a horse runs slowly.
Row 2: Pigs.
Row 3: A Broadway musical usually has two.
Row 4: A musical notes played one after the other.
Diagonal: A large bag.
Left Column: Pronoun identifies a specific thing.

Puzzle 4. FISH EAGLE

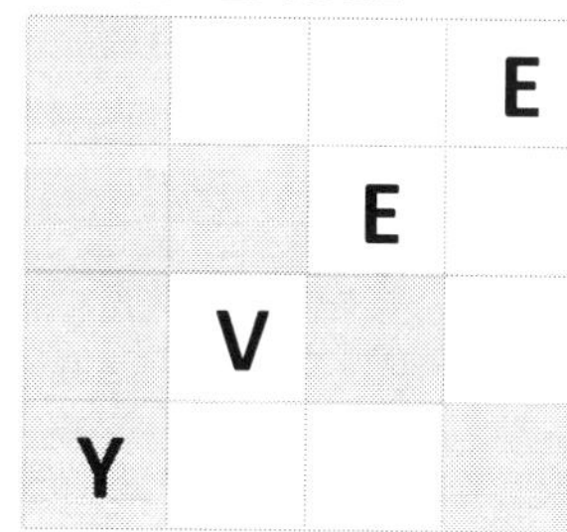

Row 1: The head priest of Catholics.
Row 2: A tall stiff grass that grows in water.
Row 3: Always; for all time.
Row 4: Something disgusting.
Diagonal: To look slyly.
Left Column: An animal that is hunted for food by a bird.

ANSWERS: 1. SUVA, LOCK, INCA, PEAK, SOCK, SLIP 2. PIKE, OURS, EATS, MARS, PUTS, POEM 3. TROT, HOGS, ACTS, TUNE, TOTE, THAT 4. POPE, REED, EVER, YUCK, PEEK, PREY

Find & Circle the First Part of a "wear" in Each Quadrant

E	A	A	B	A	B	A	C	T	O	T	O	F	F	O	F	E	S	E	E	U	R	I	U
H	B	C	C	E	C	B	A	O	O	O	O	O	F	O	O	S	R	S	L	L	E	R	S
C	A	A	A	E	A	H	B	O	F	F	F	F	O	T	F	L	E	U	R	L	L	U	L
C	A	H	C	A	B	B	E	O	O	F	T	O	F	T	O	E	U	S	S	E	E	R	U
H	A	C	C	E	A	C	E	O	O	T	O	T	T	O	O	E	R	E	L	I	E	E	E
E	H	H	C	A	B	H	A	T	O	T	O	O	O	O	F	R	U	L	E	E	E	E	R
C	B	C	A	A	E	E	A	F	T	O	O	O	T	O	O	R	L	R	I	L	U	L	I
H	H	E	B	H	C	B	B	F	T	O	T	O	O	T	T	E	U	U	E	R	E	U	I
L	E	U	E	N	O	L	G									E	N	E	N	E	N	S	M
G	O	L	E	E	O	O	N									E	M	M	E	S	S	M	N
E	U	U	N	G	O	O	E									M	N	N	M	S	S	E	N
N	U	U	N	O	L	U	L									M	E	E	E	N	E	E	S
G	N	N	U	G	G	U	L									S	N	S	N	N	E	M	S
N	G	E	G	L	E	E	U									S	S	N	E	S	E	S	E
L	E	L	O	E	E	U	O									M	M	E	S	M	N	E	E
N	E	U	U	G	N	L	E									E	E	E	M	M	M	M	N
G	G	T	T	N	I	N	H									P	E	P	E	S	P	P	S
I	T	N	G	G	N	T	N									S	E	P	P	S	S	E	S
N	H	H	I	G	H	G	G									E	P	E	H	E	H	E	E
N	I	I	N	G	T	H	H									P	S	S	P	A	S	S	P
N	T	H	I	N	H	H	I									H	P	H	E	A	H	H	H
H	N	I	G	I	G	T	H									H	E	P	E	A	P	S	H
G	N	H	T	G	G	T	T									P	H	A	P	A	A	E	E
H	G	H	N	H	N	G	H									H	H	E	A	S	P	S	S
S	P	S	T	O	R	P	P	M	I	I	I	M	I	M	I	U	R	D	R	E	N	U	U
S	S	S	S	S	O	S	R	W	I	M	M	S	M	W	I	N	R	E	D	N	R	R	U
S	S	S	T	R	R	S	S	M	I	M	M	I	S	M	S	D	R	E	U	R	N	N	D
S	O	P	S	P	T	R	O	I	W	S	I	S	S	I	M	U	D	U	N	D	D	E	U
O	O	T	S	R	T	O	P	W	S	W	I	W	W	S	W	U	U	U	D	E	N	E	E
S	S	O	O	R	R	R	S	I	I	S	I	I	S	M	W	U	R	R	R	U	N	N	N
O	T	P	T	S	S	O	R	M	S	M	W	W	W	M	W	R	R	E	D	R	D	E	D
R	S	R	T	P	S	T	S	W	M	M	I	M	S	M	W	R	U	E	E	D	N	U	E

Five Words with a 7 Letter Suffix in 5 Minutes

Find words ending with the given 7 letters.

1. Suffix BIOLOGY

2. Suffix CIATION

3. Suffix DUCTION

4. Suffix GRAPHER

5. Suffix ISHMENT

6. Suffix MENTARY

7. Suffix MISSION

8. Suffix ORATION

9. Suffix RESSION

10. Suffix STATION

11. Suffix TEDNESS

12. Suffix TRATION

ANSWERS: 1. YGOLOIBORUEN ,YGOLOIBORCIM ,YGOLOIBORDYH ,YGOLOIBOPORHTNA ,YGOLOIBORGA 2. NOITAICNUNORP ,NOITAICSAF ,NOITAICERPED ,NOITAICOSSA ,NOITAICERPPA 3. NOITCUDES ,NOITCUDORPER ,NOITCUDORP ,NOITCUDORTNI ,NOITCUDED ,NOITCUDBA 4. REHPARGONETS ,REHPARGOTOHP ,REHPARGOEG ,REHPARGOTPYRC ,REHPARGOEROHC ,REHPARGOTRAC ,REHPARGOIBOTUA 5. TNEMHSIRUONREDNU ,TNEMHSINUP ,TNEMHSILBATSE ,TNEMHSINOTSA ,TNEMHSILPMOCCA 6. YRATNEMIDES ,YRATNEMOM ,YRATNEMELE ,YRATNEMUCOD ,YRATNEMILPMOC ,YRATNEMMOC 7. NOISSIMSNART ,NOISSIMBUS ,NOISSIMREP ,NOISSIME ,NOISSIMMOC ,NOISSIMDA 8. NOITAROTSER ,NOITAROFREP ,NOITAROCED ,NOITAROPROC ,NOITAROBALLOC ,NOITARODA 9. NOISSERPER ,NOISSERPPO ,NOISSERPMI ,NOISSERPXE ,NOISSERPED ,NOISSERGGA 10. NOITATSKROW ,NOITATSELOM ,NOITATSEG ,NOITATSAVED ,NOITATSEROFED 11. SSENDETHGISTROHS ,SSENDETRAEHDNIK ,SSENDETBEDNI ,SSENDETOVED ,SSENDETRAEHGIB 12. NOITARTSIGER ,NOITARTENEP ,NOITARTSULLI ,NOITARTSURF ,NOITARTLIF ,NOITARTNECNOC ,NOITARTSINIMDA

JOHN WAYNE & KATHARINE HEPBURN MARKERS QUIZ

Which movie were they co-stars?

Boyhood ___ of JOHN WAYNE

The Clyde Morrison ___ moved ___ Winterset to this ___ in 1909 and lived here again in 1913-14. Mr. Morrison was a ___ employed by the Rainsburg ___ Store, located near the south ___ of Jackson Street on the ___ side. His ___ son, Marion, attended ___ at the Brooklyn ___ School and entered ___ grade there in the ___ of 1913.

When Mr. Morrison was ___ with ___ he moved his ___ to California in 1914. In later ___ the Morrison's ___ son, Marion, became the ___ Hollywood ___ ___ as John Wayne.

Katharine Hepburn ___ Here

"54" was ___ in 1911 ___ Dr. Sewell ___ a Johns ___ trained ___. His ___ Kate spent ___ here with the ___. Rep___, Kate's ___ had trouble ___ State Circle. Kate ___ wore ___.

ANSWERS - John Wayne: nwonk ,rotca ,yradnegel ,redlo ,sraey ,ylimaf ,sisolucrebut ,desongaid ,tsrif ,yratnemelE ,netragrednik ,redlo ,tsew ,dne ,gurd ,tsicamrahp ,esuoh ,morf ,ylimaf ,emoH

Katharine Hepburn: sresuort ,syawla ,gnitagivan ,enisuomil ,yldetropeR ,ylimaf ,emit ,ecein ,naicisyhp ,snikpoH ,nrubpeH ,yb ,tliub ,tpelS

Co-stars in: NRUBGOC RETSOOR

Words Starting with HY in 3 Minutes

What is the HY word based on the meaning?

1. A popular fragrant flower at Easter; funny lady character of the TV Britcom: Keeping up Appearances.

___

2. Mule is an example of one; Toyota Prius is another example.

___

3. A many-headed serpent or monster in the lake of Lerna (Greek mythology).

___

4. Bushy plants with large heads of pretty flowers; white & other colors; most diverse in China, Japan, & Korea.

___

5. Firefighters connect their hoses to it to put out a fire.

___

6. Your automobile brakes are assisted by this liquid system.

___

7. This is the gas which kept the Hindenburg, German passenger airship, afloat until the disaster at Lakehurst, New Jersey.

___

8. This kind of power plant shared by the United States & Canada at Niagara Falls.

___

9. A big dog-like nocturnal carnivoran mammal; commonly viewed as frightening; Africa is a major habitat.

___

10. Lyrics & music; usually sung in church to praise God.

___

11. Advertising publicity with exaggerated claims.

___

12. Healthy clean practices in medicine & personal life.

___

ANSWERS: 1. HTNICAYH 2. DIRBYH 3. ARDYH 4. AEGNARDYH 5. TNARDYH 6. CILUARDYH 7. NEGORDYH 8. CIRTCELEORDYH 9. ANEYH 10. NMYH 11. EPYH 12. ENEIGYH

Suprising Facts

State, guess or search the internet for the answer.

1. Does an airplane fly better in warm or cold weather? Dry or humid air?

2. What was the internet from the stone age to 1800? 1900? 1940? 1970? 2000?

3. What was the original nationality of Columbus? Einstein? Stalin? Hitler? Edward Teller? Emma Watson? Julie Andrews? Sean Connery?

4. How does a bird know to land in headwind?

5. What is the advantage of ordering special meals on airplanes?

6. What is the sure way of avoiding stomach issues on a foreign trip?

7. The average dog is able to learn up to 250 words & gestures. Its intelligence level is equal to a child's of what age?

8. What was the crew & passenger capacity of Amelia Earhart's Lockheed Electra 10E?

9. At what age did Dolly Parton, with 11 siblings & "dirt poor" family, start to sing?

10. Lyrics & music; usually sung in church to praise God.

11. Was Bela Lugosi, Count Dracula, born in Transylvania? When did he become Dracula?

12. How many people were employed by Blockbuster, famous home movie & video game rental services company, in 2004?

ANSWERS: 1. RIA YRD ,DLOC NI OSLA RETTEB SKROW ENIGNE RAC ;TFIL & NEGYXO EROM SAH RIA YRD & DLOC 2. BEW EDIW DLROW ;NOISIVELET ;OIDAR ;SREPAPSWEN ;SWEN GNIGNIRB SRELLEVART 3. HSITTOCS ;HSILGNE ;HCNERF ;NAIRAGNUH ;NAIRTSUA ;NAIGROEG ;NAMREG ;NAILATI 4. GNIHSINUP YLLAUSU SI DNIWLIAT HTIW GNIDNAL ;RORRE & LAIRT YB NRAEL 5. ESLE YDOBYREVE EROFEB TI TEG UOY 6. SKNIRD DELTTOB & SEGAREVEB GNILIOB ,DOOF DEGAKCAP & DENNAC ,ERUTAREPMET HGIH TA DOOF DEKOOC LLEW 7. NERDLIHC DLO-RAEY-RUOF SA TNEGILLETNI SA ERA SPMIHC ;DLIHC DLO-RAEY-OWT 8. SKNAT LEUF ARTXE HTIW DETTIFTUO SAW ENALP S'TRAHRAE ;SREGNESSAP 01 & WERC 2 :NOITARUGIFNOC LAMRON NI 9. DOG FO HCRUHC S'YLIMAF REH NI XIS EGA TA 10. REVIRD ECNALUBMA &)ENIGNE NA DLIUBER OT WOH WENK EHS(CINAHCEM KCURT 11. NOISREV EIVOM EHT NI ELOR RATS EHT TOG EH 0391 NI ;ALUCARD YALP YAWDAORB EHT NI DERRATS EH 7291 NI ;YRAGNUH FO MODGNIK EHT FO NOIGER NREHTUOS ,SOGUL NI NROB SAW EH ,ON 12. TI DELLIK DNAMED NO OEDIV & TENRETNI ,XOBDER ,XILFTEN ;000,48

Most Memorable Pop Songs of 1950s

Name the song & artist based on the lyrics segment.

1. Well, you ain't never caught a rabbit and you ain't no friend of mine / Well they said you was high-classed / Well, that was just a lie

2. I got a gal, named Sue, she knows just what to do / She rock to the East, she rock to the West / She is the gal that I love best

3. If you knew ... / Then you'd know why I feel blue without ... / My ... / Oh well, I love you gal, yes, I love you ...

4. Slander my name all over the place / Well do anything that you want to do / But uh-uh, honey lay off of them shoes

5. I never kissed a bear, I never kissed a goon / But I can shake a chicken in the middle of the room

6. I find it very, very easy to be true / I find myself alone when each day's through / Yes, I'll admit that I'm a fool for you

7. I'd tried so, not to give in / And I said to myself this affair it never will go so well / But why should I try to resist when baby I know so well

8. In a restless world like this is / Love is ended before it's begun / And too many moonlight kisses / Seem to cool in the warmth of the sun

9. Yo no soy marinero / Yo no soy marinero, soy capitan / Soy capitan, soy capitan

10. When an old friend I happened to see / I introduced her to my loved one / And while they were dancing / My friend stole my sweetheart from me

11. When I grew up and fell in love / I asked my sweetheart, what lies ahead / Will we have rainbows / Day after day

12. Other dancers may be on the floor / Dear, but my eyes will see only you / Only you have the magic technique

ANSWERS: 1. YELSERP SIVLE YB GOD DNUOH 2. DRAHCIR ELTTIL YB ITTURF ITTUT 3. YLLOH YDDUB YB EUS YGGEP 4. YELSERP SIVLE YB SEOHS EDEUS EULB 5. NOSKCAJ ADNAW YB YTRAP A EVAH S'TEL 6. HSAC YNNHOJ YB ENIL EHT KLAW I 7. ARTANIS KNARF YB NIKS YM REDNU UOY TOG EV'I 8. ELOC GNIK TAN YB EVOL NI LLAF I NEHW 9. SNELAV EIHCTIR YB ABMAB AL 10. EGAP ITTAP YB ZTLAW EESSENNET 11. YAD SIROD YB ÁRES ,ÁRES EUQ 12. NITRAM NAED YB YAWS

Puzzle Benefits for Your Brain Quiz

Enjoy & understand the magic of puzzle solving questions.

1. Why is word search puzzle solving good for your brain?

____

2. Why is picture puzzle solving good for your brain?

____

3. Why is diagonal word square puzzle solving good for your brain?

____

4. Why is mini crossword square puzzle solving good for your brain?

____

5. Why are math basic arithmetic drills good for your brain?

____

6. Why are shopping math problems good for your brain?

____

7. Why are travel math problems good for your brain?

____

8. Why is Sudoku puzzle solving good for your brain?

____

9. Why is missing vowels puzzle solving good for your brain?

____

10. Why is Hollywood themed puzzles solving good for your brain?

____

11. Why are timed quizzes good for your brain?

____

12. Why is missing word puzzles solving good for your brain?

____

ANSWERS: 1. IT REINFORCES SYSTEMATIC, ORGANIZED SEARCH; BUILDS VOCABULARY. 2. IT CONNECTS THE VISUAL PROCESSING PART OF THE BRAIN WITH SYMBOLIC PROCESSING. 3. IT REQUIRES ALTERNATIVE APPROACHES; STRENGTHENS VOCABULARY & SPELLING. 4. IT FORCES YOU TO SEARCH IN THE DEFINITION SEGMENT OF YOUR BRAIN'S DICTIONARY. 5. BASIC MATH MUST BE AUTOMATIC IN YOUR BRAIN JUST LIKE RECALLING YOUR OWN NAME. 6. SENTENCE MATH PROBLEMS CHALLENGE YOUR BRAIN TO TRANSLATE THE PROBLEM TO MATH. 7. IN ADDITION TO MATH, IT TEACHES YOU PHYSICS & GEOGRAPHY. 8. SUDOKU IS LOGIC PUZZLE NOT MATH. IT STRENGTHENS YOUR LOGICAL ABILITY. 9. IT SHARPENS YOUR PATTERN RECOGNITION SKILLS. 10. IT TAKES AWAY BOREDOM FROM DOING PUZZLES. 11. FREQUENTLY IN LIFE WE NEED TO COME UP WITH AN ANSWER FAST. 12. IT EXERCISES THE SENTENCE PATTERN STORAGE PART OF YOUR BRAIN.

Best Picture Oscar Winners Missing Vowels Puzzles 

1. Mrs. M_n_v_r; M_ F__r L_d_; _ll Q___t _n th_ W_st_rn Fr_nt; _ M_n f_r _ll S__s_ns;
2. Th_ St_ng; _m_d__s; Th_ Gr__t_st Sh_w _n __rth; W_ngs;
3. T_t_n_c; Th_ Gr__t Z__gf_ld; Pl_t__n; __t _f _fr_c_;
4. _ B___t_f_l M_nd; H_ml_t; Th_ L_rd _f th_ R_ngs: Th_ R_t_rn _f th_ K_ng; M_dn_ght C_wb__;
5. _nn__ H_ll; C_s_bl_nc_; W_st S_d_ St_r_; F_rr_st G_mp;
6. _rd_n_r_ P__pl_; ___ C_n't T_k_ _t w_th ___; M_t_n_ _n th_ B__nt_; Th_ S_l_nc_ _f th_ L_mbs;
7. R__n M_n; Sl_md_g M_ll__n__r_; Th_ D_p_rt_d; Th_ Sh_p_ _f W_t_r;

ANSWERS: 1. ;SNOSAES LLA ROF NAM A ;TNORF NRETSEW EHT NO TEIUQ LLA ;YDAL RIAF YM ;REVINIM .SRM 2. ;SGNIW ;HTRAE NO WOHS TSETAERG EHT ;SUEDAMA ;GNITS EHT 3. ;ACIRFA FO TUO ;NOOTALP ;DLEFGEIZ TAERG EHT ;CINATIT 4. ;YOBWOC THGINDIM ;GNIK EHT FO NRUTER EHT :SGNIR EHT FO DROL EHT ;TELMAH ;DNIM LUFITUAEB A 5. ;PMUG TSERROF ;YROTS EDIS TSEW ;ACNALBASAC ;LLAH EINNA 6. ;SBMAL EHT FO ECNELIS EHT ;YTNUOB EHT NO YNITUM ;UOY HTIW TI EKAT T'NAC UOY ;ELPOEP YRANIDRO 7. ;RETAW FO EPAHS EHT ;DETRAPED EHT ;ERIANOILLIM GODMULS ;NAM NIAR

Words Starting with SQU

What is the SQU word based on the meaning?

1. A park or town center with 4 corners; a kind of country dance.

____

2. Fried calamari when alive.

____

3. Air force operational unit; a group of naval warships.

____

4. An extended sports team.

____

5. People in Japan & China are more frequently in this low body position than in America.

____

6. Spend inherited wealth quickly & stupidly.

____

7. Suppress the annoying sound of channel noise in two-way radios.

____

8. Sound made by a door in need of lubrication.

____

9. To wet with a stream of liquid.

____

10. To look at something with eyes partly closed.

____

11. A shrill cry of joy, fear or pain; to inform on someone to the police.

____

12. An English country gentleman of high social standing.

____

ANSWERS: 1. ERAUQS 2. DIUQS 3. NORDAUQS 4. DAUQS 5. TAUQS 6. REDNAUQS 7. HCLEUQS 8. KAEUQS 9. TRIUQS 10. TNIUQS 11. LAEUQS 12. ERIUQS

Words Starting with KN

What is the KN word based on the meaning?

1. Collection of organized information in your brain.

____

2. Connecting joints in fingers.

____

3. Recognized & understood.

____

4. Complex, complicated, convoluted; full of knots.

____

5. Good looking; one-sided fight.

____

6. Utensils used for cutting at the dinner table.

____

7. How grandma makes pullovers for the grandchildren.

____

8. New York City basketball team.

____

9. Due to modern medicine you can replace these body parts if they get worn out.

____

10. Old-fashioned fooling around.

____

11. Stupid; a person of questionable intelligence.

____

12. To stop doing what you are doing; cheap copy of an expensive brand product.

____

ANSWERS: 1. EGDELWONK 2. ELKCUNK 3. NWONK 4. YTTONK 5. TUOKCONK 6. SEVINK 7. GNITTINK 8. SKCINK 9. SEENK 10. YREVANK 11. DAEHELKCUNK 12. FFOKCONK

Checkmate in 2 Moves, White to Move

ANSWERS: 1. ETAMKCEHC - NEEUQ dnoces ot detomorp - 8F ot NWAP ;7E ot GNIK ;5F ot NEEUQ 2. ETAMKCEHC 8G ot KOOR ;THGINK sekat THGINK ;6F ot THGINK

Words Starting with CAT

What is the CAT word based on the meaning?

1. An underground tunnel used as a tomb by the ancient Romans.

____

2. Magazines offering merchandize for sale.

____

3. An initiator who remains unscathed; platinum is one in your car's exhaust system.

____

4. Boats on floats.

____

5. Used to launch airplanes on aircraft carriers.

____

6. Caused blindness in the past, but can now be removed by an operation.

____

7. Sinking of the Titanic was one; destruction of Pompeii by the eruption of Mount Vesuvius another.

____

8. Here, Kitty, Kitty, Kitty; suggestive whistles.

____

9. A group of related words, items, things.

____

10. A rancher breeding, raising cows.

____

11. Butterfly's ancestry includes this one.

____

12. Fashion models parade on it; elevated walkway.

____

ANSWERS: 1. BMOCATAC 2. SGOLATAC 3. TSYLATAC 4. SNARAMATAC 5. TLUPATAC 6. STCARATAC 7. EHPORTSATAC 8. SLLACTAC 9. YROGETAC 10. NAMELTTAC 11. RALLIPRETAC 12. KLAWTAC

Words Starting with PARA

What is the PARA word based on the meaning?

1. You need one when jumping from an airplane.

____

2. The perfect dream place to live.

____

3. A group of sentences living together.

____

4. Tweety Bird is one.

____

5. Frequent result of injury in a car or motorcycle accident.

____

6. Someone who does first aid out of an ambulance.

____

7. Fear of Martians taking over your town.

____

8. Someone who does lawyer work for less money.

____

9. Soldier who jumps out of an airplane to fight on the ground.

____

10. Candles made out of it.

____

11. A person who exploits others and contributes nothing.

____

12. Macy's has one at Thanksgiving.

____

ANSWERS: 1. ETUHCARAP 2. ESIDARAP 3. HPARGARAP 4. TEEKARAP 5. DEZYLARAP 6. CIDEMARAP 7. AIONARAP 8. LAGELARAP 9. REPOORTARAP 10. NIFFARAP 11. ETISARAP 12. EDARAP

The Adventures of Chuckleberry Dumperdink

All the questions related to an American state or USA territory.

1. Chuckleberry Dumperdink takes the Staten Island Ferry to photograph the Statue of Liberty after visiting the World Trade Center Memorial site.

______

2. Chuckleberry strolls around Old San Juan then drives up into the mountains to visit a rain forest. Later Chuckleberry goes for a swim on El Condado beach.

______

3. Chuckleberry visits a tasting room at a winery by the Russian River before heading back across the Golden Gate bridge to the city with cable cars.

______

4. Chuckleberry tries the rides at Disney then goes to an alligator farm. It is very hot so he goes to the beach to cool down in the Atlantic Ocean.

______

5. Chuckleberry goes gambling in Atlantic City and after losing some money he can only afford coffee at a diner by going north 100 miles on the Garden State Parkway.

______

6. Chuckleberry drives to see the snow-capped Mt. Rainier then takes a boat on the Puget Sound. He has dinner at the restaurant on the top of Space Needle.

______

7. Chuckleberry visits the Smithsonian Museum then he goes by the Potomac River to admire the cherry blossoms. In the afternoon Chucky goes for a tour of the White House.

______

8. Chucky explores Acadia National Park then heads to Bar Harbor for a lobster bake lunch.

______

9. Chucky plays golf at the beautiful greens in Pinehurst, then visits the Wright Brothers Museum at Kitty Hawk. For dinner he enjoys pulled-pork barbecue.

______

10. Chucky takes the monorail from one casino to another in the 110 degree heat. He rents a car to drive out to Hoover Dam and takes a dip in Lake Mead.

______

11. Chuck goes on the Skywalk in Grand Canyon West, then take a bus trip to Sedona to see the inspiring red rock mountains & buttes.

______

12. Chuck's last trip takes him to Yellowstone National Park where he see geysers, grizzly bears & bison. He drives to Jackson Hole to see a rodeo.

______

ANSWERS: 1. KROY WEN 2. OCIR OTREUP 3. AINROFILAC 4. ADIROLF 5. YESREJ WEN 6. NOTGNIHSAW 7. CD NOTGNIHSAW 8. ENIAM 9. ANILORAC HTRON 10. ADAVEN 11. ANOZIRA 12. GNIMOYW

Incredible Facts about Planet Earth

You may know the answers without searching the web.

1. Pizza consumption per person by country: 1. __________ 2. __________ 3. __________ 4. __________ 5.__________ 6.__________ ?

2. Military planes by country: __________ 13,000 __________ 4,000 __________ 3,000

3. World Giving Index rankings by country: 1. __________ 2. __________ 3. __________ 4. __________ 5.__________ ?

4. Top 5 countries that eat the most breakfast cereal: 1. __________ 2. __________ 3. __________ 4. __________ 5.__________

5. What is the deadliest job in America historically?

____

6. If we spill out the water from Lake Superior over North & South America, how high would it be?

____

7. Cows were domesticated in Turkey over 10,000 years ago. Which countries have the most cows: 1. __________ 2. __________ 3. __________ 4. __________ 5.__________?

8. Motor vehicles per person by country (Hint: forget Germany!): 1. __________ 2. __________ 3. __________ 4. __________ 5.__________ ?

9. Does the French Foreign Legion accept murderers today?

____

10. On a hot summer day in 2018 (hot day 86 °F) a vintage German-built (1939) Junker JU52 crashed with the full load of 20 people at 9,000 feet in the Swiss Alps. What caused the accident? Why didn't Hitler's plane (same type) crash?

____

11. Top 5 world's happiest countries: 1. __________ 2. __________ 3. __________ 4. __________ 5.__________?

12. Top 5 most polluting countries: 1. __________ 2. __________ 3. __________ 4. __________ 5.__________?

ANSWERS: 1. AISSUR ;YLATI ;YNAMREG ;MODGNIK DETINU ;SETATS DETINU ;YAWRON 2. ANIHC ;AISSUR ;SETATS SETINU 3.)NOLYEC(AKNAL IRS ;DNALAEZ WEN ;AILARTSUA ;SETATS DETINU ;RAMNAYM 4. OCIXEM ;SETATS DETINU ;AILARTSUA ;ADANAC ;MODGNIK DETINU 5. SETATS DETINU EHT FO TNEDISERP 6.)M 604(TF 333,1 :HTPED MUMIXAM ;TOOF ENO 7. ANITNEGRA ;SETATS DETINU ;ANIHC ;LIZARB ;AIDNI 8. NIAPS ;ADANAC ;YLATI ;DNALAEZ WEN/AILARTSUA ;SETATS DETINU 9. .SLANIMIRC & SREREDRUM DERREFERP TCAF NI ,TSAP EHT NI DID TI TUB .ON 10. .TEEF 000,3 EKIL EDUTITLA WOL YLEVITALER WELF & DEDAOL YLTHGIL SAW ENALP S'RELTIH .YKS EHT FO TUO SLLAF ENALPRIA EHT ESLE ,YLF OT DEEPS ARTXE SERIUQER DAOL LLUF HTIW RIA NIHT TOH 11. DNALAEZ WEN/AILARTSUA ;SDNALREHTEN EHT ;ADANAC ;DNALREZTIWS ;HTRON EHT OT SEIRTNUOC LLAMS REHTO & KRAMNED 12. NAPAJ ;AISSUR ;AIDNI ;SETATS DETINU ;ANIHC

Origin of Popular Foods

What is the animal used as the food source?

1. American Buffalo Wings, French Poulet Roti & Ailes de Poulet Caramélisées

____

2. Irish Sheppard's Pie, Gigot D'agneau A La Francaise, Italian Ragù di Agnello

____

3. Whopper, Big Mac, Dave's Triple, The White Castle Slider, Carl's Jr.'s Western Bacon Cheeseburger

____

4. Hungarian Goulash with Paprika, French Boeuf Bourguignon

____

5. Fried Calamari Fra Diavolo, French Provençal Calamari Salad

____

6. Nova Scotia Lox; Spinach, Lox and Goat Cheese Omelet

____

7. Greek Cypriot Tsamarella

____

8. French Escargots à la Bourguignonne

____

9. Thanksgiving Dinner Entrée, Pot Pie a la Dinde

____

10. English Bangers, German Bockwurst

____

11. Venison, Bloody Mary Venison Jerky

____

12. Italian Osso Bucco, French Blanquette de Veau

____

ANSWERS: 1. NEKCIHC 2. PEEHS 3. ELTTAC 4. ELTTAC 5. DIUQS 6. NOMLAS 7. TAOG 8. LIANS 9. YEKRUT 10. GIP & FLAC 11. REED 12. FLAC

NOT IN A ____ MOON!

Name the items based on the pictures. They all start with the same color.

1. 

____

5. 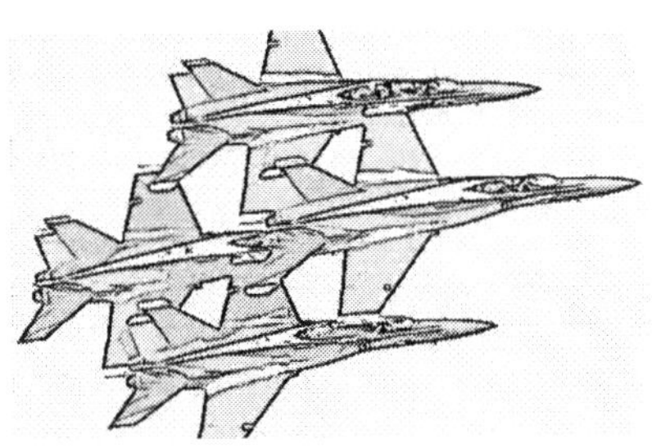

____

2. 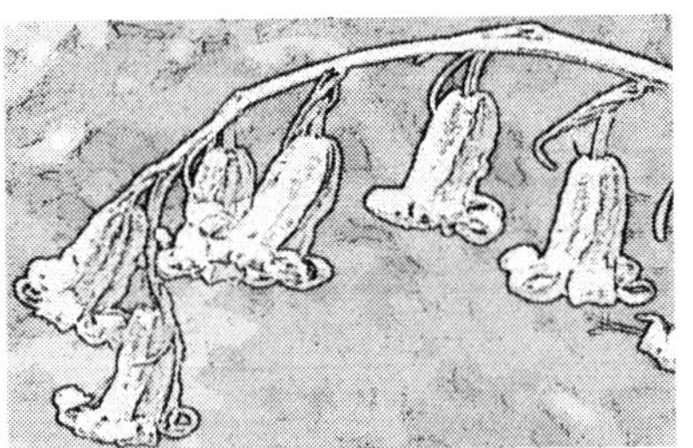

____

6. 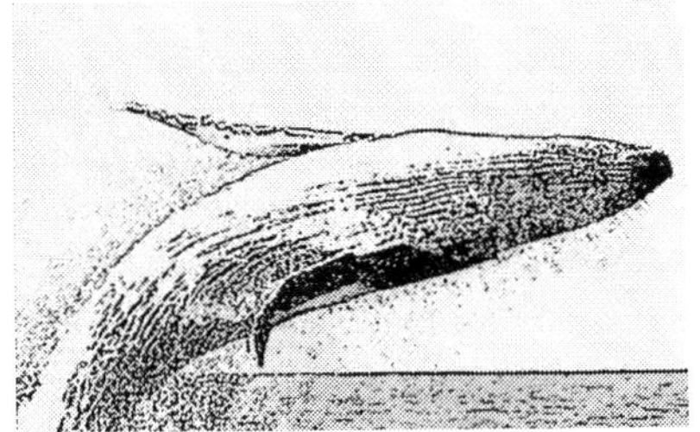

____

3. 

____

7. 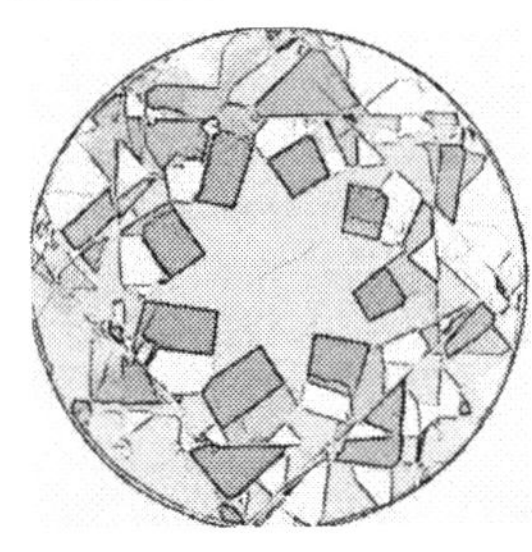

____

4. 

____

8. 

____

ANSWERS. 1. SEOHS EDEUS EULB 2. SLLEBEULB 3. YAJ EULB 4. YBOOB DETOOF-EULB 5. SLEGNA EULB 6. ELAHW EULB 7. ZAPOT EULB 8. SSORC EULB

Origin of Popular Vegetarian Foods

What is the vegetable, fruit, grain or nut used as food source?

1. Omelette, Frittata, Quiche, French Creme Brulee, Tiramisu

____

2. Nutella, French Noisette Cups, Italian Nocciola Gelato

____

3. Jiff, Skippy, Mexican Mazapanes de Cacahuate

____

4. Doritos, Taco Shells, Kellogg's Frosted Flakes

____

5. Pringles, French Fries, Russian Vodka, French Patates au Vin

____

6. Dill Pickles, Gherkins, Dosakai, French Concombre a la Menthe

____

7. Ketchup, Marinara Sauce, Salsa, French Tarte aux Moutarde

____

8. Crackers, Cookies, Bread, Baguette, French Toast, Croissant, Moroccan Couscous, Italian Pasta

____

9. Irish Porridge, Cheerios, Original Quaker Life, Lucky Charms

____

10. Raisins, Red & White Wine, Jam, Jelly, French Vins de Bordeaux

____

11. Spanish Paella, Italian Risotto, Japanese Sake & Sushi, Egyptian Pilaf

____

12. Tofu, Soy Milk, Italian Pasta Fagioli, French Salade des Haricots Verts

____

ANSWERS: 1. SGGE 2. STUNLEZAH 3. STUNAEP 4. NROC 5. OTATOP 6. REBMUCUC 7. OTAMOT 8. TAEHW 9. STAO 10. SEPARG 11. ECIR 12. SNAEB

Five Rhyming Words in 5 Minutes

What words match the pattern with one missing letter?

1. _EEPER

2. _LIGHT

3. _OBBLE

4. _UTTER

5. _ETTLE

6. FOR_ED

7. HEA_ED

8. _ECTOR

9. LOO_ED

10. _OPPER

11. S_ORES

12. _INGLE

ANSWERS: 1. REPEEW ,REPEEP ,REPEEK ,REPEED ,REPEEB 2. THGILS ,THGILP ,THGILF ,THGILB ,THGILA 3. ELBBOW ,ELBBOH ,ELBBOG ,ELBBOC ,ELBBOB 4. RETTUP ,RETTUM ,RETTUG ,RETTUC ,RETTUB 5. ELTTES ,ELTTEN ,ELTTEM ,ELTTEK ,ELTTEF 6. DEMROF ,DEKROF ,DEGROF ,DEDROF ,DECROF 7. DEVAEH ,DETAEH ,DEPAEH ,DELAEH ,DEDAEH 8. ROTCEV ,ROTCES ,ROTCER ,ROTCEL ,ROTCEH 9. DETOOL ,DESOOL ,DEPOOL ,DEMOOL ,DEKOOL 10. REPPOT ,REPPOP ,REPPOL ,REPPOH ,REPPOC 11. SEROTS ,SEROPS ,SERONS ,SEROHS ,SEROCS 12. ELGNIT ,ELGNIS ,ELGNIM ,ELGNIJ ,ELGNID

Curious Math Challenge

Math is everywhere in our lives. See for yourself below.

1. What day is Friday + 10 days? 20 days? 30 days?

____

2. What month is July + 18 months? 25 months? 35 months?

____

3. Why is kilobyte 1024 bytes and not 1000 bytes?

____

4. What country is the biggest customer of American soybeans? Corn? Wheat? Potatoes? Peaches? Beef? Chocolate Candy

____

5. In a casino you bet on red at a roulette table. If you lose you double your bet(Martingale system). Will you win eventually?

____

6. Why do months have odd (strange) number of days: 28, 29, 30, 31?

____

7. If you were born February 29 (leapling), should you celebrate on February 28 or March 1 in non-leap years?

____

8. How many ways can you change a dollar?

____

9. In "Red River" John Wayne takes on a hazardous drive of 10,000 cattle. With 12% loss factor how many cattle remained? At $20 a head, how much did he get?

____

10. Elizabeth became Queen in 1952. She is 92 years old in 2018. If she retires at 100, how long did she reign?

____

11. Arevampires, monsters & beasts good at math?

____

12. Can you make the number seven even, without adding to it or subtracting from it?

____

ANSWERS: 1. YADNUS ;YADSRUHT ;YADNOM 2. ENUJ ;TSUGUA ;REBMEVON 3. .4201 = REWOP HT01 EHT OT 2 OT ECNEREFER ETAMIXORPPA SA DESU OLIK ,YRTSUDNI RETUPMOC NI 4. ADANAC ;NAPAJ ;ADANAC ;NAPAJ ;OCIXEM ;OCIXEM ;ANIHC 5. .STIMIL TEB SAH TI & YENOM EROM SAH TI ESUACEB SNIW ONISAC EHT YLEKIL EROM .YKCUL TEG UOY FI 6. .SYAD)RAEY PAEL(63 RO 53 REBMECED & HCAE SYAD 03 VON - NAJ :EB THGIM METSYS RELPMIS A .SNOSAER CIROTSIH 7. .STNESERP EROM TEG OT EPOH UOY YAD REVEHCIHW 8. EERHT-YTENIN DERDNUH OWT 9. SRALLOD SDNASUOHT XIS-YTNEVES DERDNUH ;DERDNUH THGIE-YTHGIE 10. SRAEY RUOF YTNEVES 11. ALUCARD TNUOC :NOITPECXE ,TON YLLARENEG 12. .RETTEL TSRIF EHT EVOMER TSUJ .SEY

WHERE ON GOD'S _____ EARTH?

Name the items based on the pictures. They all start with the same color.

1.

2.

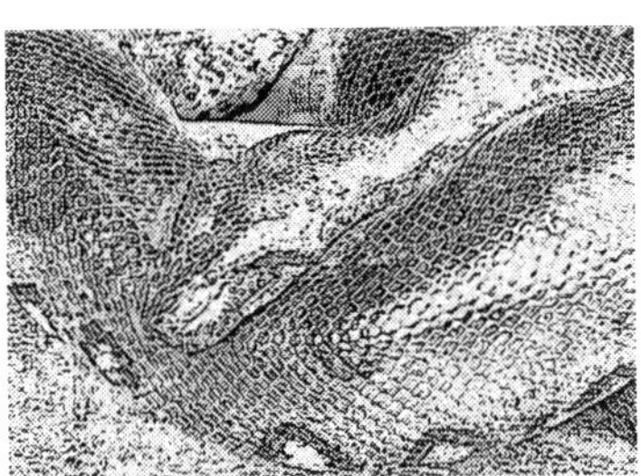

3.

4.

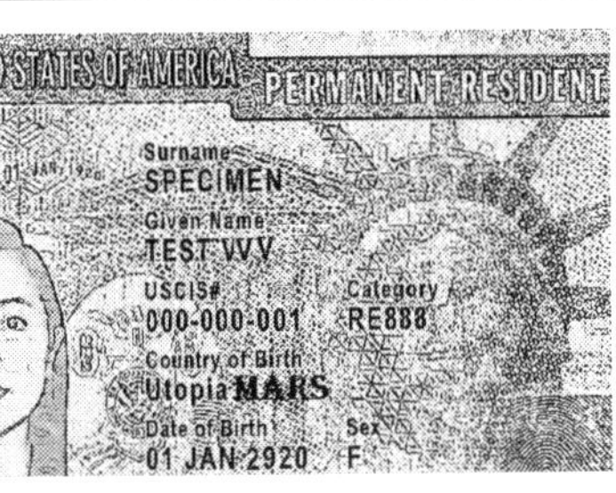

5.

6.

7.

8.

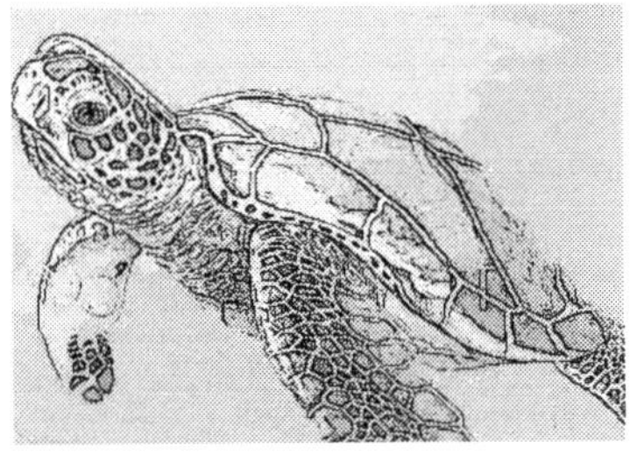

ANSWERS. 1. ESUOHNEERG 2. ADNOCANA NEERG 3. SNAEB NEERG 4. DRAC NEERG 5. YGRENE NEERG 6. NROHNEERG 7. NOITULOVER NEERG 8. ELTRUT NEERG

Seven New Words in 7 Minutes

What words match the pattern with 2 or 3 missing letters?

1. C__W

2. __OL

3. NU__

4. P__R

5. BE__ER

6. CA__ON

7. D__PER

8. SHRI__

9. CO__AGE

10. __ZZLED

11. S__MMING

12. EX___TION

ANSWERS: 1. WORC ,WERC ,WARC ,WELC ,WALC ,WOHC ,WEHC 2. LOOW ,LOIV ,LOOT ,LOOP ,LODI ,LOOF ,LOOC 3. STUN ,SNUN ,NNUN ,BMUN ,LLUN ,EKUN ,EDUN 4. RRUP ,RUOP ,ROOP ,REIP ,REEP ,RAEP ,RIAP 5. RETTEB ,REDNEB ,REPEEB ,REVAEB ,RETAEB ,RERAEB ,REKAEB 6. NOITAC ,NOTRAC ,NOSRAC ,NOBRAC ,NOYNAC ,NOTNAC ,NONNAC 7. REPMUD ,REPARD ,REPPID ,REPAID ,REPEED ,REPPAD ,REPMAD 8. KNIRHS ,ENIRHS ,PMIRHS ,LLIRHS ,EKIRHS ,TFIRHS ,KEIRHS 9. EGARUOC ,EGATTOC ,EGASROC ,EGAKROC ,EGADROC ,EGALLOC ,EGANIOC 10. DELZZIS ,DELZZUP ,DELZZUN ,DELZZUM ,DELZZUG ,DELZZIF ,DELZZAD 11. GNIMMIWS ,GNIMMETS ,GNIMMULS ,GNIMMILS ,GNIMMALS ,GNIMMIKS ,GNIMMAHS 12. NOITADUXE ,NOITROTXE ,NOITAIPXE ,NOITPMEXE ,NOITUCEXE ,NOITERCXE ,NOITPECXE

Dead Man's Pass Quiz

Complete the missing words in the Texan historical marker.

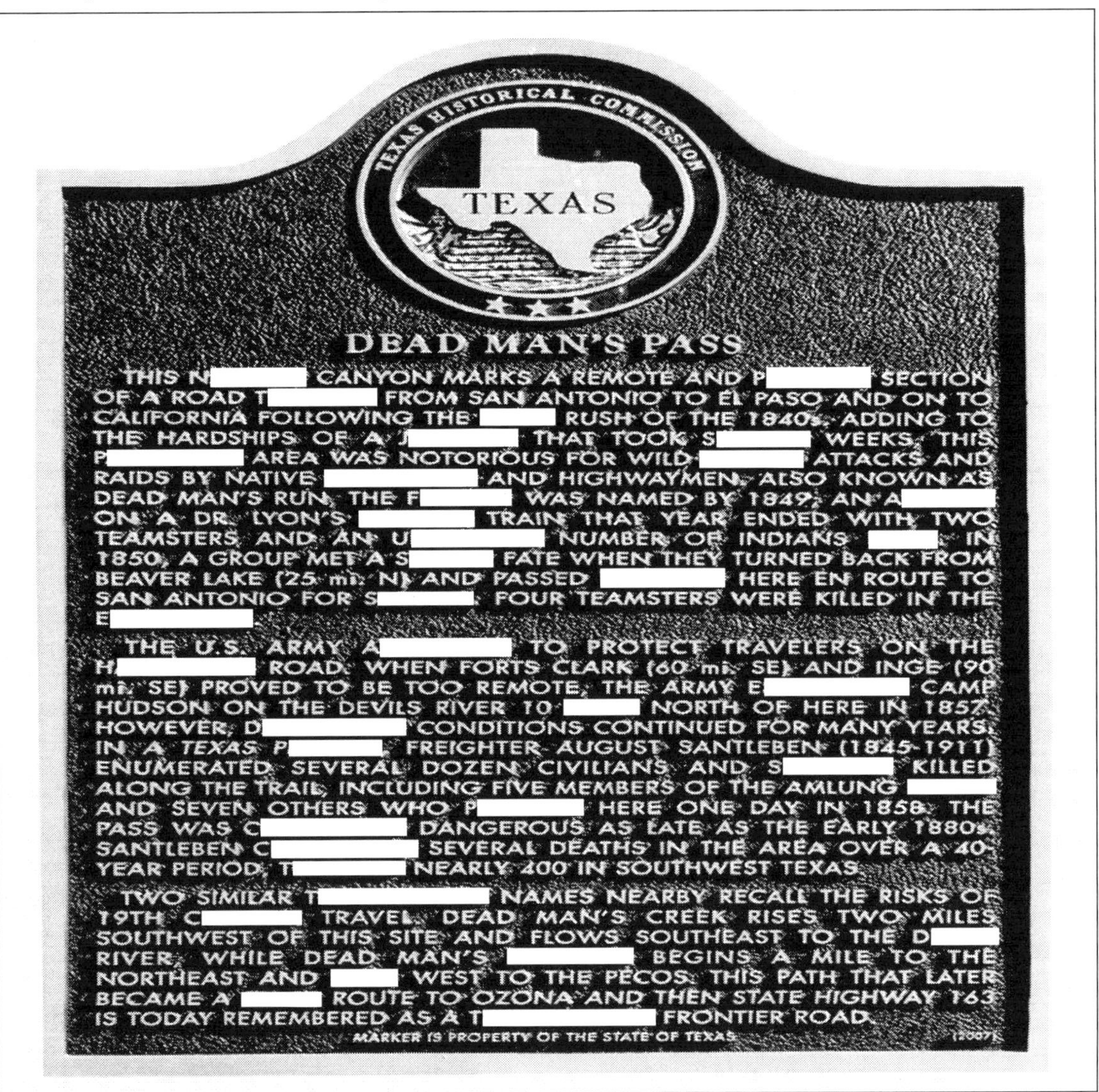

ANSWERS: SUOREHCAERT ,EGATS ,SNUR ,NOYNAC ,SLIVED ,YRUTNEC ,CIHPARGOPOT ,GNILATOT ,DELCINORHC ,DEREDISNOC ,DEHSIREP ,YLIMAF ,SREIDLOS ,REENOIP ,SUOREGNAD ,SELIM ,DEHSILBATSE ,SUODRAZAH ,DETPMETTA ,RETNUOCNE ,SEILPPUS ,HGUORHT ,RALIMIS ,DAED ,NWONKNU ,NOGAW ,HSUBMA ,ERUTAEF ,SNACIREMA ,LAMINA ,RALUCITRAP ,LAREVES ,YENRUOJ ,DLOG ,DELEVART ,SUOLIREP ,WORRAN

Name That Animal in 3 Minutes!

Find at least 3 animals that begin with each letter (if any).

1. A-B

___

2. C-D

___

3. E-F

___

4. G-H

___

5. I-J

___

6. K-L

___

7. M-N

___

8. O-P

___

9. Q-R

___

10. S-T

___

11. U-V-W

___

12. X-Y-Z

___

ANSWERS: 1. REVAEB ,RAEB ,REGDAB ,NOOBAB ,EPOLETNA ,ADNOCANA ,ACAPLA ,KRAVDRAA 2. YEKNOD ,NIHPLOD ,RUASONID ,REED ,ARBOC ,UOBIRAC ,YRANAC ,LEMAC 3. GORF ,XOF ,OGNIMALF ,NOCLAF ,UME ,KLE ,TNAHPELE ,ELGAE 4. ANEYH ,OPPIH ,GNIRREH ,GOHEGDEH ,ALLIROG ,EFFARIG ,ELLEZAG ,REDNAG 5. GUBENUJ ,YEOJ ,RAUGAJ ,SSAKCAJ ,ALAPMI ,ANAUGI ,SIBI ,XEBI 6. DRAPOEL ,RUMEL ,BMAL ,GUBYDAL ,ALAOK ,IWIK ,LUKARAK ,OORAGNAK 7. AIRTUN ,HCTAHTUN ,KRAHS ESRUN ,ELAGNITHGIN ,ESUOM ,NOLFUOM ,ESOOM ,YEKNOM 8. NIUGNEP ,KCOCAEP ,TEEKARAP ,ADNAP ,REKCEPXO ,LWO ,HCIRTSO ,SUPOTCO 9. RETSOOR ,REEDNIER ,NOOCCAR ,TIBBAR ,LLOUQ ,AKKOUQ ,LAZTEUQ ,LIAUQ 10. YEKRUT ,ESIOTROT ,TACMOT ,REGIT ,KNUKS ,KRAHS ,NOIL AES ,HSIFLIAS 11. ELAHW ,LESAEW ,GOHTRAW ,SURLAW ,ERUTLUV ,NEXIV ,REPIV ,LAIRU ,NIHCRU ,NROCINU 12. SURUASOGNOGIZ ,ORROZ ,ALLIROZ ,ROKOZ ,UBEZ ,ARBEZ ,TEKCAJWOLLEY ,KAY ,SURUASOAIX

Numbers in English in 6 Minutes

Write the math result in English like on a bank check.

1. 500+777

____

2. 888+2222

____

3. 10000-1111

____

4. 999-123

____

5. 18749+32856

____

6. 1000000-7

____

7. 4791+888

____

8. 50*41+7

____

9. 33*44+9

____

10. 100000/100+573

____

11. 200/10+2089

____

12. 9000/100+277

____

ANSWERS: 1. neveS-ytneveS derdnuH owT dnasuohT enO 2. neT derdnuH enO dnasuohT eerhT 3. eniN-ythgiE derdnuH thgiE dnasuohT thgiE 4. xiS-ytneveS derdnuH thgiE 5. eviF derdnuH xiS dnasuohT enO-ytfiF 6. eerhT-yteniN derdnuH eniN dnasuohT eniN-yteniN derdnuH eniN 7. eniN-ytneveS derdnuH xiS dnasuohT eviF 8. neveS-ytfiF dnasuohT owT 9. enO-ytxiS derdnuH ruoF dnasuohT enO 10. eerhT-ytneveS derdnuH eviF dnasuohT enO 11. eniN derdnuH enO dnasuohT owT 12. neveS-ytxiS derdnuH eerhT

Popular Songs with US States or Big Cities

Name the artist & song based on the lyrics segment.

1. I wanna wake up in a city that doesn't sleep / And find I'm king of the hill, top of the heap / These little town blues, are melting away

____

2. I dreamed about my mother dear old papa sister and brother / I dreamed about that girl who's been waiting for so long / I wanna go home I wanna go home oh how I wanna go home

____

3. Blue Ridge Mountains, Shenandoah River / Life is old there, older than the trees / Younger than the mountains, blowing like a breeze

____

4. Where the Rio Grande is flowin' / And starry skies are bright / She walks along the river / In the quiet summer night / I know that she remembers

____

5. The loveliness of Paris seems somehow sadly gray / The glory that was Rome is of another day / I've been terribly alone and forgotten in Manhattan / I'm going home to my city by the Bay

____

6. Pardon me boy, is that the Chattanooga Choo Choo? / Track twenty nine, boy you can gimme a shine / I can afford to board a Chattanooga Choo Choo / I've got my fare and just a trifle to spare

____

7. Meet me at the fair / Don't tell me the lights are shining / Any place but there / We will dance the Hoochee Koochee / I will be your tootsie wootsie

____

8. There stood a log cabin made of earth and wood / Where lived a country boy named Johnny B. Goode / Who never ever learned to read or write so well / But he could play a guitar just like a-ringin' a bell

____

9. Oh, there's black jack and poker and the roulette wheel / A fortune won and lost on ev'ry deal / All you need's a strong heart and a nerve of steel

____

10. On State Street that great street I just want to say / They do things they don't do on Broadway / They have a time, the time of their life / I saw a man, he danced with his wife

____

11. The corn is as high as an elephant's eye / And it looks like it's climbing clear up in the sky / Oh, what a beautiful mornin' / Oh, what a beautiful day / I got a beautiful feelin' / Everything's goin' my way

____

12. Come with me / While the moon is on the sea / The night is young / And so are we, so are we / Dreams come true

____

ANSWERS: 1. ARTANIS KNARF YB KROY WEN ,KROY WEN 2. SENOJ MOT & ERAB YBBOB YB YTIC TIORTED 3.)AINIGRIV TSEW(REVNED NHOJ YB SDAOR YRTNUOC ,EMOH EM EKAT 4. SAXET FO ESOR WOLLEY EHT 5. TTENNEB YNOT YB OCSICNARF NAS NI TRAEH YM TFEL I 6.)EESSENNET(SRETSIS SWERDNA EHT YB OOHC OOHC AGOONATTAHC 7.)IRUOSSIM(DNALRAG YDUJ YB SIUOL ,SIUOL .TS NI EM TEEM 8.)ANAISUOL(YRREB KCUHC YB EDOOG .B YNNHOJ 9. YELSERP SIVLE YB SAGEV SAL AVIV 10. ARTANIS KNARF YB)NWOT 'NILDDOT TAHT(OGACIHC 11. NIETSREMMAH RACSO & SREGDOR DRAHCIR YB LACISUM AMOHALKO 12. YELSERP SIVLE YB IIAWAH EULB

How Does It Work?

State, guess or search the web for the answer.

1. What is inside the long cylinder of a steam locomotive?

____

2. What is the original source of energy in a car battery?

____

3. Can the stock market keep going up without crashing ever?

____

4. Why does a Ponzi scheme always collapse?

____

5. Why doesn't US congress pass term limit legislation for senators & representatives?

____

6. Can we establish a colony on the Moon by 2050?

____

7. Can we establish a colony on the Mars by 2070?

____

8. What was the top speed of Ford Model T? How many horsepower?

____

9. Why do 4-cylinder turbo engines take the place of 6-cylinder engines in automobiles recently?

____

10. Does a vacuum cleaner throw dust in the air?

____

11. What keeps a giant airplane up in the thin air?

____

12. Why is red wine best with steak & white wine with fish?

____

ANSWERS: 1. RETAW 2. KNAT EHT NI LEUF 3. TSAP EHT NI DEHSARC SYAWLA TI ,ON 4. SREKCUS YDEERG FO TUO SNUR TI 5. TSERETNI-FLES TSNIAGA SI TI 6. NEPPAH YAM TAHT 7. SNAMUH DNES OT NOSAER ON ,STOBOR ROF YLNO 8. PH 02 ,HPM 54 9. TNEICIFFE LEUF EROM ,SSEL HGIEW 10. TCEFREP TON SI RETLIF EHT ,SEY 11. DEEPS STI 12. ETIHW SI HSIF ,DER SI KAETS :NOITIDART YRANILUC ,NOSAER ON

2 Associated Words Challenge in 10 Min

Find at least one new word based on all letters in the given words.

1. DIAPERS	LEAKS
2. HORNET	WASP
3. WOLVES	CRIED
4. BRAKES	STOP
5. SERGEANT	ARMS
6. RATTLE	SNAKE
7. TROUT	HOOKS
8. DIRECTOR	STARLET
9. CANOE	SINK
10. ANGER	CALM
11. COWS	RUSTLE
12. YELPED	SHRIEK

ANSWERS: 1. SELAK ,SEKAL ,DERIPSA ,DESIARP ,RIAPSED 2. PAWS ,SWAP ,ENORHT 3. CIRED ,REDIC ,SLEWOV 4. TOPS ,TSOP ,STOP ,SPOT ,SREKAB ,SKAERB 5. SRAM ,SMAR ,STNEGAER ,EGNARTSE 6. KAENS ,RETTAL 7. KOOHS ,ROTUT 8. SELTTAR ,ELTRATS ,ROTIDERC 9. NIKS ,SKNI ,NAECO 10. MALC ,EGNAR 11. TLUSER ,RETSUL ,WOCS 12. SREKIH ,YLPEED

MY TEETH ARE GOING ______!

Name the items based on the pictures. They all start with the same color.

1.

2.

3.

4.

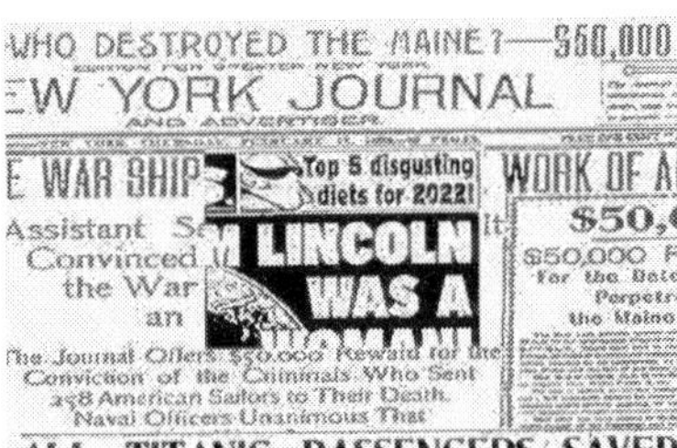

5.

6.

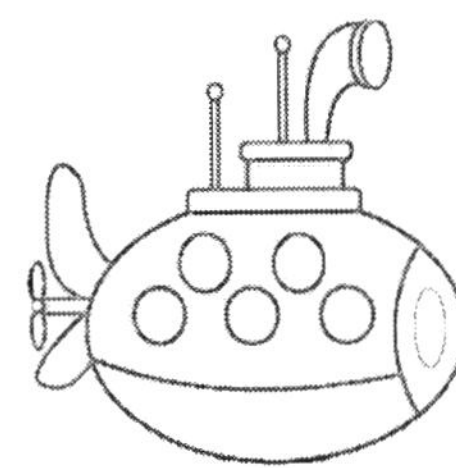

7.

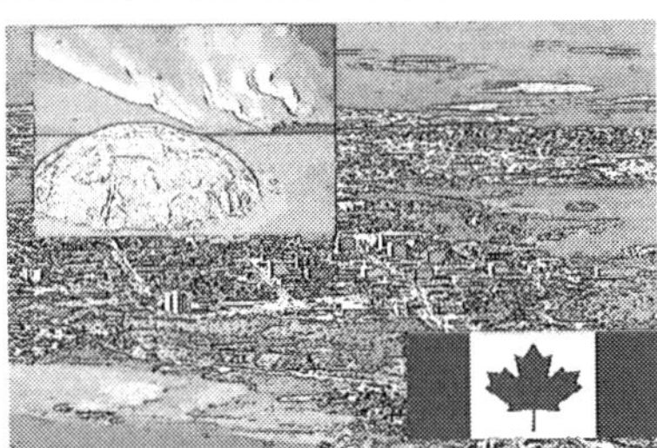

8.

ANSWERS. 1. TEKCAJWOLLEY 2. KRAP LANOITAN ENOTSWOLLEY 3. DAOR KCIRB WOLLEY 4. MSILANRUOJ WOLLEY 5. BAC WOLLEY 6. ENIRAMBUS WOLLEY 7. NWOT CITCRA NAIDANAC EFINKWOLLEY 8. HCNIF WOLLEY

Americans in Foreign City Movies

All the questions related to foreign topic movies with American heroes.

1. Who was the American in "An American in Paris" movie also starring Lise Bouvier(Leslie Caron)?

____

2. Who played the princess in "Roman Holiday" starring Gregory Peck as an American foreign correspondent in Rome?

____

3. Who played the American couple in the Hitchcock movie "The Man Who Knew Too Much" featuring the hit song "Que Sera, Sera"?

____

4. Who played the Griswald family man in National Lampoon's "European Vacation" comedy movie also starring Beverly D'Angelo?

____

5. Who played the Machinist's Mate First Class role in "The Sand Pebble" movie, also starring Candice Bergen? The plot is about the 1920s Yangtze River Patrol gunboat USS San Pablo.

____

6. Who was the actress co-starring with Bing Crosby & Bob Hope in "Road to Morocco", a 1942 American comedy film?

____

7. Who played the American ace fighter pilot during the Korean War in "Sayonara" co-starring Patricia Owens?

____

8. Who played the lead role in "Blame It on Rio" a 1984 American romantic comedy film, which also starred Valerie Harper & Demi Moore?

____

9. Who played the female lead role in "G.I. Blues", a 1960 American musical comedy film which starred Elvis Presley?

____

10. Who starred in "A Connecticut Yankee in King Arthur's Court", a 1949 movie with actress Rhonda Fleming?

____

11. Who was the lead role in "March or Die" a 1977 British film celebrating the 1920s French Foreign Legion and also starred Catherine Deneuve?

____

12. Who was the star of "Torn Curtain", a 1966 American Cold War thriller directed by Alfred Hitchcock which also starred Julie Andrews?

____

ANSWERS: 1. YLLEK ENEG YB DEYALP NAGILLUM YRREJ 2. NRUBPEH YERDUA 3. YAD SIROD & TRAWETS SEMAJ 4. ESAHC YVEHC 5. NEEUQCM EVETS 6. RUOMAL YHTOROD 7. ODNARB NILRAM 8. ENIAC LEAHCIM 9. ESWORP TEILUJ 10. YBSORC GNIB 11. NAMKCAH ENEG 12. NAMWEN LUAP

How Many Squares in a Sudoku Puzzle

Can you count them all? It is pretty challenging!

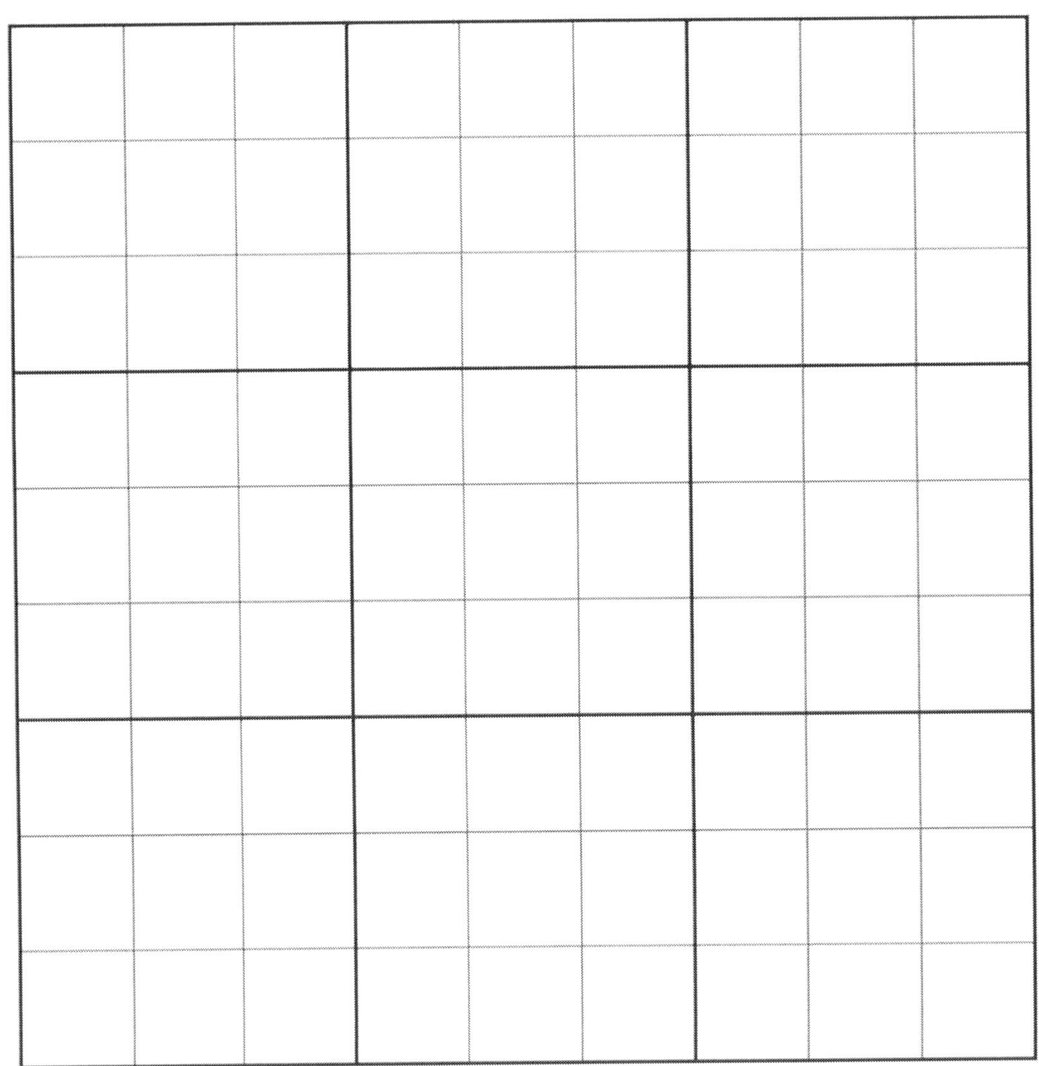

Extremely interestingly the answer is the sum of the squares of integer starting at 1 and ending at 9:

1*1+2*2+3*3+4*4+5*5+6*6+7*7+8*8+9*9

Interpretation: there is only1 9x9 square and there are 81 1x1 squares.

ANSWER: EVIF-YTHGIE DERDNUH OWT

The International Adventures of Chuckleberry Dumperdink

All the questions are related to a country on planet Earth.

1. From the large city of Colombo, Chuckleberry takes a day trip on a bus to visit 3 tea factories.

____

2. From the huge capital city of a country with huge population, Chucky takes a day trip in a private car to visit the Taj Mahal.

____

3. Chuckie lands in December on the snow-covered large airport of a big city and takes the train and subway to Red Square.

____

4. Chuckleberry flies with his girlfriend from Madrid to this beautiful capital city in 3 hours to admire the panorama on both sides of the Danube River.

____

5. Chuckie takes a train north from the imperial Vienna to this beautiful capital city with hundreds of towers.

____

6. Chucky sits on the banks of the Seine River, hugs and kisses his girlfriend after all they are in the city of lovers.

____

7. Chuckleberry sits down at the base of a statue on a Piccadilly Circus and counts the passing double-decker buses.

____

8. Chuck asks his girlfriend to put on a bikini - the smaller the better - and they go across the street from their hotel to Copacabana beach.

____

9. Chuckie and girlfriend take the Staten Island Ferry free of charge to sail passed the Statue of Liberty.

____

10. Chuckleberry grabs a taxi from his international hotel in a big city with the Nile River to see the pyramids.

____

11. Chuckie and girlfriend visit Palos de la Frontera to see the replicas of Columbus's ships.

____

12. Chuck hops into a rent-a-car with his girlfriend in NYC heading north and in seven hours they are in a big French speaking city.

____

ANSWERS: 1.)NOLYEC(AKNAL IRS 2. AIDNI 3. AISSUR 4. YRAGNUH 5. CILBUPER HCEZC 6. ECNARF 7. MODGNIK DETINU 8. LIZARB 9. SETATS DETINU 10. TPYGE 11. NIAPS 12. ADANAC

Oliver Hardy Puzzle

The Fat Man in the Laurel and Hardy Slapstick Comedy Team

GEORGIA

1776

OLIVER NORVELL HARDY

Harlem became the birthplace of the ______ member of one of Hollywood's ______ comedy ______ when Oliver Hardy was ______ January 10, 1892. After his father ______ and was buried in the Harlem ______ the year of Oliver's ______, Mrs. Hardy took the ______ to Milledgeville where she became the manager of the Baldwin ______. Young Oliver was enthralled by the ______ troupes of ______ who stayed there. Later as ______ of the town's first ______ theater, Hardy ______ regularly.

After attending Georgia ______ Academy, the Atlanta ______ of Music and for a ______ time the Univ. of Georgia, Hardy left Georgia in 1913 for the newly established film ______ in Jacksonville, ______. After working at various ______ on the ______ coast, he left for Hollywood in 1918.

"Babe" as Hardy become known to his ______, worked for ______ years as a supporting ______ until he was accidentally teamed with a young ______ Stan Laurel. Laurel and Hardy remained ______ and friends until Hardy's death in ______ in 1957.

GEORGIA HISTORIC MARKER

ANSWERS: doowylloH ,srentrap ,namhsilgnE ,rotca ,lareves ,sdneirf ,tsae ,soiduts ,adirolF ,ynoloc ,trohs ,yrotavresnoC ,yratiliM ,demrofrep ,eivom ,reganam ,sremrofrep ,gnitisiv ,letoH ,ylimaf ,htrib ,yretemeC ,deid ,nrob ,smaet ,tsetaerg ,dnutor

Most Memorable Pop Songs of All Times

Name the song & artist based on the lyrics segment.

1. Dear, as I held you close in my arms / Angels were singing a hymn to your charms / Two hearts gently beating, murmuring low / "Darling, I love you so"

____

2. You may say I'm a dreamer / But I'm not the only one / I hope some day you'll join us / And the world will be as one

____

3. Ahh you've gone to the finest schools, alright Miss Lonely / But you know you only used to get juiced in it / Nobody's ever taught you how to live out on the street

____

4. But her friend is nowhere to be seen / Now she walks through her sunken dream / To the seat with the clearest view / And she's hooked to the silver screen

____

5. When you're down and out / When you're on the street / When evening falls so hard / I will comfort you (ooo)

____

6. Are you sorry we drifted apart? / Does your memory stray to a brighter sunny day / When I kissed you and called you sweetheart?

____

7. On a dark desert highway, cool wind in my hair / Warm smell of colitas, rising up through the air / Up ahead in the distance, I saw a shimmering light

____

8. Someday, I wish upon a star / Wake up where the clouds are far behind me / Where trouble melts like lemon drops

____

9. Mama, just killed a man / Put a gun against his head / Pulled my trigger, now he's dead

____

10. People always told me be careful of what you do / And don't go around breaking young girls' hearts / And mother always told me be careful of who you love

____

11. When I'm drivin' in my car, and the man come on the radio / He's tellin' me more and more about some useless information / Supposed to fire my imagination

____

12. God save the queen / She's not a human being / and There's no future /And England's dreaming

____

ANSWERS: 1. SMAILLIW YDNA YB GNOS YRASREVINNA 2. NONNEL NHOJ YB ENIGAMI 3. NALYD BOB YB ENOTS GNILLOR A EKIL 4. EIWOB DIVAD YB ?SRAM NO EFIL 5. LEKNUFRAG & NOMIS YB RETAW DELBUORT REVO EGDIRB 6. YELSERP SIVLE YB THGINOT EMOSENOL UOY ERA 7. SELGAE YB AINROFILAC LETOH 8. DNALRAG YDUJ YB WOBNIAR EHT REVO 9. NEEUQ YB YDOSPAHR NAIMEHOB 10. NOSKCAJ LEAHCIM YB NAEJ EILLIB 11. SENOTS GNILLOR EHT YB NOITCAFSITAS)ON TEG T'NAC I(12. SLOTSIP XES YB NEEUQ EHT EVAS DOG(

Find & Circle a Bird: GOOSE(2), MACAW(2), STORK, TURKEY, FINCH, EAGLE, HOBBY(3), ROBIN, CRANE, BOOBY(2) in Each Quadrant

S	E	O	G	O	E	O	O	C	C	A	W	A	A	W	W	K	S	S	K	S	K	O	O
O	E	S	G	O	O	E	O	M	M	C	W	A	A	A	C	R	O	O	T	K	O	S	R
S	O	E	O	E	O	G	E	A	W	M	C	W	A	W	W	T	S	O	R	O	O	K	S
O	E	O	G	S	O	S	E	M	W	M	A	M	M	W	A	R	R	O	O	S	S	R	O
E	O	G	O	E	O	G	E	A	A	C	C	C	A	M	A	K	R	T	S	O	K	K	K
E	S	O	O	O	G	O	O	A	A	A	M	C	A	M	W	O	T	O	R	O	S	K	R
O	S	E	G	O	S	G	S	M	A	M	C	M	A	W	A	T	T	T	S	R	T	T	K
O	G	S	O	O	S	E	O	A	W	A	M	A	A	W	C	O	K	R	S	T	R	R	O
T	Y	T	U	T	R	Y	U									H	C	H	C	H	C	F	I
E	K	T	K	U	Y	T	R									C	H	N	H	I	I	I	F
E	Y	T	U	R	U	E	U									H	C	I	I	N	C	H	N
E	R	R	E	R	U	U	K									H	N	C	I	F	C	H	F
T	K	R	K	E	T	R	E									H	I	C	F	N	H	N	C
R	E	E	E	T	Y	R	R									N	N	H	I	N	I	N	N
R	Y	T	T	U	E	K	T									H	N	F	I	C	H	C	C
E	U	R	K	Y	R	T	R									C	F	F	H	C	H	F	H
E	G	E	G	E	A	E	A									O	B	Y	Y	H	B	B	Y
L	A	E	G	L	A	E	E									Y	H	B	B	H	H	O	B
L	E	G	A	A	E	G	A									O	B	O	O	Y	H	Y	O
E	G	A	L	G	L	E	A									B	H	B	B	B	B	Y	H
A	A	E	E	E	G	A	E									Y	B	B	H	B	B	B	B
G	E	A	A	A	E	G	E									H	O	Y	Y	B	Y	B	Y
L	A	G	L	E	G	A	E									H	O	O	O	O	B	B	O
A	A	A	E	E	G	E	G									H	H	H	Y	Y	Y	O	O
B	R	B	B	N	O	B	R	N	C	R	R	R	E	N	E	B	B	B	B	B	B	B	O
R	B	N	B	B	B	R	B	C	N	R	C	A	C	E	E	O	O	B	O	O	O	O	O
R	O	N	B	I	R	B	B	C	A	R	A	R	C	N	C	O	Y	O	B	B	O	Y	B
N	O	O	N	B	N	B	I	A	C	A	R	N	C	C	R	O	O	Y	Y	O	Y	B	B
R	B	B	N	O	B	B	R	A	A	A	C	A	E	R	N	O	O	B	B	Y	B	O	Y
B	B	N	I	O	O	N	B	N	R	R	C	N	N	A	R	O	O	B	O	O	O	Y	Y
B	O	N	B	N	I	O	O	N	A	A	N	R	E	N	E	Y	O	B	O	B	Y	O	O
B	R	I	N	O	O	N	R	C	C	C	A	E	R	R	E	Y	B	O	Y	B	Y	B	B

US States, Puerto Rico & Canadian Provinces Biggest Cities

Write the name of biggest city for each state/province.

ALABAMA	KENTUCKY	NORTH CAROLINA	WISCONSIN
ALASKA	LOUISIANA	NORTH DAKOTA	WYOMING
ARIZONA	MAINE	OHIO	PUERTO RICO
ARKANSAS	MARYLAND	OKLAHOMA	ALBERTA
CALIFORNIA	MASSACHUSETTS	OREGON	BRITISH COLUMBIA
COLORADO	MICHIGAN	PENNSYLVANIA	MANITOBA
CONNECTICUT	MINNESOTA	RHODE ISLAND	NEW BRUNSWICK
DELAWARE	MISSISSIPPI	SOUTH CAROLINA	NEWFOUNDLAND
FLORIDA	MISSOURI	SOUTH DAKOTA	NORTHWEST TERR
GEORGIA	MONTANA	TENNESSEE	NOVA SCOTIA
HAWAII	NEBRASKA	TEXAS	NUNAVUT
IDAHO	NEVADA	UTAH	ONTARIO
ILLINOIS	NEW HAMPSHIRE	VERMONT	PRINCE EDWARD ISLAND
INDIANA	NEW JERSEY	VIRGINIA	QUEBEC
IOWA	NEW MEXICO	WASHINGTON	SASKATCHEWAN
KANSAS	NEW YORK	WEST VIRGINIA	YUKON

Name That Flower in 10 Minutes!

Find at least 3 flowers for each letter (if any).

1. A-B

2. C-D

3. E-F

4. G-H

5. I-J

6. K-L

7. M-N

8. O-P

9. Q-R

10. S-T

11. U-V-W

12. X-Y-Z

ANSWERS: 1. PUCRETTUB ,TENNOBEULB ,REWOLFLLEB ,AINOGEB ,AELAZA ,AISORBMA ,SILLYRAMA ,AICACA 2. DOOWGOD ,YSIAD ,AILHAD ,LIDOFFAD ,BMOCSKCOC ,REVOLC ,SHTNASYRHC ,NOITANRAC ,AILLEMAC 3. SMUM IJUF ,AISHCUF ,AISEERF ,EVOLGXOF ,YLIL EMALF ,AIBROHPUE ,SUTPYLACUE ,ENITNALGE ,SSIEWLEDE 4. AEGNARDYH ,HTNICAYH ,YLLOH ,SUCSIBIH ,NROHTWAH ,TOOFESOOG ,DORNEDLOG ,MUINAREG ,AINEDRAG 5. REPINUJ ,LIUQNOJ ,ENIMASSEJ ,ENIMSAJ ,ACINOPAJ ,SIRI ,ENAC NAIDNI ,YLIL ACNI 6. ENRECUL ,SUTOL ,YLIL ,CALIL ,REDNEVAL ,LERUAL ,NREF ECAL ,DEEWPANK ,AIDENNEK 7. EDAHSTHGIN ,YLIL ENIREN ,SIPELORHPEN ,SUSSICRAN ,YRREBLUM ,DLOGIRAM ,RIAHNEDIAM ,AILONGAM 8. YPPOP ,AITTESNIOP ,AINUTEP ,ELKNIWIREP ,TNIMREPPEP ,YSNAP ,AET OGEWSO ,DIHCRO ,EGNARO ,REDNAELO 9. YRAMESOR ,ESOR ,REWOLF ECIR ,REVOR DER ,SNOBBIR DER ,EKANSELTTAR ,SULUCNUNAR ,ECNIUQ ,ECAL S'ENNA NEEUQ 10. AGNIRYS ,NREF DROWS ,REWOLFNUS ,HSUBRAGUS ,YLIL REDIPS ,DAEH EKANS ,EGAS ,REWOLFFAS 11. ENABSFLOW ,LEZAH HCTIW ,ELTTAW ,YLIL RETAW ,TELOIV ,HCTEV ,ACINOREV ,NAIRELAV ,AINISRU 12. AINNIZ ,HTNARYHPEZ ,NROHWOLLEY ,LLEB WOLLEY ,WORRAY ,MUIBOLYX ,MULLYHPOREX ,MUMEHTNAREX

Fifteen Puzzle Game

Numbers can slide up/down & left/right. To start move the numbers randomly. To solve move them back to the normal 1-15 sequence position.

1. Normal position

2. Solution in 3 moves

ANSWERS: 2. PU EVLEWT ;TFEL EERHT ;OSLA 31 & 9 SEVOM SIHT - NWOD EVIF

Fifteen Puzzle Game - 2 More Puzzles

Numbers can slide up/down & left/right. To start move the numbers randomly. To solve move them back to the normal 1-15 sequence position.

3. Solution in 4 moves

4. Solution in 4 moves

ANSWERS: 3. TFEL NEETFIF ;PU ENIN ;THGIR OWT ;NWOD THGIE 4. PU EVLEWT ;TFEL NEVES ;NWOD ENIN ;THGIR NEETRUOF

One-Way Trip to Mars Odd Man Out Quizzes

Find the word which does not fit with the rest of the bunch.

1. SATURN, JUPITER, MARS, VENUS, NEBULA, PLUTO

2. RED SAND, FROZEN WATER, MARTIANS, DUST STORMS, CRATERS

3. SILVER DOLLAR, DIME, QUARTER, PENNY, NICKEL, HALF DOLLAR

4. REALTORS, ASTRONAUTS, PLUMBERS, ELECTRICIANS, CONTRACTORS

5. SPIDER, LIME TICKS, DADDY LONGLEGS, SQUIDS, SCORPIONS

6. HERD, SOLAR SYSTEM, FLOCK, PARLIAMENT, SWARM

7. DAFFODILS, CORN-ON-THE-COB, SCHOOL BUSES, FIRE TRUCKS, NEW YORK CITY CABS

8. SUSHI, PIZZA, FRIED CALAMARI, MEATBALL SUBS, CALZONE

9. CAMERAMAN, DIRECTOR, GAME DESIGNER, PRODUCER, ACTRESS

10. USA, ENGLAND, HONG-KONG, AUSTRALIA, CANADA, ECUADOR

11. PEANUT BUTTER, PUMPKIN PIE, MASHED POTATOES, ALMONDS, APPLE SAUCE

12. MARS ONE, FLY ME TO THE MOON, ELON MUSK, NASA'S JOURNEY TO MARS, ASTRONAUT APPLICATION FEE

ANSWERS: 1. ALUBEN :tenalp a toN 2. SNAITRAM :sraM no tey dnuof neeb t'nsaH 3. YNNEP :roloc revlis toN 4. STUANORTSA :sesuoh htiw devlovni toN 5.)SELCATNET 01 SAH(DIUQS :sgel 8 no klaw ton seoD 6. METSYS RALOS :slamina fo puorg a toN 7. SKCURT ERIF :wolley toN 8. IHSUS :unem tnaruatser azzip no toN 9. RENGISED EMAG :noitcudorp eivom doowylloH ni devlovni toN 10. DNALGNE :yrtnuoc ycnerruc rallod a toN 11. SDNOMLA :hteet ruoy kaerb nac - doof tfos toN 12. "NOOM EHT OT EM YLF" - ARTANIS KNARF :SRAM ot pirt yaw-eno ni devlovni toN

Name That Food in 7 Minutes!

Find at least 3 foods beginning with each letter (if any).

1. A-B

____

2. C-D

____

3. E-F

____

4. G-H

____

5. I-J

____

6. K-L

____

7. M-N

____

8. O-P

____

9. Q-R

____

10. S-T

____

11. U-V-W

____

12. X-Y-Z

____

ANSWERS: 1. ILOCCORB ,SNAEB ,SLEGAB ,NOCAB ,DNOMLA ,ODACOVA ,SELPPA ,SUGARAPSA 2. STUNOD ,SGNILPMUD ,TIURF NOGARD ,SETAD ,SEIKOOC ,NEKCIHC ,STORRAC ,EGABBAC 3. TSAOT HCNERF ,HSIF ,SGIF ,LEFALAF ,SNIFFUM HSILGNE ,ADALIHCNE ,TNALPGGE ,SGGE 4. SUMMUH ,SGOD TOH ,SNWORB HSAH ,YENOH ,REGRUBMAH ,SEPARG ,ALONARG ,REGNIG ,CILRAG 5. ABOJOJ ,MAJ ,YLLEJ ,AYALABMAJ ,AOCOC TNATSNI ,RETAW ECI ,ECUTTEL GREBECI ,MAERC ECI 6. RETSBOL ,SLITNEL ,KEEL ,ANGASAL ,IBARLHOK ,IWIK ,PUHCTEK ,SBOBAK 7. SELDOON ,ENIRATCEN ,PUOS NAEB YVAN ,SOHCAN ,EKAHSKLIM ,NOLEM ,SLLABTAEM ,OGNAM 8. ELPPAENIP ,SEKACNAP ,AZZIP ,AYAPAP ,SEGNARO ,SNOINO ,ARKO ,LAEMTAO 9. BRABUHR ,NEBUER ,YRREBPSAR ,HSIDAR ,AONIUQ ,EHCIUQ ,SALLIDASEUQ ,LIAUQ 10. OTAMOT ,SPOP RETSAOT ,ARUPMET ,SOCAT ,SEIRREBWARTS ,HSAUQS ,HCANIPS ,ITTEHGAPS 11. ETALOCOHC ETIHW ,STUNLAW ,DALAS FRODLAW ,SELFFAW ,NOSINEV ,ANAIGIMRAP LAEV ,EGDUF ALLINAV ,EKAC ELPPAENIP NWOD-EDISPU 12. INIHCCUZ ,ITIZ ,WALS ELOC YMMUY ,SGOL EDITELUY ,TRUGOY ,SMAY ,SEIKOOC SAMX ,PUOS REIVAX

Mind-Grabbing Odd Man Out Quizzes

Find the word which does not fit with the rest of the bunch.

1. KITTENS, PUPPIES, TADPOLES, FAWNS, LAMBS

____

2. HERSHEY, NESTLE, DOVE, COLGATE, CADBURY

____

3. MEGA MILLIONS, WIN-4, POWERBALL, LOTTO, SOLITAIRE

____

4. FRUIT LOOPS, QUAKER OAT LIFE, FROSTED FLAKES, OATMEAL, CHEERIOS

____

5. SMART PHONE, RADIO, TELEVISION, IPAD, LAPTOP

____

6. SUV, MINI COOPER, MUSTANG, CIVIC, CHEROKEE

____

7. EYES, NOSE, WHISKERS, PAWS, EARS

____

8. PROPERTY BOTHERS, NAKED & AFRAID, FLIP OR FLOP, FIXER UPPER, THIS OLD HOUSE

____

9. FLAMINGO, CANARY, CROW, PARROT, BLUE JAY

____

10. TORNADO, TSUNAMI, THUNDERSTORM, TYPHOON, THERMOMETER

____

11. LEMON MERINGUE, GERMAN CHOCOLATE, CHERRY, CHOCOLATE CREAM, COCONUT CUSTARD

____

12. HOT FUDGE, ICE CREAM, BANANA, STRAWBERRY SYRUP, CANADIAN MAPLE SYRUP

____

ANSWERS: 1. SELOPDAT :lammam a toN 2. ETAGLOC :dnarb etalocohc a toN 3. ERIATILOS :yrettol a toN 4. LAEMTAO :laerec yrd a toN 5. OIDAR :noissimsnart erutcip oN 6. VUS :eman ledom rac a toN 7. SWAP :ecaf s'tac fo trap toN 8. DIARFA & DEKAN :wohs tnemevorpmi emoh a toN 9. WORC :lufroloc toN 10. RETEMOMREHT :tneve rehtaew a toN 11. EKAC ETALOCOHC NAMREG :eip a toN 12. PURYS ELPAM NAIDANAC :eadnus tilps ananab a fo trap toN

World Changing Discoveries, Inventions & Technologies

Figure out the missing information for each World advancement.

1. 3500 BC. Cavemen were rocking & rolling with this technological innovation.

---

2. 1781. In England this man patented the improved steam engine which kicked off the Industrial Revolution.

---

3. 1813. This man built the first steam locomotive. A few years later, established his company as builder of steam locomotives in England, America, and Europe.

---

4. 1831. The British scientist Michael Faraday discovered the principal for the generation of this form of shocking energy.

---

5. 1800. The Italian Alessandro Volta invented the first one of these electronic power source which are used in cars & mobile phones.

---

6. 1885. This French micro-biologist created a vaccine against the dreaded disease rabies.

---

7. 1957. This Soviet sattelite was launched into Earth orbit which triggered the space race between the Soviet Union and the United States.

---

8. 1928. The discovery of pennicilin by this man allowed many bacterial diseases to be cured.

---

9. 1955. The first polio vaccine was developed by this man and came into wide-spread use shortly after.

---

10. 1886. The German inventor Carl Benz developed the first of these innovative horseless carriages.

---

11. 1050 BC. The Chinese were the first to use lodestones for spiritual & navigational purposes.

---

12. 1492. Christopher Columbus lands in America with these 3 ships.

ANSWERS: 1. leehW 2. ttaW semaJ 3. nosnehpetS egroeG 4. yticirtcelE 5. yrettaB 6. ruetsaP siuoL 7. kintupS 8. gnimelF rednaxelA 9. klaS sanoJ 10. elibomotuA 11. ssapmoc citengaM 12. atniP ,aniN ,airaM atnaS

Cities with Big Towers

Name the city based on the pictures. Which has the tallest tower?

1.

4.

2.

5.

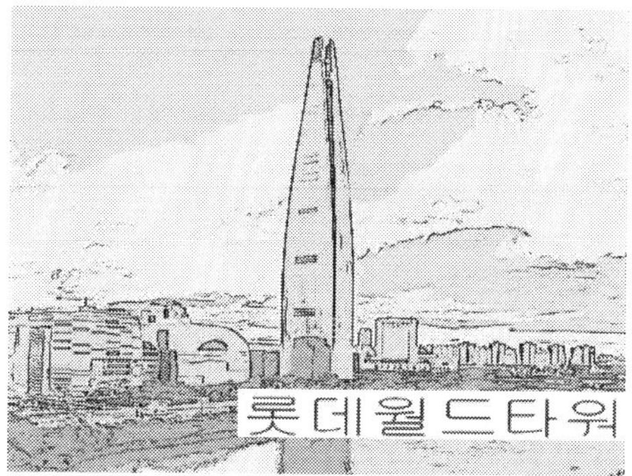

3.

6.

ANSWERS. 1. GNAYGNOYP 2. SIRAP 3. SAGEV SAL 4. !TSELLAT - IABUD 5. LUOES 6. YTIC KROY WEN

Sequences for Logic Challenge

What is the next member of the sequence?

1. Alfa, Bravo, Charlie, Delta, Echo,

___

2. 1, 2, 4, 8, 16, 32, 64, 128,

___

3. 2, 3, 5, 7, 11, 13, 17, 19,

___

4. Zulu, Yankee, X-ray, Whiskey, Victor,

___

5. 1, 4, 9, 16, 25, 36, 49,

___

6. 1, 8, 27, 64, 125,

___

7. triangle, rectangle, pentagon, hexagon, heptagon,

___

8. 0, 1, 1, 2, 3, 5, 8, 13, 21, 34, 55,

___

9. D, N, O, S, A,

___

10. Z, O, T, T, F, F, S, S,

___

11. 4, 12, 20, 28, 36,

___

12. wy, wi, wv,

___

ANSWERS: 1. TORTXOF 2. 652 3. 32 4. MROFINU 5. 46 6. 612 7. NOGATCO 8. 98 9. J 10. E 11. 44 12. AW

Word Jumbles: Unscramble the Letters

1.	A B N R
2.	B G G G I L N O
3.	A D E M P S W
4.	E E I N N R S T V
5.	A C E E I L N N N T
6.	A C E F G H I I N N N R S
7.	A C E H I N O O R R S T T
8.	C E E I N O O P R R S T T
9.	C E I R S U V
10.	A D E E I N R S T T
11.	A B C E L S
12.	G H I M N P T U
13.	A E E H L R T W Y
14.	A A I M N O R S T
15.	A A B E L L L O W
16.	A A E I L M N S T
17.	A D D E E N N P S T
18.	A G I N R R T
19.	A D O R R
20.	A D E E I M N R S T Y
21.	A D D E E H L R
22.	A E H I N P P S T U
23.	A A A C D N N O
24.	A D E G I I M N N O P R T
25.	C D E E M O O P S
26.	A A C D E L L N O T U
27.	A D D E I I L N V
28.	A H K R S S
29.	D D E G I R
30.	A B C E G H I L O P R T Y
31.	A I N O O R T
32.	A C G I I L L L O S T Y
33.	E E G I L N N U Y
34.	G I I L M M N S
35.	D E E G H I L M O S T
36.	F H I S
37.	A B C I I O T
38.	E G H O O R R T U V W
39.	A A C E N N N O S Y
40.	E E F L R S S T

ANSWERS: 1. nrab 2. gnilggob 3. depmaws 4. stnevnier 5. lainnetnec 6. gnisihcnarfne 7. noitartsehcro 8. noitcepsorter 9. evisruc 10. detatsnier 11. selbac 12. gnipmuht 13. ylrehtaew 14. srotamina 15. elbawolla 16. setanimal 17. stnadneped 18. gnirrat 19. rodra 20. yratnemides 21. dedlareh 22. tseippahnu 23. adnocana 24. gnitanimoderp 25. esopmoced 26. detacollanu 27. dedilavni 28. skrahs 29. degdir 30. elbathgirypoc 31. oiratno 32. yllacitsigol 33. yleniuneg 34. gnimmils 35. emosthgiled 36. hsif 37. citoiba 38. thguorwrevo 39. secnayonna 40. sselterf

Alpha/Text Sequences for Logic Challenge

What is the next member of the sequence?

1. H, I, J, A, Q, K, L, M, A, Q, N, O, P, A, Q,

____

2. Alaska, Texas, California, Montana,

____

3. Dog, Cat, Hamster, Fish, Mouse,

____

4. Russia, Canada, United States, China, Brazil,

____

5. African elephant, Asian elephant, Rhinoceros, Giraffe,

____

6. adore, regal, alpha, haven, enter,

____

7. Thousand, Million, Billion, Trillion,

____

8. King Creole, Viva Las Vegas, Jailhouse Rock,

____

9. positive - negative, black - white, good - bad, giant -

____

10. Adam & Eve, life & death, birds & bees, name & address, bread & butter, nice &

____

11. I, it, ivy, inch, igloo, immune, inhabit,

____

12. alive &, rough &, safe &, spick &, thick &, short &

____

ANSWERS: 1. Q 2. OCIXEM WEN 3. GIP AENIUG 4. AILARTSUA 5. SUMATOPOPPIH 6. TPURE ,RORRE ,ESARE 7. NOILLIRDAUQ 8. IIAWAH EULB 9. YNIT 10. YSAE 11. YTIDNEDI ,LATROMMI ,ETINIFNI ,ROIRETNI 12. TEEWS ,NIHT ,NAPS ,DNUOS ,HGUOT ,LLEW

2 New Words from Same Letters in 10 Min

Find other words based on all letters in the given word.

1. PAINTERS BRAKE

2. LADIES LATER

3. MEDICAL EARLY

4. EASTERN SPEAR

5. DRAWER SATIN

6. GALLERY WEIRD

7. FOREST SMILE

8. SEMINAR SPOOL

9. DIAPERS LAKE

10. PAINTER LEAP

11. ARTIST NAME

12. STRIPES WOLF

ANSWERS: 1. REKAB ,KAERB ,SEIRTNAP ,SNIATREP 2. TRELA ,RETLA ,SLAEDI ,DELIAS 3. REYAL ,YALER ,DEMIALC ,LAMICED ,MIALCED 4. ERAPS ,SRAEP ,SERAP ,ESRAP ,TSERAEN ,TSENRAE 5. NIATS ,TNIAS ,DERRAW ,WARDER ,DRAWER ,REDRAW 6. REDIW ,DERIW ,YGRELLA ,YLLAGER ,YLEGRAL 7. EMILS ,SEMIL ,SELIM ,RETFOS ,RETSOF 8. SLOOP ,SPOOL ,POOLS ,SNIAMER ,SENIRAM 9. ELAK ,KAEL ,DERIPSA ,DESIARP ,RIAPSED 10. AELP ,ELAP ,LAEP ,NIATREP ,TNIAPER 11. ENAM ,NAEM ,NEMA ,STIART ,TIARTS 12. LWOF ,WOLF ,TSISREP ,SETIRPS ,STSEIRP

Best Picture Oscar Winners Missing Vowels Puzzles 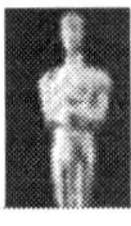

8. B_rdm_n; G_ntl_m_n's _gr__m_nt; T_rms _f _nd__rm_nt; C_v_lc_d_;

9. Th_ L_st W__k_nd; G_g_; _ll th_ K_ng's M_n; L_wr_nc_ _f _r_b__;

10. Ch_r__ts _f F_r_; Kr_m_r vs. Kr_m_r; Th_ _p_rtm_nt; _l_v_r!;

11. N_ C__ntr_ f_r _ld M_n; Th_ Fr_nch C_nn_ct__n; Th_ G_df_th_r P_rt __; H_w Gr__n W_s M_ V_ll__;

12. _t H_pp_n_d _n_ N_ght; _n _m_r_c_n _n P_r_s; Th_ H_rt L_ck_r; _m_r_c_n B___t_;

13. Fr_m H_r_ t_ _t_rn_t_; _n th_ W_t_rfr_nt; 12 ___rs _ Sl_v_; Th_ D__r H_nt_r;

14. G_n_ w_th th_ W_nd; Th_ L_f_ _f _m_l_ Z_l_; Th_ Br__dw__ M_l_d_; M__nl_ght;

ANSWERS: 8. ;EDACLAVAC ;TNEMRAEDNE FO SMRET ;TNEMEERGA S'NAMELTNEG ;NAMDRIB 9. ;AIBARA FO ECNERWAL ;NEM S'GNIK EHT LLA ;IGIG ;DNEKEEW TSOL EHT 10. ;!REVILO ;TNEMTRAPA EHT ;REMARK .SV REMARK ;ERIF FO STOIRAHC 11. ;YELLAV YM SAW NEERG WOH ;II TRAP REHTAFDOG EHT ;NOITCENNOC HCNERF EHT ;NEM DLO ROF YRTNUOC ON 12. ;YTUAEB NACIREMA ;REKCOL TRUH EHT ;SIRAP NI NACIREMA NA ;THGIN ENO DENEPPAH TI 13. ;RETNUH REED EHT ;EVALS A SRAEY 21 ;TNORFRETAW EHT NO ;YTINRETE OT EREH MORF 14. ;THGILNOOM ;YDOLEM YAWDAORB EHT ;ALOZ ELIME FO EFIL EHT ;DNIW EHT HTIW ENOG

TAKE A FUN CRUISE FROM NEW YORK CITY

What are the main vacation destinations from NYC?

ANSWER: AITOCS AVON ,SDNALSI NAEBBIRAC ,SAMAHAB ,ADUMREB

Video Poker Winning Hands

Name the winning hands based on the pictures. Which is the jackpot?

ANSWERS. 1. RENNIW A TON 2. RETTEB RO SKCAJ 3. SRIAP OWT 4. DNIK A FO EERHT 5. THGIARTS 6. HSULF 7. ESUOH LLUF 8. DNIK A FO RUOF 9. HSULF THGIARTS 10. !TOPKCAJ - HSULF LAYOR

USA Changing Discoveries, Inventions & Technologies

Figure out the missing information for each American brain-inspired progress.

1. 1836. This man developed a dots & dashes communications code for telegraphs.

____

2. 1879. This American inventor patented the first light bulb.

____

3. 1903. These two siblings created a flying machine which altered transportation forever.

____

4. 1908. The mass production of this automobile starts.

____

5. 1945. These two Japanese cities suffer umimaginable catastrophies due to atom bombs.

____

6. 1969. First time in history a man walks on this celestial body other than Earth.

____

7. 2004. The launching of this social media on the internet; originally popular with college students.

____

8. 1990s. The World Wide Web(WWW) application which truly brought this revolutionary technology into our daily life.

____

9. 1945. This modern electronic computing device was introduced at the University of Pennsylvania ushering in the computer revolution.

____

10. 2007. Steve Jobs's company, Apple, introduced this personal electronic device which revolutionizd personal communications.

____

11. 1876. Alexander Graham Bell introduces this device for distance communcations in real-time.

____

12. 1869. The completion of this construction united the Eastern & Western part of USA.

____

ANSWERS: 1. esroM leumaS 2. nosidE samohT 3. srehtorb thgirW 4. T ledoM droF 5. ikasagaN & amihsoriH 6. nooM 7. koobecaF 8. tenretnI 9. CAINE 10. enohpI 11. enohpeleT 12. ocsicnarF naS gnihcaer yawliar latnenitnocsnarT

Hollywood's 2 Comedian Don-s

1. Who played female Agent 99 in Get Smart with Maxwell Smart (Don Adams) as Secret Agent 86, a combination of James Bond & Inspector Clouseau?

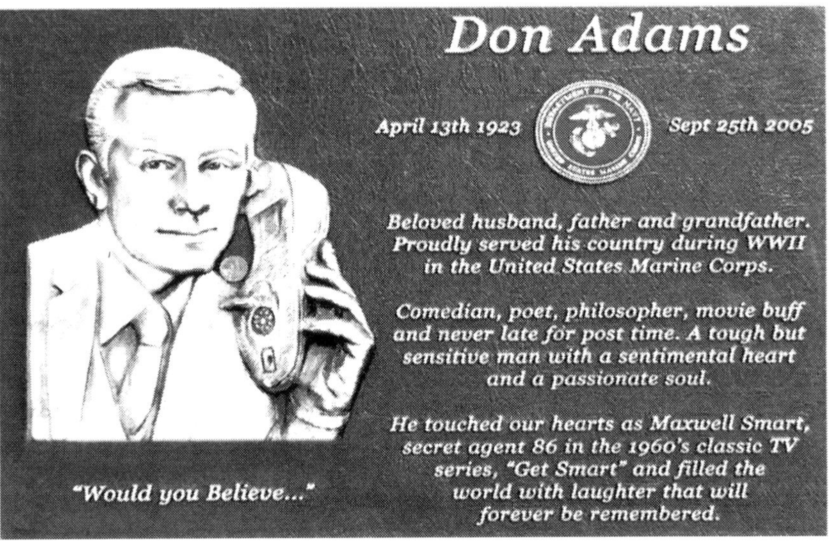

2. Who played the widowed sheriff with Don Knott as Deputy Sheriff Barney Fife in the fictional small town of Mayberry, North Carolina?

ANSWERS: 1. NODLEF ARABRAB 2. HTIFFIRG YDNA

History Making World Political Events

Figure out the missing information for each World changing event.

1. 1989. The fall of this building structure led to the unification of Germany and the end of the Cold War.

____

2. 1933. This man became Chancellor of Germany and his expansion policies led to World War II.

____

3. 1917. It began with the overthrow of the Russian Czar and ended with the establishment of Communism.

____

4. 1914. The assassination of this man by 19-year-old Bosnian Serb nationalist Gavrilo Princip in Sarajevo started a chain of events which led to World War I.

____

5. 1949. This communist leader founded the Peoples Republic of China.

____

6. 1999. The establishment of this currency marked the unification of many European countries.

____

7. 1789. During this uprising in Paris people fought to abolish monarchies in Europe.

____

8. 1947. This huge colony gets independence from the British Empire. Israel was also established in this year.

____

9. 1517. This man published his 95 THESIS which led to the protestant revolution.

____

10. 1869. This canal opens with a big celebration in Cairo shortening the shipping distance between Europe and Asia.

____

11. 1914. This canal opens in Central America shortening the shipping distance between the Atlantic & Pacific Oceans.

____

12. 1975. The long war in this Asian country, which was started by the French and finished by the Americans, ends.

____

ANSWERS: 1. llaw nilreB ehT 2. reltiH flodA 3. noituloveR teivoS naissuR 4. enorht nairagnuH-ortsuA eht ot rieh ,airtsuA fo dnanidreF znarF ekudhcrA 5. gnut-esT oaM 6. oruE 7. noituloveR hcnerF 8. aidnI 9. rehtuL nihtraM 10. zeuS 11. amanaP 12. manteiV

MATCH COUNTRIES WITH CAPITALS

Select a country then find its capital. Write it down on the following blank form.

Portugal	Bolivia	Buenos Aires	Washington D.C.
Brazil	Uruguay	Budapest	Slovakia
Thailand	Croatia	Kyiv	Belgium
Poland	Beijing	Quito	Canada
Switzerland	China	Rome	Turkey
Bern	Iceland	Denmark	Finland
Bratislava	Hungary	Bangkok	Pakistan
Santiago	New Zealand	Colombo	Ljubljana
Morocco	Montevideo	Germany	Cairo
Iran	Oslo	Bulgaria	Chile
Lisbon	Jakarta	Lima	Wellington
Japan	Uganda	Cuba	USA
Accra	Ukraine	Nairobi	Vienna
Athens	Damascus	Riyadh	Ottawa
Reykjavik	Spain	Islamabad	Sofia
Madrid	Manila	London	Baghdad
Italy	Caracas	Copenhagen	Ireland
Peru	Venezuela	Nepal	Kenya
Australia	Canberra	Brasilia	Ghana
Iraq	Moscow	Saudi Arabia	Norway
Philippines	Russia	Kathmandu	Stockholm
Ankara	Kabul	Kampala	Greece
Sweden	Austria	Egypt	Slovenia
Rabat	Zagreb	Bogota	Serbia
Tokyo	Dublin	Argentina	Syria
India	Indonesia	Belgrade	France
Colombia	Brussels	Berlin	Ecuador
Sri Lanka	Hanoi	United Kingdom	Havana
Helsinki	Paris	Warsaw	Tehran
Afghanistan	New Delhi	Vietnam	La Paz

MATCH COUNTRIES WITH CAPITALS BLANK FORM

Select a country then find its capital. Write it down on the following blank form.

1960s Popular Love Songs Celebration

Name the artist & song based on the lyrics segment.

1. Like a river flows surely to the sea / Darling so it goes / Some things are meant to be / Take my hand, take my whole life too

2. I Fell Into A Burning Ring Of Fire / I Went Down, Down, Down / And The Flames Went Higher

3. Let me sing among those stars / Let me see what spring is like / On Jupiter and Mars

4. When the night has come / And the land is dark / And the moon is the only light we'll see / No I won't be afraid, no I won't be afraid / Just as long as

5. I see trees of green red roses too / I see them bloom for me and you / And I think to myself what a

6. And when I touch you / I feel happy inside / It's such a feelin' that my love / I can't hide

7. I love the colorful clothes she wears / And the way the sunlight plays upon her hair / I hear the sound of a gentle word /On the wind that lifts her perfume through the air

8. When I'm ridin' 'round the world / And I'm doin' this and I'm signin' that / And I'm tryin' to make some girl, who tells me / Baby, better come back maybe next week

9. Well, around and round and up and down / We go again / Come on baby make me know you love me so

10. I got so much honey / the bees envy me / I got a sweeter song / than the birds in the trees / well I guess you say / what can make me feel this way

11. You'd be like heaven to touch. / I wanna hold you so much. / At long last love has arrived. /And I thank God I'm alive.

12. But then I know it's growing strong / Oh, wasn't the spring, whooo / And spring became the summer / Who'd believe you'd come along

ANSWERS: 1. YELSERP SIVLE YB EVOL NI GNILLAF PLEH T'NAC 2. HSAC YNNHOJ YB ERIF FO GNIR 3. ARTANIS KNARF YB NOOM EHT OT EM YLF 4. GNIK .E NEB YB EM YB DNATS 5. GNORTSMRA SIUOL YB DLROW LUFREDNOW A TAHW 6. SELTAEB EHT YB DNAH RUOY DLOH OT TNAW I 7. SYOB HCAEB EHT YB SNOITARBIV DOOG 8. ENOTS GNILLOR EHT YB NOITCAFSITAS)ON TEG T'NAC I(9. REKCEHC YBBUHC YB NIAGA TSIWT S'TEL 10. SNOITATPMET YB LRIG YM 11. ILLAV EIKNARF YB UOY FFO SEYE YM EKAT T'NAC 12. DNOMAID LIEN YB)DOOG OS DEMEES REVEN SEMIT DOOG(ENILORAC TEEWS

American History Making Political Events

Figure out the missing information for each nation forming event.

1. 1776. This number of English colonies declares independence and establishes the United States of America.

____

2. 1620. English Pilgrims sailing on this ship land at Plymouth Rock and establish a colony.

____

3. 2008. This African-American becomes the first non-white president of the United States.

____

4. 1773. This event in Massachusetts triggered the American revolution and the formation of the United States.

____

5. 1849. Gold discovered in this state and the gold rush starts.

____

6. 1941. The Japanese bombing of this harbor brought the US into World War II.

____

7. 1963. The assassination of this US president in Texas shocked the world.

____

8. 1863. In this Pennsylvanian city there was a defining battle of the Civil War which ended with a Union (North) victory.

____

9. 2001. This terrorist attack on this date resulted in 3000 deaths and lead to a global war on terrorism.

____

10. 1929. This financial event led the world into the great depression.

____

11. 2016. This non-politician becomes the president of the Unites States by defeating Hillary Clinton in the electoral college.

____

12. 1621. The Pilgrims invited this tribe of Indians to celebrate the first Thanksgiving with roasted wild turkey following the first successful harvest.

____

ANSWERS: 1. 31 2. rewolfyaM 3. amabO kcaraB 4. ytrap aet notsoB 5. ainrofilaC 6. robraH lraeP 7. ydenneK dlaregztiF nhoJ 8. grubsytteG 9. 11/9 10. hsarc tekram kcotS 11. pmurT dlanoD 12. gaonapmaW

Dubai - the Middle-Eastern Shangri-La

Can you answer the interesting & entertaining questions?

1. How many millions are citizens from Dubai's (UAE) population of 10 million?

____

2. What are the main foreign nationalities in Dubai(UAE)?

____

3. How many foreign taxi drivers live in one apartment in Dubai (to save money for the family at home)?

____

4. Can you become a Dubai(UAE) citizen if you are a foreign worker?

____

5. What are the main perks of being a Dubai (UAE) citizen?

____

6. Can you have a glass of wine at the very expensive Billionaire Mansion Dubai restaurant?

____

7. Does the Dubai police force use super-expensive automobiles like Ferrari FF ($500,000)?

____

8. Why people in Dubai love shopping malls?

____

9. What floors are used for observation in Burj Khalifa tower?

____

10. Can you see very far from the Burj Khalifa observation deck?

____

11. Can women wear shorts in Dubai?

____

12. Can women wear bikinis on Dubai beaches?

____

ANSWERS: 1. NOILLIM ENO 2. NAKNAL IRS DNA IHSEDALGNAB ,ONIPILIF ,INATSIKAP ,NAIDNI 3. NET 4. YLPPA YAM REKROW NGIEROF A YCNEDISER LAGEL FO SRAEY 03 RETFA 5. NOITACUDE EERF ,SNAOL EERF-TSERETNI ,SEXAT EMOCNI ON ,ERACHTLAEH EERF ,YTICIRTCELE EERF ,RETAW EERF :SKREP EHT GNOMA ;YNAM 6. DEVRES SI ENIW EERF)ECAPS RIA IABUD EDISTUO NEHW(ENILRIA SETARIME NO ;IABUD NI NOITPMUSNOC LOHOCLA ON 7. 819 EHCSROP ,GMA 36LS ZNEB-SEDECREM ,SG SUXEL ,TG GNATSUM DROF ,REPIV EGDOD ,ETTEVROC TELORVEHC ,8I WMB ,8R IDUA :SELIBOMOTUA EVISNEPXE EMOS ,SEY 8. EDISTUO TOH OOT 9. THGIE YTROF DERDNUH LEVEL & EVIF YTNEWT DERDNUH LEVEL 10. YAD RAELC YREV A NO YLNO 11. EENK OT REDLUOHS MORF PU REVOC OT RETTEB TUB ,OD EMOS 12. SLOOP LETOH EMOS NI NEVE ,SEHCAEB NO INIKIB A GNIRAEW ENIF YLLATOT

Best Picture Oscar Winners Missing Vowels Puzzles 

15. Th_ K_ng's Sp__ch; T_m J_n_s; Sp_tl_ght; _nf_rg_v_n;

16. B_n-H_r; Dr_v_ng M_ss D__s_; P_tt_n; Sh_k_sp__r_ _n L_v_;

17. Th_ G_df_th_r; Br_v_h__rt; _n th_ H__t _f th_ N_ght; R_b_cc_;

18. _n_ Fl_w _v_r th_ C_ck__'s N_st; M_rt_; Th_ Br_dg_ _n th_ R_v_r Kw__; R_ck_;

19. Gl_d__t_r; Th_ L_st _mp_r_r; D_nc_s w_th W_lv_s; Sch_ndl_r's L_st;

20. C_m_rr_n; Ch_c_g_; Th_ _ngl_sh P_t__nt; G_ndh_;

21. Gr_nd H_t_l; _rg_; Cr_sh; G__ng M_ W__;

ANSWERS: 15. ;NEVIGROFNU ;THGILTOPS ;SENOJ MOT ;HCEEPS S'GNIK EHT 16. ;EVOL NI ERAEPSEKAHS ;NOTTAP ;YSIAD SSIM GNIVIRD ;RUH-NEB 17. ;ACCEBER ;THGIN EHT FO TAEH EHT NI ;TRAEHEVARB ;REHTAFDOG EHT 18. ;YKCOR ;IAWK REVIR EHT NO EGDIRB EHT ;YTRAM ;TSEN S'OOKCUC EHT REVO WELF ENO 19. ;TSIL S'RELDNIHCS ;SEVLOW HTIW SECNAD ;ROREPME TSAL EHT ;ROTAIDALG 20. ;IHDNAG ;TNEITAP HSILGNE EHT ;OGACIHC ;NORRAMIC 21. ;YAW YM GNIOG ;HSARC ;OGRA ;LETOH DNARG

Surprising Airplane Facts Quiz

Don't be surprised if you can't answer them.

1. When you fly the Airbus 380 double-decker giant plane on tourist class, do you see a difference from a regular airplane deck?

____

2. Did the Wright Brothers get rich from their invention of the airplane?

____

3. What is the cheapest way to learn flying?

____

4. Did WWI contribute to the development of aviation?

____

5. Did WWII contribute to the development of aviation?

____

6. People see birds flying for thousands of years. Why did it take so long for man to fly?

____

7. Is it safer to fly in the front or back of an airliner?

____

8. Is it safer to fly than drive?

____

9. What if I, living in NYC, afraid to fly & was invited to my Goddaughter's wedding in California?

____

10. How many Boeing 747 jumbo jets (weighing as much as 70 African elephants) were produced?

____

11. What was the most deadly airplane accident?

____

12. The cost of how many millions of new cars is equivalent to flying a few people to Mars?

____

ANSWERS: 1. .KCAB DNA TNORF EHT TA SRIATS DNUOR EES UOY TPECXE KCED TFARCRIA ELSIA-NIWT YDOB-EDIW A EKIL SI TI ,ON 2. .NOILLIM 01$ FO HTROW TEN A HTIW 8491 NI DEID ELLIVRO ;2191 NI GNUOY DEID RUBLIW ;YHTLAEW EMACEB YEHT 3. EGAKCAP ROTALUMIS THGILF A YUB 4. .SETATS DETINU EHT NI DERUTCAFUNAM EREW SENALPRIA 000,21 ,9191 YB .YLSUODNEMERT SEY 5. .YNAMREG IZAN NI DEPOLEVED TSRIF SAW ENIGNE TEJ EHT .YLSUOMRONE SEY 6. .YRUTNEC HT02 FO GNINNIGEB EHT TA DEPOLEVED YLNO EREW SENIGNE THGIL EHT 7. KCAB YREV EHT NI SEHSARC DEVIVRUS ELPOEP EMOS ;ECNEREFFID ON SI EREHT YLLACITCARP 8. YLF OT REFAS HCUM 9. NAC UOY SA NOOS SA SKNIRD WEF A ROF KSA 10. DERDNUH NEETFIF 11. GOF NI 747 MA-NAP GNIIXAT A HTIW DEDILLOC FFO GNIKAT 747 MLK ;DEHSIREP 006 OT ESOLC ;)DLROW WEN EHT EROFEB POTS TSAL S'SUBMULOC - NIAPS ,SDNALSI YRANAC(7791 EFIRENET 12. SRAC WEN NOILLIM EVIF

Name That Car Model in 10 Minutes!

Find at least 3 automobile models for each letter if any.

1. A-B ______________________________
2. C-D ______________________________
3. E-F ______________________________
4. G-H ______________________________
5. I-J ______________________________
6. K-L ______________________________
7. M-N ______________________________
8. O-P ______________________________
9. Q-R ______________________________
10. S-T ______________________________
11. U-V-W ______________________________
12. X-Y-Z ______________________________

ANSWERS: 1. OCNORB ,ADAVARB ,TLOB ,ADUMREB ,NOLAVA ,STA ,AMITLA ,DROCCA 2. OGNARUD ,TTEUD ,ETNAMAID ,XAM-C ,ETTEVROC ,LATNENITNOC ,ORAMAC 3. ATSEIF ,REITNORF ,SUCOF ,NOCLAF ,EVALCNE ,REROLPXE ,NOITIDEPXE ,EPACSE 4. REMMUH ,TENROH ,XULIH ,REDNALHGIH ,OMSIRUTNARG ,NILMERG ,ADANARG 5. EKUJ ,YMMIJ ,AMARAJ ,APLAJ ,MUSPI ,AZERPMI ,ALAPMI 6. ENRECUL ,YCAGEL ,FAEL ,ESSORCAL ,ANOK ,IHSAZIK 7. ORIN ,TROPWEN ,ROTAGIVAN ,OJAVAN ,GNATSUM ,T LEDOM ,AMIXAM ,UBILAM 8. RASLUP ,ADNAP ,TOLIP ,ALAPO ,KCABTUO ,YESSYDO ,AIVATCO 9. EUGOR ,ENILEGDIR ,TNAILER ,REGNAR ,06XQ ,ORTTAUQ ,IAQHSAQ 10. TISNART ,EOHAT ,SURUAT ,AMOCAT ,NABRUBUS ,ODAREVLIS ,AIOUQES 11. RELGNARW ,HTIARW ,RATSDNIW ,TLOV ,REPIV ,REGALLIV ,SELLIASREV ,ASREV ,ZURCAREV ,ARTCEV ,ONU 12. 8Z ,RYHPEZ ,STEHZOROPAZ ,OGUY ,NOCUY ,NOLISPY ,SIRAY ,5X ,ARRETX

HUMPHREY BOGART & IRENE DUNNE HISTORIC MARKERS

Which movies with the same title did they star in separately?

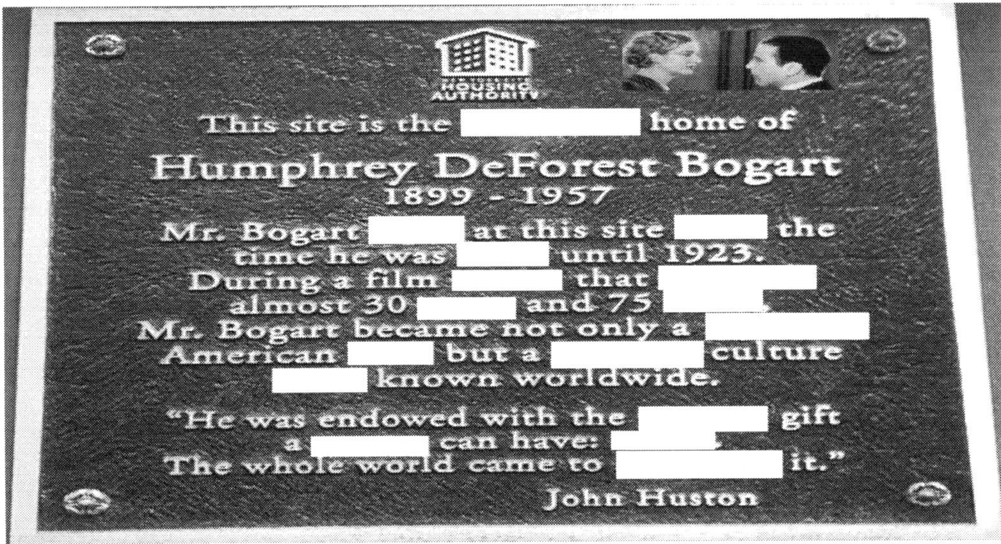

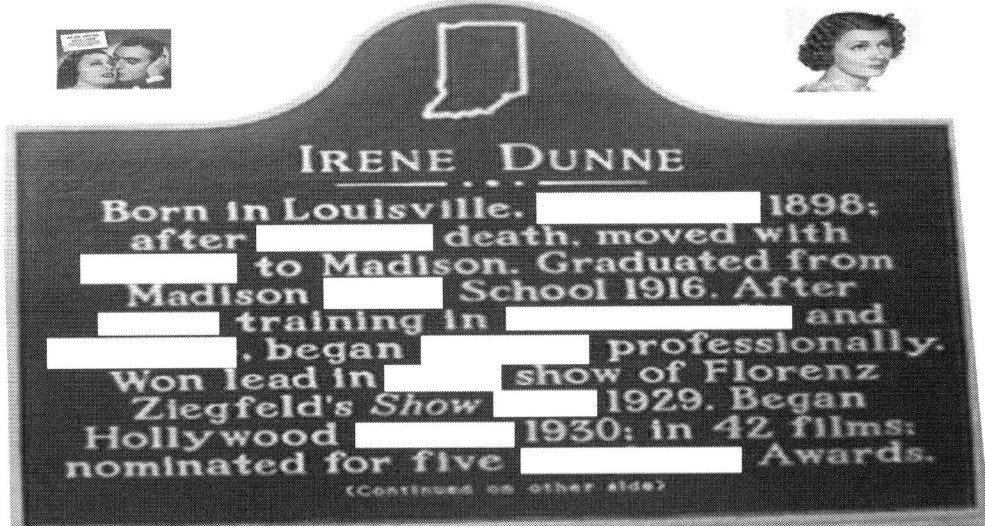

ANSWERS: BOGART: EZINGOCER ,TNELAT ,NOSREP ,TSETAERG ,NOCI ,RALUPOP ,OREH ,LACIHTYM ,SMLIF ,SRAEY ,DENNAPS ,REERAC ,NROB ,MORF ,DEVIL ,DOOHDLIHC
DUNNE: YMEDACA ,REERAC ,TAOB ,DAOR ,GNIGNIS ,OGACIHC ,SILOPANAIDNI ,ECIOV ,HGIH ,YLIMAF ,S'REHTAF ,YKCUTNEK
SAME MOVIE TITLE: SEIVOM DETALERNU ,)9391(RIAFFA EVOL NI ENNUD ENERI ,)2391(RIAFFA EVOL NI TRAGOB YERHPMUH

Brain Teaser Word Find Puzzle

Find & circle all occurrences of ORYX(2), HARE(2), COLT(2),DUCK(1), GOAT(2), LYNX(2)

Y	R	O	O	O	Y					E	H	R	A	E	A	R	R	H	H
X	Y	R	Y	O	X					E	E	A	A	A	E	H	H	R	R
R	Y	O	R	X	O					R	R	A	H	H	R	H	E	H	H
O	Y	R	R	Y	O					E	A	A	A	A	E	H	H	E	A
X	O	Y	O	R	O					E	R	A	E	H	H	A	A	H	E
R	O	Y	X	Y	O	X	R	X	X	A	R	R	R	R	E	E	A	R	E
Y	Y	R	R	X	X	O	X	O	O	A	A	E	H	R	H	H	E	E	E
R	R	R	R	Y	X	R	R	X	X	R	E	H	R	H	E	E	A	H	A
Y	X	Y	O	Y	Y	Y	R	Y	Y	R	A	R	A	A	R	H	E	E	R
O	Y	O	Y	O	Y	O	R	R	X	A	H	H	H	E	H	E	E	E	R
C	C	L	L	O	C	L	C	C	C					D	D	C	K	U	K
L	L	L	C	C	T	O	C	L	T					U	C	U	C	C	K
T	C	O	C	O	T	C	O	L	L					C	C	U	K	K	C
T	T	L	L	T	T	T	O	O	T					D	D	C	U	C	D
T	C	O	L	C	L	C	T	C	O					K	U	C	C	K	K
T	C	O	L	L	L	L	T	T	L					K	K	C	D	C	K
T	L	T	O	L	L	O	C	O	O	C	C	U	D	C	K	D	K	K	D
C	O	O	O	T	C	C	C	T	C	C	K	U	U	C	K	K	K	C	K
C	L	C	C	L	O	L	L	T	O	C	D	U	C	C	D	D	U	U	K
O	L	O	O	L	C	O	O	C	L	D	C	D	D	K	C	D	D	U	K
G	T	O	A	G	A	G	G	T	T	Y	X	X	X	X	N	X	L	N	N
A	A	A	A	O	O	O	T	A	O	X	L	X	Y	L	Y	Y	N	Y	L
T	T	O	G	G	T	O	T	O	A	N	Y	Y	L	X	X	L	Y	L	L
G	A	A	T	A	G	A	T	A	G	Y	Y	N	L	L	Y	X	X	L	N
G	A	O	O	O	T	G	O	G	T	X	Y	Y	L	N	X	X	L	L	Y
A	T	G	G	O	A	G	A	A	G	L	N	L	L	Y	N	Y	N	X	Y
A	T	T	A	O	O	A	G	T	G	Y	N	Y	L	N	X	Y	N	N	X
O	G	T	O	A	A	O	T	T	A	L	X	L	L	N	X	X	Y	N	L
T	G	A	A	O	G	G	A	G	T	L	L	N	L	X	N	X	Y	L	N
A	G	T	A	T	A	A	T	O	G	L	Y	L	Y	N	Y	L	Y	Y	Y

STATUE OF LIBERTY IN NEW YORK HARBOR

U.S. CITIZENSHIP QUIZZES

U.S. Citizenship Test 1

All the questions are related to the official test required for citizenship.

1. What is the supreme law of the land?

____

2. What does the Constitution do?

____

3. What are the first three words of the Constitution?

____

4. What is an amendment to the Constitution?

____

5. What do we call the first ten amendments to the Constitution?

____

6. What is one right or freedom from the First Amendment?

____

7. What did the Declaration of Independence do?

____

8. What are two rights in the Declaration of Independence?

____

9. What is freedom of religion?

____

10. What is the economic system in the United States?

____

11. What is the "rule of law"?

____

12. Name one branch or part of the government.

____

ANSWERS: 1. NOITUTITSNOC EHT 2. SNACIREMA FO STHGIR CISAB STCETORP ;TNEMNREVOG EHT SENIFED ;TNEMNREVOG EHT PU STES 3. ELPOEP EHT EW 4. NOITIDDA NA ;EGNAHC A 5. STHGIR FO LLIB EHT 6. TNEMNREVOG EHT NOITITEP ;SSERP ;YLBMESSA ;NOIGILER ;HCEEPS 7. EERF SI SETATS DETINU EHT TAHT DIAS ;)NIATIRB TAERG MORF(ECNEDNEPEDNI RUO DERALCED 8. SSENIPPAH FO TIUSRUP ;YTREBIL ;EFIL 9. .NOIGILER A ECITCARP TON RO ,NOIGILER YNA ECITCARP NAC UOY 10. YMONOCE TEKRAM ;YMONOCE TSILATIPAC 11. WAL EHT EVOBA SI ENO ON ;WAL EHT YEBO TSUM TNEMNREVOG ;WAL EHT YEBO TSUM SREDAEL ;WAL EHT WOLLOF TSUM ENOYREVE 12. LAICIDUJ ;STRUOC EHT ;EVITUCEXE ;TNEDISERP ;EVITALSIGEL ;SSERGNOC

U.S. Citizenship Test 2

All the questions are related to the official test required for citizenship.

1. What stops one branch of government from becoming too powerful?

____

2. Who is in charge of the executive branch?

____

3. Who makes federal laws?

____

4. What are the two parts of the U.S. Congress?

____

5. How many U.S. Senators are there?

____

6. We elect a U.S. Senator for how many years?

____

7. Who is one of your state's U.S. Senators now?

____

8. The House of Representatives has how many voting members?

____

9. We elect a U.S. Representative for how many years?

____

10. Name your U.S. Representative.

____

11. Who does a U.S. Senator represent?

____

12. Why do some states have more Representatives than other states?

____

ANSWERS: 1. SREWOP FO NOITARAPES ;SECNALAB DNA SKCEHC 2. TNEDISERP EHT 3. ERUTALSIGEL)LANOITAN RO .S.U(;SEVITATNESERPER FO ESUOH DNA ETANES ;SSERGNOC 4. SEVITATNESERPER FO ESUOH DNA ETANES EHT 5. ETATS HCAE ROF SROTANES OWT ;)001(DERDNUH ENO 6.)6(XIS 7.].SROTANES .S.U ON EVAH SEIROTIRRET .S.U DNA .C.D NOTGNIHSAW[.YRAV LLIW SREWSNA 8.)534(EVIF-YTRIHT DERDNUH RUOF 9.)2(OWT 10. .YRAV LLIW SREWSNA 11. ETATS EHT FO ELPOEP LLA 12. ELPOEP EROM EVAH SETATS EMOS)ESUACEB(;ELPOEP EROM EVAH YEHT)ESUACEB(;NOITALUPOP S'ETATS EHT)FO ESUACEB(

U.S. Citizenship Test 3

All the questions are related to the official test required for citizenship.

1. We elect a President for how many years?

____

2. In what month do we vote for President?

____

3. What is the name of the President of the United States now?

____

4. What is the name of the Vice President of the United States now?

____

5. If the President can no longer serve, who becomes President?

____

6. If both the President and the Vice President can no longer serve, who becomes President?

____

7. Who is the Commander in Chief of the military?

____

8. Who signs bills to become laws?

____

9. Who vetoes bills?

____

10. What does the President's Cabinet do?

____

11. What are two Cabinet-level positions?

____

12. What does the judicial branch do?

____

ANSWERS: 1.)4(RUOF 2. REBMEVON 3. YRAV LLIW SREWSNA 4. YRAV LLIW SREWSNA 5. TNEDISERP ECIV EHT 6. ESUOH EHT FO REKAEPS EHT 7. TNEDISERP EHT 8. TNEDISERP EHT 9. TNEDISERP EHT 10. TNEDISERP EHT SESIVDA 11. TNEDISERP ECIV ;LARENEG YENROTTA ;SRIAFFA SNARETEV ,YRUSAERT EHT ,NOITATROPSNART ,ETATS ,ROBAL ,ROIRETNI EHT ,TNEMPOLEVED NABRU DNA GNISUOH ,YTIRUCES DNALEMOH ,SECIVRES NAMUH DNA HTLAEH ,YGRENE ,NOITACUDE ,ESNEFED ,ECREMMOC ,ERUTLUCIRGA FO YRATERCES 12. NOITUTITSNOC EHT TSNIAGA SEOG WAL A FI SEDICED ;SETUPSID SEVLOSER ;SWAL SNIALPXE ;SWAL SWEIVER

U.S. Citizenship Test 4

All the questions are related to the official test required for citizenship.

1. What is the highest court in the United States?

2. How many justices are on the Supreme Court?

3. Who is the Chief Justice of the United States now?

4. Under our Constitution, some powers belong to the federal government. What is one power of the federal

5. Under our Constitution, some powers belong to the states. What is one power of the states?

6. Who is the Governor of your state now?

7. What is the capital of your state?

8. What are the two major political parties in the United States?

9. What is the political party of the President now?

10. What is the name of the Speaker of the House of Representatives now?

11. There are four amendments to the Constitution about who can vote. Describe one of them.

12. What is one responsibility that is only for United States citizens?

ANSWERS: 1. TRUOC EMERPUS EHT 2.)9(ENIN 3. YRAV LLIW SREWSNA 4. SEITAERT EKAM OT ;YMRA NA ETAERC OT ;RAW ERALCED OT ;YENOM TNIRP OT 5. ESU DNAL DNA GNINOZ EVORPPA ;ESNECIL S'REVIRD A EVIG ;)STNEMTRAPED ERIF(YTEFAS EDIVORP ;)ECILOP(NOITCETORP EDIVORP ;NOITACUDE DNA GNILOOHCS EDIVORP 6. YRAV LLIW SREWSNA 7. YRAV LLIW SREWSNA 8. NACILBUPER DNA CITARCOMED 9. YRAV LLIW REWSNA 10. YRAV LLIW REWSNA 11. .)ETOV NAC(ECAR YNA FO NEZITIC ELAM A ;).ETOV NAC NEM DNA NEMOW(.ETOV NAC NEZITIC YNA ;ETOV OT)XAT LLOP A(YAP OT EVAH T'NOD UOY ;)ETOV NAC(REDLO DNA)81(NEETHGIE SNEZITIC 12. NOITCELE LAREDEF A NI ETOV ;YRUJ A NO EVRES

U.S. Citizenship Test 5

All the questions are related to the official test required for citizenship.

1. Name one right only for United States citizens.

____

2. What are two rights of everyone living in the United States?

____

3. What do we show loyalty to when we say the Pledge of Allegiance?

____

4. What is one promise you make when you become a United States citizen?

____

5. How old do citizens have to be to vote for President?

____

6. What are two ways that Americans can participate in their democracy?

____

7. When is the last day you can send in federal income tax forms?

____

8. When must all men register for the Selective Service?

____

9. What is one reason colonists came to America?

____

10. Who lived in America before the Europeans arrived?

____

11. What group of people was taken to America and sold as slaves?

____

12. Why did the colonists fight the British?

____

ANSWERS: 1. ECIFFO LAREDEF ROF NUR ;NOITCELE LAREDEF A NI ETOV 2. SMRA RAEB OT THGIR EHT ;NOIGILER FO MODEERF ;TNEMNREVOG EHT NOITITEP OT MODEERF ;YLBMESSA FO MODEERF ;HCEEPS FO MODEERF ;NOISSERPXE FO MODEERF 3. GALF EHT ;SETATS DETINU EHT 4. SETATS DETINU EHT OT LAYOL EB ;)DEDEEN FI(NOITAN EHT)ROF KROW TNATROPMI OD(EVRES ;)DEDEEN FI(YRATILIM .S.U EHT NI EVRES ;SETATS DETINU EHT FO SWAL EHT YEBO ;SETATS DETINU EHT FO SWAL DNA NOITUTITSNOC EHT DNEFED ;SEIRTNUOC REHTO OT YTLAYOL PU EVIG 5. REDLO DNA)81(NEETHGIE 6. AIDEM LAICOS NO ETIRW ;REPAPSWEN A OT ETIRW ;ECIFFO ROF NUR ;YCILOP RO EUSSI NA ESOPPO RO TROPPUS YLCILBUP ;SEVITATNESERPER DNA SROTANES LLAC ;EUSSI NA NO NOINIPO RUOY LAICIFFO DETCELE NA EVIG ;PUORG YTINUMMOC A NIOJ ;PUORG CIVIC A NIOJ ;NGIAPMAC A HTIW PLEH ;YTRAP LACITILOP A NIOJ ;ETOV 7. 51 LIRPA 8.)62(XIS-YTNEWT DNA)81(NEETHGIE NEEWTEB ;)81(NEETHGIE EGA TA 9. NOITUCESREP EPACSE ;NOIGILER RIEHT ECITCARP ;YTINUTROPPO CIMONOCE ;MODEERF SUOIGILER ;YTREBIL LACITILOP ;MODEERF 10. SNACIREMA EVITAN ;SNAIDNI NACIREMA 11. ACIRFA MORF ELPOEP ;SNACIRFA 12. TNEMNREVOG-FLES EVAH T'NDID YEHT ESUACEB ;)GNIRETRAUQ ,GNIDRAOB(SESUOH RIEHT NI DEYATS YMRA HSITIRB EHT ESUACEB ;)NOITATNESERPER TUOHTIW NOITAXAT(SEXAT HGIH FO ESUACEB

U.S. Citizenship Test 6

All the questions are related to the official test required for citizenship.

1. Who wrote the Declaration of Independence?

____

2. When was the Declaration of Independence adopted?

____

3. There were 13 original states. Name three.

____

4. What happened at the Constitutional Convention?

____

5. When was the Constitution written?

____

6. The Federalist Papers supported the passage of the U.S. Constitution. Name one of the writers.

____

7. What is one thing Benjamin Franklin is famous for?

____

8. Who is the "Father of Our Country"?

____

9. Who was the first President?

____

10. What territory did the United States buy from France in 1803?

____

11. Name one war fought by the United States in the 1800s.

____

12. Name the U.S. war between the North and the South.

____

ANSWERS: 1. NOSREFFEJ)SAMOHT(2. 6771 ,4 YLUJ 3. AIGROEG ;ANILORAC HTUOS ;ANILORAC HTRON ;AINIGRIV ;DNALYRAM ;ERAWALED ;AINAVLYSNNEP ;YESREJ WEN ;KROY WEN ;TUCITCENNOC ;DNALSI EDOHR ;STTESUHCASSAM ;ERIHSPMAH WEN 4. NOITUTITSNOC EHT ETORW SREHTAF GNIDNUOF EHT ;NETTIRW SAW NOITUTITSNOC EHT 5. 7871 6. SUILBUP ;YAJ)NHOJ(;NOTLIMAH)REDNAXELA(;NOSIDAM)SEMAJ(7. SEIRARBIL EERF TSRIF EHT DETRATS ;"CANAMLA S'DRAHCIR ROOP" FO RETIRW ;SETATS DETINU EHT FO LARENEG RETSAMTSOP TSRIF ;NOITNEVNOC LANOITUTITSNOC EHT FO REBMEM TSEDLO ;TAMOLPID .S.U 8. NOTGNIHSAW)EGROEG(9. NOTGNIHSAW)EGROEG(10. ANAISIUOL ;YROTIRRET ANAISIUOL EHT 11. RAW NACIREMA-HSINAPS ;RAW LIVIC ;RAW NACIREMA-NACIXEM ;2181 FO RAW 12. SETATS EHT NEEWTEB RAW EHT ;RAW LIVIC EHT

U.S. Citizenship Test 7

All the questions are related to the official test required for citizenship.

1. Name one problem that led to the Civil War.

____

2. What was one important thing that Abraham Lincoln did?

____

3. What did the Emancipation Proclamation do?

____

4. What did Susan B. Anthony do?

____

5. Name one war fought by the United States in the 1900s.

____

6. Who was President during World War I?

____

7. Who was President during the Great Depression and World War II?

____

8. Who did the United States fight in World War II?

____

9. Before he was President, Eisenhower was a general. What war was he in?

____

10. During the Cold War, what was the main concern of the United States?

____

11. What movement tried to end racial discrimination?

____

12. What did Martin Luther King, Jr. do?

____

ANSWERS: 1. STHGIR 'SETATS ;SNOSAER CIMONOCE ;YREVALS 2. RAW LIVIC EHT GNIRUD SETATS DETINU EHT DEL ;NOINU EHT)DEVRESERP RO(DEVAS ;)NOITAMALCORP NOITAPICNAME(SEVALS EHT DEERF 3. SETATS NREHTUOS TSOM NI SEVALS DEERF ;SETATS ETAREDEFNOC EHT NI SEVALS DEERF ;YCAREDEFNOC EHT NI SEVALS DEERF ;SEVALS EHT DEERF 4. STHGIR LIVIC ROF THGUOF ;STHGIR S'NEMOW ROF THGUOF 5. RAW FLUG)NAISREP(RAW MANTEIV ;RAW NAEROK ;II RAW DLROW ;I RAW DLROW 6. NOSLIW)WORDOOW(7. TLEVESOOR)NILKNARF(8. YLATI DNA ,YNAMREG ,NAPAJ 9. II RAW DLROW 10. MSINUMMOC 11.)TNEMEVOM(STHGIR LIVIC 12. SNACIREMA LLA ROF YTILAUQE ROF DEKROW ;STHGIR LIVIC ROF THGUOF

U.S. Citizenship Test 8

All the questions are related to the official test required for citizenship.

1. What major event happened on September 11, 2001, in the United States?

____

2. Name one American Indian tribe in the United States.

____

3. Name one of the two longest rivers in the United States.

____

4. What oceans are on the coasts of the United States?

____

5. Name one U.S. territory.

____

6. Name one state that borders Canada.

____

7. Name one state that borders Mexico.

____

8. Why does the flag have 13 stripes?

____

9. Why does the flag have 50 stars?

____

10. What is the name of the national anthem?

____

11. When do we celebrate Independence Day?

____

12. Name two national U.S. holidays.

____

ANSWERS: 1. .SETATS DETINU EHT DEKCATTA STSIRORRET 2. TIUNI ;IPOH ;NOTET ;WORC ;ATOKAL ;ADIENO ;NORUH ;NAGEHOM ;EENWAHS ;KAWARA ;ENNEYEHC ;ELONIMES ;TEEFKCALB ;KEERC ;SIOUQORI ;EHCAPA ;OLBEUP ;WATCOHC ;AWEPPIHC ;XUOIS ;OJAVAN ;EEKOREHC 3. REVIR(IPPISSISSIM ;)REVIR(IRUOSSIM 4. NAECO CIFICAP DNA NAECO CITNALTA 5. MAUG ;SDNALSI ANAIRAM NREHTRON ;AOMAS NACIREMA ;SDNALSI NIGRIV .S.U ;OCIR OTREUP 6. AKSALA ;NOTGNIHSAW ;OHADI ;ANATNOM ;ATOKAD HTRON ;ATOSENNIM ;NAGIHCIM ;OIHO ;AINAVLYSNNEP ;KROY WEN ;TNOMREV ;ERIHSPMAH WEN ;ENIAM 7. SAXET ;OCIXEM WEN ;ANOZIRA ;AINROFILAC 8. SEINOLOC LANIGIRO EHT TNESERPER SEPIRTS EHT ESUACEB ;SEINOLOC LANIGIRO 31 EREW EREHT ESUACEB 9. SETATS 05 ERA EREHT ESUACEB ;ETATS A STNESERPER RATS HCAE ESUACEB ;ETATS HCAE ROF RATS ENO SI EREHT ESUACEB 10. RENNAB DELGNAPS-RATS EHT 11. YLUJ FO HTRUOF ;4 YLUJ 12. SAMTSIRHC ;GNIVIGSKNAHT ;YAD SNARETEV ;YAD SUBMULOC ;YAD ROBAL ;YAD ECNEDNEPEDNI ;YAD LAIROMEM ;YAD 'STNEDISERP ;YAD .RJ ,GNIK REHTUL NITRAM ;YAD S'RAEY WEN

PICTURE PUZZLE 3. NEW WORLD TRADE CENTER ONE NEAR FINISH

PICTURE PUZZLE 3. CIRCLE THE TEN DIFFERENCES

MINI CROSSWORD SQUARES

3x3 MINI CROSSWORD SQUARES

Puzzle 1. REMEMBER THE LAST CENTURY?

Row 1: Perform in a play, movie or TV show.
Row 2: A light two-wheeled horse carriage; a musical job.
Row 3: Having been alive or on earth for a long time.
Diagonal: To support, help or supply with money.
Left Column: In the past, gone by.

Puzzle 2. NEVER TOO OLD TO PLAY!

Row 1: Something kids enjoy playing with.
Row 2: The lacy net that spiders spin.
Row 3: A single unit and no more.
Diagonal: A holder to prop up a golf ball.
Left Column: One plus one.

Puzzle 3. ARE YOU HUNGRY?

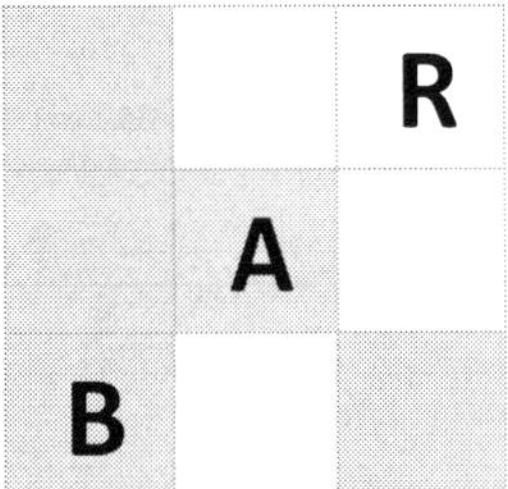

Row 1: Make a mistake.
Row 2: A paper or plastic sack for holding things.
Row 3: A small piece of something.
Diagonal: To chew and swallow food.
Left Column: Movement of the tide out to the sea; to lessen.

Puzzle 4. SLEEP HERE TONITE!

Row 1: The time between sunrise and sunset.
Row 2: A small hotel where travelers stay and eat.
Row 3: Neither solid nor liquid; oxygen for example.
Diagonal: Abbreviation for Domain Name System.
Left Column: To make a hole in the ground; to like a lot.

Puzzle 5. ARE YOU AFRAID OF SNAKES?

		T
	I	
E		

Row 1: Appropriate, proper, suitable or likely.
Row 2: A container for corn, bread, coal, or rubbish.
Row 3: A long snake-like fish.
Diagonal: To supply with help.
Left Column: Abbreviation for Adult Basic Education.

Puzzle 6. VENEZUELA NEEDS HELP!

		M
	I	
S		

Row 1: Tastes good with Swiss on a sandwich.
Row 2: To support, help or give money.
Row 3: USA iconic "Uncle".
Diagonal: The boy with her.
Left Column: Owns or possesses.

Puzzle 7. DINNER TIME?

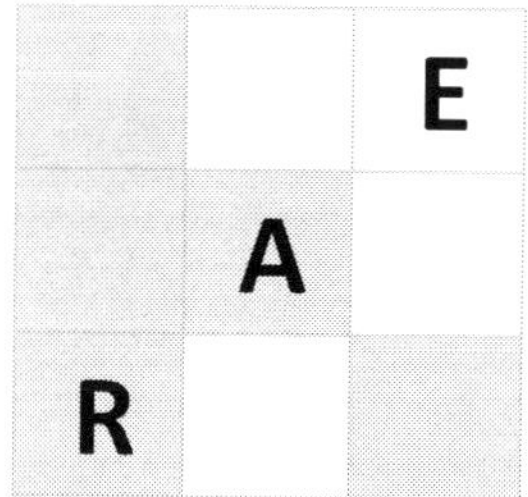

Row 1: Food made of pastry outside, and filled with fruit or meat.
Row 2: To chew and swallow food.
Row 3: What you did in a race yesterday.
Diagonal: A metal container with a handle, used for cooking.
Left Column: In the opinion of.

Puzzle 8. HOW OLD ARE YOU?

Row 1: Something you don't ask a woman.
Row 2: One plus one.
Row 3: A ram's wife. Baaaaa!
Diagonal: Fear, wonder or great respect for.
Left Column: Chewed and swallowed.

Puzzle 9. OMELETTE FOR BREAKFAST?

		D
	G	
R		

Row 1: Grand finale.
Row 2: The number of years lived.
Row 3: To fix in a hurry; an arrangement of sails.
Diagonal: Fried, over easy, scrambled or poached.
Left Column: If not deaf, you hear with it.

Puzzle 10. SOMETHING FISHY?

Row 1: Cheerie-O's grain.
Row 2: Advertisements.
Row 3: Fishermen attach it to a reel.
Diagonal: Not even.
Left Column: Used to row, row, row your boat.

Puzzle 11. LONDON HAS MANY!

		T
	U	
A		

Row 1: Matching group of dishes.
Row 2: A place to drink wine, beer and ale with friends.
Row 3: A tool used by Paul Bunyan.
Diagonal: To file in court for damages.
Left Column: A place for massages and other body pampering.

Puzzle 12. SEED WITH A SHELL?

		G
	E	
N		

Row 1: A cup for hot drinks.
Row 2: A slippery snake-like fish.
Row 3: Pea, hazel, chest or wal for instance.
Diagonal: To meet yesterday.
Left Column: Two and a Half ___.

Puzzle 13. BIRD OF NIGHT

		E
	W	
L		

Row 1: Being a single unit.
Row 2: World Wide Web
Row 3: Speak falsely.
Diagonal: To need to pay.
Left Column: A bird with big eyes and a sharp curved beak.

Puzzle 14. IT GOES WITH CARROT

		E
	P	
P		

Row 1: To use your eyes.
Row 2: Appropriate, proper.
Row 3: A green seeds used as food.
Diagonal: A place to swim in mineral water.
Left Column: Juice in plants and trees.

Puzzle 15. STAY OVERNIGHT

		Y
	N	
M		

Row 1: Nothing specific.
Row 2: Place of lodging in the country.
Row 3: Soft wet dirt.
Diagonal: Also.
Left Column: To point a weapon.

Puzzle 16. CAT ENEMY

Row 1: Man's best friend.
Row 2: A climbing plant, some are poison.
Row 3: The Creator of everything.
Diagonal: Movies are on it.
Left Column: To make a hole in the ground.

Puzzle 17. HOLD THE WATER

		Y
	I	
D		

Row 1: You there!
Row 2: Roman numeral 3.
Row 3: A wall which checks a flow of water.
Diagonal: The boy with her.
Left Column: To hide yesterday.

Puzzle 18. MADAME, COFFEE OR

Row 1: Roman Numeral equal to 104.
Row 2: To point a gun at a target.
Row 3: A hot drink made with boiling water and dried leaves.
Diagonal: By way of.
Left Column: A large vessel used to make wine.

Puzzle 19. STRAWBERRY RHUBARB DELICACY

		E
	A	
T		

Row 1: A pastry shell filled with something sweet.
Row 2: What Van Gogh cut off.
Row 3: To attempt.
Diagonal: Monetary reward from your boss.
Left Column: A domesticated animal kept at home.

Puzzle 20. OPPOSITE OF NIGHT

Row 1: Father.
Row 2: Plus.
Row 3: The word you use to show you agree.
Diagonal: Domain Name System (internet).
Left Column: 24 hours.

Puzzle 21. ELEPHANT HAS THE BIGGEST

		R
	A	
E		

Row 1: "___ he's a Jolly Good Fellow."
Row 2: You row with it.
Row 3: The part of the body you hear with.
Diagonal: A long way away.
Left Column: An enemy.

Puzzle 22. SUPERMARKET CHECKOUT

Row 1: What you do at the cashier.
Row 2: You use it to listen.
Row 3: A girl or young woman.
Diagonal: A friend you hang with.
Left Column: Small dowel.

Puzzle 23. SHARPEN KNIFE

		T
	E	
U		

Row 1: To use a scissors.
Row 2: Used for writing with ink.
Row 3: Unidentified Flying Object
Diagonal: Chief Executive Officer
Left Column: The heart of a computer.

Puzzle 24. BIG TREE

		W
	A	
E		

Row 1: Belonging to the tribe or kingdom of Judah.
Row 2: A tree with acorns.
Row 3: What you put your phone near to hear.
Diagonal: Glass container for pickles or mayonnaise.
Left Column: Common name for a GI.

Puzzle 25. OPEN AND SEE

		E
	Y	
E		

Row 1: A popular brand of denim jeans.
Row 2: Part of your face with a lid.
Row 3: A female sheep.
Diagonal: A caustic alkaline solution.
Left Column: The general of the Confederate Army.

Puzzle 26. TIME TO CLEAN

		S
	I	
M		

Row 1: Contracted as in a disease.
Row 2: To suffer a sickness.
Row 3: Swiffer has a wet one.
Diagonal: Large joint that allows your whole leg to move.
Left Column: Meat often in pea soup.

Puzzle 27. LONG FISH STORY

		D
	E	
T		

Row 1: Where peas grow up.
Row 2: Elongated fish, sometimes electric.
Row 3: A thick black liquid used on a roof.
Diagonal: Prefix for fect, fume and culator.
Left Column: Dog, cat, or hamster for example.

Puzzle 28. LATIN ALPHABET

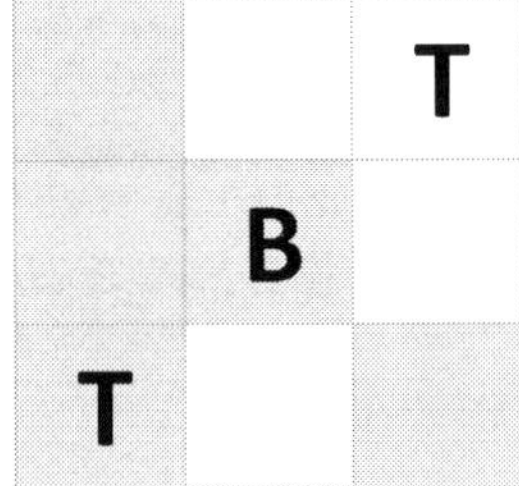

Row 1: Do it when you also "drink" and "be merry".
Row 2: Easy as ....
Row 3: To move over when typing to create columns.
Diagonal: What a tide does to move away from the shore.
Left Column: Consume food.

Puzzle 29. NOT SEVEN

		N
	I	
S		

Row 1: A male human being when he is grown up.
Row 2: Bunch of sails on a boat.
Row 3: Two times three.
Diagonal: To put different things together.
Left Column: The title of a married woman.

Puzzle 30. MAMMA MIA

Row 1: An ugly witch or sorceress.
Row 2: A Turkic word for village.
Row 3: Mother.
Diagonal: To make a musical sound in your nose.
Left Column: Salty meat from a pig.

Puzzle 31. EAT SPAM FOR LUNCH

Row 1: Read Only Memory.
Row 2: Something belonging to us.
Row 3: A small airtight metal container for food.
Diagonal: To move quickly on your feet.
Left Column: A monstrous bird of Arabian mythology.

Puzzle 32. HIDE YOUR PASSWORDS

		E
	P	
W		

Row 1: To use your eyes to look at something.
Row 2: Choose to be IN or OUT.
Row 3: A little twisted from normal, as in humor.
Diagonal: Someone who secretly watches what other people are doing.
Left Column: To plant seeds in the ground.

Puzzle 33. JUMP IN

Row 1: Put in and out of something quickly.
Row 2: To intend, as in "to please".
Row 3: Husband of a woman.
Diagonal: Loud unpleasant prolonged noise.
Left Column: There is a big one in Boulder, CO.

Puzzle 34. POPULAR IN ENGLAND

Row 1: Neither solid nor liquid.
Row 2: The mixture of gases which we breathe.
Row 3: Spanish word for "saint".
Diagonal: Against; nearby; also a card game & alcoholic drinks.
Left Column: Type of home heating. Hint: not electric, coal or solar.

Puzzle 35. GO TO AN EXHIBIT

		E
	R	
T		

Row 1: Money paid for a service.
Row 2: Drawing, painting and sculpture, or the creation thereof.
Row 3: Three minus one.
Diagonal: To be tossed away from.
Left Column: Bacon has a lot of it!

Puzzle 36. BALLERINA DANCE

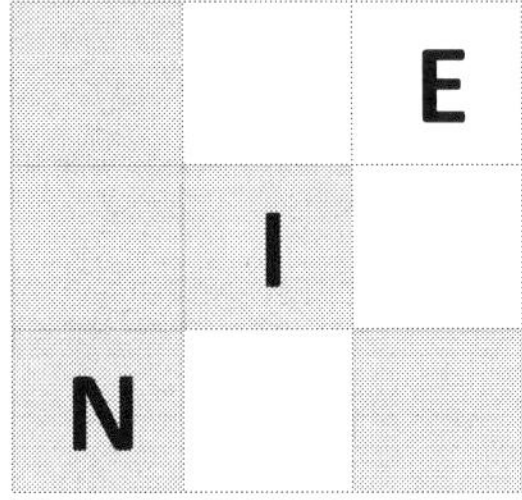

Row 1: A digit of your foot. One is called "big" another "pinky".
Row 2: Used with "less" to mean lacking direction.
Row 3: A short sleep.
Diagonal: The point of a pen.
Left Column: The brown color of skin when exposed to sunlight.

4x4 MINI CROSSWORD SQUARES

Puzzle 1. RUTH & BASEBALL

			E
		A	
	H		
S			

Row 1: Another word for infant.
Row 2: Verbally.
Row 3: Who,____ , when & where?
Row 4: As a bug in a rug.
Diagonal: To boast about.
Left Column: Pretty knots of ribbon.

Puzzle 2. CHILD'S PLAY

			K
		C	
	P		
T			

Row 1: Public garden and play area.
Row 2: The shapes of rainbows.
Row 3: Feature found on a Dalmatian's coat. Woof!
Row 4: Added to the check amounts at restaurants for good service.
Diagonal: Experts.
Left Column: Not present or future.

Puzzle 3. TWO NICKELS

			S
		A	
	I		
S			

Row 1: How old people are, in years.
Row 2: Country in the Middle East.
Row 3: A silver ten-cent coin.
Row 4: Chinese dish Chop ____.
Diagonal: Soldiers in a large group.
Left Column: Those that help nurses.

Puzzle 4. SAILSHIP ON HORIZON!

			Z
		I	
	X		
S			

Row 1: A canal connecting the Mediterranean and the Red Seas.
Row 2: A poem recounting heroic deeds; slang: impressive
Row 3: A line through the middle; the Earth rotates around one.
Row 4: Shakespeare's Lady Macbeth - "Out damned ____!"
Diagonal: Something unpleasant llamas & camels do when annoyed.
Left Column: Includes Red, Dead, Mediterranean & Bering.

Puzzle 5. YOU ARE PICKY!

			L
		N	
	A		
T			

Row 1: The opposite of empty.
Row 2: Mom or Dad's sister.
Row 3: No credit cards accepted, _____ only!
Row 4: Not "THAT".
Diagonal: To make a stink about something trivial.
Left Column: Something true and uncontestable.

Puzzle 6. PAY IT MONTHLY!

			Y
		S	
	I		
T			

Row 1: Exciting, titillating or even arousing.
Row 2: Bar during prohibition: Speak ____.
Row 3: Synonym for "HITHER"; near, close to, or almost.
Row 4: Plant with leaves and branches; one grows in Brooklyn.
Diagonal: Tremendous anger or fury.
Left Column: "Trailers for Sale or ____ , Rooms to Lent 50 cents".

Puzzle 7. NOT USED TO CATCH FISH?

			E
		S	
	O		
S			

Row 1: To push someone's buttons; purposefully irritate or enrage.
Row 2: Too.
Row 3: Inside section of a house; space.
Row 4: Lots of flakes,
Diagonal: You do it to candles on your birthday.
Left Column: Bad guys are behind them in jails.

Puzzle 8. FLAP YOUR WINGS!

			D
		S	
	U		
B			

Row 1: Tie together with rope.
Row 2: So that you won't, for fear of or in case.
Row 3: Unpleasant facial affliction for teenagers.
Row 4: A feathered friend.
Diagonal: A curve in the road.
Left Column: Thoughtlessly tell a secret; snitch.

Puzzle 9. WRESTLING MANIA

			O
		E	
	H		
K			

Row 1: Wrestling Japanese style.
Row 2: A sign or indication of what is to happen in the future.
Row 3: Served in the Army Mess Hall; Cowboys get it from the Chuck Wagon.
Row 4: A great ruler who sits on a throne.
Diagonal: Dirty air.
Left Column: Foot clothing.

Puzzle 10. OH TITANIC!

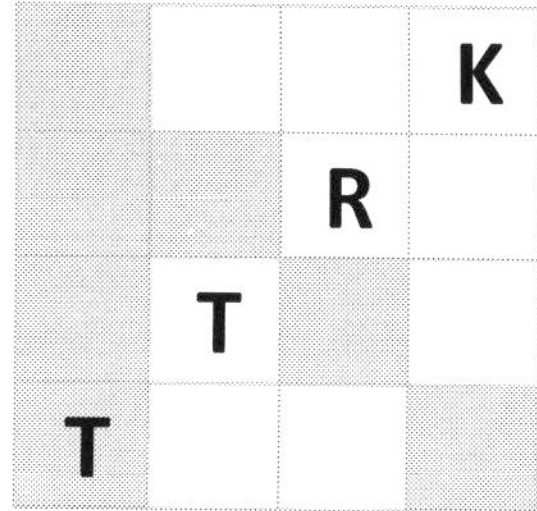

Row 1: It happened to an unsinkable boat after an iceberg encounter.
Row 2: A role in a play.
Row 3: Makes you want to scratch!
Row 4: A job or chore that must be completed.
Diagonal: A bag which may have flour, beans or potatoes inside.
Left Column: Nasty projection of saliva.

Puzzle 11. DRINK IT EVERY DAY

			E
		R	
	N		
M			

Row 1: A "happening" place.
Row 2: To hang around watching, without being seen, perhaps for evil purpose.
Row 3: 1/12th of a foot.
Row 4: A key ingredient in shakes.
Diagonal: What a baby does to ingest milk.

Puzzle 12. STOP STARING!

			W
		S	
	T		
G			

Row 1: Defrost.
Row 2: "A word to the ____."
Row 3: Empire in ancient Peru.
Row 4: To stare at rudely.
Diagonal: Sound made by a clock. Hint: not tock.
Left Column: A tiny tree branch.

Puzzle 13. LIFE NOT ALL WORK

			S
		A	
	M		
R			

Row 1: Talks.
Row 2: To have fun; to join in a game.
Row 3: Within the group.
Row 4: To wander about, buffalo do it.
Diagonal: Thin; often followed by "Jim".
Left Column: Done in a practice boxing match.

Puzzle 14. GONE FISHING

Row 1: Kind; friendly, but not exceptionally wonderful.
Row 2: ".... and every one."
Row 3: Targets.
Row 4: A word for highway following "turn".
Diagonal: What a person is called.
Left Column: A tide when high and low are the same depth.

Puzzle 15. GARDENING NECESSITY

			S
		D	
	A		
T			

Row 1: Manager to employee.
Row 2: Helps, sometimes with money.
Row 3: A garden tool with a long handle and metal teeth.
Row 4: To wear down; often used before "out".
Diagonal: A manually powered vehicle, sometimes "built for two".

Puzzle 16. TOO MANY CARS ON EARTH

			M
		O	
	E		
G			

Row 1: Unwanted email.
Row 2: He was partners with ANDY.
Row 3: Bright decorative lights. (Think Las Vegas)
Row 4: Mike Myers hosted this zany talent "Show".
Diagonal: Dirty air over city.
Left Column: "SING, ..., SUNG."

Puzzle 17. EASY TO DRIVE

			D
		E	
	A		
O			

Row 1: In or on a bed.
Row 2: Takes advantage; employs for the task at hand.
Row 3: To get hold: or to carry away.
Row 4: In debt; mortgaged.
Diagonal: Inquires; "does it with questions".
Left Column: Machine works by itself; used with "matic".

Puzzle 18. BUILT FOR TWO

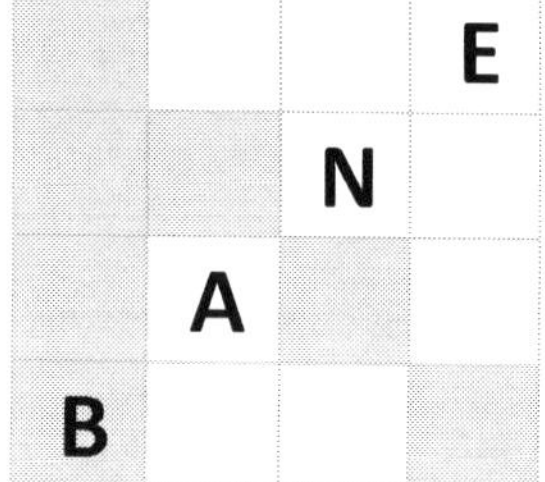

Row 1: An infant; sometimes "in the woods"?
Row 2: Pig singing.
Row 3: To produce, to build.
Row 4: Cause contention verbally.
Diagonal: Unicycle with 2 wheels?
Left Column: A nasty device which explodes.

Puzzle 19. TICKER-TAPE?

Row 1: The opposite of thick.
Row 2: Has the legal rights to.
Row 3: Uttered words.
Row 4: A kind of snail without a shell. (yuck)
Diagonal: A little branch on a tree or bush.
Left Column: To throw something carelessly into the air.

Puzzle 20. LOBSTER FOR DINNER

Row 1: In a short time.
Row 2: A sharp curved nail on the foot of an animal.
Row 3: A nation on the Arabian Peninsula.
Row 4: Rising and swelling repeatedly, like the ocean.
Diagonal: To kill a dragon.
Left Column: A large flat-bottomed boat, having broad, square ends.

Puzzle 21. GOLF ANYONE?

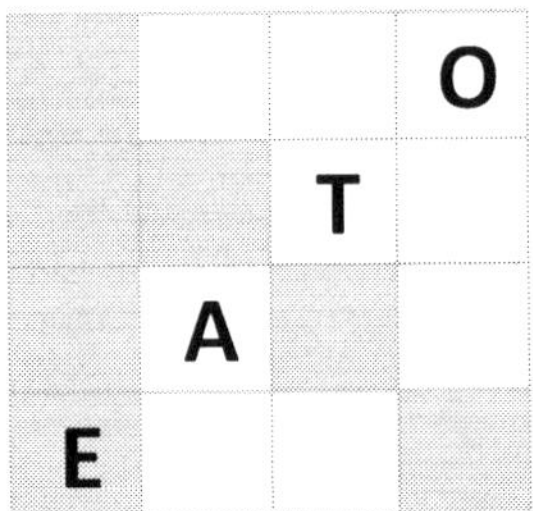

Row 1: A ring of light around the heads of an angel.
Row 2: A kind of grain used mostly to feed animals.
Row 3: The parts of the earth that are not covered by water.
Row 4: Takes food.
Diagonal: Main ethnic group of China.
Left Column: An opening in or through something.

Puzzle 22. WHAT A STORY!

Row 1: The distance between the ends of a bridge.
Row 2: A poem celebrating heroic achievements, in formal verse.
Row 3: The object of a verb.
Row 4: A particle expressing comparison; e.g. "bigger or smaller ...".
Diagonal: Made cotton into yarn.
Left Column: Forwarded an e-mail.

Puzzle 23. IT STOPS HERE

Row 1: Olden days word for dagger.
Row 2: The back part.
Row 3: Bends of a rainbow.
Row 4: Slang for "the responsibility", used with "stops here".
Diagonal: The flooring on a boat of ship.
Left Column: Not bright or exciting.

Puzzle 24. CHEERIO?

Row 1: Slick; dripping with fatty calories.
Row 2: A narrow walk-way may be unpaved.
Row 3: First part of a long name for car.
Row 4: Allows; does not prohibit.
Diagonal: A grain used by QUAKER.
Left Column: A mineral consisting of silica.

Puzzle 25. I NEED A NEW SHIRT

			P
		N	
	I		
E			

Row 1: A small place where you can buy things.
Row 2: The sister of your father or mother.
Row 3: The appearance or manner of a person.
Row 4: Not difficult; not hard to do or understand.
Diagonal: Chop is the first part of this Chinese dish.
Left Column: Not different; like something else.

Puzzle 26. PARTNER OF ICE

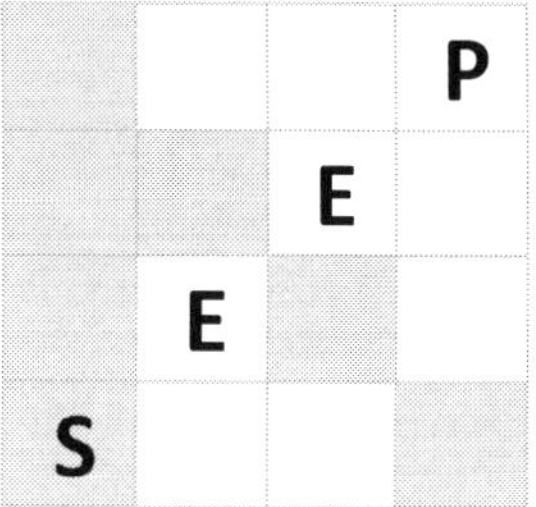

Row 1: To hit with the palm, sometimes "across the face".
Row 2: Single-file marching - not in two's.
Row 3: Element with atomic number 10; bright lights.
Row 4: To slay a dragon yesterday.
Diagonal: Drops of water that become flakes in winter.
Left Column: Like daughters only boys.

Puzzle 27. LIGHT MEAL STOP

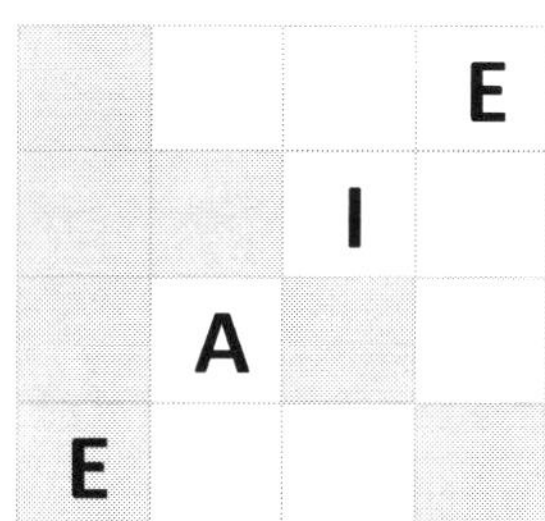

Row 1: Small restaurant where you can buy coffee and food.
Row 2: Neighbor of Pennsylvania.
Row 3: The high or principal table, at the end of a hall.
Row 4: Like Homer's Iliad and Odyssey.
Diagonal: In fancy current style.
Left Column: Secret words or signals used to send messages.

Puzzle 28. IT NEEDS CLEAN AIR

Row 1: To be in need of you need.
Row 2: The sister of your father or mother.
Row 3: A member of a religious group living in a monastery.
Row 4: A wave of extreme pain or anguish.
Diagonal: A body organ for respiration.
Left Column: A light, usually on a desk or end table.

Puzzle 29. WINTER FUN

			S
		S	
	C		
S			

Row 1: Inky writing instruments.
Row 2: As well as, in addition.
Row 3: A barge sometimes with sails.
Row 4: A vehicle with metal runners and moves easily in snow.
Diagonal: To walk heavily and slowly.
Left Column: To move ahead of something in front of you.

Puzzle 30. A TASK FOR PAY

			P
		L	
	N		
W			

Row 1: Sound make when the palm of the hand meets someone's face.
Row 2: Where soldiers hide preceded by "fox".
Row 3: For one time only; "..... in a lifetime"
Row 4: To do something useful or difficult.
Diagonal: Cloth covering for a foot and ankle.
Left Column: A presentation or play that "must go on!".

Puzzle 31. OH DADDY!

			A
		S	
	T		
T			

Row 1: A child's word for father.
Row 2: To fail to have something that you had before.
Row 3: Beetle Bailey's dog; German name spelled the same forward and back.
Row 4: Therefore; in this way.
Diagonal: Goes with pans, usually somewhat deeper.
Left Column: A small piece of land.

Puzzle 32. WHAT A FOOL!

			E
		G	
	O		
B			

Row 1: To tolerate a bad situation.
Row 2: To try to persuade strongly.
Row 3: A loud deep noise made by lions and tigers.
Row 4: A foolish or stupid person; dunce, idiot.
Diagonal: Ocean animal with a hard shell and big claws.
Left Column: To hold something back.

Puzzle 33. WINTER IS OVER

			S
		C	
	L		
T			

Row 1: The sign which shows that numbers are to be added.
Row 2: Parts of a circle, curved lines.
Row 3: T block up something like a drainpipe.
Row 4: To melt or soften something frozen.
Diagonal: The fore part of a vessel; the bow.
Left Column: A covenant; joint agreement.

Puzzle 34. MAKES IT TASTE BETTER

			N
		O	
	O		
T			

Row 1: To move round and round in one place.
Row 2: On or upon; not below or under.
Row 3: All that can be carried at one time.
Row 4: English name short for Tobias.
Diagonal: To be in one place and not leave.
Left Column: A white powder we get from sea water.

Puzzle 35. UNBOUND AT LAST!

			D
		I	
	I		
L			

Row 1: Resist an attacker, as in ".... off".
Row 2: Kingly name as in ".... the Great".
Row 3: Did not tell the truth.
Row 4: To reside in a certain place.
Diagonal: Commerce unrestricted by tariff or customs.
Left Column: To fall yesterday.

Puzzle 36. SEND MONEY VIA A BANK

Row 1: Hair not straight or curly.
Row 2: To add to your staff with a salary.
Row 3: Old fashioned word for homeland or Earth.
Row 4: Not wild; able to live as pets.
Diagonal: A thin, long piece of metal; to connect to electricity.
Left Column: To make more keen or eager for, as in an appetite.

5x5 MINI CROSSWORD SQUARES

Puzzle 1. NO HUFFING

				T
			F	
		L		
	A			
M				

Row 1: A piece of cloth on a bed; could be used to make a GHOST costume.
Row 2: The wolf huffs and he _____, and he blows the house down!
Row 3: Metal mixture.
Row 4: Weasely animal with a gorgeous coat.
Row 5: Unclear, hard to see through.
Diagonal: Pouty, uncommunicative after one's feelings are hurt.
Left Column: Uncontrollable jerky movement.

Puzzle 2. HOLY COWS?

				C
			S	
		D		
	E			
P				

Row 1: Community minded as in governmental duties.
Row 2: Abrasive or unkind, usually related to verbal criticism.
Row 3: Which way is the TAJ MAHAL?
Row 4: To freshen-up or to continue a subscription.
Row 5: Use your finger to identify the guilty party.
Diagonal: A student at West Point Academy.
Left Column: Sound made by a bird.

Puzzle 3. MOVIE TRICK

				T
			E	
		A		
	E			
S				

Row 1: A silly act to get attention; to prevent from reaching full potential.
Row 2: One plus one plus one.
Row 3: Knowing about something, danger for instance.
Row 4: Coral home for beautiful fish.
Row 5: To process metal until it melts; to smell yesterday.
Diagonal: The longest part of an arrow.
Left Column: Famous actors and actresses.

Puzzle 4. YOU'RE ON THE EDGE!

				S
			A	
		I		
	B			
S				

Row 1: Musical groups that play at concerts, weddings & during parades.
Row 2: Portions of space with a distinct purpose.
Row 3: The tip of the steeple.
Row 4: A fancy name for the color black.
Row 5: A tiny spot or piece.
Diagonal: The edge of or very close to some major change; verge.
Left Column: Where Armies and Navies live.

Puzzle 5. THAT'S ROYAL?

				T
			A	
		A		
	H			
S				

Row 1: To wish for with eagerness; to desire possession of.
Row 2: Of or pertaining to a king; kingly; royal.
Row 3: To rub or scrape out, as letters or characters written.
Row 4: The possessive case of who or which.
Row 5: Afraid.
Diagonal: To stop.
Left Column: Airline staff workers.

Puzzle 6. GOING IN CIRCLES

Row 1: To damage or spoil something; a rest between tasks.
Row 2: A lasso does this around a horse's or cows's neck.
Row 3: To love intensely, worship.
Row 4: The opposite of cloudy.
Row 5: A faint trace of color.
Diagonal: Town in North Carolina named after pioneer Daniel.
Left Column: An explosion; to turn up music so it is too loud.

Puzzle 7. TIME TO CELEBRATE

				S
			C	
		E		
	W			
T				

Row 1: Things you buy in a grocery store or market to consume.
Row 2: To vote into office.
Row 3: White poplar tree.
Row 4: To use a broom to clean the floor.
Diagonal: Runs from danger.
Left Column: Special meal with lots of good things to eat and drink.

Puzzle 8. PEEPING TOM?

				K
			E	
		A		
	M			
T				

Row 1: Often used with "taken" meaning surprised.
Row 2: Watched someone who did not know you were there.
Row 3: Does not leave.
Row 4: Type of board used to beautify fingernails
Row 5: Speckled game fish which lives in fresh water.
Diagonal: Not together, separate.
Left Column: A valuable possession.

Puzzle 9. HAPPY HALLOWEEN!

				S
			P	
		R		
	N			
R				

Row 1: Male/female name, Everet or Cuomo for example.
Row 2: Small masses of irregular shape.
Row 3: Frightening especially on Halloween.
Row 4: The corner made when two lines meet at a point.
Row 5: To answer an invitation.
Diagonal: Hair that is not straight; going around in curves.
Left Column: "I can see _____ ly now, the rain is gone."

Puzzle 10. LOVE RIVER IN PARIS

				C
			A	
		I		
	R			
S				

Row 1: Shape of childrens' blocks.
Row 2: To calm the violence; mitigate.
Row 3: A large net, one edge of which is provided with sinkers.
Row 4: Footprint of an animal.
Row 5: The head of an Arab family.
Diagonal: A short snappy sound.
Left Column: Staffs up for a movie or play.

Puzzle 11. APPLE A DAY

				S
			E	
		D		
	A			
T				

Row 1: Underground chambers.
Row 2: To become mature and ready to eat; fruit for example.
Row 3: Intense passion or love.
Row 4: Lost color or brightness.
Row 5: A small wax candle.
Diagonal: Beverage made from apples in the fall.
Left Column: A hobby or profession, jewelry-making for instance.

Puzzle 12. CUBAN PRIDE

				R
			B	
		I		
	L			
S				

Row 1: Tobacco leaves rolled together for smoking.
Row 2: Middle Eastern, North African nationality.
Row 3: A wish to be cruel.
Row 4: Popular glue brand; Mr. Fudd of cartoon fame.
Row 5: Separating into like categories.
Diagonal: Yells for help; sheds tears.
Left Column: Boxes of wine bottles, great for a party.

Puzzle 13. ROPE LIKE ANIMAL

				E
			M	
		E		
	Y			
E				

Row 1: A reptile with a long body and no legs.
Row 2: A weight suspended by a string check for verticality.
Row 3: Future plans which you think of; some may be brilliant.
Row 4: A goddess of the mountains, forests, meadows, or waters; sprite.
Row 5: Country of the Pharaohs.
Diagonal: Dozed off.
Left Column: The backbone of a person or animal.

Puzzle 14. USA HAS FIFTY

Row 1: The lengths of bridges.
Row 2: The ones over there.
Row 3: Parallel in the same direction; from one to another as in "passed"
Row 4: Next after second; one of three.
Row 5: To be; to continue to live.
Diagonal: Not very long; not very tall.
Left Column: Condition one is in, as in "..... of exhaustion".

Puzzle 15. EVERY CHURCH HAS ONE

				T
			A	
		U		
	R			
S				

Row 1: A stone which gives off sparks when you struck.
Row 2: Any raised place or structure for religious purposes.
Row 3: Cavemen's tools for hunting by blunt force.
Row 4: The act of rubbing off a word or picture.
Row 5: Melting snow; soft mud.
Diagonal: To send something down quickly; in line with.
Left Column: Body locations of people's eyes, nose and mouth.

Puzzle 16. COMPANY PEOPLE

				E
			O	
		E		
	L			
F				

Row 1: To keep something until it is needed food for instance.
Row 2: To release a ball or a stone out of your hand.
Row 3: Actors or performers manager.
Row 4: To rest on top of liquid or air. Boats and clouds do it.
Row 5: Nicer; of better quality.
Diagonal: To cut, clip, or sever with scissors, especially cloth.
Left Column: A group of people working together in an office.

Puzzle 17. PUZZLES MAKE IT SHARPER

				N
			E	
		G		
	N			
R				

Row 1: The part inside your head that controls everything.
Row 2: Strings used for fishing.
Row 3: A large bird of prey, some are bald.
Row 4: To irritate someone with constant interruptions.
Row 5: Worn around the neck of Priests; Moroccan capital city.
Diagonal: One partial to his own group and intolerant of those who differ.
Left Column: To blur, dim or redden, often applied to the eyesight.

Puzzle 18. LONG LEGGED WHITE BIRD

				S
			S	
		K		
	H			
H				

Row 1: Distinct and meaningful groups of letters.
Row 2: To lift up; to care for until grown.
Row 3: Awry; askance; not right; not balanced or properly fitted.
Row 4: To throw yesterday.
Row 5: Any wading bird usually white-feathered.
Diagonal: To cease to sleep; happens every morning hopefully?
Left Column: Great anger; especially of the Gods.

Puzzle 19. SHE WEARS THE PANTS

				Y
			E	
		O		
	A			
S				

Row 1: Trait of someone who constantly tells others what to do.
Row 2: Little people who work for Santa or Keebler; leprecons.
Row 3: Pretty close to; sort of as in "..... the same"
Row 4: Element with atomic number 86, tested for in basements.
Row 5: Avoided or stayed at a distance. As in "..... away from".
Diagonal: The red liquid which circulates round your body.
Left Column: Large animals that love to eat honey.

Puzzle20. AUSTRALIAN CUTIE BEAR

				A
			G	
		N		
	I			
T				

Row 1: A tailless marsupial, found in Australia.
Row 2: The cry a horse makes, when it is frightened or excited.
Row 3: A feeling of weariness and disgust; dullness and languor.
Row 4: Country next to Egypt.
Row 5: A drug useful in neuralgia, derived from a Fijian plant.
Diagonal: African country with wildlife refuges and parks.
Left Column: To kneel yesterday.

Puzzle 21. THIS TRADE KILLS ELEPHANTS

				Y
			N	
		A		
	X			
S				

Row 1: The hard, white substance of rhino and elephant tusks.
Row 2: A period of time spent doing something, in the Army for example.
Row 3: A large camel-like animal with that spits.
Row 4: To raise high; to elevate; to lift up; hold in high honor.
Row 5: Moodily silent; sullen or obstinate after a disappointment.
Diagonal: Boot shaped country.
Left Column: Poetic plural of "islands".

Puzzle 22. NOMADIC PEOPLE GROUPS

				S
			E	
		I		
	N			
S				

Row 1: You need 4 of these on your car.
Row 2: Furnished with weapons of offense or defense.
Row 3: A flat piece cut from something, bread or meat for example.
Row 4: Round handles to open something.
Row 5: Thin slippery coating of mud or other unpleasant substance.
Diagonal: A group of families who live together with one chief.
Left Column: Things you have to do, take out the garbage, for example.

Puzzle 23. A CHICK POPS OUT

				P
			C	
		V		
	M			
D				

Row 1: A long thin piece of leather, usually with a buckle.
Row 2: To break out of the eggshell, as when baby birds enter the world.
Row 3: One who pursues the same object as another, a competitor.
Row 4: A lighted coal, smoldering amid ashes.
Row 5: Great fear of something unpleasant.
Diagonal: Rescued; took out of danger; stored for later use.
Left Column: A scarp or strip torn off something; a small amount e.g. evidence?

Puzzle 24. DOMINOS HAVE PLENTY

Row 1: A rectangular piece of something, like wood, metal or stone.
Row 2: Makes a shirt smooth with a hot tool.
Row 3: Attempts something.
Row 4: To turn or incline from straight or level.
Row 5: Not old; in the early part of life.
Diagonal: To carry something with you when you come.
Left Column: Second part of the "Itsy, ... Spider".

Puzzle 25. SOLDIERS LIVE HERE

				S
			N	
		U		
	R			
S				

Row 1: Lives outdoors in a tent.
Row 2: A large open space with seats all around.
Row 3: The opening in your face where tasting occurs.
Row 4: To push against or push down.
Row 5: Sound made while rinsing the mouth.
Diagonal: To press together or squash something.
Left Column: Accommodations in nature around a fire.

Puzzle 26. TWO-PIECE WEAPON

				R
			C	
		A		
	E			
S				

Row 1: One who gives monetary punishment.
Row 2: Vote into office.
Row 3: To look forward to or anticipate.
Row 4: To send back; to give up.
Row 5: To move in a circling movement; vanilla and chocolate in a cone.
Diagonal: An instrument for threshing; move about without control.
Left Column: Things you are afraid of.

Puzzle 27. FIX YOUR HAIR FOR THE PARTY

				Y
			I	
		A		
	A			
S				

Row 1: To send out fine drops of liquid.
Row 2: Postmen dread it; replaces "snail mail".
Row 3: Behind; toward the stern from.
Row 4: A tree which has cones and long thin leaves like needles.
Row 5: To say something; present verbally.
Diagonal: To hit with the open hand; sometime on baby's bottom.
Left Column: Aquatic mammals that balance balls on their snouts.

Puzzle 28. TV REMEDY FOR PAIN RELIEF

				H
			E	
		A		
	P			
S				

Row 1: A small piece of cloth to cover a hole in clothes.
Row 2: The one of greater age.
Row 3: To break something into pieces, usually with a crashing noise.
Row 4: Opposite of closes.
Row 5: Supplies of food and other goods stored by shopkeepers.
Diagonal: A long flat heavy piece of wood, thicker than a board.
Left Column: Mexicans earn them.

Puzzle 29. SOFT END OF THE PENCIL

				N
			S	
		I		
	A			
Y				

Row 1: Author of "TOM SAWYER" and "HUCKLEBERRY FIN"
Row 2: To rub or something written in pencil.
Row 3: Bees do this when angered.
Row 4: Long stories of yesteryear.
Row 5: Opens mouth wide when sleepy.
Diagonal: Makes and attempt in good faith.
Left Column: Fretful; easily irritated.

Puzzle 30. DRUMS & RHYTHM

				S
			P	
		R		
	U			
S				

Row 1: Drummer does it to his drum.
Row 2: Small masses of irregular shape, bumps.
Row 3: Ahead of time; near the beginning.
Row 4: Full of natural light; Eggs ".....-side up"
Row 5: Protection for your feet
Diagonal: To injure with hot water.
Left Column: To make holy; to ask God to show favor to someone.

Puzzle 31. GREAT BRITAIN

				T
			H	
		L		
	L			
Y				

Row 1: A person who wears a plaid kilt.
Row 2: Ways, trails sometimes unpaved.
Row 3: Kings did this.
Row 4: To calm the violence; delay; mitigate.
Row 5: Showed fatigue or boredom by opening mouth.
Diagonal: A mixture of cold vegetables, such as lettuce and tomatoes.
Left Column: Water gently with a hose.

Puzzle 32. SCHEDULE YOURSELF

				N
			S	
		E		
	A			
T				

Row 1: Ladies; group of female grown-ups.
Row 2: Utilize it again.
Row 3: Not fit or suitable; unqualified.
Row 4: Large bags made of cloth, paper or plastic.
Row 5: Platter used in serving food.
Diagonal: Groups of 7 days.
Left Column: The thin part of your arm close to your hand.

Puzzle 33. HEAVEN IN SAND

				E
			I	
		F		
	E			
D				

Row 1: To relinquish, especially temporarily, as a right or claim.
Row 2: A fertile spot of refuge in a desert.
Row 3: Out of shape; incompetent.
Row 4: Another word for flat; with no slant.
Row 5: Someone who goes down into very deep water.
Diagonal: A very thin biscuit.
Left Column: To be willing to under certain circumstances.

Puzzle 34. STEAK VARIATION

				S
			I	
		C		
	T			
S				

Row 1: Rain has many of them.
Row 2: A small wild bird with a red breast and grey feathers.
Row 3: A master of ceremonies; host and announcer.
Row 4: A strong pointed stick or post; a claimed miming site.
Row 5: Bricks and boxes have 4 of them.
Diagonal: Ship does this when at the port.
Left Column: To put on clothes; a garment worn by women.

Puzzle 35. SHAKESPEARE

				E
			E	
		P		
	O			
H				

Row 1: To copy using transparent paper; small evidence of.
Row 2: Juliet was his love.
Row 3: The first letter in the Greek alphabet, dominate member.
Row 4: Hard and firm all through, not hollow or liquid.
Row 5: Devastation; often wrecked upon something.
Diagonal: Any subject people choose to speak, write or argue about.
Left Column: That which is worthless; rubbish; refuse.

Puzzle 36. MASTERS OF WORDS & SOULS

				N
			U	
		R		
	L			
P				

Row 1: Country on west central African coast.
Row 2: A mode of expressing words by pictures.
Row 3: A TV show does it, usually weekly.
Row 4: Covered in a slippery substance.
Row 5: Lord Byron for example.
Diagonal: Wash your hand with soap.
Left Column: To seize and hold tightly.

6X6 MINI CROSSWORD SQUARES

Puzzle 1. ENDANGERED BIG CAT

					N
				R	
			I		
		V			
	N				
T					

Row 1: To lament.
Row 2: A luminous phenomenon in the upper regions of the atmosphere.
Row 3: The act of stacking bricks together.
Row 4: Crowbars for instance.
Row 5: To suffer through trouble or pain.
Row 6: Big cats with stripes.
Diagonal: Shoppers who make purchases.
Left Column: Classic dancing in tights.

Puzzle 2. GIDDY-UP!

					E
				E	
			I		
		N			
	Q				
S					

Row 1: The capital of the Republic of Macedonia.
Row 2: Lots & lots of ordinary people.
Row 3: A name designating the East & West groups of Southeast Asian islands.
Row 4: Having an estate in land; what a plane did at the end of the flight.
Row 5: Is the same as; adds up to be.
Row 6: A small spirit or fairy; a young mischievous child.
Diagonal: A leather seat for an equestrian rider.
Left Column: Happy facial expressions.

Puzzle 3. IN THE FAST LANE?

					E
				S	
			E		
		A			
	Y				
S					

Row 1: A color made by mixing red and blue.
Row 2: To wake someone or stir him into action.
Row 3: Drives too fast.
Row 4: Hires employees for a new company.
Row 5: Exposed only when blinking or sleeping.
Row 6: The part added to the end of a word.
Diagonal: To attach at the beginning.
Left Column: Goes by or around a car.

Puzzle 4. GOLD RUSH

					G
				I	
			M		
		S			
	U				
E					

Row 1: The act of digging valuables from a cave or panning them from a river.
Row 2: A city in eastern Texas.
Row 3: Popular spice starts with the suffix of walnut.
Row 4: To take upon one's self; to guess without checking.
Row 5: Elvis Presley played it.
Row 6: A hard shiny paint used on bathtubs.
Diagonal: Reciprocally acting or related; an agreement for example.
Left Column: To be responsible for or take charge of.

Puzzle 5. UPPER CHAMBER OF CONGRESS

					R
				P	
			A		
		L			
	N				
L					

Row 1: To come into sight.
Row 2: When the boss gives you too much work.
Row 3: The legislative body in ancient Rome.
Row 4: Armies fighting together.
Row 5: Leave spaces before the first line of a paragraph.
Row 6: Not dead.
Diagonal: A roof like cover, usually of canvas.
Left Column: To attack with violence, or in a hostile manner.

Puzzle 6. BEYOND JUPITER

					S
				E	
			W		
		J			
	E				
N					

Row 1: Performs slowly on purpose; often used with "off".
Row 2: Two a day, keep the doctor away?
Row 3: A little gardening shovel with a curved blade.
Row 4: Acting contrary to the standard of right.
Row 5: Negligent.
Row 6: To deny or give counter testimony.
Diagonal: A husband or wife.
Left Column: One of the elder and principal deities, the son of Coelus.

Puzzle 7. LIGHT BULBS & PHONOGRAPHS

					C
				N	
			E		
		N			
	D				
S					

Row 1: " ______ Woman", popular TV show where body parts are replaced.
Row 2: Rats and mice.
Row 3: Descent off a vertical drop.
Row 4: A point equally distant from all sides.
Row 5: Great American inventor and industrialist who lived in NJ.
Row 6: Scandinavian country known for chocolate.
Diagonal: Famous for it's Tea Party!

Puzzle 8. I NEED YOUR OPINION

					Y
				O	
			I		
		P			
	M				
S					

Row 1: To take a careful look over something or some place.
Row 2: Where boats rest.
Row 3: To offer a requested opinion.
Row 4: To mend; to put back together.
Row 5: To come into existence from below or inside. (Think of the ALIEN movies)
Row 6: Funny mocking play.
Diagonal: A wild and uncivilized human being; ruthless.
Left Column: Gives some to everybody.

Puzzle 9. HAPPENS ON SOME NIGHTS

					Y
				S	
			I		
		E			
	V				
T					

Row 1: Pitifully small or despicable.
Row 2: A place set back in a wall; time to play outside.
Row 3: Complete; whole.
Row 4: Talks a language.
Row 5: The same amount throughout.
Row 6: Clothes to dry yourself.
Diagonal: Pretty flower parts.
Left Column: Adjust in advance of its use.

Puzzle 10. FAMOUS WHALER PORT

					E
				M	
			H		
		K			
	Y				
S					

Row 1: Capable of being done.
Row 2: To give a new name to.
Row 3: One or the other.
Row 4: Capital of Turkey
Row 5: One who claims direct divine illumination.
Row 6: Where you see the action in a movie theatre or on TV.
Diagonal: To keep back or from; to stop from leaving.
Left Column: Vivid images during sleep - hopefully pleasant!

Puzzle 11. WEDDING BELLS?

					S
				A	
			G		
		A			
	I				
T					

Row 1: Accepts or goes along with.
Row 2: Type of shower before a wedding.
Row 3: A mark of infamy or token of disgrace attached to a person.
Row 4: Rubs out or makes less visible.
Row 5: Young female children of siblings.
Row 6: The pieces of something cut into three parts.
Diagonal: Emerges; gets up in the morning.
Left Column: Missing; away; not present.

Puzzle 12. 007 AND MAXWELL SMART

					S
				R	
			N		
		M			
	R				
T					

Row 1: A contagious continued fever caught in the tropics.
Row 2: Mistakes or boo-boos.
Row 3: Secret government spies.
Row 4: To hit over and over again.
Row 5: One who delivers an elaborate, formal speech.
Row 6: The mood you are in. A bad one may lead to violence.
Diagonal: An involuntary trembling or shivering.
Left Column: "I'm a little ______ , short and stout"; Hint: holds a hot beverage.

Puzzle 13. SMALL WOMEN'S SIZE

					E
				E	
			R		
		E			
	N				
L					

Row 1: Size in clothing store for small, short and thin women.
Row 2: Ten and one added; convenience store name 7-......
Row 3: Very close; almost, as in "...... there"; not far off.
Row 4: Long, showy feathers on birds' heads.
Row 5: The money you make must be declared on taxes.
Row 6: Capital of Angola.
Diagonal: Blood without red and white cells.
Left Column: You write with it and it can be erased.

Puzzle 14. WEATHER CAN BE NASTY

					S
				D	
			L		
		T			
	O				
S					

Row 1: FBI men and women.
Row 2: Overcast skies.
Row 3: Restaurants have many with chairs or booths; can be turned?
Row 4: The interval of a musical note above or below any other.
Row 5: Propelling a boat using oars.
Row 6: Cloudy, rainy, windy kind of weather.
Diagonal: Capital of New York State.
Left Column: Hollywood has lots of them.

Puzzle 15. SOME SALT HAS IT

					T
				L	
			I		
		E			
	O				
E					

Row 1: Predicament; problems that must be endured in life.
Row 2: Seldom; not often; the way I like my steak cooked.
Row 3: Element with atomic number 53 and used by the thyroid gland.
Row 4: Must have it yesterday.
Row 5: Expensive; not cheap. Describes diamond jewelry and mink coats.
Row 6: Suitable to be consumed by mouth.
Diagonal: What you do to move a canoe on water.
Left Column: The son of a king or queen.

Puzzle 16. WHAT A FOOL!

					G
				I	
			I		
		P			
	O				
T					

Row 1: Performing in a play, movie or TV show.
Row 2: Foolish; silly; slow to think.
Row 3: Towns with large populations.
Row 4: Someone who knows a lot about a particular subject.
Row 5: Writing it down or wanting to remember something.
Row 6: Like a wedding cake; large layers on the bottom, smallest at top.
Diagonal: To be present; listen carefully to what is said.
Left Column: A rising, soaring, or climbing up.

Puzzle 17. YOU CAN DONATE THEM

					S
				N	
			A		
		E			
	B				
N					

Row 1: Rests between activities.
Row 2: Parts of the body with important roles, e.g. heart, lungs.
Row 3: A rectangle whose four sides are equal in length.
Row 4: Belief in God.
Row 5: To think about something constantly.
Row 6: A slight degree of difference in anything perceptible to the mind.
Diagonal: A dark mark where the skin has been hit but not broken. OUCH!
Left Column: The home of the "Red Socks".

Puzzle 18. MONEY MATTERS

					L
				E	
			U		
		E			
	I				
T					

Row 1: Pertaining to the treasury or finances.
Row 2: What music becomes when you turn up the volume.
Row 3: Disregarding restraint; out of control.
Row 4: Free, clear, or released, as from some rules or laws.
Row 5: Young female relatives of a brother or sister.
Row 6: Having the sediment disturbed; roiled; muddy; thick.
Diagonal: Arranged, created; clay pots on a potter wheel.
Left Column: Speaking and understanding a language.

Puzzle 19. EXCUSE ME

					Y
				O	
			N		
		T			
	O				
S					

Row 1: Worn out; almost ragged as of clothes or furniture for example.
Row 2: When a President forgives a crime or overturns a conviction.
Row 3: Of a certain heritage or people.
Row 4: To gain, accomplish, achieve, obtain. Usually something good.
Row 5: Common name, Rob or Bob for short.
Row 6: A short sleep taken in the middle of the day in Mexico.
Diagonal: Lots of sand in this part of North Africa.
Left Column: Stone Age weapons for hunting; a pole with a sharp point.

Puzzle 20. IBM SELECTRIC HAD IT

					G
				H	
			I		
		L			
	C				
R					

Row 1: Termination or finale.
Row 2: Of a small importance or significance.
Row 3: One who believes in the existence of a God.
Row 4: The pieces of something cut into 2 equal parts.
Row 5: You get these when you yell in a tunnel.
Row 6: A narrow piece of colorful cloth used to tie up a gift.
Diagonal: The number before twelve.
Left Column: Jewish queen of the Persian king Ahasuerus.

Puzzle 21. YUMMY OR YUCKY?

					S
				N	
			I		
		A			
	I				
S					

Row 1: Taj Mahal has 4 of these tall constructions.
Row 2: A roof like canvas cover which creates shade.
Row 3: A large sled usually pulled by a horse.
Row 4: What a hypnotist puts you into.
Row 5: Eight times ten; fourscore.
Row 6: In a careful manner to avoid danger or injury.
Diagonal: One more that nineteen; one score?
Left Column: What the buds on your tongue help you do.

Puzzle 22. EXPRESS TO ISTANBUL

					N
				D	
			E		
		P			
	E				
Y					

Row 1: To call by authority; invite strongly.
Row 2: The pieces of something cut into 3 parts.
Row 3: The Express on which Agatha Christie penned Murder.
Row 4: To say or do over again.
Row 5: To interfere with what someone else is trying to do.
Row 6: Open your mouth sleepily, yesterday.
Diagonal: Something you hold up to protect yourself; a police badge.
Left Column: Description of the sea as a hurricane approaches.

Puzzle 23. GET WINE FROM THE BARREL

					T
				N	
			H		
		J			
	N				
L					

Row 1: To take what is offered.
Row 2: To spring, yesterday.
Row 3: To take fuel out of the gas tank with a hose.
Row 4: Sunk to a low condition; worthless; contemptible.
Row 5: To mean or hope to do something.
Row 6: It remained till today; did not expire or run out.
Diagonal: To add or attach later.
Left Column: To attack with violence, or in a hostile manner.

Puzzle 24. RICH & FAMOUS LIFE

					D
				R	
			U		
		P			
	A				
S					

Row 1: He was held responsible for something bad.
Row 2: Living in richness.
Row 3: A reason for not doing something.
Row 4: A square piece of cloth or paper used to wipe your mouth.
Row 5: Dashed in and out.
Row 6: Confesses to a priest.
Diagonal: The list of things you want to do before you die.
Left Column: Merges with the background to be unnoticed. Used with "in".

Puzzle 25. TURKISH SULTAN

					N
				E	
			R		
		E			
	N				
S					

Row 1: A long piece of cloth wound round the head and worn as a hat
Row 2: People live in them.
Row 3: What you do to gifts with colorful paper.
Row 4: The part of your shirt or jacket that covers your arm.
Row 5: To take out a policy for compensation if something is lost.
Row 6: Used after "our" to refer to you and me.
Diagonal: Some are "leaning" some have a "clock" some are "Fawlty"
Left Column: An essay or treatise on a particular subject.

Puzzle 26. NEED TO CHARGE MY MOBILE!

					N
				E	
			K		
		B			
	M				
L					

Row 1: You "take" this to get something done!
Row 2: They tell you how many pounds you weigh.
Row 3: A hollow place that you fit something into.
Row 4: The lady superior of a nunnery.
Row 5: Show up uninvited and expect to stay.
Row 6: Broadway and Las Vegas have many which make them bright.
Diagonal: Cyber thieves do this to your personal information.
Left Column: Word from the 1500's that mean "to attack with words".

Puzzle 27. COMPUTER PROGRAM

					T
				U	
			I		
		V			
	U				
S					

Row 1: A category for priests, nuns and other Christians.
Row 2: Of an oil rig its crude; of a mine it may be coal or gold.
Row 3: The liquid that keeps the inside of your mouth moist.
Row 4: Storing for use in the future.
Row 5: The old world.
Row 6: These with stone could break your bones.
Diagonal: Holland has many colorful ones.
Left Column: Throws gently and slowly.

Puzzle 28. TOMATO BUDDY

					N
				E	
			E		
		A			
	V				
R					

Row 1: Agitated as in an earthquake.
Row 2: Usually right next to the salt.
Row 3: Most slippery road in the winter.
Row 4: Originally, an ornamental head band or jeweled crown.
Row 5: To avoid or get out of the way, yesterday.
Row 6: For beverages you can get them free at McDonald's.
Diagonal: A measurement for beer; beer mug or glass.
Left Column: A small web-spinning animal with eight legs.

Puzzle 29. CHAMPS ELYSEES

					N
				T	
			N		
		N			
	L				
S					

Row 1: To put all your strength into it; overdo the effort.
Row 2: Three times ten; one more than twenty-nine.
Row 3: A wide street or pathway, usually with trees on both sides.
Row 4: To get to the end; to complete.
Row 5: Large groups of birds or sheep.
Row 6: One in time, saves nine.
Diagonal: Arabic: the elder of a tribe.
Left Column: Hires employees. Often used with "up".

Puzzle 30. GOVERNMENT HAS MANY

					T
				L	
			W		
		M			
	U				
E					

Row 1: Something you don't tell anybody.
Row 2: Feeling slightly cold.
Row 3: Term used change the subject, or resumes a subject after interruption.
Row 4: That which cures a disease, to cure, redress, repair.
Row 5: A downward movement of the body by bending the knees.
Row 6: A young or small eagle.
Diagonal: Most timid.
Left Column: Not enough of; difficult to find.

Puzzle 31. ROSE PARADE

					S
				I	
			P		
		T			
	E				
S					

Row 1: Colorful flower parts.
Row 2: A tincture; a liquid remedy.
Row 3: American Indian dwelling
Row 4: To involve; necessitate.
Row 5: To struggle or fight against someone or something.
Row 6: An artificial passage for water, with a valve or gate.
Diagonal: To make someone feel happy; polite way to make a request.
Left Column: Piper, Pan and Pumpkin Eater for example.

Puzzle 32. BETWEEN NORWAY & FINLAND

					S
				L	
			M		
		I			
	R				
S					

Row 1: A number of things, TV shows or events following one another.
Row 2: A building in which people pray and worship.
Row 3: He wondered about; buffalo did it in on the range.
Row 4: Animating spirit; intention; temper.
Row 5: To drive, throw, push or urge forward.
Row 6: Nordic country with aurora borealis!
Diagonal: Sailors.
Left Column: A seatbelt?

Puzzle 33. OVERPAY YOUR TAXES

					R
				N	
			U		
		F			
	O				
H					

Row 1: More easily yielding to pressure; not harder.
Row 2: A multitude of persons or living beings.
Row 3: To have plenty; to be very prevalent.
Row 4: Money you get back when you overpay.
Row 5: A part or section of a country; bigger than a city.
Row 6: Dwelling structures.
Diagonal: Yells at the top of your lungs.
Left Column: Substance that makes shirts stiff.

Puzzle 34. DO YOU LIKE MOUNTAINS?

					T
				L	
			L		
		I			
	C				
S					

Row 1: A rising, soaring, or climbing up.
Row 2: A roll of paper or parchment; a writing formed into a roll.
Row 3: Weighing machines; found on the skin of a snake.
Row 4: To evoke or extract or draw out gradually or without violence.
Row 5: With beautiful views; often used with "drive".
Row 6: A mark of infamy or token of disgrace.
Diagonal: A thorny bush or tree.
Left Column: To determine the amount of a tax to be paid.

Puzzle 35. COMMUNISTS HAD MANY

					N
				I	
			A		
		U			
	T				
D					

Row 1: Advertising phrase for a product, e.g. "Just do it!"
Row 2: A sloping typeface used for emphasis.
Row 3: Small country in South America.
Row 4: Carted it away, usually in a truck.
Row 5: Carved a design into glass.
Row 6: Tool used to makes a hole, often in wood when building.
Diagonal: Fashion has many different ones.
Left Column: Breathed out heavily when you were tired or sad.

Puzzle 36. WEMBLEY STADIUM IN LONDON

					T
				N	
			C		
		R			
	X				
R					

Row 1: To look forward to as certain or probable.
Row 2: The process of climbing up a mountain.
Row 3: European football.
Row 4: Jewish homeland.
Row 5: Leave out or apart from.
Row 6: A shelter or safe place.
Diagonal: To get free. Usually from something unpleasant.
Left Column: Less difficult.

PICTURE PUZZLE 4. RADIO CITY MUSIC HALL AT 50th STREET IN NYC

PICTURE PUZZLE 4. CIRCLE THE TEN DIFFERENCES

HOLLYWOOD STARS MOVIES SEARCH

HOLLYWOOD STARS MOVIES SEARCH

Puzzle 1 : Arnold Schwarzenegger 

K	I	O	M	D	N	A	T	S	T	S	A	L	E	H	T	T	P	E	I
L	L	Q	K	N	E	D	O	J	Z	U	N	F	E	E	V	E	R	G	J
T	J	M	T	O	Y	A	V	T	Q	D	B	N	R	A	E	E	O	Y	O
J	L	D	K	R	Q	Y	Y	Y	M	N	D	Y	E	I	Y	C	Y	R	N
M	F	P	V	I	B	F	L	E	M	O	G	S	T	O	O	Q	E	T	E
K	J	B	V	G	J	Z	M	G	F	Z	M	Y	R	N	C	H	Y	G	E
B	C	O	Y	N	V	W	S	D	U	L	R	T	A	T	N	P	A	S	S
Q	A	Q	M	I	S	B	A	M	E	G	S	N	H	O	D	T	T	Y	U
H	Y	D	W	P	H	Y	T	S	N	E	T	E	I	Z	O	F	H	A	N
Z	K	U	Z	M	S	U	C	U	D	H	T	T	H	B	I	S	E	O	B
K	F	I	O	U	R	A	H	E	E	E	C	J	A	F	T	G	R	H	H
S	F	S	H	P	P	Y	H	B	R	A	U	S	D	W	T	Z	U	Z	K
I	P	O	U	E	A	T	A	M	T	N	S	Z	I	H	E	T	N	T	C
T	Z	O	P	T	N	R	I	S	I	Z	D	N	E	S	D	A	N	R	K
U	K	L	S	A	B	N	A	O	A	B	S	6	M	B	F	E	I	U	G
V	A	K	N	A	A	L	R	A	G	Z	T	Q	S	O	P	H	N	E	H
N	D	O	R	T	Z	Z	Q	E	V	H	D	D	J	S	D	D	G	L	N
D	C	I	O	O	K	B	P	T	D	F	S	R	S	D	M	E	M	I	F
U	A	R	N	U	M	Y	U	A	B	I	Z	R	T	Z	A	R	A	E	B
N	A	O	R	Q	A	M	Y	H	Q	E	H	L	Z	V	A	U	N	S	Z

☐ CONAN THE BARBARIAN	☐ CONAN THE DESTROYER
☐ END OF DAYS	☐ ESCAPE PLAN
☐ JUNIOR	☐ LAST ACTION HERO
☐ PUMPING IRON	☐ RED HEAT
☐ SABOTAGE	☐ STAY HUNGRY
☐ THE 6TH DAY	☐ THE LAST STAND
☐ THE RUNNING MAN	☐ THE TERMINATOR
☐ TRUE LIES	☐ TWINS

Puzzle 2 : Meryl Streep

D	I	Q	M	Y	C	M	R	J	S	S	S	S	O	M	W	Z	Q	Y	E
O	W	C	A	I	Z	Q	O	Q	C	Y	O	A	S	Z	T	A	R	S	D
I	A	B	R	L	B	V	H	M	D	P	S	I	K	H	G	E	B	V	Y
F	H	H	V	P	B	R	J	Z	H	E	L	R	E	H	H	B	S	T	S
Q	Y	M	I	I	Y	V	R	I	Z	K	A	P	Z	S	C	U	N	D	H
H	N	L	N	Y	F	P	E	C	W	M	O	P	E	A	F	U	O	F	F
M	J	E	S	U	M	S	G	O	E	S	F	M	W	F	O	O	U	I	A
P	D	V	R	F	C	D	O	R	T	A	O	F	R	C	W	P	C	T	L
J	P	C	O	H	Q	D	V	I	C	C	R	A	E	E	P	Z	G	S	L
S	D	A	O	Z	L	S	R	I	E	E	G	G	H	A	Q	Q	C	C	I
E	O	I	M	S	K	O	R	B	V	E	A	T	V	B	Q	O	L	O	N
Q	C	C	E	R	N	F	H	I	T	S	O	R	F	Q	Q	P	T	M	G
E	R	Z	A	W	A	T	G	T	O	T	Y	P	D	Y	P	U	Z	P	I
Z	L	M	E	F	A	E	E	:	N	Z	I	G	Z	U	T	L	F	L	N
S	E	E	O	E	H	H	T	I	Z	J	F	F	F	S	F	U	I	I	L
R	D	T	D	T	N	S	O	V	V	M	A	M	M	A	M	I	A	C	O
F	U	U	F	V	U	M	K	V	H	M	V	Z	Z	Z	A	C	F	A	V
O	C	Y	I	G	S	F	M	V	T	G	G	Y	D	O	N	G	S	T	E
S	Z	C	U	T	Q	Z	P	E	J	T	A	O	D	O	S	D	S	E	G
D	J	A	B	U	E	H	E	A	R	T	B	U	R	N	W	Z	N	D	F

☐	AUGUST: OSAGE COUNTY	☐	DEATH BECOMES HER
☐	FALLING IN LOVE	☐	HEARTBURN
☐	INTO THE WOODS	☐	IRONWEED
☐	IT'S COMPLICATED	☐	KRAMER VS. KRAMER
☐	MAMMA MIA!	☐	MARVIN'S ROOM
☐	OUT OF AFRICA	☐	SILKWOOD
☐	SOPHIE'S CHOICE	☐	SUFFRAGETTE
☐	THE GIVER	☐	THE POST

Puzzle 3 : Sean Connery

U S L O V B G T Q T S T O E Y L T Z D O
C B R B V J N H Z L E I N S D T R R H U
S R R V V L R E I I P M I F U C A Z S T
V O Y E P J E U D I A E U Y W L E L A L
D B M C T G V N B O T B W K A E H T F A
C I A I H E T T D T N A T S T H Y H A N
G N B W U I W O B F O N N P O D B E M D
J A K T N N Z U S C S D E Y J F G N I T
M N R E D R I C H O R I M T Z I N A L U
S D O V E A S H T Z E T P T W T I M Y T
C M F I R M Q A K N D S A N R T Y E B D
K A B L B J Q B Z L N I R N D H A O U S
K R M Y A K K L V L A R T Z W E L F S F
C I Z L L J D E C I E K N N G R P T I O
O A W N L T B S Z H H L E E I O V H N N
T N D O Q V L Z B E T G Z Z R C B E E R
J M E U D Z H Z O H O C J Q M K Z R S D
C Z Z O S Q Y J Z T F F R Y G B L O S Q
Z C E Y Z K F I R S T K N I G H T S Z F
D D K W C Q C G V N O L M C M K V E O D

☐ DR. NO
☐ FAMILY BUSINESS
☐ MARNIE
☐ PLAYING BY HEART
☐ THE ANDERSON TAPES
☐ THE NAME OF THE ROSE
☐ THE UNTOUCHABLES
☐ TIME BANDITS
☐ ENTRAPMENT
☐ FIRST KNIGHT
☐ OUTLAND
☐ ROBIN AND MARIAN
☐ THE HILL
☐ THE ROCK
☐ THUNDERBALL
☐ YOU ONLY LIVE TWICE

Puzzle 4 : Katharine Hepburn

Z	J	P	J	S	L	E	B	E	R	N	A	M	O	W	A	V	G	M	Z
B	I	Q	Z	T	H	T	S	V	O	K	P	U	D	B	R	U	S	E	D
H	H	O	L	I	D	A	Y	S	D	K	N	E	E	I	T	K	D	S	H
H	O	Z	D	P	K	Q	V	E	A	D	E	Y	I	A	F	S	R	T	E
M	A	T	R	V	F	Z	E	K	E	R	R	G	O	R	U	R	M	A	I
W	Z	N	H	B	Z	S	N	R	C	O	G	C	J	M	I	Z	N	G	N
Q	L	K	I	S	N	V	C	N	L	I	I	F	M	Z	T	T	Z	E	P
W	O	O	R	O	P	U	A	G	Q	T	K	E	O	J	V	V	C	D	W
U	U	D	G	T	R	C	G	M	T	P	R	A	O	A	B	Z	S	O	I
S	K	A	Y	R	I	N	B	E	U	T	R	R	A	V	E	P	D	O	T
Q	R	Q	E	R	I	H	P	A	I	R	E	P	K	B	C	S	V	R	H
D	G	N	E	N	L	N	W	M	O	G	T	T	J	E	Z	G	E	H	O
R	T	M	R	M	O	V	E	W	F	D	G	G	Z	B	B	E	M	H	U
Q	A	O	N	R	U	B	G	O	C	R	E	T	S	O	O	R	S	N	T
F	M	B	I	R	L	E	H	O	U	N	Q	V	H	U	E	R	T	O	L
Z	Z	E	O	B	R	I	A	F	F	A	E	V	O	L	P	F	O	Y	O
V	H	T	H	E	A	F	R	I	C	A	N	Q	U	E	E	N	Z	J	V
T	I	H	N	H	W	B	Z	T	E	S	K	S	E	D	U	M	W	Z	E
M	Q	B	M	A	L	Y	B	F	Y	Z	R	Q	Y	D	G	Y	A	H	S
I	G	A	A	G	K	O	N	G	O	L	D	E	N	P	O	N	D	R	N

☐	A WOMAN REBELS	☐	AMERICAN CREED
☐	DESK SET	☐	DRAGON SEED
☐	HOLIDAY	☐	LOVE AFFAIR
☐	MORNING GLORY	☐	ON GOLDEN POND
☐	ROOSTER COGBURN	☐	STAGE DOOR
☐	SUMMERTIME	☐	THE AFRICAN QUEEN
☐	THE IRON PETTICOAT	☐	THE SEA OF GRASS
☐	UNDERCURRENT	☐	WITHOUT LOVE

Puzzle 5 : Tom Hanks

Z	E	W	E	D	O	C	I	C	N	I	V	A	D	E	H	T	U	C	R
C	U	D	E	T	H	E	M	O	N	E	Y	P	I	T	Z	E	M	R	R
B	C	F	L	R	C	P	J	Z	G	Y	I	D	E	Z	K	N	H	I	N
E	W	D	C	U	N	A	N	G	E	L	S	D	E	M	O	N	S	S	W
Q	P	H	S	A	L	P	S	G	I	D	Q	L	V	Z	S	Z	N	J	P
Z	U	Q	B	I	T	H	A	T	T	H	I	N	G	Y	O	U	D	O	F
G	M	Q	L	O	Y	V	S	R	U	S	Z	S	F	Z	Q	N	T	R	M
P	W	T	H	E	P	O	L	A	R	E	X	P	R	E	S	S	K	L	F
O	R	T	S	C	M	Y	3	Y	R	O	T	S	Y	O	T	C	Q	O	Y
S	B	R	U	B	E	H	T	L	K	S	R	D	R	B	Z	H	S	N	A
O	D	J	Q	Y	U	M	A	U	V	B	V	E	J	U	N	L	J	R	W
G	V	W	H	L	E	L	I	M	N	E	E	R	G	E	H	T	O	E	A
Z	L	E	N	U	B	R	I	D	G	E	O	F	S	P	I	E	S	F	T
S	L	E	E	P	L	E	S	S	I	N	S	E	A	T	T	L	E	N	S
L	A	Z	J	Z	I	D	Z	H	J	W	T	A	W	Y	A	B	Y	I	A
C	S	F	O	R	R	E	S	T	G	U	M	P	I	J	Y	N	I	D	C
Z	U	L	I	A	M	T	O	G	E	V	U	O	Y	N	S	J	M	G	V
A	L	S	A	L	T	A	D	U	O	L	C	Z	L	H	J	Z	Z	W	D
U	C	O	S	N	O	S	L	N	C	K	H	J	F	R	E	V	U	T	C
H	V	P	F	Z	C	R	U	C	B	B	D	A	R	K	D	H	N	Z	W

☐ ANGELS - DEMONS	☐ BRIDGE OF SPIES
☐ CAST AWAY	☐ CLOUD ATLAS
☐ FORREST GUMP	☐ INFERNO
☐ SLEEPLESS IN SEATTLE	☐ SPLASH
☐ THAT THING YOU DO!	☐ THE 'BURBS
☐ THE DA VINCI CODE	☐ THE GREEN MILE
☐ THE MONEY PIT	☐ THE POLAR EXPRESS
☐ TOY STORY 3	☐ YOU'VE GOT MAIL

Puzzle 6 : Elizabeth Taylor

T	A	E	S	S	R	E	V	I	R	D	E	H	T	A	J	E	G	I	L
R	A	I	N	T	R	E	E	C	O	U	N	T	Y	B	I	B	A	M	P
O	N	V	Y	B	M	S	G	Y	U	Y	K	R	L	S	W	T	A	I	H
M	M	R	S	H	J	O	D	T	Z	O	L	F	S	M	U	L	V	I	W
T	M	I	H	V	L	O	Z	L	O	C	Q	A	B	O	I	A	T	N	R
Q	Q	S	Z	T	S	Z	P	I	A	I	L	U	S	C	N	G	P	I	T
F	B	F	B	P	U	D	K	N	J	F	Z	I	E	H	I	J	I	N	H
Y	V	P	A	O	P	O	N	L	O	Q	H	I	O	J	Y	I	W	A	E
T	G	H	B	Q	O	H	Y	E	A	T	N	E	T	D	V	O	V	C	S
S	R	Z	B	F	T	M	G	F	I	W	C	B	V	A	C	B	E	S	E
W	N	Y	M	E	B	A	H	M	O	R	T	A	S	H	U	W	E	O	O
G	H	B	O	V	R	T	S	N	S	D	F	N	U	J	K	J	H	T	L
P	P	N	E	U	H	R	D	V	I	I	R	N	A	Z	O	N	V	G	D
U	T	Z	O	E	E	E	W	R	R	S	E	I	E	H	P	T	W	N	B
O	I	C	V	M	R	V	M	Y	F	B	Y	L	B	E	P	K	B	U	R
S	D	I	M	L	F	V	O	Y	V	K	E	S	H	T	W	E	Q	O	O
F	P	A	A	L	T	T	J	L	D	R	L	Z	Z	O	E	T	L	Y	A
S	H	N	U	S	T	L	L	G	V	Z	B	H	W	H	I	E	E	E	D
Z	D	I	T	N	I	G	H	T	W	A	T	C	H	R	Q	O	W	B	S
A	P	L	A	C	E	I	N	T	H	E	S	U	N	R	Z	J	I	S	M

- ☐ A PLACE IN THE SUN
- ☐ BOOM!
- ☐ ELEPHANT WALK
- ☐ IVANHOE
- ☐ NIGHT WATCH
- ☐ RHAPSODY
- ☐ THE DRIVER'S SEAT
- ☐ THESE OLD BROADS
- ☐ BETWEEN FRIENDS
- ☐ COURAGE OF LASSIE
- ☐ HAMMERSMITH IS OUT
- ☐ MALICE IN WONDERLAND
- ☐ RAINTREE COUNTY
- ☐ SWEET BIRD OF YOUTH
- ☐ THE V.I.P.S
- ☐ YOUNG TOSCANINI

Puzzle 7 : Clint Eastwood

K	C	O	O	G	A	N	S	B	L	U	F	F	M	C	C	M	D	A	C
W	H	E	R	E	E	A	G	L	E	S	D	A	R	E	I	D	P	Q	R
R	I	E	L	C	D	W	Q	W	Q	H	G	C	R	L	I	E	Y	A	V
M	F	B	C	M	C	V	J	I	G	N	A	L	L	K	R	U	M	R	E
S	H	K	J	R	V	O	N	I	U	L	Y	I	E	F	P	T	C	R	B
J	D	G	H	S	H	K	H	M	L	C	O	O	E	Q	H	Y	I	Z	A
C	F	P	Z	I	N	M	F	I	R	N	J	C	R	E	Q	F	T	V	A
N	F	L	B	Y	E	O	D	E	D	W	T	E	E	G	F	H	Q	N	Y
R	T	K	Y	G	R	A	D	O	H	W	C	I	D	O	E	Z	A	S	I
G	A	T	N	C	C	I	L	A	O	R	G	E	E	G	V	M	J	Z	G
Z	I	A	E	K	R	L	H	R	O	E	M	N	A	U	K	Y	U	E	K
H	H	P	N	E	A	R	L	F	R	I	I	U	O	N	Z	Y	C	P	A
U	D	I	L	R	Q	D	N	S	R	L	N	F	O	V	U	F	S	Z	B
A	P	A	B	N	A	E	A	C	E	T	V	T	J	U	G	Z	M	L	S
J	P	A	Z	H	E	N	E	H	L	G	Y	W	E	P	Z	H	W	Z	B
E	B	M	R	H	C	U	T	E	C	K	G	K	F	O	S	I	H	V	L
Y	D	V	T	T	R	N	T	Y	N	K	G	I	T	D	Q	Y	I	T	N
U	U	A	I	T	I	D	I	O	M	H	W	A	W	S	A	U	N	Q	K
P	L	O	Z	W	Z	S	H	Z	C	G	U	F	M	F	H	I	L	K	Z
Z	N	G	L	S	H	N	B	L	O	O	D	W	O	R	K	F	H	W	B

☐	A PERFECT WORLD	☐	BLOOD WORK
☐	COOGAN'S BLUFF	☐	HANG 'EM HIGH
☐	HONKYTONK MAN	☐	IN THE LINE OF FIRE
☐	JOE KIDD	☐	MAGNUM FORCE
☐	MILLION DOLLAR BABY	☐	PALE RIDER
☐	PINK CADILLAC	☐	THE EIGER SANCTION
☐	THE ENFORCER	☐	THE GAUNTLET
☐	TRUE CRIME	☐	WHERE EAGLES DARE

Puzzle 8 : Audrey Hepburn

D	A	O	R	E	H	T	R	O	F	O	W	T	I	L	W	R	S	K	M
K	V	Z	N	D	A	G	O	Y	E	Q	G	R	T	Y	U	E	W	J	U
N	A	G	P	D	V	R	D	N	W	G	Q	G	T	O	C	T	I	C	M
A	L	Q	Q	Q	C	R	I	P	O	Z	R	Y	H	R	H	W	J	Y	W
I	A	P	Z	Z	W	L	O	A	S	T	R	S	E	E	E	D	F	D	C
R	G	M	Z	W	D	M	C	I	F	O	N	T	Y	G	S	A	H	A	H
A	H	Q	A	O	Q	Q	I	U	T	E	P	A	O	N	I	N	G	D	W
M	B	K	O	N	F	H	N	S	R	E	L	T	O	R	A	C	D	A	R
D	L	L	A	F	L	N	S	D	O	L	O	I	L	J	T	R	I	Z	A
N	B	F	A	D	Y	N	L	P	L	M	S	A	W	W	O	T	K	L	W
A	H	F	P	F	U	I	L	A	O	N	D	S	Y	M	U	K	D	A	H
N	J	A	A	N	H	E	U	N	A	Y	A	V	A	N	Y	J	R	I	U
I	E	C	E	C	Y	G	T	M	E	I	U	N	T	P	E	A	S	O	B
B	E	H	E	L	H	E	N	C	E	W	H	I	I	Y	N	A	F	C	Q
O	T	H	N	E	C	E	H	O	F	O	L	E	O	D	B	V	A	E	J
R	T	L	D	A	E	A	K	Z	L	D	U	B	P	R	S	S	G	V	N
L	P	E	R	R	R	B	Q	I	A	I	T	E	I	J	O	C	Z	J	T
Z	M	L	G	A	W	N	D	R	A	M	A	N	M	Z	Y	D	G	V	L
C	O	P	D	A	V	A	K	F	Z	C	A	F	W	J	B	V	N	M	R
Z	W	E	C	G	Y	F	P	J	E	S	U	T	L	S	Q	B	U	Y	G

☐	BLOODLINE	☐	CHARADE
☐	FUNNY FACE	☐	GREEN MANSIONS
☐	MY FAIR LADY	☐	ROBIN AND MARIAN
☐	ROMAN HOLIDAY	☐	SABRINA
☐	SECRET PEOPLE	☐	THE CHILDREN'S HOUR
☐	THE NUN'S STORY	☐	THEY ALL LAUGHED
☐	TWO FOR THE ROAD	☐	WAIT UNTIL DARK
☐	WAR AND PEACE	☐	WE GO TO MONTE CARLO

Puzzle 9 : John Wayne

N C U Y Q Q L C T W V Z E D P C N Y N P
C Z P T T M J Z H D B W U O A A L Q P A
D H L K Y R E Y E Z N G P G R H O Z B O
N S I W I R S L L J R B A Y A I R V S I
E A I S R M I I O F T W L E D L O Y O A
S G G N U E T Q N W S M S F I L R L R C
E E D I Q M H O G Q I Z O T S U R K E T
R B P A L M E T V Q T Z F Q E S E Q H H
U R T L D J S W O W O J T F C M T H C R
T U Z C U Z E H Y M O C H H A A S B N E
N S F M Z N A R A R H F E E N R A N A E
E H G M W Q R K G Y S H S W Y S X T M F
V T M I D K C K E E E W A U O H E D O A
D R D J D A H U H H H O D A N A T H C C
A A O G B Z E A O T T D D C Z L Z R E E
P I L I Q F R M M Y Z N L S H K W R H S
K L D B P M S J E S Z O E C J N U H T W
V K E A L A Z C U K F H H I I O E C S E
L I A R T Y L E N O L E H T E K C Z M S
V G Y T H E L U C K Y T E X A N I I I T

- ☐ ADVENTURE'S END
- ☐ CAHILL U.S. MARSHAL
- ☐ HONDO
- ☐ PARADISE CANYON
- ☐ TEXAS TERROR
- ☐ THE LONELY TRAIL
- ☐ THE LUCKY TEXAN
- ☐ THE SHOOTIST
- ☐ BIG JIM MCLAIN
- ☐ CHISUM
- ☐ PALS OF THE SADDLE
- ☐ SAGEBRUSH TRAIL
- ☐ THE COMANCHEROS
- ☐ THE LONG VOYAGE HOME
- ☐ THE SEARCHERS
- ☐ THREE FACES WEST

Puzzle 10 : Reese Witherspoon

R	E	E	Q	C	D	Z	T	G	F	N	C	N	F	S	H	A	F	M	E
L	E	H	O	W	D	O	Y	O	U	K	N	O	W	N	A	U	Q	K	A
S	S	L	I	N	K	O	D	Z	S	S	N	I	D	O	F	S	R	Z	T
W	N	S	E	B	J	Y	V	G	T	N	W	T	M	I	R	D	S	A	H
W	F	E	T	C	K	N	H	P	N	A	A	I	U	T	E	F	E	W	E
W	K	F	I	W	T	T	I	M	A	J	O	D	M	N	E	O	V	A	M
Y	E	J	Z	L	T	I	K	Z	H	G	P	N	Q	E	W	U	P	A	A
E	T	R	Q	B	A	Z	O	H	P	G	V	E	E	T	A	R	Z	C	N
L	H	A	W	H	F	S	W	N	E	Z	D	R	A	N	Y	C	R	F	I
L	G	W	B	S	R	P	V	V	L	O	P	F	I	I	J	H	W	N	N
I	I	S	W	V	Z	K	C	S	E	A	A	W	D	L	F	R	A	L	T
V	L	N	R	B	W	P	Y	R	R	R	Z	U	R	E	O	I	L	C	H
T	I	A	Y	R	J	F	V	R	O	E	C	V	S	U	Q	S	K	S	E
N	W	E	C	V	O	S	S	F	F	Y	T	N	P	R	H	T	T	P	M
A	T	M	A	G	A	S	F	W	R	T	V	S	W	C	B	M	H	P	O
S	D	S	V	A	K	P	G	S	E	N	M	E	N	U	D	A	E	J	O
A	U	I	A	F	L	M	M	P	T	C	F	O	D	O	E	S	L	B	N
E	F	H	R	A	H	H	Q	W	A	C	J	B	Z	S	M	E	I	O	N
L	Z	T	C	H	D	N	V	Z	W	C	K	B	Y	Q	V	S	N	E	L
P	C	E	J	U	S	T	L	I	K	E	H	E	A	V	E	N	E	E	C

☐	A FAR OFF PLACE	☐	CRUEL INTENTIONS
☐	ELECTION	☐	FOUR CHRISTMASES
☐	FREEWAY	☐	HOW DO YOU KNOW
☐	JUST LIKE HEAVEN	☐	MONSTERS VS. ALIENS
☐	PLEASANTVILLE	☐	RENDITION
☐	S.F.W.	☐	THE MAN IN THE MOON
☐	THIS MEANS WAR	☐	TWILIGHT
☐	WALK THE LINE	☐	WATER FOR ELEPHANTS

Puzzle 11 : Humphrey Bogart

S	B	K	S	U	T	H	E	B	A	D	S	I	S	T	E	R	K	Q	V
S	B	W	Z	R	E	C	R	O	F	N	E	E	H	T	W	D	R	Z	Z
N	J	M	R	Q	B	L	A	C	K	L	E	G	I	O	N	J	Q	N	F
E	L	L	I	E	S	R	A	M	O	T	E	G	A	S	S	A	P	B	W
P	G	Y	Y	N	E	E	U	Q	N	A	C	I	R	F	A	E	H	T	L
W	N	M	A	R	K	E	D	W	O	M	A	N	J	L	E	I	B	K	H
S	B	B	Z	Z	K	L	D	A	R	K	P	A	S	S	A	G	E	E	A
V	S	F	Y	O	I	K	S	O	J	B	U	P	D	T	N	T	M	Y	D
K	R	T	V	O	C	Q	V	Q	K	Q	Q	Z	P	G	P	M	V	L	E
S	W	Z	B	U	T	B	D	B	O	H	P	Z	C	B	D	Z	Y	A	A
Y	P	B	C	B	I	T	Q	I	R	B	P	U	K	N	W	J	U	R	D
U	G	W	T	K	N	O	C	K	O	N	A	N	Y	D	O	O	R	G	E
Q	C	P	E	E	L	S	G	I	B	E	H	T	E	Z	E	T	A	O	N
Y	M	O	G	C	S	A	H	A	R	A	P	Z	M	J	F	Z	I	R	D
Z	U	T	Y	G	B	K	D	O	L	D	A	H	A	L	A	G	D	I	K
L	K	C	H	S	L	I	V	E	D	E	H	T	T	A	E	B	U	G	E
S	L	Y	Z	R	A	Z	T	M	M	L	D	Z	I	P	G	N	J	Y	J
R	T	H	E	D	E	S	P	E	R	A	T	E	H	O	U	R	S	C	E
S	C	I	Z	G	D	A	R	K	V	I	C	T	O	R	Y	I	T	G	G
B	Y	Q	I	F	T	D	F	D	G	H	P	S	J	U	L	A	H	D	Z

☐	BEAT THE DEVIL	☐	BLACK LEGION
☐	DARK PASSAGE	☐	DARK VICTORY
☐	DEAD END	☐	KEY LARGO
☐	KID GALAHAD	☐	KNOCK ON ANY DOOR
☐	MARKED WOMAN	☐	PASSAGE TO MARSEILLE
☐	SAHARA	☐	THE AFRICAN QUEEN
☐	THE BAD SISTER	☐	THE BIG SLEEP
☐	THE DESPERATE HOURS	☐	THE ENFORCER

Puzzle 12 : Nicole Kidman

F	V	C	A	I	Z	Z	J	E	O	M	C	H	E	E	N	B	C	O	Z
A	F	G	Z	B	N	W	I	A	W	V	C	G	E	B	I	J	D	B	U
R	T	R	E	S	P	A	S	S	I	C	U	F	V	R	D	N	I	B	N
Z	S	I	S	Z	I	E	P	G	E	O	I	S	T	Z	I	B	J	H	O
S	E	T	P	I	T	J	Q	L	R	L	I	H	R	G	A	A	H	L	I
N	Y	L	O	I	N	P	L	N	Y	L	M	E	H	I	T	H	D	K	S
P	E	O	I	F	F	I	I	M	W	N	D	T	L	L	E	E	H	A	A
N	R	C	E	G	V	L	F	B	K	I	M	A	Q	R	H	M	C	Z	V
E	I	A	H	G	U	P	B	E	R	A	R	Y	E	C	V	O	L	D	N
T	E	A	O	O	D	V	S	D	S	T	F	K	T	M	L	G	Z	Z	I
D	H	D	M	U	Z	C	N	T	S	A	A	I	T	D	O	T	Y	Y	E
P	T	S	Z	N	Y	I	E	U	Z	M	W	H	M	W	C	C	Y	A	H
W	N	I	A	D	W	R	A	E	E	E	E	O	Q	F	S	K	F	W	T
P	I	H	H	J	Y	R	R	C	B	H	U	M	L	E	A	Z	M	A	B
D	T	V	G	Z	V	A	A	G	O	N	Z	I	V	V	Q	U	Q	D	G
K	E	K	F	D	N	E	W	U	T	G	R	M	C	N	Z	U	H	N	L
F	R	N	T	G	P	V	R	A	U	T	N	W	S	E	P	E	S	A	A
F	C	O	B	E	Z	S	I	R	I	W	G	D	V	P	B	F	C	R	Z
G	E	T	H	T	M	N	C	N	S	Q	Z	V	R	L	O	I	F	A	Y
B	S	T	Z	L	H	O	G	A	Q	E	K	G	A	M	D	B	U	F	K

☐	AUSTRALIA	☐	BEWITCHED
☐	BIRTH	☐	COLD MOUNTAIN
☐	DOGVILLE	☐	FAR AND AWAY
☐	FLIRTING	☐	MOULIN ROUGE!
☐	MY LIFE	☐	NIGHTMASTER
☐	SECRET IN THEIR EYES	☐	THE HOURS
☐	THE INVASION	☐	THE PEACEMAKER
☐	TRESPASS	☐	WINDRIDER

Best Pop Songs of All Times

Name the song based on the lyrics segment & artist.

1. Something evil's lurking from the dark / Under the moonlight / You see a sight that almost stops your heart / You try to scream / But terror takes the sound before you make it / You start to freeze (Michael Jackson)

____

2. I hear your voice, it's like an angel sighing / I have no choice, I hear your voice / Feels like flying / I close my eyes, oh God I think I'm falling (Madonna)

____

3. Oh baby, baby, I shouldn't have let you go / And now you're out of sight, yeah / Show me how want it to be (Britney Spears)

____

4. I stay out too late, got nothin' in my brain / That's what people say, mmm hmm, that's what people say, mmm hmm / I go on too many dates, but I can't make 'em stay (Taylor Swift)

____

5. Do you ever feel already buried deep / Six feet under scream / But no one seems to hear a thing (Katy Perry)

____

6. One, don't pick up the phone / You know he's only calling 'cause he's drunk and alone / Two, don't let him in / You'll have to kick him out again (Dua Lipa)

____

7. Now I'm rising from the ground / Rising up to you / Filled with all the strength I found / There's nothing I can't do! (John Newman)

____

8. Friday night and the lights are low / Looking out for a place to go / Where they play the right music / Getting in the swing (ABBA)

____

9. You were made to go out and get her / The minute you let her under your skin / Then you begin to make it better (The Beatles)

____

10. Round and around and / Up and down we go / (Yeah, oh, baby) / Making with the /Shaking to and fro (Chubby Checker)

____

11. If I should stay / I would only be in your way / So I'll go but I know / I'll think of you every step of the way (Whitney Houston)

____

12. Is for a little respect when you get home (just a little bit) / Hey baby (just a little bit) when you get home / (just a little bit) mister (just a little bit) (Aretha Franklin)

____

ANSWERS: 1. RELLIRHT 2. 3. EMIT EROM ENO YBAB... 4. FFO TI EKAHS 5. KROWERIF 6. SELUR WEN 7. NIAGA EM EVOL 8. NEEUQ GNICNAD 9. EDUJ YEH 10. TSIWT EHT 11. UOY EVOL SYAWLA LLIW I 12. TCEPSER

Puzzle 13 : Marlon Brando

Z	T	Z	I	S	W	R	K	I	Y	S	R	M	C	N	U	L	S	O	M
P	E	N	O	D	L	I	W	E	H	T	H	A	O	T	Z	N	C	Y	U
E	Z	E	R	C	G	G	V	Z	V	L	F	P	H	R	O	M	M	Z	T
O	N	V	B	S	V	I	U	O	Q	B	S	E	H	I	I	U	F	U	A
Y	J	A	Z	T	H	H	C	Y	P	M	F	L	L	P	T	T	O	J	S
E	Z	R	C	K	A	U	W	S	S	O	N	G	N	I	G	K	U	Q	U
N	J	B	Q	I	P	R	U	T	R	A	N	E	N	C	Y	Y	P	R	N
O	H	E	T	P	R	O	A	M	E	U	N	Y	M	R	A	R	K	A	I
M	M	H	P	H	H	E	U	N	O	B	O	D	O	E	A	Z	P	D	M
E	W	T	L	A	E	L	M	Y	O	N	T	T	D	S	H	O	C	G	J
E	N	U	F	Y	A	S	E	A	T	Y	S	T	E	O	C	T	M	D	N
R	C	D	N	O	U	H	C	H	Y	E	A	A	C	A	L	R	V	P	J
F	V	R	Q	Z	T	O	E	O	M	L	C	S	L	A	G	L	L	H	G
Q	Q	O	I	P	L	B	V	I	R	S	G	Y	M	L	N	Y	S	B	Z
O	P	P	U	B	O	E	T	B	U	E	P	U	J	W	A	D	E	Y	V
N	J	M	L	U	D	D	N	I	S	S	H	A	E	U	N	T	Y	J	U
Z	P	Q	N	E	E	I	L	N	E	Z	D	M	B	H	I	U	Y	H	I
M	G	T	G	B	G	U	Y	N	M	V	A	H	B	H	T	O	P	I	V
J	Y	G	V	O	J	M	O	A	Q	R	P	A	M	U	W	D	P	S	S
R	F	T	T	G	Z	W	U	Q	P	Y	F	B	N	L	U	M	B	N	L

☐	APOCALYPSE NOW	☐	BEDTIME STORY
☐	CANDY	☐	FREE MONEY
☐	GUYS AND DOLLS	☐	JULIUS CAESAR
☐	MORITURI	☐	MUTINY ON THE BOUNTY
☐	SAYONARA	☐	THE BRAVE
☐	THE FORMULA	☐	THE MEN
☐	THE SCORE	☐	THE UGLY AMERICAN
☐	THE WILD ONE	☐	THE YOUNG LIONS

Puzzle 14 : Kate Winslet

N	F	U	V	G	Z	S	G	I	H	E	G	A	N	R	A	C	C	R	I
L	E	I	B	N	P	U	B	B	T	L	G	H	L	P	T	E	I	A	I
D	O	R	N	H	H	Z	V	Y	C	H	Y	I	T	V	D	D	N	C	E
H	A	C	D	D	T	S	T	C	Z	Z	E	U	H	P	O	S	A	H	K
E	P	O	W	L	I	H	B	E	H	K	Z	R	G	T	U	C	T	R	O
A	M	P	R	J	I	N	E	O	L	Q	O	E	E	E	J	M	I	I	M
V	G	I	D	Y	Q	H	G	H	J	M	K	Z	Y	A	S	P	T	S	S
E	A	H	J	E	R	R	C	N	O	E	A	M	G	Y	D	Z	Z	T	Y
N	L	R	K	R	B	A	I	E	E	L	V	H	U	E	F	E	Q	M	L
L	O	P	J	D	G	B	N	D	L	V	I	E	D	Z	P	P	R	A	O
Y	D	O	Z	E	Q	B	G	O	T	T	E	D	T	T	C	B	Z	S	H
C	M	I	D	V	H	N	T	O	I	N	T	R	A	S	N	B	J	C	C
R	D	N	V	D	D	G	S	J	L	T	E	I	L	Y	U	V	T	A	L
E	J	H	H	E	G	K	Q	L	Z	W	U	G	L	A	Y	T	H	R	G
A	W	P	P	C	R	W	S	K	L	I	J	L	R	O	N	E	G	O	A
T	C	V	V	L	W	G	P	R	G	I	L	N	O	U	K	D	J	L	F
U	G	R	F	E	K	H	E	O	O	H	U	Z	E	V	S	L	D	Q	K
R	J	S	R	E	K	S	L	N	R	A	Q	Q	I	S	E	N	Z	L	U
E	Z	K	I	P	D	Z	G	C	T	T	W	B	A	L	O	R	I	P	Z
S	S	C	P	H	L	R	E	K	A	M	S	S	E	R	D	E	H	T	M

☐	A CHRISTMAS CAROL	☐	CARNAGE
☐	DIVERGENT	☐	FINDING NEVERLAND
☐	HAMLET	☐	HEAVENLY CREATURES
☐	HOLY SMOKE	☐	INSURGENT
☐	LITTLE CHILDREN	☐	QUILLS
☐	REVOLUTIONARY ROAD	☐	STEVE JOBS
☐	THE DRESSMAKER	☐	THE HOLIDAY
☐	THE READER	☐	TITANIC

Puzzle 15 : Leonardo DiCaprio

H	C	A	E	B	E	H	T	E	J	E	E	Z	R	Z	D	A	H	S	L
T	I	T	A	N	I	C	P	Z	Q	F	E	Z	B	J	F	T	O	T	Y
L	P	N	N	G	O	J	U	Y	I	I	O	Z	A	V	H	A	D	D	K
L	P	T	J	H	A	Q	N	L	Q	C	Z	N	R	E	Z	D	A	R	D
J	E	D	G	A	R	N	S	U	E	S	G	F	G	L	P	O	P	N	A
R	R	J	S	E	D	Y	G	L	A	O	S	R	Y	P	R	C	A	M	G
E	O	Z	L	Y	O	Z	E	S	U	R	E	W	B	Y	U	L	A	U	P
Y	E	H	L	B	Z	B	T	N	O	A	I	L	R	Z	S	R	I	N	T
A	W	K	S	C	R	S	C	T	T	F	O	A	I	I	V	S	Q	J	A
Q	I	I	Q	I	C	H	A	G	A	O	N	N	R	I	A	V	L	M	Y
H	H	S	T	R	A	I	A	L	D	O	C	E	N	M	Q	J	S	F	T
T	V	Y	C	I	V	T	I	D	I	E	T	S	W	Y	L	J	W	M	H
Z	U	A	N	A	S	K	I	T	P	T	R	R	D	Y	T	B	Z	Q	D
B	C	E	E	B	Z	A	U	T	U	O	Y	R	H	R	O	I	V	G	C
W	D	H	Y	Y	M	L	I	H	O	T	K	F	Y	U	D	R	Q	N	I
Y	T	V	I	O	O	O	S	M	M	P	O	Z	U	K	E	E	K	L	Z
Q	R	O	N	V	N	M	W	V	V	Z	R	Y	H	M	B	T	E	Z	K
Q	H	D	E	Z	A	U	S	Y	S	E	I	L	F	O	Y	D	O	B	D
D	N	R	W	Z	S	M	C	M	E	G	K	Z	W	E	Z	H	Z	P	T
G	B	S	S	K	N	A	C	U	O	Y	F	I	E	M	H	C	T	A	C

☐	BLOOD DIAMOND	☐	BODY OF LIES
☐	CATCH ME IF YOU CAN	☐	CELEBRITY
☐	DJANGO UNCHAINED	☐	GANGS OF NEW YORK
☐	INCEPTION	☐	J. EDGAR
☐	MARVIN'S ROOM	☐	REVOLUTIONARY ROAD
☐	SHUTTER ISLAND	☐	THE AVIATOR
☐	THE BEACH	☐	THE GREAT GATSBY
☐	THIS BOY'S LIFE	☐	TITANIC

Puzzle 16 : Sandra Bullock

O B J E G A O Q G Z B Z W Z C T D Y G Z
G Z E E V A A S J H R S M R H Q E C C N
N E I O W R M L T P L V U E K N K S T E
A V Q Y D E M P Q H Q M B T O Q T W Q S
K E S G T T E F I S E L N M F W T T A M
A T K T T I A S H K I P S D O R P O U K
T S G Y A O L T U N Y I R W M Y T R D R
A T N N K O L A D O H T E O G F D N U H
P U F H I Y L S I D H E Q E P E R W I P
T O Y A Z H I F N N K E F W R O L G Z A
O B R R I D S A E S E O K B H L S Q K R
H A M U E P L I N P E G Y A N C L A C R
S L R A V O Y O N C O N N R L Z E P L G
O L M L O Z T W N A U H R O Q E Z I Y S
H A V F I I G I Y M V W Q P C H H K P N
W P A K C H R H B O H E L R Z S G T Z O
Z K B E S P S E U F J C H T O D S C G I
P V W A E N R U W Q I B L T H Q T I A N
L W R H U S T W O I F B Y S E A P E M I
P C T G B Y B C V K F Z B I I A K Z Q M

☐	A FOOL AND HIS MONEY	☐	ALL ABOUT STEVE
☐	CRASH	☐	GUN SHY
☐	HOPE FLOATS	☐	MINIONS
☐	MISS CONGENIALITY	☐	MURDER BY NUMBERS
☐	THE BLIND SIDE	☐	THE LAKE HOUSE
☐	THE PRINCE OF EGYPT	☐	THE PROPOSAL
☐	THE VANISHING	☐	TWO IF BY SEA
☐	TWO WEEKS NOTICE	☐	WHO SHOT PATAKANGO?

Puzzle 17 : Cary Grant

R	N	R	E	P	W	S	R	A	C	H	O	J	W	P	Z	C	I	Q	Z
E	D	A	O	Y	A	S	F	M	O	U	L	T	H	R	D	S	G	P	S
D	E	Z	T	B	Y	I	U	J	P	Z	A	Z	E	Q	F	Y	C	M	E
I	S	H	H	E	F	S	J	O	E	C	D	O	N	T	Y	L	K	L	Y
M	T	P	A	D	Q	I	A	O	R	P	I	U	Y	H	A	V	P	E	E
W	I	E	T	A	A	R	O	K	A	M	E	D	O	I	D	I	B	G	N
I	N	E	T	N	V	C	E	J	T	S	S	W	U	S	R	A	H	N	W
F	A	D	O	E	R	T	P	K	I	S	S	E	R	I	U	S	C	A	O
E	T	E	U	R	N	I	B	Z	O	E	H	C	E	S	T	C	U	O	R
I	I	H	C	E	R	K	J	H	N	N	O	F	I	T	A	A	S	N	B
H	O	T	H	S	K	E	V	U	P	I	U	K	N	H	S	R	B	M	G
T	N	D	O	Y	Z	O	H	E	E	S	L	Z	L	E	T	L	S	I	I
A	T	N	F	N	Y	Z	C	E	T	U	D	E	O	N	O	E	L	Z	B
H	O	A	M	N	Q	W	Q	N	T	B	L	T	V	I	H	T	P	N	M
C	K	L	I	E	K	S	Y	Y	I	Y	I	V	E	G	Q	T	S	W	J
T	Y	I	N	P	P	R	B	P	C	E	S	S	U	H	J	O	L	E	D
A	O	V	K	K	S	O	C	N	O	K	T	B	U	T	W	I	V	B	E
C	U	E	H	Z	Y	Z	L	E	A	N	E	A	E	M	U	W	E	K	T
O	Q	D	Y	R	E	P	P	O	T	O	N	M	D	R	L	Z	Y	Q	D
T	I	I	V	M	U	O	L	W	W	M	I	F	D	N	G	O	R	E	V

- ☐ BIG BROWN EYES
- ☐ DESTINATION TOKYO
- ☐ HOT SATURDAY
- ☐ LADIES SHOULD LISTEN
- ☐ OPERATION PETTICOAT
- ☐ SYLVIA SCARLETT
- ☐ THIS IS THE NIGHT
- ☐ TOPPER
- ☐ CRISIS
- ☐ DEVIL AND THE DEEP
- ☐ I'M NO ANGEL
- ☐ MONKEY BUSINESS
- ☐ PENNY SERENADE
- ☐ THAT TOUCH OF MINK
- ☐ TO CATCH A THIEF
- ☐ WHEN YOU'RE IN LOVE

Puzzle 18 : Angelina Jolie

C	O	V	G	N	I	L	E	G	N	A	H	C	Z	B	J	S	H	O	F
N	U	C	Y	W	N	H	M	M	C	M	R	K	N	E	O	B	B	G	M
T	S	A	A	M	V	E	O	A	O	J	U	A	Z	O	R	T	T	F	Y
E	H	F	U	K	S	M	H	J	L	N	K	I	E	W	U	N	W	O	F
O	K	E	E	S	G	L	A	C	G	E	I	U	S	U	O	H	R	H	K
B	U	T	B	J	G	V	H	F	T	K	F	R	J	L	G	D	F	U	M
R	Z	2	O	O	E	B	U	K	J	I	E	I	U	F	E	V	N	Q	S
F	L	H	A	M	N	P	A	C	Z	D	K	J	C	T	N	G	F	Q	Y
O	Q	A	O	D	A	E	Z	M	R	Z	O	S	P	E	F	N	N	E	E
T	E	O	L	N	N	U	C	O	I	K	B	U	L	U	N	Z	F	W	G
N	N	N	D	E	Q	A	B	O	M	G	R	J	P	L	T	T	D	U	U
L	B	A	O	V	X	D	P	S	L	R	H	A	K	H	E	E	R	P	Q
J	F	E	C	G	N	A	U	U	E	L	N	T	E	P	T	H	L	O	U
V	T	U	I	O	Y	J	N	T	F	D	E	T	Y	N	K	L	J	I	H
W	P	B	Y	T	K	E	N	D	A	G	O	C	A	H	V	E	A	Q	T
K	Q	E	L	H	N	I	V	3	E	U	N	W	T	C	E	S	V	U	L
C	B	A	C	H	L	Z	G	C	R	R	Y	U	L	O	J	A	M	H	F
B	H	B	Y	R	Z	R	O	I	H	K	T	M	K	V	R	U	R	F	S
S	K	M	I	F	C	N	S	B	T	P	Z	F	H	A	Z	P	S	T	L
A	A	G	R	O	T	T	H	A	C	K	E	R	S	Z	F	Q	Q	Z	I

☐	A MIGHTY HEART	☐	ALEXANDER
☐	BEOWULF	☐	BEYOND BORDERS
☐	CHANGELING	☐	GIRL, INTERRUPTED
☐	HACKERS	☐	HELL'S KITCHEN
☐	KUNG FU PANDA	☐	KUNG FU PANDA 2
☐	KUNG FU PANDA 3	☐	MALEFICENT
☐	MOJAVE MOON	☐	THE BONE COLLECTOR
☐	THE TOURIST	☐	WANTED

Puzzle 19 : Gregory Peck

H	C	C	O	B	E	H	F	P	R	L	Z	O	Z	S	Z	U	H	R	V
A	A	V	F	C	I	Z	M	R	Z	Y	G	M	T	H	U	O	D	I	D
M	N	H	N	H	Z	M	G	E	F	E	J	J	Q	Q	W	R	E	A	Z
I	K	S	O	L	D	G	R	I	N	G	O	F	O	T	E	S	V	R	D
N	O	O	M	G	N	I	K	L	A	T	S	E	H	T	A	I	S	E	W
T	B	J	D	P	Z	D	T	I	L	H	N	E	H	C	D	E	S	P	H
Q	F	R	G	Z	T	G	Y	B	S	I	W	G	E	A	V	I	E	N	G
E	U	Q	S	E	B	A	R	A	L	E	I	N	N	L	G	L	M	H	L
C	P	K	H	Q	V	P	G	E	S	F	I	D	O	N	P	A	Z	O	Y
L	N	B	S	Z	Z	K	H	T	N	D	B	W	I	O	C	E	M	T	G
H	V	A	W	E	Q	T	W	U	A	A	A	N	E	A	H	I	V	C	N
R	I	F	J	L	K	A	G	R	T	E	G	P	R	H	Z	F	J	O	I
L	Z	F	B	L	S	E	A	H	S	W	T	T	N	Z	I	U	Q	T	L
O	B	T	A	W	H	P	S	E	O	H	H	U	T	M	T	P	G	V	R
Q	F	W	O	T	E	H	H	M	G	U	Y	T	H	A	G	M	T	B	A
U	I	N	F	H	E	T	A	I	R	W	I	V	T	Z	U	K	U	B	E
Z	A	I	T	B	Z	N	N	C	H	S	N	C	T	A	G	Z	T	D	Y
N	A	H	A	D	T	H	E	P	U	R	P	L	E	P	L	A	I	N	E
L	G	E	N	O	R	A	V	A	N	F	O	S	N	U	G	E	H	T	H
M	A	R	O	O	N	E	D	W	W	C	Q	Y	R	A	I	R	N	E	T

☐	ARABESQUE	☐	DAVID AND BATHSHEBA
☐	DESIGNING WOMAN	☐	HOW THE WEST WAS WON
☐	I WALK THE LINE	☐	MACARTHUR
☐	MAROONED	☐	NIGHT PEOPLE
☐	OLD GRINGO	☐	THE GUNFIGHTER
☐	THE GUNS OF NAVARONE	☐	THE PARADINE CASE
☐	THE PURPLE PLAIN	☐	THE SEA WOLVES
☐	THE STALKING MOON	☐	THE YEARLING

Puzzle 20 : Bette Davis

T	P	T	K	E	W	R	E	T	F	A	M	I	E	V	O	L	S	T	I
V	S	D	N	A	H	Q	A	Y	H	K	S	A	M	I	T	M	J	Y	U
T	T	U	L	P	D	V	L	B	D	R	I	C	P	M	N	J	L	N	V
H	Q	S	G	D	N	A	M	E	D	N	O	T	N	E	M	Y	A	P	G
E	F	M	D	U	N	T	H	E	C	O	R	N	I	S	G	R	E	E	N
S	R	O	T	R	A	J	J	B	K	E	E	J	T	O	I	E	Y	O	T
T	E	O	K	F	J	F	W	U	M	Q	D	L	T	O	T	U	L	W	E
A	P	R	E	D	R	Z	O	Q	M	Z	W	N	G	H	C	D	E	A	P
R	M	G	P	I	L	O	R	S	W	Z	O	Z	E	Z	A	I	W	F	I
V	U	N	L	Z	D	B	N	N	E	I	W	S	O	C	A	A	J	V	M
B	J	I	K	E	T	S	O	T	T	L	C	F	Q	K	Y	K	T	G	V
O	E	T	Q	Q	Z	R	R	P	P	O	A	U	J	B	V	H	R	R	H
R	T	C	J	A	D	B	E	E	P	A	A	H	A	G	E	J	I	U	P
D	U	E	V	S	S	C	Q	O	M	I	G	C	W	M	V	G	V	Y	B
E	H	N	S	H	E	V	N	I	N	M	K	E	E	E	Q	Q	Q	D	T
R	C	N	U	D	I	E	E	T	S	H	U	N	W	N	H	O	Y	A	U
T	A	O	N	N	G	Y	A	T	O	Z	A	S	Z	O	M	T	G	L	J
O	R	C	W	A	P	N	W	M	Q	C	U	R	S	B	M	S	C	X	K
W	A	N	M	W	C	A	E	E	E	Q	C	V	Y	A	Z	A	Q	E	I
N	P	E	T	E	E	F	Q	U	K	J	P	T	F	Z	P	Z	N	F	L

☐	AS SUMMERS DIE	☐	BORDERTOWN
☐	CONNECTING ROOMS	☐	DECEPTION
☐	EX-LADY	☐	FRONT PAGE WOMAN
☐	IT'S LOVE I'M AFTER	☐	OLD ACQUAINTANCE
☐	PARACHUTE JUMPER	☐	PAYMENT ON DEMAND
☐	THE CORN IS GREEN	☐	THE MENACE
☐	THE SCOPONE GAME	☐	THE STAR
☐	THE WHALES OF AUGUST	☐	WAY BACK HOME

Puzzle 21 : Brad Pitt

D	Q	N	G	J	S	W	W	J	O	S	F	J	F	B	G	A	L	P	S
N	Z	E	F	Z	Y	J	T	R	O	H	S	G	I	B	E	H	T	D	Q
I	O	E	A	T	E	T	K	J	Z	S	Q	D	Z	U	T	Z	R	B	O
M	B	T	J	J	K	C	H	L	W	A	C	U	S	F	M	E	U	R	Z
A	S	R	Z	H	N	D	M	E	K	O	H	Z	P	H	T	P	U	M	Q
G	B	I	V	V	O	O	K	R	T	T	R	T	Z	S	T	S	M	G	V
E	F	H	E	U	M	H	A	N	M	R	W	L	A	W	A	J	S	W	A
M	B	T	D	D	E	M	O	E	Q	R	E	B	D	B	N	Z	G	Y	S
R	U	S	G	D	V	I	T	K	E	F	S	E	Y	W	D	F	T	C	L
Z	L	N	M	U	L	W	D	R	D	U	E	S	O	P	A	D	Q	C	E
B	C	A	Q	G	E	R	Y	Z	O	E	N	Y	M	F	T	R	S	T	E
Q	T	E	D	A	W	L	A	I	F	W	Z	O	F	I	L	C	Z	Z	P
H	H	C	Z	E	T	I	R	S	N	A	T	C	H	R	T	I	L	D	E
Z	G	O	M	I	Z	U	L	P	C	L	E	Q	T	B	H	H	F	S	R
Y	I	K	Z	D	O	O	C	E	A	N	S	T	W	E	L	V	E	E	S
C	F	J	Z	L	M	B	C	P	T	T	H	E	M	E	X	I	C	A	N
K	L	E	G	E	N	D	S	O	F	T	H	E	F	A	L	L	Y	W	G
G	J	N	D	I	Q	A	I	N	R	O	F	I	L	A	K	D	K	F	W
T	I	S	F	V	E	K	Y	R	W	Z	T	L	V	H	K	N	R	J	E
M	E	E	T	J	O	E	B	L	A	C	K	H	Y	Z	C	U	L	Y	Q

- ☐ FIGHT CLUB
- ☐ KALIFORNIA
- ☐ MEET JOE BLACK
- ☐ MR. - MRS. SMITH
- ☐ OCEAN'S TWELVE
- ☐ SNATCH
- ☐ THE MEXICAN
- ☐ TWELVE MONKEYS
- ☐ INGLOURIOUS BASTERDS
- ☐ LEGENDS OF THE FALL
- ☐ MEGAMIND
- ☐ OCEAN'S THIRTEEN
- ☐ SLEEPERS
- ☐ THE BIG SHORT
- ☐ THE TREE OF LIFE
- ☐ WORLD WAR Z

Puzzle 22 : Julia Roberts

F N S H S B K W Q I N F E S S F R Y Q M
H R A N T H M A U T R R P E N D B H L O
C P I O L N F Z C E K B V C F O Y N M U
M U L T Z A H L H Q T S V R L R T A I I
T V O T T M D I A E J N L E V M N C R Y
S S N I B O U Z R R P E B T A U U I R A
N V G N V W P O L I K V O I L O O X O Z
I S A G R Y L W I N W E O N E V C E R V
L C M H W T I H E B C L Q T N N E M M B
L E L I E T C A W R F E D H T J G E I S
O S E L Q E I G I O P S P E I S A H R B
C N E L Z R T S L C W N Y I N R S T R R
L O T D K P Y R S K M A F R E E O Y O M
E B S E R I J Q O O S E Q E S N : T R O
A I U O E Z G Y N V A C H Y D I T E P S
H Z Z J S Z D I S I J O E E A L S M P D
C Z P A O S T W W C Y Z I S Y T U V R T
I L A K L V C N A H L D R M A A G U P D
M M Z U C O A Y R A D C J C V L U P T M
W C R A E W O T Y D A E R R Y F A S U W

- ☐ AUGUST: OSAGE COUNTY
- ☐ CLOSER
- ☐ ERIN BROCKOVICH
- ☐ MICHAEL COLLINS
- ☐ NOTTING HILL
- ☐ PRETTY WOMAN
- ☐ SECRET IN THEIR EYES
- ☐ THE MEXICAN
- ☐ CHARLIE WILSON'S WAR
- ☐ DUPLICITY
- ☐ FLATLINERS
- ☐ MIRROR MIRROR
- ☐ OCEAN'S ELEVEN
- ☐ READY TO WEAR
- ☐ STEEL MAGNOLIAS
- ☐ VALENTINE'S DAY

Puzzle 23 : Tom Cruise

E	F	D	T	R	C	S	G	S	N	A	S	Y	N	U	E	W	S	Y	Q
K	W	C	A	E	K	B	I	Q	G	G	Q	N	N	G	N	E	T	K	F
J	O	V	L	G	W	M	G	F	Y	M	T	M	U	D	A	L	F	S	Q
U	D	D	L	L	O	A	J	E	A	I	S	U	D	M	M	B	F	A	F
W	Y	M	T	T	R	L	H	Z	E	N	U	P	A	A	N	I	Y	L	I
C	L	U	H	L	R	R	U	Z	C	O	N	D	Y	K	I	S	E	L	C
Q	T	U	E	Q	O	O	U	F	H	R	N	L	S	W	A	S	N	I	Y
A	I	N	R	N	M	F	W	J	P	I	E	I	O	E	R	O	O	N	V
C	B	W	I	U	O	S	L	G	B	T	M	V	F	C	C	P	M	A	M
K	M	Y	G	G	T	N	D	C	C	Y	D	K	T	O	P	M	F	V	Q
J	N	J	H	P	F	O	C	V	U	R	O	W	H	L	G	I	O	A	N
R	M	V	T	O	O	I	O	N	A	E	O	K	U	L	M	:	R	I	D
F	K	S	M	T	E	L	C	T	I	P	G	U	N	A	J	N	O	A	G
Z	N	H	O	Z	G	M	K	H	L	O	W	R	D	T	Z	O	L	T	K
Y	O	O	V	N	D	T	T	S	O	R	E	U	E	E	Z	I	O	G	O
W	C	S	E	H	E	D	A	O	N	T	F	G	R	R	H	S	C	W	R
M	S	T	S	F	E	T	I	T	G	Z	A	H	E	A	D	S	E	K	P
D	R	D	Q	L	P	H	L	K	A	T	L	Q	Z	L	Y	I	H	E	B
U	A	M	E	R	I	C	A	N	M	A	D	E	C	B	U	M	T	K	D
V	A	L	K	Y	R	I	E	D	H	Z	N	K	H	Q	E	Z	Q	E	W

☐	A FEW GOOD MEN	☐	ALL THE RIGHT MOVES
☐	AMERICAN MADE	☐	COCKTAIL
☐	COLLATERAL	☐	DAYS OF THUNDER
☐	EDGE OF TOMORROW	☐	LIONS FOR LAMBS
☐	MAGNOLIA	☐	MINORITY REPORT
☐	MISSION: IMPOSSIBLE	☐	RAIN MAN
☐	THE COLOR OF MONEY	☐	TOP GUN
☐	VALKYRIE	☐	VANILLA SKY

Puzzle 24 : Jane Fonda

W	I	K	S	T	A	N	L	E	Y	I	R	I	S	R	J	H	U	D	W
S	C	K	K	M	H	D	Z	Z	B	Z	I	J	T	Q	U	U	O	G	I
W	D	M	R	W	I	A	O	V	O	I	A	H	K	R	H	G	Z	I	I
M	N	N	K	A	P	D	Y	L	K	G	E	M	R	C	F	Q	H	U	T
I	J	Q	O	A	P	I	K	B	L	C	N	Y	E	O	H	S	D	A	B
W	Q	M	R	P	H	E	L	Y	H	S	S	I	S	G	P	O	S	S	C
E	C	O	E	S	N	F	H	A	A	U	H	E	R	I	P	C	J	B	W
O	Y	W	T	D	M	E	S	T	N	D	N	O	R	G	I	E	Z	G	R
V	G	B	F	O	R	E	D	D	N	G	S	I	U	Z	D	M	V	R	O
K	A	L	A	Z	G	I	O	L	A	I	T	E	Y	S	O	L	E	Z	S
I	U	O	G	C	E	W	B	V	O	S	T	P	N	N	E	V	O	E	J
M	Y	T	N	F	N	A	L	E	O	G	K	O	S	D	O	M	Y	C	P
J	C	I	I	K	H	M	H	F	U	D	N	T	O	L	E	W	Q	R	Z
Q	I	V	N	A	M	U	T	N	K	L	E	O	L	F	S	W	I	T	C
M	P	Z	R	U	P	H	E	D	Y	R	B	O	P	K	E	F	Y	D	M
M	R	Z	O	O	E	M	K	B	I	E	R	E	F	A	I	R	Y	N	K
P	H	G	M	D	Y	Q	D	N	L	T	E	G	H	F	I	O	A	V	A
Z	U	G	E	S	O	H	L	E	W	T	I	P	H	T	U	L	F	B	Y
H	L	A	H	Z	K	A	Y	M	L	R	Z	F	J	T	Y	Z	U	Z	U
O	D	U	T	I	W	M	B	M	S	L	F	S	H	A	H	U	C	J	V

☐	A DOLL'S HOUSE	☐	AGNES OF GOD
☐	ANY WEDNESDAY	☐	BAREFOOT IN THE PARK
☐	HURRY SUNDOWN	☐	JULIA
☐	MONSTER-IN-LAW	☐	OLD GRINGO
☐	ON GOLDEN POND	☐	ROLLOVER
☐	SPIRITS OF THE DEAD	☐	STANLEY - IRIS
☐	THE BLUE BIRD	☐	THE CHASE
☐	THE MORNING AFTER	☐	YOUTH

PICTURE PUZZLE 5. LAS VEGAS STRATOSPHERE WITH RIDES ON THE TOP

PICTURE PUZZLE 5. CIRCLE THE TEN DIFFERENCES

DIAGONAL WORD SQUARE PUZZLES

INSTRUCTIONS

Each row and the **diagonal** contain an English word in the square puzzles. **For the 3x3, 4x4 & 5x5 puzzles, the left column is also a word.** The following instructions assumes that the left column is not a word. Find the missing letters and write them in. For example, S_CK pattern can be satisfied by 4 words: SACK, SICK, SOCK and SUCK. The D_AL pattern can be solved by 3 words: DEAL, DIAL and DUAL. That means two solutions: SICK – DIAL and SUCK – DUAL.

In the solution section only a single solution is given.

Solving Word Puzzles Is a Fun Activity!

Improve & Expand Your Vocabulary!

Improve Your English Spelling!

Improve Your Memory the Easy Way!

Solving a Diagonal Word Square Puzzle

In the **diagonal word square puzzle**, the rows and the diagonal (upper left to lower right) contain words. The columns hold no words since very few puzzles can be constructed that way. When we see a word with missing first letter such as _IKE, our brain automatically jumps to a frequently used word with the same suffix: LIKE. But that may not be the correct word for the puzzle; therefore, we should consider other possibilities by going down the alphabet letter by letter: BIKE, DIKE, HIKE, MIKE, PIKE and RIPE. It is helpful to write down the list of possibilities on a scratchpad.

If two letters are missing, we may get a combinatorial explosion. Let's consider all the words for the **_I_E** two missing letters pattern.

1.	AIDE	28.	NICE
2.	BIKE	29.	NINE
3.	BITE	30.	PIKE
4.	DICE	31.	PILE
5.	DIKE	32.	PINE
6.	DIME	33.	PIPE
7.	DINE	34.	RICE
8.	DIRE	35.	RIDE
9.	DIVE	36.	RIPE
10.	FIDE	37.	RISE
11.	FINE	38.	SIDE
12.	FIRE	39.	SINE
13.	FIVE	40.	SITE
14.	GIVE	41.	SIZE
15.	HIDE	42.	TIDE
16.	HIKE	43.	TILE
17.	HIRE	44.	TIME
18.	KITE	45.	TINE
19.	LIFE	46.	TIRE
20.	LIKE	47.	VICE
21.	LIME	48.	VISE
22.	LINE	49.	WIDE
23.	LIVE	50.	WIFE
24.	MICE	51.	WINE
25.	MILE	52.	WIPE
26.	MINE	53.	WIRE
27.	MIRE	54.	WISE

That is a huge number of choices. Therefore when we work on a diagonal word square puzzle, we should select first the word pattern with the least possibilities.

Let's take an example puzzle and find a solution the easiest way possible.

	H	I	P
		O	W
C		I	
		U	R

It is promising to start with the first row. Let's go through the alphabet to find word matching the _HIP pattern. **CHIP SHIP WHIP**

Let's try CHIP first. Using a pencil, write"C"into the upper left box.

C	H	I	P
		O	W
C		I	
		U	R

Unfortunately, we cannot find a word match for the C_IR diagonal pattern. Therefore we should erase C and try S for SHIP.

S	H	I	P
		O	W
C		I	
		U	R

If we try the letters of the alphabet, we find one word for the diagonal: STIR. Let's pencil it in.

S	H	I	P
	T	O	W
C		I	
		U	R

We a created a new 3 letter pattern _TOW in the second row. One word matches the pattern: STOW.

S	H	I	P
S	T	O	W
C		I	
		U	R

For the 3rd and 4th row patterns (C_I_ & __UR), we can use any match if there are multiple matches since the dependency on the diagonal STIR is already satisfied.

List of C_I_ words:

CHIN CHIP CLIP COIL COIN CRIB

We can use any of the words, example COIN.

S	H	I	P
S	T	O	W
C	O	I	N
		U	R

List of __UR words:

BLUR FOUR HOUR POUR SOUR SPUR TOUR YOUR

We can use anyone of the words to satisfy the puzzle, for example"TOUR".

S	H	I	P
S	T	O	W
C	O	I	N
T	O	U	R

That completes the diagonal word square puzzle.

Note that the book solution section shows only one solution even when multiple solutions are available.

Let's return the list of first row words and try the third one (WHIP).

W	H	I	P
		O	W
C		I	
		U	R

There is no word find for the diagonal pattern W_IR. Therefore we found all the solutions for this diagonal word square puzzle.

3x3 DIAGONAL WORD SQUARE PUZZLES

Wise sayings: "YOU REAP WHAT YOU SOW."

Rows, Diagonal & Left Column contain words.

Puzzle 1.

	B	
	T	
D		

Puzzle 2.

	N	Y
		N
M		L

Puzzle 3.

		E
		L
T		N

Puzzle 4.

	E	N
V		
	I	G

Puzzle 5.

	E	N
A		
M	R	

Puzzle 6.

	U	B
	A	R
		B

Puzzle 7.

F	I	
A		
	U	O

Puzzle 8.

		G
O	A	
	E	T

Puzzle 9.

	N	D
		E
	A	B

Puzzle 10.

	A	R
A		T
R		

Puzzle 11.

B	O	
		R
	O	N

Puzzle 12.

O	F	
	I	P
	E	

4x4 DIAGONAL WORD SQUARE PUZZLES

"YOU CAN'T TEACH AN OLD DOG NEW TRICKS."

Puzzle 1.

O		L	
		U	E
R		L	E
	U		E

Puzzle 2.

	X	E	
		T	S
T			K
S	H		E

Puzzle 3.

E	X		T
	M	I	
R	A		
S			A

Puzzle 4.

S	P		Y
		I	C
A	L		
	E		M

Puzzle 5.

F			K
A			H
C		O	
	R	A	M

Puzzle 6.

B			Y
L		S	
A	G		D
	A		N

Puzzle 7.

	U	V	
		N	E
	L	O	
K	N	E	

Puzzle 8.

	E		E
A	R		
		E	M
		E	W

Puzzle 9.

S			D
I			H
T		A	N
	L	A	

Puzzle 10.

P	I		
L		N	
O			S
	E	A	M

Puzzle 11.

	O	N	E
		E	S
	O		F
	A		Y

Puzzle 12.

O		A	L
		N	E
	E	C	
S			E

5x5 DIAGONAL WORD SQUARE PUZZLES

"KEEP YOUR FRIENDS CLOSE & YOUR ENEMIES CLOSER."

Puzzle 1.

T		N	E	
	A		L	Y
L		M		T
	I	K		D
		O	L	D

Puzzle 2.

S	E		V	
	T	O	M	
N			S	Y
D	R	U		
S	H			K

Puzzle 3.

B	I	R		
A	I	R		
R			E	R
G		B		
	X	A	L	

Puzzle 4.

P	O	K		
	R	M		R
N			C	E
E		M		R
	O		I	N

Puzzle 5.

	X	A		S
L			D	
	A	T		M
E		V		S
		V	E	N

Puzzle 6.

F	A		M	
A		O		T
L			K	S
S			U	T
E		E	C	

Puzzle 7.

	R	I		K
		B	I	N
I	R		T	
E	R	A		
F		O		

Puzzle 8.

	A	I	S	
A	R	R		
	H	O	D	
T		B		O
S	T		I	

Puzzle 9.

	A		E	L
		L	E	N
S			L	
E		U		E
	T	O	L	

"LOOK BEFORE YOU LEAP."

Puzzle 10.

	L	U	S	
	E			Y
		T	I	C
	A		C	H
N			P	H

Puzzle 11.

C	L		P	
A		P	H	
	K	I		
T		U	M	
	H	R	U	

Puzzle 12.

		N	E	
	D	U		T
		O	N	Y
E	V		R	
	H	O	E	

Puzzle 13.

		M	M	
	U	D	I	
	A	S		S
	H	R	I	
H	A			C

Puzzle 14.

S	W	I		
T	H		O	
E		E	N	
A				Y
M			O	R

Puzzle 15.

	O	L	D	
	O		E	
E	L			R
W			M	S
		M	O	

Puzzle 16.

C	H	I		
	I		L	
V	I			D
E	D		I	
S		E	A	

Puzzle 17.

C	O		L	
A		D		R
	T	U		F
	X	A		
S		R		

Puzzle 18.

		A	S	
E	Q			L
	A		G	H
L		T	I	
	P	E		D

"IT'S NO USE CRYING OVER SPILLED MILK."

Puzzle 19.

			R	Y
	R		A	N
S	H		L	
	I	R	E	
S		N	U	

Puzzle 20.

G	O	L		
	A	K		S
		B	O	T
D	O		B	
	S	S		

Puzzle 21.

	D	R		M
R			G	S
U	R			D
M	O			R
		I	E	R

Puzzle 22.

	R	O		E
	L		C	T
	D		P	T
	O	U	N	
H	O			S

Puzzle 23.

		A		S
O			L	Y
		R	L	
T		M	O	
S	A	L		

Puzzle 24.

S	O			D
		D	R	O
A		L		Y
S	C			E
M	U			S

Puzzle 25.

T	R			
H	A			H
	O	C		
E	V			E
	A		K	

Puzzle 26.

		N	E	S
	A		N	S
		B	E	S
		U	A	L
S	H			L

Puzzle 27.

			R	Y
	L	L		N
		E	C	T
	I	N	E	
S			L	T

"ONLY THE STUPID NEVER CHANGE."

Puzzle 28.

P			M	S
	E	A	F	
E	X		L	
A	W	A		
D	A		T	

Puzzle 29.

P			N	
L	A			E
	P		L	Y
N			E	D
E		D		R

Puzzle 30.

F	A	I		
I		O		S
R		I	N	
	E	A	L	
		E	L	L

Puzzle 31.

		X	I	S
	R	M	E	
S		A		Y
		T	I	E
	L		I	N

Puzzle 32.

	A		C	
	A	N		S
	C		R	
P	O			S
S		L	E	

Puzzle 33.

	W	E	L	
E	R	U		
A		I	C	
L		R		A
S				E

Puzzle 34.

	U	M	O	
R		D	E	
E	R		O	
A			E	R
T			N	D

Puzzle 35.

	L	I		E
	W		N	G
N		E		E
	L	T		R
R		L	E	

Puzzle 36.

	I	G	H	
L	O			S
A			I	N
M			E	D
A	B		S	

Find & Circle: PUPPY(2), ZEBRA, SNAIL, CAMEL, SHEEP(2), RHINO, OTTER(2), HORSE, GECKO, BONGO(2) in Each Quadrant

U	P	P	P	P	U	P	U	E	A	A	E	R	E	Z	Z	L	S	A	S	A	L	N	L
P	P	P	P	P	Y	P	P	A	Z	A	B	Z	Z	Z	R	L	S	I	A	S	N	S	L
P	U	U	P	P	U	P	Y	E	B	R	B	Z	Z	E	A	S	I	S	L	A	N	L	N
U	Y	P	P	P	U	P	P	E	Z	A	Z	B	A	A	E	I	I	N	L	A	S	N	L
P	Y	U	P	P	U	P	P	B	E	A	R	R	E	A	E	S	A	L	I	N	A	L	S
U	P	U	Y	U	Y	P	P	A	Z	R	Z	B	R	Z	Z	I	A	L	A	A	A	I	S
Y	P	U	Y	P	P	Y	P	Z	B	R	Z	Z	E	Z	A	S	S	S	S	L	I	A	S
P	P	P	P	Y	Y	P	U	R	Z	E	R	B	A	Z	E	L	L	L	L	L	L	I	I
A	M	E	E	E	A	C	E									P	H	P	H	S	S	H	H
L	C	M	C	L	A	A	C									S	E	E	E	S	S	P	E
E	L	L	E	M	L	C	L									H	P	H	P	E	E	H	E
A	A	M	L	L	E	C	M									S	E	S	E	E	H	E	P
L	A	M	C	L	M	E	C									E	E	E	H	S	E	S	H
C	L	A	C	M	L	C	M									E	P	H	H	H	S	H	S
A	L	E	E	A	C	E	L									P	P	P	H	E	E	E	S
E	A	E	M	C	M	C	C									E	H	E	H	H	E	H	S
I	R	O	R	I	H	N	N									R	T	E	T	T	R	R	E
N	R	O	O	H	I	R	I									E	O	O	E	R	T	T	E
O	O	H	R	O	I	N	I									T	T	R	T	T	R	O	T
R	H	I	H	R	N	N	H									T	T	O	E	E	E	R	T
O	H	H	R	I	H	O	O									E	R	T	T	T	E	O	T
N	H	N	H	H	H	H	I									T	T	T	T	T	T	T	T
N	H	I	R	H	H	I	N									E	O	E	E	R	T	O	T
N	R	I	I	O	R	N	O									T	R	T	R	O	O	T	T
S	R	R	R	E	H	R	E	C	C	K	C	C	C	E	K	G	O	O	O	O	B	O	O
E	E	R	S	O	R	O	S	K	K	K	K	C	E	G	E	N	O	G	B	G	O	B	B
E	H	E	H	S	S	S	H	K	K	C	E	C	E	E	C	G	O	O	N	G	G	O	B
O	R	O	S	S	S	R	S	E	E	K	O	C	G	G	C	B	B	O	N	O	G	G	G
S	S	O	S	R	S	H	O	G	K	C	K	O	E	C	K	O	N	O	O	B	B	O	G
S	H	E	R	S	O	H	O	O	C	O	C	K	K	C	E	O	B	N	N	O	O	N	G
H	E	S	S	R	S	H	E	C	G	G	O	E	E	C	E	N	O	O	G	O	G	G	G
S	O	S	H	S	O	S	H	C	K	O	C	C	C	C	C	O	G	N	G	G	B	O	G

6x6 DIAGONAL WORD SQUARE PUZZLES

"ALL GOOD THINGS MUST COME TO AN END."

Puzzle 1.

	R	T		S	
B	L		O		
O	P	T			
	E		E	S	S
T			A	R	D
S		E		L	S

Puzzle 2.

S	O			E	N
			K	L	E
E	I			T	
	S	C	H	E	
			O	T	A
	P		R	T	

Puzzle 3.

S	I		I		E
			H	E	D
	A		I	U	S
		M		N	D
I			A		E
		S	S		U

Puzzle 4.

C		U	R	S	
		B		I	D
	X	P	E	C	
S		I			L
T		Y		U	S
S		A	R		

"THERE'S NO PLACE LIKE HOME."

Puzzle 5.

S	N				H
T		R	A		H
A			D	E	
	O	B	U	S	
C	A	N		L	
	E	L			D

Puzzle 6.

D	E		I		
	A	T		R	S
	O	Z		E	
A				O	N
D		A	B	L	
	S			P	E

Puzzle 7.

S		I		E	S
L			G	T	
		W		R	D
E		S		Y	S
P		L		G	
	I	Z		L	E

Puzzle 8.

P	O		N	D	
A		T	E		
S	I			T	
S				T	S
E		I	S	T	
	U	N		A	Y

"EASY COME, EASY GO."

Puzzle 9.

A	R	C			
S	P	E			H
T	R		O	P	
H		N	G		R
	A	R	R		
A	R	O			

Puzzle 10.

D		P	O		T
R	E		A		E
	S		A		S
A	C	T			
M		N		G	
S	H		K		N

Puzzle 11.

	O		I	E	D
	A	I			D
O	N	L	I		
C	R	A			
U	N				D
S		R	U		S

Puzzle 12.

S	A			A	L
P			K	E	
	E			E	R
I	M		I		E
		E	N	T	Y
	M		O		Y

7x7 DIAGONAL WORD SQUARE PUZZLES

"A CHAIN IS ONLY AS STRONG AS ITS WEAKEST LINK."

Rows & Diagonal contain words.

Puzzle 1.

	E			C	L	E
	E	N		I	O	
		V		R	E	D
A		T		N		O
R	E	C			L	
R			O	L	V	
	E	R	B		S	E

Puzzle 2.

L			K	J	A	
	E	F	E	N		
		N	N	I		S
	N		G	G		D
C	O	U	N			Y
D	R			G	H	
R	E		E		L	

Puzzle 3.

B	I	Z			R	
C	E		A			C
H	Y	D			N	T
E	M			I		D
F			D	I		G
S	C		E			S
	B	T		U		E

Puzzle 4.

	E			G	O	N
R	A			O		N
R		T	U	R		
C		N			A	L
	A	R	S	H		S
A	P		L		E	
	T	R	I		E	

"TIME IS MONEY."

Puzzle 5.

	Q	U	A		O	
L	A				R	D
	L	U			E	R
		U	N	T	E	
F		A			E	R
B	R	U	I		E	
G	R	A	Z			

Puzzle 6.

		E	C	U	T	
E		I	N	E		
	O	B		E	B	
	S	S	A			T
A	R		U	S	E	
		T	C	A		T
T	H		R		L	

Puzzle 7.

	R	A		P	E	
	R	D		R	E	D
R	O			I		G
A	L		M	N		
F		R	E		A	
C		U	C			L
C		A	V	I		

Puzzle 8.

S	U		M			G
S		O	U	R		
P	R	O	C			
	M	A	L		A	
	O	R		D	L	Y
B		A		G	E	
B	L	O			E	

"TWO IS COMPANY, THREE IS A CROWD."

Puzzle 9.

		I	L		Z	E
	N		E	R		E
	R	C	H			Y
	O		A		C	O
I	S	L		N		
H	O	L			N	
L		O	S		L	Y

Puzzle 10.

K	E		C	H		
E	N	Q				E
		O	T	T		D
C	O	B	W	E		
	E		T	I	N	
P			F	I		G
H	A		G	I		

Puzzle 11.

		T	C	H		R
P	R	E		A		D
		U	C	H	E	
	R		S	Q		E
P		T	C		E	
M	U			I		R
F	L			P	E	

Puzzle 12.

M	I		R	O		
M			I	M	A	
I	N		I	A		
P	E		T	I		G
B	U		K		R	
W		N	N		R	
	N	T	O		Y	

8x8 DIAGONAL WORD SQUARE PUZZLES

"WISE SAYING:"A BIRD IN THE HAND IS WORTH TWO IN THE BUSH."

Puzzle 1.

S		I		M	E		T
	T		A	P		E	
E			N	O	M		C
			C	I	O	U	S
C		E		K	E		S
S				K	I	N	G
C	U		H		O		S
C			I		I	N	

Puzzle 2.

		L	E		T	E	D
S		R	A	D	D		
B		A			I	N	
		E		R	I	E	S
M	E	A		T		M	
S		U		T		E	
D	A	R		E	N		
P		O	F	I			D

Puzzle 3.

C	H	O			I		G
W	O		D	S			P
		M	P	O			D
		R	M	I	N		
		C	T	U		U	S
S	O		I	E			L
	E			C	L		S
P		L	L	S	T		

Puzzle 4.

	N	L	A	R		E	
	N		O	N		M	S
E		T		T	L	E	
	P	E		A	T		R
N	E			A		K	A
H	A		I				A
	R		P	H			Y
A	U	D		E			E

"IT'S NOT OVER 'TILL THE FAT LADY SINGS."

Puzzle 5.

			D	U	C	E	S
				R	A	S	T
A	P		E			I	
D	I	S		E			E
N	A		T	I			L
B	A	R	B				E
V		L			B		E
P			T		C	L	

Puzzle 6.

I	N	E	D	I			
I	N		I			N	G
	T		I	O		I	
W	A	T	E			A	
T			E	R	I	N	
	O	M		S		C	
B	L			K		T	S
	I	N		S	H	E	

Puzzle 7.

				L	I	N	G
		S	C	O		O	
		O		G	H	T	S
			G	H	T	L	Y
	U	M	E	R			S
	O		T	R		C	T
			D	P		P	E
C	H	I			I	S	

Puzzle 8.

R	E	L		A	S		
		C		R		N	G
	N	Q	U	I			D
T	R	O	U			E	
	U		S	I		E	D
S	U	P		O	R		
T		X		A	Y		R
R	A		C	H			

"NEVER LOOK A GIFT HORSE IN THE MOUTH."

Puzzle 9.

A		J	A		E		
E	P	I		E	M		
B	E	H	E		O		
C		R	E	L			S
S	A			L		N	G
	A		E	R	I	N	
G			N		S		N
H			G	H	T		N

Puzzle 10.

T		O	U			N	D
	R	I		I	N		L
			R	T	I		G
R			U			E	D
D	O		M		D		Y
	A	R	E	W		L	
A			W	H		R	E
	A	I	N	L	E		

Puzzle 11.

		I	N		A		N
				O	O	D	Y
K		N		N	E	S	
A	C	Q			R		D
P			R	M		C	Y
Q		O	T			N	T
M	I	D	P	O			
	U	M	O	R		S	

Puzzle 12.

		D	C	O		E	R
S	E	P			A	T	
Q	U	A	G	M			
	L	O				C	E
H	E			I	E		T
	U	T			N		S
B	E		R	U			E
		U		N	E	Y	S

9x9 DIAGONAL WORD SQUARE PUZZLES

"DON'T BITE THE HAND THAT FEEDS YOU."

Puzzle 1.

E	N			E	S	S		
		E			I	S	E	S
C		E	R	G		M		
S		A	C		W	A		K
D	I		C	R	E			
U				L	A	T		D
	E		C	R	I	B	E	
	I	T	I			L	L	Y
S		A	I				S	E

Puzzle 2.

U	N					A	K	E
	N	H	E			T	H	
	E		U			I	V	E
	L	U	E			R	R	Y
	E		A	R	A		E	S
T	R		N	C		A		T
	M	B		R			S	S
A		S		S		A	N	
		R	F	B		A		D

Puzzle 3.

D	I		P			S		L
D		F	E	N			N	G
	I		W	A	U		E	E
P			I	T	I		A	
	X	P	A			I	N	
D	I	S	P		E		S	
	S			I	L	A		T
	E				A	N	T	S
	I		H	T	R	O		

Puzzle 4.

		S	H	E		M		N
R		S		N	T		U	L
P	E			A	N			T
	N	I				L	L	Y
O	B	E				N	C	E
	A		K		L	I	D	E
		T		C	T		V	E
E	T	I	Q	U				
				F	U	L	L	Y

"GOOD THINGS COME TO THOSE WHO WAIT."

Puzzle 5.

E				U	N		E	R
E	L			E	M		N	
	T	I	N	E	R		R	
A		A	Z				N	T
D	I	S			R			D
S			L	A	B			S
	N	D			W	E	A	
		T	O		I	E	T	Y
W	O		K	B	E	N		

Puzzle 6.

D	E	P				I		N
D		V	I	L		E		T
I			R		S	S		D
		D	E		T	A	R	
T	E			N	I		A	
	R	O	C	E		U		E
I	N			P		E	N	
	T	R	I			E	N	T
C		N	F			A		T

Puzzle 7.

	O		B			E	S	S
P		N		T			T	E
C	E	L	E	S				
	E	L	I	G		O	U	
N		S		V	I		L	
		F	L	U	E			E
D			N	W		R	D	S
	R	G		N	I	Z		S
E		E	R	C	I			

Puzzle 8.

S	U					A	S	H
S	Y	N	T	H	E			
T	O	M		T	I			
S	U	S	P					N
C		M		O	T		O	
P	U	R		O				Y
C	L	U			H	I		G
	N	G	E			O		S
	E	T	R	O			U	M

"SLOW AND STEADY WINS THE RACE."

Puzzle 9.

F		E	N			M	E	
	E	S	P		C	T		D
B	L		M	E			S	S
		N	R		N	D	O	
B	U	L		F	R			
S	U	R	R	O				S
	I				U	L	L	Y
S		R	I	O		S		
D	O		E	F				Y

Puzzle 10.

				E	S	T	E	R
	R		D	U	C	I		
P	R		B	O		C	I	
D			F	E			N	G
C	O		Q	U		R		
	X		U	I	S	I		E
A		T		O	R			E
		O	C	E	S			R
A	D		I	S				N

Puzzle 11.

D				I	C	U	L	T
	I	L	L	I		E	S	
P		S	S				E	R
	R		G			N	C	E
			T	U	T	O		Y
I				L	I	T	I	C
W	I	S	C			S		
B					R	R	E	D
	L	E		E	L		N	

Puzzle 12.

C		N		I		E	N	T
	R	O				N	C	E
		U	G	A		I	T	
F	A		S	E		O		
	E	E		A		E	R	
T	O	R	N	A				S
N		R		H			S	T
N	E	I		H	B		R	
	R		H	R	I			S

PICTURE PUZZLE 6. STATUE OF LIBERTY WITH TOURIST BOAT

PICTURE PUZZLE 6. CIRCLE THE TEN DIFFERENCES

HOLLYWOOD MOVIE TRIVIA QUIZZES

"WISE SAYING:"A BIRD IN THE HAND IS WORTH TWO IN THE BUSH."

1. Which of the following movies: Divorce American Style; Royal Wedding; Susan Slept Here; This Happy Feeling; did not star Debbie Reynolds?

2. Which of the following movies: Baby Driver; Buffalo Bill; The Black Swan; The Hunchback of Notre Dame; did not co-star Maureen O'Hara & Thomas Mitchell?

3. Which of the following movies: Judge Hardy and Son; Out West with the Hardys; Say One for Me; The Hardys Ride High; did not co-star Cecilia Parker & Lewis Stone?

4. Which of the following movies: American Creed; The Black Cat; The Raven; You'll Find Out; did not star Boris Karloff?

5. Which of the following movies: Boccaccio '70; Island of Lost Souls; Jamaica Inn; The Hunchback of Notre Dame; did not star Charles Laughton?

6. Which of the following movies: Hard Candy; Miracle on 34th Street; To the Shores of Tripoli; Tripoli; did not co-star John Payne & Maureen O'Hara?

7. Which of the following movies: Léon: The Professional; Star Wars: Episode II - Attack of the Clones; The Bounty; V for Vendetta; did not star Natalie Portman?

ANSWERS: 1. GNIDDEW LAYOR 2. REVIRD YBAB 3. EM ROF ENO YAS 4. DEERC NACIREMA 5. 07' OICCACCOB 6. YDNAC DRAH 7. YTNUOB EHT

"IT'S NOT OVER 'TILL THE FAT LADY SINGS."

8. Which of the following movies: Dirty Harry; Magic; Misconduct; The Good Father; did not star Anthony Hopkins?

9. Which of the following movies: Brokeback Mountain; Donnie Darko; Love & Other Drugs; The Rocketeer; did not star Jake Gyllenhaal?

10. Which of the following movies: Aftermath (IV); Doctor Faustus; The V.I.P.s; Under Milk Wood; did not star Richard Burton?

11. Which of the following movies: A Time to Kill; June Night; The Lincoln Lawyer; The Paperboy; did not star Matthew McConaughey?

12. Which of the following movies: Inside Man; Killer Elite; The Bank Dick; The Bourne Identity; did not star Clive Owen?

13. Which of the following movies: Criss Cross; Escape Me Never; Judgment at Nuremberg; The Professionals; did not star Burt Lancaster?

14. Which of the following movies: Looking for Mr. Goodbar; Role Models; Something's Gotta Give; The Godfather; did not star Diane Keaton?

ANSWERS: 8. YRRAH YTRID 9. REETEKCOR EHT 10.)VI(HTAMRETFA 11. THGIN ENUJ 12. KCID KNAB EHT 13. REVEN EM EPACSE 14. SLEDOM ELOR

"YOU CAN NEVER EAT A PIE IN THE SKY."

15. Which of the following movies: Broken Lance; No Way Out; The Alamo; Zoolander; did not star Richard Widmark?

16. Which of the following movies: June Night; The Children's Hour; The Evening Star; These Old Broads; did not star Shirley MacLaine?

17. Which of the following movies: Flying Tigers; Marooned; Rambo: First Blood Part II; Wait Until Dark; did not star Richard Crenna?

18. Which of the following movies: Lust for Life; Man of the Year; The Fisher King; What Dreams May Come; did not star Robin Williams?

19. Which of the following movies: Key Largo; Save the Tiger; The Big Sleep; To Have and Have Not; did not co-star Humphrey Bogart & Lauren Bacall?

20. Which of the following movies: Carefree; Mister Cory; The Story of Vernon and Irene Castle; Top Hat; did not co-star Fred Astaire & Ginger Rogers?

21. Which of the following movies: Lover Come Back; Pillow Talk; Send Me No Flowers; White Heat; did not co-star Doris Day, Rock Hudson & Tony Randall?

ANSWERS: 15. REDNALOOZ 16. THGIN ENUJ 17. SREGIT GNIYLF 18. EFIL ROF TSUL 19. REGIT EHT EVAS 20. YROC RETSIM 21. TAEH ETIHW

"THE BEST THINGS IN LIFE ARE FREE."

22. Which of the following movies: Captain Ron; Ocean's 11; Robin and the 7 Hoods; Sergeants 3; did not co-star Dean Martin, Frank Sinatra & Sammy Davis Jr.?

23. Which of the following movies: A Bronx Tale; Rocky II; Rocky III; Rocky IV; did not co-star Burt Young & Sylvester Stallone?

24. Which of the following movies: Maytime; Naughty Marietta; Rose-Marie; The Class of 92; did not co-star Jeanette MacDonald & Nelson Eddy?

25. Which of the following movies: Happy Feet; The Fountain; The Freshman; X-Men 2; did not star Hugh Jackman?

26. Which of the following movies: Judge Hardy's Children; Out West with the Hardys; Swept Away; The Hardys Ride High; did not star Fay Holden?

27. Which of the following movies: Cactus Flower; Randy Rides Alone; Sagebrush Trail; The Star Packer; did not co-star John Wayne & Yakima Canutt?

28. Which of the following movies: All the King's Men; Closer; Gattaca; Johnny Guitar; did not star Jude Law?

ANSWERS: 22. NOR NIATPAC 23. ELAT XNORB A 24. 29 FO SSALC EHT 25. NAMHSERF EHT 26. YAWA TPEWS 27. REWOLF SUTCAC 28. RATIUG YNNHOJ

Hollywood Movie Actors & Actresses Search Puzzle 1.

D	Y	S	U	G	E	F	F	I	O	S	M	B	D	Z	E	S	P	O	Y	O
C	E	K	K	H	T	G	C	R	A	P	U	S	A	I	V	O	U	E	T	C
A	N	U	H	K	S	A	H	E	C	A	H	J	V	C	T	B	A	O	J	R
T	G	R	E	N	E	Z	G	K	H	U	C	M	I	L	G	Y	N	R	A	S
E	A	T	N	E	G	D	I	R	B	D	T	F	D	I	C	R	A	N	C	R
B	C	R	R	E	D	R	E	A	H	R	I	E	N	N	H	O	M	O	K	E
L	S	U	Y	U	I	O	L	P	L	E	M	C	I	T	T	B	W	M	N	G
A	E	S	F	Q	R	C	N	A	L	Y	T	I	V	E	I	I	E	N	I	O
N	M	S	O	C	B	K	E	I	A	H	R	R	E	A	E	N	N	Y	C	R
C	A	E	N	M	F	H	I	L	B	E	E	P	N	S	K	W	L	L	H	R
H	J	L	D	E	F	U	V	I	E	P	B	T	F	T	N	I	U	I	O	E
E	R	L	A	V	E	D	I	C	L	B	O	N	N	W	A	L	A	R	L	G
T	Z	T	L	E	J	S	V	E	L	U	R	E	W	O	I	L	P	A	S	N
T	R	M	C	T	T	O	S	C	I	R	H	C	I	O	R	I	B	M	O	I
Z	S	N	Z	S	U	N	W	A	C	N	V	N	U	D	B	A	T	Y	N	G
F	A	Y	H	O	L	D	E	N	U	V	M	I	J	R	H	M	Q	J	H	D
E	N	Y	A	W	N	H	O	J	L	G	N	V	N	K	R	S	B	K	W	M
H	K	C	Y	W	N	A	T	S	A	R	A	B	R	A	B	U	Q	Q	Z	I
B	R	A	D	P	I	T	T	L	E	T	I	E	K	Y	E	V	R	A	H	B
S	N	H	O	I	U	R	I	C	H	A	R	D	B	U	R	T	O	N	I	S
M	W	A	L	T	E	R	M	A	T	T	H	A	U	A	Y	L	J	C	D	B

☐ AUDREY HEPBURN	☐ BARBARA STANWYCK	☐ BRAD PITT	☐ BRIAN KEITH
☐ CATE BLANCHETT	☐ CECILIA PARKER	☐ CLINT EASTWOOD	☐ DAVID NIVEN
☐ FAY HOLDEN	☐ GINGER ROGERS	☐ HARVEY KEITEL	☐ HENRY FONDA
☐ JACK NICHOLSON	☐ JAMES CAGNEY	☐ JEFF BRIDGES	☐ JOHN WAYNE
☐ KURT RUSSELL	☐ LUCILLE BALL	☐ MARILYN MONROE	☐ PAUL NEWMAN
☐ RICHARD BURTON	☐ ROBERT MITCHUM	☐ ROBIN WILLIAMS	☐ ROCK HUDSON
☐ STEVE MCQUEEN	☐ VINCENT PRICE	☐ VIVIEN LEIGH	☐ WALTER MATTHAU

"DON'T PUT THE CART BEFORE THE HORSE."

29. Which of the following movies: Newsies; Slap Shot; The Train Robbers; The Villain; did not star Ann-Margret?

30. Which of the following movies: From the Terrace; Matthew and Son; The Drowning Pool; Winning; did not co-star Joanne Woodward & Paul Newman?

31. Which of the following movies: Hannah and Her Sisters; Little Man Tate; The Birdcage; The Purple Mask; did not star Dianne Wiest?

32. Which of the following movies: Adventureland; Divorce His - Divorce Hers; The V.I.P.s; Under Milk Wood; did not co-star Elizabeth Taylor & Richard Burton?

33. Which of the following movies: Deception; Juarez; Now, Voyager; The Master; did not co-star Bette Davis & Claude Rains?

34. Which of the following movies: Haven; Pirates of the Caribbean: Dead Man's Chest; The Blue Bird; The Lord of the Rings: The Fellowship of the Ring; did not star Orlando Bloom?

35. Which of the following movies: Bedtime for Bonzo; Crossed Swords; Girls on Probation; The Girl from Jones Beach; did not star Ronald Reagan?

ANSWERS: 29. TOHS PALS 30. NOS DNA WEHTTAM 31. KSAM ELPRUP EHT 32. DNALERUTNEVDA 33. RETSAM EHT 34. DRIB EULB EHT 35. SDROWS DESSORC

"A GOOD WOMAN IS THE CROWN JEWEL OF A HOUSEHOLD."

36. Which of the following movies: Road to Singapore; Road to Utopia; Star Spangled Rhythm; Taking Lives; did not co-star Bing Crosby & Bob Hope?

37. Which of the following movies: A Doll's House; Kelly's Heroes; Peace, Love & Misunderstanding; This Is Where I Leave You; did not star Jane Fonda?

38. Which of the following movies: 3 Godfathers; Dersu Uzala; The Searchers; The Wings of Eagles; did not star Ward Bond?

39. Which of the following movies: Fancy Pants; Forever, Darling; On Golden Pond; Yours, Mine and Ours; did not star Lucille Ball?

40. Which of the following movies: August: Osage County; Bad Lieutenant; Confessions of a Dangerous Mind; Valentine's Day; did not star Julia Roberts?

41. Which of the following movies: Rocky; Rocky II; Rocky IV; The Bears and I; did not co-star Carl Weathers & Sylvester Stallone?

42. Which of the following movies: Invictus; Masquerade; The Departed; The Martian; did not star Matt Damon?

ANSWERS: 36. SEVIL GNIKAT 37. SEOREH S'YLLEK 38. ALAZU USRED 39. DNOP NEDLOG NO 40. TNANETUEIL DAB 41. I DNA SRAEB EHT 42. EDAREUQSAM

"THE APPLE DOESN'T FALL FAR FROM THE TREE."

43. Which of the following movies: Days of Thunder; Halloween; Open Range; Wrestling Ernest Hemingway; did not star Robert Duvall?

44. Which of the following movies: Midnight Lace; On Moonlight Bay; Taxi Driver; The Ballad of Josie; did not star Doris Day?

45. Which of the following movies: Andy Hardy Meets Debutante; How Do You Know; Judge Hardy and Son; The Courtship of Andy Hardy; did not co-star Cecilia Parker, Fay Holden & Lewis Stone?

46. Which of the following movies: ffolkes; Forever, Darling; Kagemusha; The Verdict; did not star James Mason?

47. Which of the following movies: Dangerous; Hideous Kinky; Of Human Bondage; Special Agent; did not star Bette Davis?

48. Which of the following movies: Detective Story; Strangers When We Meet; The Bad and the Beautiful; Too Many Girls; did not star Kirk Douglas?

49. Which of the following movies: Girl, Interrupted; Maleficent; Taking Lives; True Grit; did not star Angelina Jolie?

ANSWERS: 43. NEEWOLLAH 44. REVIRD IXAT 45. WONK UOY OD WOH 46. AHSUMEGAK 47. YKNIK SUOEDIH 48. SLRIG YNAM OOT 49. TIRG EURT

"THE PEN IS MIGHTIER THAN THE SWORD."

50. Which of the following movies: Frankenstein Meets the Wolf Man; MacArthur; Night Monster; Son of Frankenstein; did not co-star Bela Lugosi & Lionel Atwill?

51. Which of the following movies: 10 to Midnight; Andy Hardy Gets Spring Fever; Andy Hardy Meets Debutante; Out West with the Hardys; did not co-star Cecilia Parker, Lewis Stone & Mickey Rooney?

52. Which of the following movies: A Woman's Face; Casablanca; Hello, Dolly!; Under Capricorn; did not star Ingrid Bergman?

53. Which of the following movies: Death to Smoochy; Home Alone; Peace, Love & Misunderstanding; Synecdoche, New York; did not star Catherine Keener?

54. Which of the following movies: Death Wish II; Meet John Doe; The Mechanic; The Valachi Papers; did not star Jill Ireland?

55. Which of the following movies: Seven Samurai; The Quiet Duel; Throne of Blood; Trading Places; did not star Toshirô Mifune?

56. Which of the following movies: Birthday Girl; Jet Pilot; The Manchurian Candidate; The Perfect Furlough; did not star Janet Leigh?

ANSWERS: 50. RUHTRACAM 51. THGINDIM OT 01 52. !YLLOD ,OLLEH 53. ENOLA EMOH 54. EOD NHOJ TEEM 55. SECALP GNIDART 56. LRIG YADHTRIB

Hollywood Movie Actors & Actresses Search Puzzle 2.

A	L	P	A	C	I	N	O	S	P	E	N	C	E	R	T	R	A	C	Y	I
F	R	E	D	M	A	C	M	U	R	R	A	Y	Y	A	D	S	I	R	O	D
U	D	D	E	A	N	M	A	R	T	I	N	Q	M	Z	E	F	D	Z	L	Y
A	D	K	U	Y	J	O	K	E	O	J	E	I	J	L	U	P	W	O	A	W
G	K	A	I	A	F	B	A	T	Z	C	R	E	I	H	K	N	P	L	U	O
L	N	M	Y	E	I	J	T	S	K	E	I	W	L	U	Q	E	J	I	R	D
Z	C	R	E	L	S	O	H	A	C	Z	A	E	L	J	W	T	A	V	E	Y
D	F	O	N	I	O	D	A	C	O	Y	T	Q	I	I	F	T	M	I	N	S
L	H	B	O	Z	G	I	R	N	L	B	S	M	R	E	J	O	E	A	C	N
A	W	E	O	A	U	E	I	A	L	S	A	L	E	W	O	C	S	D	E	O
R	O	R	R	B	L	F	N	L	U	O	D	E	L	A	H	H	M	E	O	V
A	O	T	Y	E	A	O	E	T	B	R	E	W	A	N	N	P	A	H	L	X
H	D	D	E	T	L	S	H	R	A	C	R	I	N	M	N	E	S	A	I	A
O	Y	U	K	H	E	T	E	U	R	G	F	S	D	C	Y	S	O	V	V	M
N	A	V	C	T	B	E	P	B	D	N	Q	S	B	G	D	O	N	I	I	Y
E	L	A	I	A	E	R	B	R	N	I	S	T	D	R	E	J	L	L	E	Z
E	L	L	M	Y	H	K	U	Q	A	B	I	O	T	E	P	B	Y	L	R	A
R	E	L	L	L	F	F	R	Q	S	J	Z	N	H	G	P	I	V	A	M	Q
U	N	D	L	O	F	P	N	F	Q	M	Z	E	Q	O	O	O	U	N	K	Q
A	P	C	A	R	Y	G	R	A	N	T	F	P	D	R	E	U	B	D	D	Z
M	J	J	C	T	E	L	S	N	I	W	E	T	A	K	W	E	N	B	H	I

☐ AL PACINO	☐ BELA LUGOSI	☐ BING CROSBY	☐ BURT LANCASTER
☐ CARY GRANT	☐ DEAN MARTIN	☐ DORIS DAY	☐ ELIZABETH TAYLOR
☐ EWAN MCGREGOR	☐ FRED ASTAIRE	☐ FRED MACMURRAY	☐ JAMES MASON
☐ JILL IRELAND	☐ JODIE FOSTER	☐ JOHNNY DEPP	☐ JOSEPH COTTEN
☐ KATE WINSLET	☐ KATHARINE HEPBURN	☐ LAURENCE OLIVIER	☐ LEWIS STONE
☐ MAUREEN O'HARA	☐ MAX VON SYDOW	☐ MICKEY ROONEY	☐ OLIVIA DE HAVILLAND
☐ ROBERT DUVALL	☐ SANDRA BULLOCK	☐ SPENCER TRACY	☐ WOODY ALLEN

"STRIKE WHILE THE IRON IS HOT."

57. Which of the following movies: Lucky Lady; Oliver Twist; The Conversation; Twilight; did not star Gene Hackman?

58. Which of the following movies: End of Days; Grumpier Old Men; Luv; The Great Race; did not star Jack Lemmon?

59. Which of the following movies: Dark Command; Mr. Lucky; Stagecoach; The High and the Mighty; did not co-star Claire Trevor & John Wayne?

60. Which of the following movies: Changeling; Hell or High Water (II); Iron Man; The Big Lebowski; did not star Jeff Bridges?

61. Which of the following movies: Out West with the Hardys; The Exorcist; The Hardys Ride High; You're Only Young Once; did not co-star Fay Holden, Lewis Stone & Mickey Rooney?

62. Which of the following movies: Pirates of the Caribbean: At World's End; Pirates of the Caribbean: On Stranger Tides; Pirates of the Caribbean: The Curse of the Black Pearl; The Searchers; did not co-star Geoffrey Rush & Johnny Depp?

63. Which of the following movies: Pals of the Saddle; Red River Range; The Comedian; Three Texas Steers; did not co-star John Wayne & Max Terhune?

ANSWERS: 57. TSIWT REVILO 58. SYAD FO DNE 59. YKCUL .RM 60. GNILEGNAHC 61. TSICROXE EHT 62. SREHCRAES EHT 63. NAIDEMOC EHT

"THERE'S NO BIZ LIKE SHOWBIZ."

64. Which of the following movies: Burnt Offerings; The Lord of the Rings: The Fellowship of the Ring; The Lord of the Rings: The Return of the King; The Lord of the Rings: The Two Towers; did not co-star Elijah Wood, Ian McKellen & Orlando Bloom?

65. Which of the following movies: A High Wind in Jamaica; La Strada; Off Limits; Viva Zapata!; did not star Anthony Quinn?

66. Which of the following movies: Shrek 2; The Holiday; The Prestige; Vanilla Sky; did not star Cameron Diaz?

67. Which of the following movies: Dark Shadows; Lady Jane; Suffragette; The Far Country; did not star Helena Bonham Carter?

68. Which of the following movies: Bad Day at Black Rock; Billy Budd; Bloodline; The Longest Day; did not star Robert Ryan?

69. Which of the following movies: Don't Bother to Knock; Ladies of the Chorus; Shock Corridor; The Prince and the Showgirl; did not star Marilyn Monroe?

70. Which of the following movies: Death Wish II; How Sweet It Is!; My Fellow Americans; Victor Victoria; did not star James Garner?

ANSWERS: 64. SGNIREFFO TNRUB 65. STIMIL FFO 66. EGITSERP EHT 67. YRTNUOC RAF EHT 68. ENILDOOLB 69. RODIRROC KCOHS 70. II HSIW HTAED

"HASTE MAKES WASTE."

71. Which of the following movies: Charley and the Angel; Father Was a Fullback; Follow Me, Boys!; Stalag 17; did not star Fred MacMurray?

72. Which of the following movies: Elizabeth; Elizabeth: The Golden Age; Escape Me Never; Shine; did not star Geoffrey Rush?

73. Which of the following movies: Blue Skies; Marvin's Room; Pennies from Heaven; Road to Singapore; did not star Bing Crosby?

74. Which of the following movies: Camelot; The Cassandra Crossing; The Front; Unforgiven; did not star Richard Harris?

75. Which of the following movies: Love and Bullets; The Party; The Pawnbroker; The Specialist; did not star Rod Steiger?

76. Which of the following movies: Mister Cory; Road to Bali; Star Spangled Rhythm; The Cat and the Canary; did not star Bob Hope?

77. Which of the following movies: Hostile Waters; Now You See Him, Now You Don't; The Computer Wore Tennis Shoes; The Strongest Man in the World; did not co-star Cesar Romero, Joe Flynn & Kurt Russell?

ANSWERS: 71. 71 GALATS 72. REVEN EM EPACSE 73. MOOR S'NIVRAM 74. TNORF EHT 75. YTRAP EHT 76. YROC RETSIM 77. SRETAW ELITSOH

"HINDSIGHT IS 20/20."

78. Which of the following movies: F for Fake; Monte Carlo; The Lady from Shanghai; The Long, Hot Summer; did not star Orson Welles?

79. Which of the following movies: Guns of Diablo; John Wick; Master of the World; You Can't Win 'Em All; did not star Charles Bronson?

80. Which of the following movies: Eyes Wide Shut; Gold Diggers of 1935; Little Miss Marker; Paths of Glory; did not star Adolphe Menjou?

81. Which of the following movies: Bells Are Ringing; Sergeants 3; Some Came Running; The Sea Wolves; did not star Dean Martin?

82. Which of the following movies: Bronco Billy; Inside Daisy Clover; Sex and the Single Girl; Splendor in the Grass; did not star Natalie Wood?

83. Which of the following movies: Sorrowful Jones; Star Wars: Episode IV - A New Hope; Star Wars: Episode V - The Empire Strikes Back; Star Wars: The Last Jedi; did not co-star Carrie Fisher & Mark Hamill?

84. Which of the following movies: Now You See Him, Now You Don't; Superdad; The 'Burbs; The Computer Wore Tennis Shoes; did not co-star Joe Flynn & Kurt Russell?

ANSWERS: 78. OLRAC ETNOM 79. KCIW NHOJ 80. TUHS EDIW SEYE 81. SEVLOW AES EHT 82. YLLIB OCNORB 83. SENOJ LUFWORROS 84. SBRUB' EHT

Hollywood Movie Actors & Actresses Search Puzzle 3.

M	L	M	K	E	W	N	T	Q	P	S	I	R	C	D	L	A	N	O	D	U
O	J	R	O	I	I	M	E	G	E	O	R	G	E	B	R	E	N	T	D	E
R	N	A	N	I	Z	J	E	D	T	S	V	F	Y	Q	M	O	F	H	V	N
G	A	Z	N	Y	R	N	V	R	L	O	O	R	I	J	H	R	E	F	Y	I
A	R	Z	H	E	T	P	N	A	Y	O	N	V	M	L	C	L	F	T	H	A
N	T	A	B	E	F	L	A	I	Q	L	H	Y	G	W	E	N	Y	O	B	L
F	A	E	N	D	G	O	N	C	U	T	S	M	C	N	Z	F	Z	M	O	C
R	N	L	G	D	Z	Z	N	A	I	Q	F	T	A	U	H	V	W	H	R	A
E	I	V	E	I	O	Q	G	D	M	D	Y	B	R	I	R	M	E	A	I	M
E	S	I	N	E	F	L	U	E	A	F	O	N	D	E	L	T	B	N	S	Y
M	K	S	E	M	S	O	P	E	O	N	F	D	O	D	E	L	I	K	K	E
A	N	P	K	U	S	I	L	H	H	R	N	O	R	H	S	P	I	S	A	L
N	A	R	E	R	P	O	V	A	S	W	G	O	H	A	T	U	A	W	R	R
E	R	E	L	P	C	V	M	A	E	C	O	E	M	N	N	N	I	P	L	I
P	F	S	L	H	V	C	O	K	D	U	O	R	S	M	I	O	A	U	O	H
O	V	L	Y	Y	A	Z	S	E	S	E	S	T	R	A	E	T	E	D	F	S
H	J	E	Q	R	H	F	K	H	O	D	T	Q	T	A	N	L	S	L	F	J
B	T	Y	T	D	I	A	N	E	K	E	A	T	O	N	F	D	K	U	S	V
O	A	E	C	L	A	R	K	G	A	B	L	E	E	A	H	A	E	C	D	I
B	R	K	C	E	P	Y	R	O	G	E	R	G	D	B	Y	H	I	R	A	U
D	O	R	I	N	E	D	T	R	E	B	O	R	B	C	G	C	Q	M	S	J

☐ ANTHONY QUINN	☐ BETTE DAVIS	☐ BOB HOPE	☐ BORIS KARLOFF
☐ CLARK GABLE	☐ DIANE KEATON	☐ DONALD CRISP	☐ DUSTIN HOFFMAN
☐ EDDIE MURPHY	☐ ELVIS PRESLEY	☐ FRANK SINATRA	☐ GENE KELLY
☐ GEORGE BRENT	☐ GEORGE SANDERS	☐ GREGORY PECK	☐ HELENA BONHAM CARTER
☐ JACK LEMMON	☐ JANE FONDA	☐ LEONARDO DICAPRIO	☐ MERYL STREEP
☐ MIA FARROW	☐ MORGAN FREEMAN	☐ RANDOLPH SCOTT	☐ ROBERT DE NIRO
☐ SHIRLEY MACLAINE	☐ TOM HANKS	☐ TONY CURTIS	☐ WILLIAM HOLDEN

"COFFEE & LOVE TASTE BEST WHEN HOT."

85. Which of the following movies: Frenzy; Strangers on a Train; The Chief; To Catch a Thief; did not direct Alfred Hitchcock?

86. Which of the following movies: City of God; Dial M for Murder; Green Fire; The Bridges at Toko-Ri; did not star Grace Kelly?

87. Which of the following movies: Captain Horatio Hornblower R.N.; Mirage; Savage Sam; The World in His Arms; did not star Gregory Peck?

88. Which of the following movies: Andy Hardy Gets Spring Fever; Andy Hardy's Double Life; Judge Hardy and Son; Young at Heart; did not co-star Cecilia Parker & Fay Holden?

89. Which of the following movies: Adam's Rib; State of the Union; The Wild Bunch; Without Love; did not co-star Katharine Hepburn & Spencer Tracy?

90. Which of the following movies: A Yank at Oxford; Deception; Gentlemen's Agreement; That Hamilton Woman; did not star Vivien Leigh?

91. Which of the following movies: Harper; Murder on the Orient Express; Tombstone; Young Man with a Horn; did not star Lauren Bacall?

ANSWERS: 85. FEIHC EHT 86. DOG FO YTIC 87. MAS EGAVAS 88. TRAEH TA GNUOY 89. HCNUB DLIW EHT 90. NOITPECED 91. ENOTSBMOT

"THE ROAD TO HELL IS PAVED WITH GOOD INTENTIONS."

92. Which of the following movies: Bullets or Ballots; Double Indemnity; Harry Brown; The Prize; did not star Edward G. Robinson?

93. Which of the following movies: Overland Stage Raiders; The Jazz Singer; The Night Riders; Wyoming Outlaw; did not co-star John Wayne & Ray Corrigan?

94. Which of the following movies: A Double Life; The Great Muppet Caper; The Muppet Movie; The Muppets Take Manhattan; did not co-star Frank Oz & Jim Henson?

95. Which of the following movies: Agatha; Edison, the Man; Lenny; Straw Dogs; did not star Dustin Hoffman?

96. Which of the following movies: Babes in Arms; Easter Parade; Meet Me in St. Louis; The Great Lover; did not star Judy Garland?

97. Which of the following movies: Charade; Eraser; Pat Garrett & Billy the Kid; The Big Red One; did not star James Coburn?

98. Which of the following movies: Piranha 3D; Sudden Impact; The Gauntlet; The Outlaw Josey Wales; did not co-star Clint Eastwood & Sondra Locke?

ANSWERS: 92. NWORB YRRAH 93. REGNIS ZZAJ EHT 94. EFIL ELBUOD A 95. NAM EHT ,NOSIDE 96. REVOL TAERG EHT 97. ENO DER GIB EHT 98. D3 AHNARIP

"ACTIONS SPEAK LOUDER THAN WORDS."

99. Which of the following movies: Ghostbusters II; Mad Dog and Glory; The Admiral; Where the Buffalo Roam; did not star Bill Murray?

100. Which of the following movies: Phantom of the Opera; The Celebration; The Prince and the Pauper; The Sea Hawk; did not star Claude Rains?

101. Which of the following movies: Best Laid Plans; Inherit the Wind; Mary of Scotland; The Iceman Cometh; did not star Fredric March?

102. Which of the following movies: Any Which Way You Can; Bronco Billy; Every Which Way But Loose; Kiss of Death; did not co-star Clint Eastwood, Geoffrey Lewis & Sondra Locke?

103. Which of the following movies: A Man Escaped; Billy Bathgate; God Grew Tired of Us; The Invasion; did not star Nicole Kidman?

104. Which of the following movies: Cinema Paradiso; Killer Elite; Raging Bull; The Last Tycoon; did not star Robert De Niro?

105. Which of the following movies: Burnt Offerings; Junior Bonner; The Great Escape; The Thomas Crown Affair; did not star Steve McQueen?

ANSWERS: 99. LARIMDA EHT 100. NOITARBELEC EHT 101. SNALP DIAL TSEB 102. HTAED FO SSIK 103. DEPACSE NAM A 104. OSIDARAP AMENIC 105. SGNIREFFO TNRUB

"LIFE DOES NOT CHANGE UNLESS YOU MAKE IT CHANGE."

106. Which of the following movies: 4 for Texas; Next Goal Wins; Ocean's 11; Robin and the 7 Hoods; did not co-star Dean Martin & Frank Sinatra?

107. Which of the following movies: Brannigan; Spider-Man; The English Patient; To Live and Die in L.A.; did not star Willem Dafoe?

108. Which of the following movies: All About Steve; Bataan; Broadway Melody of 1938; Camille; did not star Robert Taylor?

109. Which of the following movies: Andy Hardy Comes Home; Judge Hardy and Son; Psych-Out; You're Only Young Once; did not co-star Cecilia Parker, Fay Holden & Mickey Rooney?

110. Which of the following movies: Bullets or Ballots; Footlight Parade; Fourteen Hours; The Perfect Specimen; did not star Joan Blondell?

111. Which of the following movies: Swept Away; The Kid Stays in the Picture; The Roots of Heaven; The Teahouse of the August Moon; did not star Eddie Albert?

112. Which of the following movies: 21 Grams; Carlito's Way; Dead Man Walking; Tall Tale; did not star Sean Penn?

ANSWERS: 106. SNIW LAOG TXEN 107. NAGINNARB 108. EVETS TUOBA LLA 109. TUO-HCYSP 110. SRUOH NEETRUOF 111. YAWA TPEWS 112. ELAT LLAT

Hollywood Movie Actors & Actresses Search Puzzle 4.

F	D	S	U	J	O	N	R	O	G	E	R	M	O	O	R	E	G	A	J	Y
P	W	A	N	B	N	O	E	E	R	R	O	L	F	L	Y	N	N	R	U	K
K	C	N	I	I	A	S	K	R	E	P	O	O	C	Y	R	A	G	N	L	I
I	H	T	C	L	M	R	V	G	I	N	I	P	C	Z	R	R	P	O	I	R
R	A	H	O	L	K	A	T	S	L	Z	K	E	Q	E	F	W	J	L	E	K
G	R	O	L	M	C	C	L	Y	O	H	U	Z	E	I	L	D	A	D	A	D
R	L	N	E	U	A	K	U	L	J	V	E	S	F	Z	C	E	M	S	N	O
Q	E	Y	K	R	H	C	H	V	A	V	E	L	I	R	Q	B	E	C	D	U
Z	S	H	I	R	E	A	U	E	N	W	N	A	N	N	O	B	S	H	R	G
C	B	O	D	A	N	J	M	S	I	S	S	U	A	A	D	I	S	W	E	L
L	R	P	M	Y	E	M	P	T	L	O	E	R	N	G	N	E	T	A	W	A
A	O	K	A	K	G	K	H	E	E	P	A	E	N	R	A	R	E	R	S	S
U	N	I	N	L	C	E	R	R	G	H	N	N	E	O	R	E	W	Z	T	N
D	S	N	T	I	R	E	E	S	N	I	C	B	R	M	B	Y	A	E	O	I
E	O	S	Z	S	R	N	Y	T	A	A	O	A	B	K	N	N	R	N	M	V
R	N	N	P	Q	O	A	B	A	B	L	N	C	R	N	O	O	T	E	C	R
A	Y	O	W	W	R	N	O	L	M	O	N	A	E	A	L	L	S	G	R	A
I	O	M	U	S	N	W	G	L	A	R	E	L	T	R	R	D	Z	G	U	M
N	L	S	K	F	I	Y	A	O	I	E	R	L	L	F	A	S	L	E	I	E
S	H	S	S	U	D	N	R	N	P	N	Y	P	A	Z	M	J	P	R	S	E
L	A	W	S	U	B	N	T	E	Q	A	M	J	W	G	K	C	S	U	E	L

☐ ANGELINA JOLIE	☐ ANTHONY HOPKINS	☐ ARNOLD SCHWARZENEGGER	☐ BILL MURRAY
☐ CHARLES BRONSON	☐ CLAUDE RAINS	☐ DEBBIE REYNOLDS	☐ ERROL FLYNN
☐ FRANK MORGAN	☐ GARY COOPER	☐ GENE HACKMAN	☐ HUMPHREY BOGART
☐ JACK CARSON	☐ JAMES STEWART	☐ JULIE ANDREWS	☐ KEENAN WYNN
☐ KIRK DOUGLAS	☐ LAUREN BACALL	☐ LEE MARVIN	☐ MARLON BRANDO
☐ NICOLE KIDMAN	☐ REESE WITHERSPOON	☐ ROGER MOORE	☐ SEAN CONNERY
☐ SOPHIA LOREN	☐ SYLVESTER STALLONE	☐ TOM CRUISE	☐ WALTER BRENNAN

"A PENNY SAVED IS A PENNY EARNED."

113. Which of the following movies: Another Dawn; Caught in the Draft; Road to Bali; Road to Singapore; did not co-star Bob Hope & Dorothy Lamour?

114. Which of the following movies: A Midsummer Night's Dream; Almost Famous; Another Dawn; That Certain Woman; did not star Ian Hunter?

115. Which of the following movies: King Creole; Never So Few; Ocean's 11; Sergeants 3; did not co-star Frank Sinatra & Peter Lawford?

116. Which of the following movies: Hit the Deck; How Green Was My Valley; Monkey Business; Voyage to the Bottom of the Sea; did not star Walter Pidgeon?

117. Which of the following movies: Dark Victory; Into the Abyss; Kid Galahad; The Petrified Forest; did not co-star Bette Davis & Humphrey Bogart?

118. Which of the following movies: Davy Crockett and the River Pirates; High Fidelity; The Great Locomotive Chase; Westward Ho, the Wagons!; did not co-star Fess Parker & Jeff York?

119. Which of the following movies: Andy Hardy's Double Life; Black Narcissus; Life Begins for Andy Hardy; The Courtship of Andy Hardy; did not co-star Lewis Stone & Mickey Rooney?

ANSWERS: 113. NWAD REHTONA 114. SUOMAF TSOMLA 115. ELOERC GNIK 116. SSENISUB YEKNOM 117. SSYBA EHT OTNI 118. YTILEDIF HGIH 119. SUSSICRAN KCALB

"GOD HELPS THOSE WHO HELP THEMSELVES."

120. Which of the following movies: Brief Encounter; Mutiny on the Bounty; The Furies; The Sea Wolves; did not star Trevor Howard?

121. Which of the following movies: All Through the Night; Crime School; In Cold Blood; The Caine Mutiny; did not star Humphrey Bogart?

122. Which of the following movies: Road to Bali; Road to Morocco; Road to Rio; Say One for Me; did not co-star Bing Crosby, Bob Hope & Dorothy Lamour?

123. Which of the following movies: Meet John Doe; The Odd Couple; The Plainsman; Vera Cruz; did not star Gary Cooper?

124. Which of the following movies: A Time to Kill; Agnes of God; Captain America: The First Avenger; Sphere; did not star Samuel L. Jackson?

125. Which of the following movies: Abandon Ship; Casino Royale; The Asphalt Jungle; The Maltese Falcon; did not direct John Huston?

126. Which of the following movies: Always; Beyond the Sea; Doctor Dolittle; The Artist; did not star John Goodman?

ANSWERS: 120. SEIRUF EHT 121. DOOLB DLOC NI 122. EM ROF ENO YAS 123. ELPUOC DDO EHT 124. DOG FO SENGA 125. PIHS NODNABA 126. ELTTILOD ROTCOD

"ONE MAN'S TRASH IS ANOTHER MAN'S TREASURE."

127. Which of the following movies: A Special Day; Adaptation.; Marriage Italian Style; The Priest's Wife; did not co-star Marcello Mastroianni & Sophia Loren?

128. Which of the following movies: Being Flynn; Boogie Nights; Children of Men; Stablemates; did not star Julianne Moore?

129. Which of the following movies: San Francisco; Tortilla Flat; Viridiana; Woman of the Year; did not star Spencer Tracy?

130. Which of the following movies: Sunset Boulevard; The Front Page; The Major and the Minor; Wait Until Dark; did not direct Billy Wilder?

131. Which of the following movies: Honkytonk Man; The Adventures of Ichabod and Mr. Toad; The Adventures of Robin Hood; The Black Sleep; did not star Basil Rathbone?

132. Which of the following movies: Dark Command; Edison, the Man; Northern Pursuit; The Big Trail; did not direct Raoul Walsh?

133. Which of the following movies: Moon Over Miami; Road to Morocco; The Littlest Rebel; The Princess and the Pirate; did not direct David Butler?

ANSWERS: 127. .NOITATPADA 128. SETAMELBATS 129. ANAIDIRIV 130. KRAD LITNU TIAW 131. NAM KNOTYKNOH 132. NAM EHT ,NOSIDE 133. IMAIM REVO NOOM

"PRACTICE MAKES PERFECT."

134. Which of the following movies: Bataan; Love Nest; The Big Wheel; The Black Swan; did not star Thomas Mitchell?

135. Which of the following movies: No Room for the Groom; Son of Ali Baba; The Long Riders; The Prince Who Was a Thief; did not co-star Piper Laurie & Tony Curtis?

136. Which of the following movies: A Shot in the Dark; Murder by Death; The Longest Day; The Party; did not star Peter Sellers?

137. Which of the following movies: American Beauty; Bordertown; Fog Over Frisco; Jezebel; did not co-star Bette Davis & Margaret Lindsay?

138. Which of the following movies: Rocky II; Rocky III; Rocky IV; The Hobbit; did not co-star Burt Young, Carl Weathers & Talia Shire?

139. Which of the following movies: Blood and Wine; Pirates of the Caribbean: At World's End; Pirates of the Caribbean: Dead Men Tell No Tales; Pirates of the Caribbean: The Curse of the Black Pearl; did not co-star Geoffrey Rush, Johnny Depp & Orlando Bloom?

140. Which of the following movies: Drive a Crooked Road; Stage Fright; The Adventures of Huckleberry Finn; The Private Lives of Adam and Eve; did not star Mickey Rooney?

ANSWERS: 134. TSEN EVOL 135. SREDIR GNOL EHT 136. YAD TSEGNOL EHT 137. YTUAEB NACIREMA 138. TIBBOH EHT 139. ENIW DNA DOOLB 140. THGIRF EGATS

"IF AT FIRST YOU DON'T SUCCEED, TRY, TRY AGAIN."

141. Which of the following movies: I'll See You in My Dreams; Kid Galahad; The Case of the Curious Bride; The Nice Guys; did not direct Michael Curtiz?

142. Which of the following movies: Dream Wife; Marriage on the Rocks; Roger & Me; The Life and Death of Colonel Blimp; did not star Deborah Kerr?

143. Which of the following movies: Marathon Man; Mother Wore Tights; The Little Princess; Week-End in Havana; did not direct Walter Lang?

144. Which of the following movies: Jimmy the Gent; Something to Sing About; The War Lover; The West Point Story; did not star James Cagney?

145. Which of the following movies: Eraserhead; Manhattan; Manhattan Murder Mystery; Sleeper; did not co-star Diane Keaton & Woody Allen?

146. Which of the following movies: Front Page Woman; In This Our Life; Jezebel; The Purple Mask; did not co-star Bette Davis & George Brent?

147. Which of the following movies: Anchors Aweigh; Take Me Out to the Ball Game; The Last Detail; The Three Musketeers; did not star Gene Kelly?

ANSWERS: 141. SYUG ECIN EHT 142. EM & REGOR 143. NAM NOHTARAM 144. REVOL RAW EHT 145. DAEHRESARE 146. KSAM ELPRUP EHT 147. LIATED TSAL EHT

PICTURE PUZZLE 7. SPACE SHUTTLE ENTERPRISE ON INTREPID IN NYC

PICTURE PUZZLE 7. CIRCLE THE TEN DIFFERENCES

MATH DRILLS TO KEEP YOUR BRAIN SPINNING

1.	13 - (5 - 4) + 3 = _____	21.	14 * 13 + 8 - 6 = _____
2.	(22 + 17) + (16 + 4) = _____	22.	(21 - 20) + (17 - 3) = _____
3.	23 + 19 * (9 - 6) = _____	23.	18 * 17 - 12 * 4 = _____
4.	19 * 17 + (15 - 13) = _____	24.	20 * 12 + 4 - 3 = _____
5.	23 + 22 + (18 + 6) = _____	25.	22 + (18 + 17) - 13 = _____
6.	14 - (12 - 11) + 9 = _____	26.	(23 + 15) - (10 - 5) = _____
7.	20 * 18 - (12 * 11) = _____	27.	(17 * 13) + (12 * 3) = _____
8.	23 - 15 + (9 - 7) = _____	28.	20 - 16 + (5 + 4) = _____
9.	(14 - 11) * (10 + 4) = _____	29.	21 + (17 * 9) - 8 = _____
10.	21 - 14 / (11 - 10) = _____	30.	(23 + 19) - 7 - 4 = _____
11.	17 - 11 + 9 - 7 = _____	31.	21 + (17 - 16) - 14 = _____
12.	21 - (19 - 7) + 5 = _____	32.	20 + (15 - 7) / 4 = _____
13.	(17 - 16) * (15 * 3) = _____	33.	(19 - 17) * (11 + 9) = _____
14.	(22 - 19) + (16 * 11) = _____	34.	18 + 12 - (10 - 3) = _____
15.	(23 + 15) + (11 * 9) = _____	35.	10 * 7 / 5 + 4 = _____
16.	19 / (7 - 6) + 5 = _____	36.	(23 * 13) - (12 + 11) = _____
17.	22 - 21 + (19 - 13) = _____	37.	22 - 15 - 4 + 3 = _____
18.	18 * 14 - (10 + 9) = _____	38.	(23 + 22) - 21 - 20 = _____
19.	23 - 22 + 15 * 13 = _____	39.	19 + 17 - 16 + 6 = _____
20.	18 * 15 / (10 - 8) = _____	40.	(22 - 11) + 7 * 5 = _____

41.	15 + 9 - 5 + 3 = _____	61.	16 + 14 * (9 - 5) = _____
42.	23 * (22 - 13) + 8 = _____	62.	(20 + 18) + 14 - 4 = _____
43.	12 + 9 + (7 + 5) = _____	63.	(23 - 8) - (7 + 3) = _____
44.	(21 + 19) + (8 + 3) = _____	64.	22 + 18 * (16 - 14) = _____
45.	(20 - 14) * (9 * 4) = _____	65.	19 - (15 - 14) * 6 = _____
46.	(12 + 7) + (5 + 3) = _____	66.	22 * 12 / (7 - 4) = _____
47.	(19 * 15) + 9 + 5 = _____	67.	(18 + 17) + 14 + 7 = _____
48.	18 + (14 - 8) + 3 = _____	68.	15 * 14 / (12 - 5) = _____
49.	20 * 10 - (9 + 4) = _____	69.	(23 - 22) * (20 * 16) = _____
50.	22 + (18 + 13) * 5 = _____	70.	11 * 9 * 8 / 6 = _____
51.	21 - 10 - (9 - 7) = _____	71.	21 + (17 + 9) - 8 = _____
52.	22 * 12 / 4 / 3 = _____	72.	22 + (20 - 18) * 17 = _____
53.	15 / (11 - 10) + 4 = _____	73.	17 * 9 - (7 * 5) = _____
54.	(23 + 22) - 16 - 5 = _____	74.	11 + (7 - 6) * 3 = _____
55.	18 - (17 - 15) + 11 = _____	75.	(23 - 15) * (13 + 10) = _____
56.	21 * 20 / (18 - 4) = _____	76.	(15 + 10) + 8 + 5 = _____
57.	12 + (5 * 4) + 3 = _____	77.	17 + (13 - 10) * 7 = _____
58.	23 + 19 + (12 - 9) = _____	78.	21 * (17 - 13) + 3 = _____
59.	(21 - 14) + (13 * 5) = _____	79.	(20 * 16) - (11 - 5) = _____
60.	(19 - 17) * (15 + 3) = _____	80.	23 - 17 - (12 / 6) = _____

81.	19 + 12 * (10 - 3) = ____	101.	22 - (20 - 14) + 13 = ____
82.	(16 - 13) + 11 - 7 = ____	102.	23 + (18 / 9) - 3 = ____
83.	23 - (19 - 14) / 5 = ____	103.	18 * 16 / (13 - 12) = ____
84.	17 + 13 + (9 + 4) = ____	104.	17 + 10 + (6 / 3) = ____
85.	23 - (11 + 8) - 3 = ____	105.	21 + (19 + 9) * 7 = ____
86.	(22 - 21) * (19 * 10) = ____	106.	(14 - 10) * 8 - 3 = ____
87.	19 * 17 - (11 + 5) = ____	107.	(18 - 16) * (15 - 13) = ____
88.	(18 - 15) * 12 * 8 = ____	108.	(21 - 20) + 11 * 3 = ____
89.	21 - (12 + 11) + 9 = ____	109.	20 * (19 - 15) * 4 = ____
90.	(23 - 19) * (9 * 8) = ____	110.	(23 + 21) - (6 * 5) = ____
91.	16 + 10 + 6 - 5 = ____	111.	(17 - 5) / (4 - 3) = ____
92.	(22 + 12) * (10 - 9) = ____	112.	15 + (9 * 7) - 5 = ____
93.	15 - 11 + (8 * 5) = ____	113.	23 * (21 - 14) / 7 = ____
94.	16 * (15 - 5) / 4 = ____	114.	14 * 11 + (6 / 3) = ____
95.	(15 * 11) - 10 - 9 = ____	115.	17 * (16 / 8) + 6 = ____
96.	(22 - 15) + 8 - 7 = ____	116.	19 * (14 - 11) - 5 = ____
97.	23 + 14 * 13 - 8 = ____	117.	23 * 17 - 15 * 8 = ____
98.	17 + 15 * 6 - 5 = ____	118.	20 + (19 + 18) - 14 = ____
99.	(21 + 18) - 7 * 4 = ____	119.	(21 - 16) + 13 + 8 = ____
100.	20 - 17 + 11 * 9 = ____	120.	23 - (20 - 12) + 5 = ____

121.	17 * 15 - 14 * 7 = _____	141.	(14 - 13) * (12 + 3) = _____
122.	(18 + 12) - (5 * 3) = _____	142.	20 / 10 + (8 * 5) = _____
123.	(22 + 21) + 17 * 5 = _____	143.	21 + 20 + 16 - 15 = _____
124.	18 / 9 + 7 * 3 = _____	144.	19 * 18 - 8 - 4 = _____
125.	19 + (13 + 11) + 8 = _____	145.	15 * (12 + 10) - 6 = _____
126.	(15 + 12) / 9 * 6 = _____	146.	23 - (22 + 17) / 3 = _____
127.	23 + 22 - 6 * 4 = _____	147.	21 * 8 / (7 * 6) = _____
128.	21 + (19 * 15) - 8 = _____	148.	18 * 15 * 6 / 5 = _____
129.	(17 * 10) - 7 * 4 = _____	149.	(22 * 10) + (7 * 3) = _____
130.	(23 - 13) + 10 - 7 = _____	150.	19 * 11 - (10 + 8) = _____
131.	(20 * 16) - (11 - 9) = _____	151.	(23 + 18) * (9 - 6) = _____
132.	(23 + 21) + 5 + 4 = _____	152.	13 * 11 - 10 + 4 = _____
133.	22 + 7 * (6 + 3) = _____	153.	23 + 20 - 6 * 3 = _____
134.	(18 + 17) - (13 + 11) = _____	154.	22 - 16 + 14 * 8 = _____
135.	(21 + 18) + 15 + 5 = _____	155.	23 - 22 + (10 + 3) = _____
136.	13 + 6 + (5 + 4) = _____	156.	12 * (11 - 5) / 4 = _____
137.	(19 + 18) - (13 + 9) = _____	157.	22 + 15 + 8 * 5 = _____
138.	9 * 7 + 4 + 3 = _____	158.	20 + 19 - 12 - 7 = _____
139.	19 - 17 + (14 * 12) = _____	159.	(21 - 17) + (10 + 4) = _____
140.	17 + 8 + 7 * 4 = _____	160.	(23 - 19) + 13 + 9 = _____

161.	20 * (10 - 5) - 4 = _____	181.	(19 - 9) + (8 - 3) = _____
162.	(18 * 17) - (16 + 10) = _____	182.	21 * (19 - 17) * 4 = _____
163.	23 - 21 + (10 - 3) = _____	183.	(22 - 20) * (18 * 5) = _____
164.	18 + 9 + 8 - 5 = _____	184.	23 + (9 + 7) * 6 = _____
165.	22 - 16 + (15 + 14) = _____	185.	(21 * 20) / 12 * 9 = _____
166.	23 * 12 - (11 + 3) = _____	186.	(18 + 17) - 16 + 14 = _____
167.	(21 * 16) - 8 - 4 = _____	187.	22 - 21 + 14 - 11 = _____
168.	(20 * 10) - 6 / 3 = _____	188.	19 - 18 + (16 * 8) = _____
169.	21 + (19 - 18) * 13 = _____	189.	(16 + 12) + 7 + 5 = _____
170.	(20 * 18) - 12 * 10 = _____	190.	(17 * 6) + 4 * 3 = _____
171.	(22 - 7) / (4 - 3) = _____	191.	23 + (12 - 9) + 6 = _____
172.	(20 / 10) * (7 + 5) = _____	192.	(18 + 7) + 6 * 5 = _____
173.	22 + 20 - 12 + 3 = _____	193.	(23 - 18) + (8 - 4) = _____
174.	23 - (22 - 15) - 8 = _____	194.	(19 - 10) + (9 - 6) = _____
175.	(20 - 18) + (11 - 10) = _____	195.	20 + 16 - (11 - 5) = _____
176.	21 + (6 - 4) - 3 = _____	196.	22 - (17 - 16) + 12 = _____
177.	14 - 8 + 6 - 4 = _____	197.	(17 + 13) - 6 * 4 = _____
178.	(21 * 16) / 14 - 6 = _____	198.	22 + 19 + 15 * 13 = _____
179.	(17 * 7) - (6 * 4) = _____	199.	(18 * 11) - 6 * 5 = _____
180.	(16 + 15) + (12 * 9) = _____	200.	20 + 19 + (17 + 11) = _____

1.	13 - (5 - 4) + 3 = 15	21.	14 * 13 + 8 - 6 = 184
2.	(22 + 17) + (16 + 4) = 59	22.	(21 - 20) + (17 - 3) = 15
3.	23 + 19 * (9 - 6) = 80	23.	18 * 17 - 12 * 4 = 258
4.	19 * 17 + (15 - 13) = 325	24.	20 * 12 + 4 - 3 = 241
5.	23 + 22 + (18 + 6) = 69	25.	22 + (18 + 17) - 13 = 44
6.	14 - (12 - 11) + 9 = 22	26.	(23 + 15) - (10 - 5) = 33
7.	20 * 18 - (12 * 11) = 228	27.	(17 * 13) + (12 * 3) = 257
8.	23 - 15 + (9 - 7) = 10	28.	20 - 16 + (5 + 4) = 13
9.	(14 - 11) * (10 + 4) = 42	29.	21 + (17 * 9) - 8 = 166
10.	21 - 14 / (11 - 10) = 7	30.	(23 + 19) - 7 - 4 = 31
11.	17 - 11 + 9 - 7 = 8	31.	21 + (17 - 16) - 14 = 8
12.	21 - (19 - 7) + 5 = 14	32.	20 + (15 - 7) / 4 = 22
13.	(17 - 16) * (15 * 3) = 45	33.	(19 - 17) * (11 + 9) = 40
14.	(22 - 19) + (16 * 11) = 179	34.	18 + 12 - (10 - 3) = 23
15.	(23 + 15) + (11 * 9) = 137	35.	10 * 7 / 5 + 4 = 18
16.	19 / (7 - 6) + 5 = 24	36.	(23 * 13) - (12 + 11) = 276
17.	22 - 21 + (19 - 13) = 7	37.	22 - 15 - 4 + 3 = 6
18.	18 * 14 - (10 + 9) = 233	38.	(23 + 22) - 21 - 20 = 4
19.	23 - 22 + 15 * 13 = 196	39.	19 + 17 - 16 + 6 = 26
20.	18 * 15 / (10 - 8) = 135	40.	(22 - 11) + 7 * 5 = 46

FILM TRIVIA. Fill in the missing words for 4 movie titles
1. The Case of the _______ Bride; Merry _______ Mr. Lawrence; _______ The Legend of Ron Burgundy; Star Wars: _______ II - Attack of the Clones;
2. The _______ of Emily; _______ of a Shopaholic; The Young and _______ T.S. Spivet; Hearts of Darkness: A _______ Apocalypse;
3. Star Wars: _______ I - The Phantom Menace; The Man with the _______ Arm; _______ His - _______ Hers; What Ever _______ to Baby Jane?;
4. The _______, the Bad and the Ugly; Horatio _______ The Duchess and the Devil; Dear _______ A Letter to a Son About His Father; _______ Once Upon a Time in India;
5. Every Girl Should Be _______; The Lord of the _______ The Two Towers; Mr. _______ Wonder Emporium; They Shoot _______, Don't They?;
6. _______ to the Bottom of the Sea; The _______ of Being Earnest; Peace, Love & _______; The Roman _______ of Mrs. Stone;
7. The _______ of Joan of Arc; Life _______ for Andy Hardy; Pirates of the _______ The Curse of the Black Pearl; The World _______ to Garp;
ANSWERS: 1. ;EDOSIPE ;:NAMROHCNA ;SAMTSIRHC ;SUOIRUC 2. ;S'REKAMMLIF ;SUOIGIDORP ;SNOISSEFNOC ;NOITAZINACIREMA 3. ;DENEPPAH ;ECROVID ;NEDLOG ;EDOSIPE 4. ;:NAAGAL ;:YRAHCAZ ;:REWOLBNROH ;DOOG 5. ;SESROH ;S'MUIROGAM ;:SGNIR ;DEIRRAM 6. ;GNIRPS ;GNIDNATSREDNUSIM ;ECNATROPMI ;EGAYOV 7. ;GNIDROCCA ;:NAEBBIRAC ;SNIGEB ;NOISSAP

41.	15 + 9 - 5 + 3 = 22	61.	16 + 14 * (9 - 5) = 72
42.	23 * (22 - 13) + 8 = 215	62.	(20 + 18) + 14 - 4 = 48
43.	12 + 9 + (7 + 5) = 33	63.	(23 - 8) - (7 + 3) = 5
44.	(21 + 19) + (8 + 3) = 51	64.	22 + 18 * (16 - 14) = 58
45.	(20 - 14) * (9 * 4) = 216	65.	19 - (15 - 14) * 6 = 13
46.	(12 + 7) + (5 + 3) = 27	66.	22 * 12 / (7 - 4) = 88
47.	(19 * 15) + 9 + 5 = 299	67.	(18 + 17) + 14 + 7 = 56
48.	18 + (14 - 8) + 3 = 27	68.	15 * 14 / (12 - 5) = 30
49.	20 * 10 - (9 + 4) = 187	69.	(23 - 22) * (20 * 16) = 320
50.	22 + (18 + 13) * 5 = 177	70.	11 * 9 * 8 / 6 = 132
51.	21 - 10 - (9 - 7) = 9	71.	21 + (17 + 9) - 8 = 39
52.	22 * 12 / 4 / 3 = 22	72.	22 + (20 - 18) * 17 = 56
53.	15 / (11 - 10) + 4 = 19	73.	17 * 9 - (7 * 5) = 118
54.	(23 + 22) - 16 - 5 = 24	74.	11 + (7 - 6) * 3 = 14
55.	18 - (17 - 15) + 11 = 27	75.	(23 - 15) * (13 + 10) = 184
56.	21 * 20 / (18 - 4) = 30	76.	(15 + 10) + 8 + 5 = 38
57.	12 + (5 * 4) + 3 = 35	77.	17 + (13 - 10) * 7 = 38
58.	23 + 19 + (12 - 9) = 45	78.	21 * (17 - 13) + 3 = 87
59.	(21 - 14) + (13 * 5) = 72	79.	(20 * 16) - (11 - 5) = 314
60.	(19 - 17) * (15 + 3) = 36	80.	23 - 17 - (12 / 6) = 4

81.	19 + 12 * (10 - 3) = 103	101.	22 - (20 - 14) + 13 = 29
82.	(16 - 13) + 11 - 7 = 7	102.	23 + (18 / 9) - 3 = 22
83.	23 - (19 - 14) / 5 = 22	103.	18 * 16 / (13 - 12) = 288
84.	17 + 13 + (9 + 4) = 43	104.	17 + 10 + (6 / 3) = 29
85.	23 - (11 + 8) - 3 = 1	105.	21 + (19 + 9) * 7 = 217
86.	(22 - 21) * (19 * 10) = 190	106.	(14 - 10) * 8 - 3 = 29
87.	19 * 17 - (11 + 5) = 307	107.	(18 - 16) * (15 - 13) = 4
88.	(18 - 15) * 12 * 8 = 288	108.	(21 - 20) + 11 * 3 = 34
89.	21 - (12 + 11) + 9 = 7	109.	20 * (19 - 15) * 4 = 320
90.	(23 - 19) * (9 * 8) = 288	110.	(23 + 21) - (6 * 5) = 14
91.	16 + 10 + 6 - 5 = 27	111.	(17 - 5) / (4 - 3) = 12
92.	(22 + 12) * (10 - 9) = 34	112.	15 + (9 * 7) - 5 = 73
93.	15 - 11 + (8 * 5) = 44	113.	23 * (21 - 14) / 7 = 23
94.	16 * (15 - 5) / 4 = 40	114.	14 * 11 + (6 / 3) = 156
95.	(15 * 11) - 10 - 9 = 146	115.	17 * (16 / 8) + 6 = 40
96.	(22 - 15) + 8 - 7 = 8	116.	19 * (14 - 11) - 5 = 52
97.	23 + 14 * 13 - 8 = 197	117.	23 * 17 - 15 * 8 = 271
98.	17 + 15 * 6 - 5 = 102	118.	20 + (19 + 18) - 14 = 43
99.	(21 + 18) - 7 * 4 = 11	119.	(21 - 16) + 13 + 8 = 26
100.	20 - 17 + 11 * 9 = 102	120.	23 - (20 - 12) + 5 = 20

121.	17 * 15 - 14 * 7 = 157	141.	(14 - 13) * (12 + 3) = 15
122.	(18 + 12) - (5 * 3) = 15	142.	20 / 10 + (8 * 5) = 42
123.	(22 + 21) + 17 * 5 = 128	143.	21 + 20 + 16 - 15 = 42
124.	18 / 9 + 7 * 3 = 23	144.	19 * 18 - 8 - 4 = 330
125.	19 + (13 + 11) + 8 = 51	145.	15 * (12 + 10) - 6 = 324
126.	(15 + 12) / 9 * 6 = 18	146.	23 - (22 + 17) / 3 = 10
127.	23 + 22 - 6 * 4 = 21	147.	21 * 8 / (7 * 6) = 4
128.	21 + (19 * 15) - 8 = 298	148.	18 * 15 * 6 / 5 = 324
129.	(17 * 10) - 7 * 4 = 142	149.	(22 * 10) + (7 * 3) = 241
130.	(23 - 13) + 10 - 7 = 13	150.	19 * 11 - (10 + 8) = 191
131.	(20 * 16) - (11 - 9) = 318	151.	(23 + 18) * (9 - 6) = 123
132.	(23 + 21) + 5 + 4 = 53	152.	13 * 11 - 10 + 4 = 137
133.	22 + 7 * (6 + 3) = 85	153.	23 + 20 - 6 * 3 = 25
134.	(18 + 17) - (13 + 11) = 11	154.	22 - 16 + 14 * 8 = 118
135.	(21 + 18) + 15 + 5 = 59	155.	23 - 22 + (10 + 3) = 14
136.	13 + 6 + (5 + 4) = 28	156.	12 * (11 - 5) / 4 = 18
137.	(19 + 18) - (13 + 9) = 15	157.	22 + 15 + 8 * 5 = 77
138.	9 * 7 + 4 + 3 = 70	158.	20 + 19 - 12 - 7 = 20
139.	19 - 17 + (14 * 12) = 170	159.	(21 - 17) + (10 + 4) = 18
140.	17 + 8 + 7 * 4 = 53	160.	(23 - 19) + 13 + 9 = 26

161.	20 * (10 - 5) - 4 = 96	181.	(19 - 9) + (8 - 3) = 15
162.	(18 * 17) - (16 + 10) = 280	182.	21 * (19 - 17) * 4 = 168
163.	23 - 21 + (10 - 3) = 9	183.	(22 - 20) * (18 * 5) = 180
164.	18 + 9 + 8 - 5 = 30	184.	23 + (9 + 7) * 6 = 119
165.	22 - 16 + (15 + 14) = 35	185.	(21 * 20) / 12 * 9 = 315
166.	23 * 12 - (11 + 3) = 262	186.	(18 + 17) - 16 + 14 = 33
167.	(21 * 16) - 8 - 4 = 324	187.	22 - 21 + 14 - 11 = 4
168.	(20 * 10) - 6 / 3 = 198	188.	19 - 18 + (16 * 8) = 129
169.	21 + (19 - 18) * 13 = 34	189.	(16 + 12) + 7 + 5 = 40
170.	(20 * 18) - 12 * 10 = 240	190.	(17 * 6) + 4 * 3 = 114
171.	(22 - 7) / (4 - 3) = 15	191.	23 + (12 - 9) + 6 = 32
172.	(20 / 10) * (7 + 5) = 24	192.	(18 + 7) + 6 * 5 = 55
173.	22 + 20 - 12 + 3 = 33	193.	(23 - 18) + (8 - 4) = 9
174.	23 - (22 - 15) - 8 = 8	194.	(19 - 10) + (9 - 6) = 12
175.	(20 - 18) + (11 - 10) = 3	195.	20 + 16 - (11 - 5) = 30
176.	21 + (6 - 4) - 3 = 20	196.	22 - (17 - 16) + 12 = 33
177.	14 - 8 + 6 - 4 = 8	197.	(17 + 13) - 6 * 4 = 6
178.	(21 * 16) / 14 - 6 = 18	198.	22 + 19 + 15 * 13 = 236
179.	(17 * 7) - (6 * 4) = 95	199.	(18 * 11) - 6 * 5 = 168
180.	(16 + 15) + (12 * 9) = 139	200.	20 + 19 + (17 + 11) = 67

Find & Circle DUCK, GOAT, LION, MULE , TOAD, HARE, KUDU, CRAB, MOLE, WOLF in the Quadrants

U	C	U	K	C	D	U	D	T	G	T	O	G	A	G	O	I	O	L	N	O	N	I	N
D	D	C	C	D	C	K	K	A	G	T	O	O	G	G	G	O	I	N	N	L	O	L	N
K	C	U	K	D	U	K	D	G	A	A	O	A	T	T	T	I	O	O	O	I	N	L	L
U	D	C	D	D	D	K	K	G	G	T	T	O	O	G	G	I	N	N	N	O	I	N	I
K	U	C	D	C	U	U	K	A	T	G	A	T	T	O	G	L	I	L	I	I	O	O	L
U	D	C	K	U	U	C	C	A	O	T	A	A	A	A	O	O	O	L	L	L	L	N	I
D	C	K	D	K	U	U	K	O	O	O	O	A	G	G	T	N	I	I	L	L	O	N	I
U	D	K	D	C	D	D	C	A	A	G	T	T	T	G	G	L	I	L	I	N	L	N	L
M	U	E	U	E	E	E	U									A	D	D	T	D	T	T	O
U	L	E	L	M	L	U	L									D	O	T	O	O	A	T	A
U	L	E	U	U	L	E	L									T	A	T	D	T	T	A	A
M	L	M	E	U	M	E	L									O	O	T	O	O	A	D	O
U	U	L	L	M	L	L	U									T	A	O	A	A	T	D	A
E	U	M	L	L	M	M	U									A	O	D	T	O	T	O	D
L	U	E	U	U	E	L	E									T	O	A	A	A	O	D	D
L	E	M	E	M	M	U	L									A	O	A	T	A	O	A	D
E	E	R	H	R	E	H	H									U	U	D	D	U	D	K	D
A	H	R	H	R	H	H	R									D	U	U	D	D	D	K	K
E	E	H	E	H	A	H	R									K	U	U	K	K	D	D	K
H	A	H	H	H	R	R	A									K	U	U	K	D	U	U	D
H	A	A	H	R	A	R	H									U	D	U	U	U	K	K	K
E	E	R	E	H	E	E	H									U	U	K	K	K	K	K	D
A	A	H	E	A	E	A	A									D	U	U	D	D	K	U	U
H	A	A	A	E	A	R	R									D	U	U	U	U	D	U	D
R	R	R	A	C	C	B	C	E	O	L	L	O	M	L	M	W	O	F	W	L	L	O	O
C	C	A	C	C	B	R	B	L	M	L	M	M	M	M	M	W	O	W	W	W	O	F	F
R	C	R	B	A	C	R	R	L	M	O	M	L	L	L	M	L	L	F	L	W	W	O	W
R	A	A	R	C	C	A	R	O	O	E	L	E	E	E	E	F	F	O	F	F	W	F	F
R	C	C	C	B	A	R	A	M	O	L	L	E	E	O	L	O	L	O	L	L	F	O	F
C	B	A	A	B	B	R	A	E	E	L	O	O	E	E	E	O	L	L	L	W	O	L	L
B	C	B	C	A	B	C	B	O	M	L	L	L	L	E	L	F	W	L	F	W	F	W	L
B	A	R	B	B	B	C	A	L	L	L	M	E	L	L	O	W	L	L	W	L	F	L	O

1.	13 - (5 - _____) + 3 = 15	21.	_____ * 13 + 8 - 6 = 184
2.	(22 + 17) + (16 + _____) = 59	22.	(21 - 20) + (_____ - 3) = 15
3.	_____ + 19 * (9 - 6) = 80	23.	18 * 17 - 12 * _____ = 258
4.	19 * _____ + (15 - 13) = 325	24.	_____ * 12 + 4 - 3 = 241
5.	23 + 22 + (_____ + 6) = 69	25.	22 + (_____ + 17) - 13 = 44
6.	14 - (12 - 11) + _____ = 22	26.	(23 + 15) - (10 - _____) = 33
7.	_____ * 18 - (12 * 11) = 228	27.	(17 * _____) + (12 * 3) = 257
8.	23 - _____ + (9 - 7) = 10	28.	20 - _____ + (5 + 4) = 13
9.	(14 - 11) * (10 + _____) = 42	29.	21 + (17 * _____) - 8 = 166
10.	21 - 14 / (11 - _____) = 7	30.	(23 + 19) - 7 - _____ = 31
11.	17 - 11 + 9 - _____ = 8	31.	21 + (_____ - 16) - 14 = 8
12.	21 - (_____ - 7) + 5 = 14	32.	_____ + (15 - 7) / 4 = 22
13.	(17 - 16) * (_____ * 3) = 45	33.	(19 - _____) * (11 + 9) = 40
14.	(22 - _____) + (16 * 11) = 179	34.	18 + 12 - (10 - _____) = 23
15.	(23 + _____) + (11 * 9) = 137	35.	10 * 7 / 5 + _____ = 18
16.	19 / (7 - 6) + _____ = 24	36.	(23 * 13) - (_____ + 11) = 276
17.	22 - 21 + (_____ - 13) = 7	37.	_____ - 15 - 4 + 3 = 6
18.	18 * _____ - (10 + 9) = 233	38.	(_____ + 22) - 21 - 20 = 4
19.	23 - 22 + _____ * 13 = 196	39.	19 + _____ - 16 + 6 = 26
20.	18 * 15 / (_____ - 8) = 135	40.	(22 - 11) + 7 * _____ = 46

41.	15 + _____ - 5 + 3 = 22	61.	16 + 14 * (9 - _____) = 72
42.	23 * (22 - _____) + 8 = 215	62.	(20 + 18) + 14 - _____ = 48
43.	_____ + 9 + (7 + 5) = 33	63.	(23 - 8) - (_____ + 3) = 5
44.	(21 + _____) + (8 + 3) = 51	64.	22 + 18 * (16 - _____) = 58
45.	(20 - 14) * (_____ * 4) = 216	65.	19 - (15 - 14) * _____ = 13
46.	(_____ + 7) + (5 + 3) = 27	66.	_____ * 12 / (7 - 4) = 88
47.	(19 * 15) + _____ + 5 = 299	67.	(18 + _____) + 14 + 7 = 56
48.	_____ + (14 - 8) + 3 = 27	68.	15 * 14 / (12 - _____) = 30
49.	20 * 10 - (9 + _____) = 187	69.	(23 - 22) * (20 * _____) = 320
50.	22 + (18 + 13) * _____ = 177	70.	11 * 9 * 8 / _____ = 132
51.	21 - 10 - (_____ - 7) = 9	71.	21 + (17 + _____) - 8 = 39
52.	22 * 12 / _____ / 3 = 22	72.	22 + (_____ - 18) * 17 = 56
53.	15 / (_____ - 10) + 4 = 19	73.	_____ * 9 - (7 * 5) = 118
54.	(_____ + 22) - 16 - 5 = 24	74.	11 + (7 - _____) * 3 = 14
55.	18 - (_____ - 15) + 11 = 27	75.	(23 - _____) * (13 + 10) = 184
56.	21 * _____ / (18 - 4) = 30	76.	(_____ + 10) + 8 + 5 = 38
57.	12 + (5 * 4) + _____ = 35	77.	17 + (13 - _____) * 7 = 38
58.	23 + _____ + (12 - 9) = 45	78.	21 * (_____ - 13) + 3 = 87
59.	(_____ - 14) + (13 * 5) = 72	79.	(20 * 16) - (_____ - 5) = 314
60.	(19 - _____) * (15 + 3) = 36	80.	23 - _____ - (12 / 6) = 4

81.	19 + 12 * (_____ - 3) = 103	101.	22 - (20 - 14) + _____ = 29
82.	(16 - 13) + _____ - 7 = 7	102.	23 + (18 / 9) - _____ = 22
83.	23 - (19 - 14) / _____ = 22	103.	18 * 16 / (13 - _____) = 288
84.	17 + _____ + (9 + 4) = 43	104.	17 + 10 + (6 / _____) = 29
85.	23 - (11 + 8) - _____ = 1	105.	21 + (_____ + 9) * 7 = 217
86.	(_____ - 21) * (19 * 10) = 190	106.	(14 - _____) * 8 - 3 = 29
87.	19 * _____ - (11 + 5) = 307	107.	(18 - 16) * (_____ - 13) = 4
88.	(18 - 15) * 12 * _____ = 288	108.	(21 - _____) + 11 * 3 = 34
89.	_____ - (12 + 11) + 9 = 7	109.	20 * (_____ - 15) * 4 = 320
90.	(23 - 19) * (_____ * 8) = 288	110.	(23 + 21) - (_____ * 5) = 14
91.	16 + 10 + _____ - 5 = 27	111.	(17 - 5) / (4 - _____) = 12
92.	(22 + 12) * (10 - _____) = 34	112.	15 + (9 * _____) - 5 = 73
93.	15 - 11 + (8 * _____) = 44	113.	_____ * (21 - 14) / 7 = 23
94.	16 * (15 - _____) / 4 = 40	114.	14 * 11 + (6 / _____) = 156
95.	(15 * 11) - _____ - 9 = 146	115.	17 * (16 / 8) + _____ = 40
96.	(_____ - 15) + 8 - 7 = 8	116.	19 * (14 - _____) - 5 = 52
97.	23 + 14 * 13 - _____ = 197	117.	_____ * 17 - 15 * 8 = 271
98.	17 + 15 * _____ - 5 = 102	118.	_____ + (19 + 18) - 14 = 43
99.	(21 + _____) - 7 * 4 = 11	119.	(21 - 16) + _____ + 8 = 26
100.	20 - 17 + _____ * 9 = 102	120.	23 - (20 - 12) + _____ = 20

121.	17 * _____ - 14 * 7 = 157	141.	(_____ - 13) * (12 + 3) = 15
122.	(18 + 12) - (5 * _____) = 15	142.	_____ / 10 + (8 * 5) = 42
123.	(22 + 21) + 17 * _____ = 128	143.	21 + 20 + 16 - _____ = 42
124.	_____ / 9 + 7 * 3 = 23	144.	19 * _____ - 8 - 4 = 330
125.	_____ + (13 + 11) + 8 = 51	145.	15 * (_____ + 10) - 6 = 324
126.	(15 + 12) / 9 * _____ = 18	146.	23 - (22 + _____) / 3 = 10
127.	23 + _____ - 6 * 4 = 21	147.	21 * 8 / (_____ * 6) = 4
128.	21 + (19 * _____) - 8 = 298	148.	18 * 15 * _____ / 5 = 324
129.	(_____ * 10) - 7 * 4 = 142	149.	(22 * 10) + (7 * _____) = 241
130.	(23 - 13) + 10 - _____ = 13	150.	19 * _____ - (10 + 8) = 191
131.	(20 * 16) - (_____ - 9) = 318	151.	(23 + _____) * (9 - 6) = 123
132.	(23 + _____) + 5 + 4 = 53	152.	_____ * 11 - 10 + 4 = 137
133.	_____ + 7 * (6 + 3) = 85	153.	23 + 20 - _____ * 3 = 25
134.	(_____ + 17) - (13 + 11) = 11	154.	22 - _____ + 14 * 8 = 118
135.	(21 + _____) + 15 + 5 = 59	155.	_____ - 22 + (10 + 3) = 14
136.	13 + 6 + (5 + _____) = 28	156.	12 * (_____ - 5) / 4 = 18
137.	(19 + _____) - (13 + 9) = 15	157.	_____ + 15 + 8 * 5 = 77
138.	9 * _____ + 4 + 3 = 70	158.	20 + 19 - 12 - _____ = 20
139.	19 - _____ + (14 * 12) = 170	159.	(_____ - 17) + (10 + 4) = 18
140.	17 + _____ + 7 * 4 = 53	160.	(_____ - 19) + 13 + 9 = 26

161.	20 * (10 - _____) - 4 = 96	181.	(19 - _____) + (8 - 3) = 15
162.	(18 * 17) - (_____ + 10) = 280	182.	21 * (_____ - 17) * 4 = 168
163.	23 - 21 + (_____ - 3) = 9	183.	(22 - 20) * (18 * _____) = 180
164.	18 + 9 + 8 - _____ = 30	184.	23 + (9 + 7) * _____ = 119
165.	22 - _____ + (15 + 14) = 35	185.	(_____ * 20) / 12 * 9 = 315
166.	_____ * 12 - (11 + 3) = 262	186.	(_____ + 17) - 16 + 14 = 33
167.	(_____ * 16) - 8 - 4 = 324	187.	22 - 21 + 14 - _____ = 4
168.	(20 * 10) - _____ / 3 = 198	188.	19 - 18 + (16 * _____) = 129
169.	21 + (19 - _____) * 13 = 34	189.	(_____ + 12) + 7 + 5 = 40
170.	(_____ * 18) - 12 * 10 = 240	190.	(_____ * 6) + 4 * 3 = 114
171.	(22 - 7) / (4 - _____) = 15	191.	23 + (12 - 9) + _____ = 32
172.	(20 / _____) * (7 + 5) = 24	192.	(_____ + 7) + 6 * 5 = 55
173.	22 + _____ - 12 + 3 = 33	193.	(23 - 18) + (8 - _____) = 9
174.	23 - (_____ - 15) - 8 = 8	194.	(_____ - 10) + (9 - 6) = 12
175.	(20 - 18) + (_____ - 10) = 3	195.	20 + 16 - (_____ - 5) = 30
176.	21 + (6 - _____) - 3 = 20	196.	22 - (17 - 16) + _____ = 33
177.	14 - _____ + 6 - 4 = 8	197.	(17 + 13) - _____ * 4 = 6
178.	(21 * _____) / 14 - 6 = 18	198.	_____ + 19 + 15 * 13 = 236
179.	(17 * 7) - (_____ * 4) = 95	199.	(_____ * 11) - 6 * 5 = 168
180.	(_____ + 15) + (12 * 9) = 139	200.	20 + 19 + (_____ + 11) = 67

1.	Three x Fourteen = ____	21.	Nineteen x Seventeen = ____
2.	Nineteen x Twelve = ____	22.	Ten x Three = ____
3.	Thirteen x Seven = ____	23.	Eighteen x Eight = ____
4.	Sixteen x Eleven = ____	24.	Four x Six = ____
5.	Thirteen x Twelve = ____	25.	Twenty x Three = ____
6.	Fifteen x Thirteen = ____	26.	Sixteen x Five = ____
7.	Eighteen x Sixteen = ____	27.	Five x Twenty- = ____
8.	Seven x Eight = ____	28.	Eleven x Eighteen = ____
9.	Nine x Sixteen = ____	29.	Thirteen x Eight = ____
10.	Twenty x Eighteen = ____	30.	Sixteen x Five = ____
11.	Six x Twelve = ____	31.	Fourteen x Seven = ____
12.	Nine x Sixteen = ____	32.	Twenty x Eight = ____
13.	Thirteen x Seven = ____	33.	Fifteen x Two = ____
14.	Sixteen x Nineteen = ____	34.	Thirteen x Eight = ____
15.	Nine x Thirteen = ____	35.	Seventeen x Nine = ____
16.	Eighteen x Sixteen = ____	36.	Three x Five = ____
17.	Two x Six = ____	37.	Sixteen x Eight = ____
18.	Seventeen x Two = ____	38.	Eight x Ten = ____
19.	Six x Fifteen = ____	39.	Fourteen x Five = ____
20.	Eight x Four = ____	40.	Five x Two = ____

41.	Seventeen x Three = ____	61.	Five x Five = ____
42.	Eleven x Nineteen = ____	62.	Four x Nine = ____
43.	Nine x Eleven = ____	63.	Fifteen x Three = ____
44.	Eight x Eight = ____	64.	Sixteen x Fourteen = ____
45.	Nine x Seventeen = ____	65.	Ten x Sixteen = ____
46.	Ten x Twelve = ____	66.	Nineteen x Nineteen = ____
47.	Twelve x Five = ____	67.	Two x Seven = ____
48.	Ten x Sixteen = ____	68.	Eleven x Five = ____
49.	Twelve x Eleven = ____	69.	Twenty x Twenty- = ____
50.	Eight x Three = ____	70.	Sixteen x Two = ____
51.	Seven x Ten = ____	71.	Ten x Twelve = ____
52.	Six x Nine = ____	72.	Nine x Sixteen = ____
53.	Eleven x Eight = ____	73.	Fifteen x Two = ____
54.	Eight x Two = ____	74.	Fourteen x Sixteen = ____
55.	Twelve x Fourteen = ____	75.	Fifteen x Nineteen = ____
56.	Fourteen x Nineteen = ____	76.	Eleven x Fifteen = ____
57.	Four x Four = ____	77.	Four x Fourteen = ____
58.	Eleven x Twelve = ____	78.	Two x Twelve = ____
59.	Five x Five = ____	79.	Three x Two = ____
60.	Sixteen x Ten = ____	80.	Twenty x Eight = ____

1.	Three x Fourteen = Forty-Two	17.	Two x Six = Twelve
2.	Nineteen x Twelve = Two Hundred Twenty-Eight	18.	Seventeen x Two = Thirty-Four
3.	Thirteen x Seven = Ninety-One	19.	Six x Fifteen = Ninety
4.	Sixteen x Eleven = One Hundred Seventy-Six	20.	Eight x Four = Thirty-Two
5.	Thirteen x Twelve = One Hundred Fifty-Six	21.	Nineteen x Seventeen = Three Hundred Twenty-Three
6.	Fifteen x Thirteen = One Hundred Ninety-Five	22.	Ten x Three = Thirty-
7.	Eighteen x Sixteen = Two Hundred Eighty-Eight	23.	Eighteen x Eight = One Hundred Forty-Four
8.	Seven x Eight = Fifty-Six	24.	Four x Six = Twenty-Four
9.	Nine x Sixteen = One Hundred Forty-Four	25.	Twenty x Three = Sixty
10.	Twenty x Eighteen = Three Hundred Sixty	26.	Sixteen x Five = Eighty
11.	Six x Twelve = Seventy-Two	27.	Five x Twenty- = One Hundred
12.	Nine x Sixteen = One Hundred Forty-Four	28.	Eleven x Eighteen = One Hundred Ninety-Eight
13.	Thirteen x Seven = Ninety-One	29.	Thirteen x Eight = One Hundred Four
14.	Sixteen x Nineteen = Three Hundred Four	30.	Sixteen x Five = Eighty
15.	Nine x Thirteen = One Hundred Seventeen	31.	Fourteen x Seven = Ninety-Eight
16.	Eighteen x Sixteen = Two Hundred Eighty-Eight	32.	Twenty x Eight = One Hundred Sixty

33.	Fifteen x Two = Thirty	49.	Twelve x Eleven = One Hundred Thirty-Two
34.	Thirteen x Eight = One Hundred Four	50.	Eight x Three = Twenty-Four
35.	Seventeen x Nine = One Hundred Fifty-Three	51.	Seven x Ten = Seventy
36.	Three x Five = Fifteen	52.	Six x Nine = Fifty-Four
37.	Sixteen x Eight = One Hundred Twenty-Eight	53.	Eleven x Eight = Eighty-Eight
38.	Eight x Ten = Eighty	54.	Eight x Two = Sixteen
39.	Fourteen x Five = Seventy	55.	Twelve x Fourteen = One Hundred Sixty-Eight
40.	Five x Two = Ten	56.	Fourteen x Nineteen = Two Hundred Sixty-Six
41.	Seventeen x Three = Fifty-One	57.	Four x Four = Sixteen
42.	Eleven x Nineteen = Two Hundred Nine	58.	Eleven x Twelve = One Hundred Thirty-Two
43.	Nine x Eleven = Ninety-Nine	59.	Five x Five = Twenty-Five
44.	Eight x Eight = Sixty-Four	60.	Sixteen x Ten = One Hundred Sixty
45.	Nine x Seventeen = One Hundred Fifty-Three	61.	Five x Five = Twenty-Five
46.	Ten x Twelve = One Hundred Twenty	62.	Four x Nine = Thirty-Six
47.	Twelve x Five = Sixty	63.	Fifteen x Three = Forty-Five
48.	Ten x Sixteen = One Hundred Sixty	64.	Sixteen x Fourteen = Two Hundred Twenty-Four

65.	Ten x Sixteen = One Hundred Sixty	1.	____ x Fourteen = Forty-Two
66.	Nineteen x Nineteen = Three Hundred Sixty-One	2.	____ x Twelve = Two Hundred Twenty-Eight
67.	Two x Seven = Fourteen	3.	____ x Seven = Ninety-One
68.	Eleven x Five = Fifty-Five	4.	____ x Eleven = One Hundred Seventy-Six
69.	Twenty x Twenty- = Four Hundred	5.	____ x Twelve = One Hundred Fifty-Six
70.	Sixteen x Two = Thirty-Two	6.	____ x Thirteen = One Hundred Ninety-Five
71.	Ten x Twelve = One Hundred Twenty	7.	____ x Sixteen = Two Hundred Eighty-Eight
72.	Nine x Sixteen = One Hundred Forty-Four	8.	____ x Eight = Fifty-Six
73.	Fifteen x Two = Thirty	9.	____ x Sixteen = One Hundred Forty-Four
74.	Fourteen x Sixteen = Two Hundred Twenty-Four	10.	____ x Eighteen = Three Hundred Sixty
75.	Fifteen x Nineteen = Two Hundred Eighty-Five	11.	____ x Twelve = Seventy-Two
76.	Eleven x Fifteen = One Hundred Sixty-Five	12.	____ x Sixteen = One Hundred Forty-Four
77.	Four x Fourteen = Fifty-Six	13.	____ x Seven = Ninety-One
78.	Two x Twelve = Twenty-Four	14.	____ x Nineteen = Three Hundred Four
79.	Three x Two = Six	15.	____ x Thirteen = One Hundred Seventeen
80.	Twenty x Eight = One Hundred Sixty	16.	____ x Sixteen = Two Hundred Eighty-Eight

17.	____ x Six = Twelve	33.	____ x Two = Thirty
18.	____ x Two = Thirty-Four	34.	____ x Eight = One Hundred Four
19.	____ x Fifteen = Ninety	35.	____ x Nine = One Hundred Fifty-Three
20.	____ x Four = Thirty-Two	36.	____ x Five = Fifteen
21.	____ x Seventeen = Three Hundred Twenty-Three	37.	____ x Eight = One Hundred Twenty-Eight
22.	____ x Three = Thirty	38.	____ x Ten = Eighty
23.	____ x Eight = One Hundred Forty-Four	39.	____ x Five = Seventy
24.	____ x Six = Twenty-Four	40.	____ x Two = Ten
25.	____ x Three = Sixty	41.	____ x Three = Fifty-One
26.	____ x Five = Eighty	42.	____ x Nineteen = Two Hundred Nine
27.	____ x Twenty- = One Hundred	43.	____ x Eleven = Ninety-Nine
28.	____ x Eighteen = One Hundred Ninety-Eight	44.	____ x Eight = Sixty-Four
29.	____ x Eight = One Hundred Four	45.	____ x Seventeen = One Hundred Fifty-Three
30.	____ x Five = Eighty	46.	____ x Twelve = One Hundred Twenty
31.	____ x Seven = Ninety-Eight	47.	____ x Five = Sixty
32.	____ x Eight = One Hundred Sixty	48.	____ x Sixteen = One Hundred Sixty

FILM TRIVIA. Fill in the missing words for 4 movie titles

8. George Stevens: A _______ Journey; The _______ Love of Martha Ivers; G.I. Joe: The Rise of _______; The Great _______ Chase;

9. Bobby _______ Against the World; Rebecca of _______ Farm; Long Day's _______ Into Night; _______ First Blood Part II;

10. The _______ That Time Forgot; _______ Bobby: The True Story of a Dog; Star Wars: _______ III - Revenge of the Sith; The Curse of the Jade _______;

11. _______ from the Black Lagoon; Miracle of the White _______; Where _______ Fear to Tread; The League of _______ Gentlemen;

12. Once in a Lifetime: The _______ Story of the New York Cosmos; Captain _______ The Winter Soldier; A Woman of _______ A Drama of Fate; 1492: _______ of Paradise;

13. Big _______ in Little China; One of Our _______ Is Missing; Once _______ a Time in the West; Divine Secrets of the Ya-Ya _______;

14. Return from Witch _______; Star Wars: _______ V - The Empire Strikes Back; Fast Times at _______ High; Harry Potter and the _______ of Secrets;

ANSWERS: 8. ;EVITOMOCOL ;ARBOC ;EGNARTS ;S'REKAMMLIF 9. ;:OBMAR ;YENRUOJ ;KOORBYNNUS ;REHCSIF 10. ;NOIPROCS ;EDOSIPE ;SRAIRFYERG ;ELPOEP 11. ;YRANIDROARTXE ;SLEGNA ;SNOILLATS ;ERUTAERC 12. ;TSEUQNOC ;:SIRAP ;:ACIREMA ;YRANIDROARTXE 13. ;DOOHRETSIS ;NOPU ;SRUASONID ;ELBUORT 14. ;REBMAHC ;TNOMEGDIR ;EDOSIPE ;NIATNUOM

49.	____ x Eleven = One Hundred Thirty-Two	65.	____ x Sixteen = One Hundred Sixty
50.	____ x Three = Twenty-Four	66.	____ x Nineteen = Three Hundred Sixty-One
51.	____ x Ten = Seventy	67.	____ x Seven = Fourteen
52.	____ x Nine = Fifty-Four	68.	____ x Five = Fifty-Five
53.	____ x Eight = Eighty-Eight	69.	____ x Twenty- = Four Hundred
54.	____ x Two = Sixteen	70.	____ x Two = Thirty-Two
55.	____ x Fourteen = One Hundred Sixty-Eight	71.	____ x Twelve = One Hundred Twenty
56.	____ x Nineteen = Two Hundred Sixty-Six	72.	____ x Sixteen = One Hundred Forty-Four
57.	____ x Four = Sixteen	73.	____ x Two = Thirty
58.	____ x Twelve = One Hundred Thirty-Two	74.	____ x Sixteen = Two Hundred Twenty-Four
59.	____ x Five = Twenty-Five	75.	____ x Nineteen = Two Hundred Eighty-Five
60.	____ x Ten = One Hundred Sixty	76.	____ x Fifteen = One Hundred Sixty-Five
61.	____ x Five = Twenty-Five	77.	____ x Fourteen = Fifty-Six
62.	____ x Nine = Thirty-Six	78.	____ x Twelve = Twenty-Four
63.	____ x Three = Forty-Five	79.	____ x Two = Six
64.	____ x Fourteen = Two Hundred Twenty-Four	80.	____ x Eight = One Hundred Sixty

1.	Three x ____ = Forty-Two	17.	Two x ____ = Twelve
2.	Nineteen x ____ = Two Hundred Twenty-Eight	18.	Seventeen x ____ = Thirty-Four
3.	Thirteen x ____ = Ninety-One	19.	Six x ____ = Ninety-
4.	Sixteen x ____ = One Hundred Seventy-Six	20.	Eight x ____ = Thirty-Two
5.	Thirteen x ____ = One Hundred Fifty-Six	21.	Nineteen x ____ = Three Hundred Twenty-Three
6.	Fifteen x ____ = One Hundred Ninety-Five	22.	Ten x ____ = Thirty
7.	Eighteen x ____ = Two Hundred Eighty-Eight	23.	Eighteen x ____ = One Hundred Forty-Four
8.	Seven x ____ = Fifty-Six	24.	Four x ____ = Twenty-Four
9.	Nine x ____ = One Hundred Forty-Four	25.	Twenty x ____ = Sixty
10.	Twenty x ____ = Three Hundred Sixty	26.	Sixteen x ____ = Eighty
11.	Six x ____ = Seventy-Two	27.	Five x ____ = One Hundred
12.	Nine x ____ = One Hundred Forty-Four	28.	Eleven x ____ = One Hundred Ninety-Eight
13.	Thirteen x ____ = Ninety-One	29.	Thirteen x ____ = One Hundred Four
14.	Sixteen x ____ = Three Hundred Four	30.	Sixteen x ____ = Eighty
15.	Nine x ____ = One Hundred Seventeen	31.	Fourteen x ____ = Ninety-Eight
16.	Eighteen x ____ = Two Hundred Eighty-Eight	32.	Twenty x ____ = One Hundred Sixty

33.	Fifteen x ____ = Thirty	49.	Twelve x ____ = One Hundred Thirty-Two
34.	Thirteen x ____ = One Hundred Four	50.	Eight x ____ = Twenty-Four
35.	Seventeen x ____ = One Hundred Fifty-Three	51.	Seven x ____ = Seventy
36.	Three x ____ = Fifteen	52.	Six x ____ = Fifty-Four
37.	Sixteen x ____ = One Hundred Twenty-Eight	53.	Eleven x ____ = Eighty-Eight
38.	Eight x ____ = Eighty	54.	Eight x ____ = Sixteen
39.	Fourteen x ____ = Seventy	55.	Twelve x ____ = One Hundred Sixty-Eight
40.	Five x ____ = Ten	56.	Fourteen x ____ = Two Hundred Sixty-Six
41.	Seventeen x ____ = Fifty-One	57.	Four x ____ = Sixteen
42.	Eleven x ____ = Two Hundred Nine	58.	Eleven x ____ = One Hundred Thirty-Two
43.	Nine x ____ = Ninety-Nine	59.	Five x ____ = Twenty-Five
44.	Eight x ____ = Sixty-Four	60.	Sixteen x ____ = One Hundred Sixty
45.	Nine x ____ = One Hundred Fifty-Three	61.	Five x ____ = Twenty-Five
46.	Ten x ____ = One Hundred Twenty	62.	Four x ____ = Thirty-Six
47.	Twelve x ____ = Sixty	63.	Fifteen x ____ = Forty-Five
48.	Ten x ____ = One Hundred Sixty	64.	Sixteen x ____ = Two Hundred Twenty-Four

65.	Ten x ____ = One Hundred Sixty	73.	Fifteen x ____ = Thirty
66.	Nineteen x ____ = Three Hundred Sixty-One	74.	Fourteen x ____ = Two Hundred Twenty-Four
67.	Two x ____ = Fourteen	75.	Fifteen x ____ = Two Hundred Eighty-Five
68.	Eleven x ____ = Fifty-Five	76.	Eleven x ____ = One Hundred Sixty-Five
69.	Twenty x ____ = Four Hundred	77.	Four x ____ = Fifty-Six
70.	Sixteen x ____ = Thirty-Two	78.	Two x ____ = Twenty-Four
71.	Ten x ____ = One Hundred Twenty	79.	Three x ____ = Six
72.	Nine x ____ = One Hundred Forty-Four	80.	Twenty x ____ = One Hundred Sixty

LAS VEGAS WELCOME SIGN

PICTURE PUZZLE 8. PALACE OF VERSAILLES , 1 HR TRAIN RIDE FROM PARIS

PICTURE PUZZLE 8. CIRCLE THE TEN DIFFERENCES

SUDOKU LOGIC PUZZLES

INSTRUCTIONS

The goal of Sudoku puzzle is to fill a 9×9 grid with numbers so that each row, column and 3×3 group of cells (nonet) contain all of the digits between 1 and 9. Sudoku is an excellent logic puzzle which fortifies your brain. Solution section follows the puzzles.

Most Sudoku logic puzzles can be solved the following way: make a first pass through the puzzle placing all the numbers you can, then go back & repeat, seeing if any more numbers can now be placed. Continue, and eventually you complete the logic puzzle. There are two more sophisticated techniques one can use to solve a Sudoku logic puzzle: Crosshatching & Pencil Marks.

Sudoku improves your brain, your memory, your concentration & stimulates your mind.

Puzzle 1. US STATE FLOWERS - ALABAMA: C_M_LL__

6			7		2	3		
					9		4	1
4				5				
					6			
					1	7	8	
7			9	3			5	
		2			8			4
	3						6	7

Puzzle 2. ALASKA: F_RG_T-M_-N_T

3			1	8			9	
	2							
7				6		4		
			4					7
		8				3		2
	9			2	3		5	
			8	9		5		
6				5		1		4

Puzzle 3. ARIZONA: S_G__R_ C_CT_S BL_SS_M

	1		5				9	
4		7						
			1			3	7	2
	2	6		3				
			7					1
9								4
		8		2				6
		5					2	
3	9			5				

Puzzle 4. ARKANSAS: _PPL_ BL_SS_M

1			7				6	
		9		1		4		
			2					
		8					4	
		1	5		6		7	2
	5	2			9		3	
4	2	3		8				9
				7				

Puzzle 5. CALIFORNIA: C_L_F_RN__ P_PP_

	3	9				8		
			5		4			7
				9			3	
				5			4	
	6	4				2		
	7			1				3
		6				5	2	
	8				1			9
	2							1

Puzzle 6. COLORADO: R_CK_ M__NT__N C_L_MB_N_

					8		4	
		3				8	2	
8	1	9			6			3
4				6		1		
						7		
9		6					8	
	2		7		5			
5		1	2					
	7			9				

Puzzle 7. CONNECTICUT: M__NT__N L__R_L

		6	1		4		7	
5	9							
			5		9			2
4			9		3			8
							3	
		9			2		1	5
1		5						6
8	3					7		1

Puzzle 8. DELAWARE: P__CH BL_SS_M

					1			5
	5			8			4	
	7	1	4			8	2	
	6	2	3					
			6		2	7	3	
		8						
	4	3		5	7			9
			9	4			7	

Puzzle 9. FLORIDA: _R_NG_ BL_SS_M

			6					
8			2	4				
	1	7		5	8			
	8					1	6	
3				7	6			
9		1				5		
					4			
		4		8	2			1
			9			3		

Puzzle 10. GEORGIA: CH_R_K__ R_S_

		8		7				
			2		9			
3	7		5					
4								9
6	3					5	7	
		5	3		8	1		
	1		6		5			2
8			4		1		3	7

Puzzle 11. HAWAII: H_B_SC_S

			2		4	3		7
	8				1	6		
			8					9
		6					3	2
3		8	7	9	2			5
		7						1
	1				3	4	2	

Puzzle 12. IDAHO: M_CK _R_NG_

	8		6					7
	7			5		4		
			9	1		2		
	1				4	3		
3	2			9		7		
			5		6	8		2
1			3			6		8
	9							
					9			

Puzzle 13. ILLINOIS: P_RPL_ V__L_T

					8			
	1						9	3
	3		1					
5					4			
	2						3	5
4					7	8	6	
		7	9					6
1			6					
		9			3		5	2

Puzzle 14. INDIANA: P__N_

		2				1	5	9
1							4	
		8				3		
3			1					2
6		7			5			
				4	3			
	5		4	9				
	8							7
	3				7	8		

Puzzle 15. IOWA: W_LD PR__R__ R_S_

				1	8	6		
2		7		5				
		1		6			3	
8						2		
	1			9			5	
			6		1			
9							2	
3		8	2				1	
				4	3	5		

Puzzle 16. KANSAS: S_NFL_W_R

	1		9		2		8	
8					5			1
				7				5
7	4	9						
6	3			4	9		1	
					3			7
1	7		6					
2	8						9	3

Puzzle 17. KENTUCKY: G_LD_NR_D

6	7							
			9					
	9	1	6				4	3
		6					8	
		4			8		2	
4		8	7	2				9
5					3	2		
		9	1				3	4

Puzzle 18. LOUISIANA: M_GN_L__

2	3			4	6		5	
	9							
				1	9		3	
6				5		4	2	
					1			7
4	6					1		
			8			7		5
		8						3

Puzzle 19. MAINE: WH_T_ P_N_ T_SS_L _ND C_N_

	9		1					
	6							4
	2	5	4		3			7
				3	4			6
					1	9	3	8
					7	5		
						2		
		1	5	6	9	4		
	5	9						

Puzzle 20. MARYLAND: BL_CK-____D S_S_N

			6					9
8	7	9	2					
4	2						1	
7		5						
	3			1				
				3	5			
		4			9		5	8
5						2		
		2	7					4

Puzzle 21. MASSACHUSETTS: M__FL_W_R

								3
2					5			
	9		8			6		
	6		1	4				9
	7						2	
9	5			2	8		4	
					7			
						5		8
3	1		5			9		

Puzzle 22. MICHIGAN: _PPL_ BL_SS_M

	7	8		3		6	5	
					4		2	3
		3				9		5
	2		4					
		4	5	9	6	3		
		6				5		
			3	8				1
	9				1	7		

FILM TRIVIA. Fill in the missing words for 4 movie titles

15. _______ Or My Mom Will Shoot; The Inn of the Sixth _______; Harry Potter and the _______ of Azkaban; The _______ Band of Misfits;

16. _______ The Secret Service; The Story of _______ and Irene Castle; An Officer and a _______; _______ in a Golden Eye;

17. Not with My Wife, You _______; There Was a _______ Man...; Once Upon a Time in _______; The Three Lives of _______;

18. _______ Tiger, Hidden Dragon; _______ They Gave a War and Nobody Came?; The _______ of Ichabod and Mr. Toad; The Bad News _______ Go to Japan;

19. Please Don't Eat the _______; _______ Fauss and Big Halsy; Boy, Did I Get a Wrong _______; The Girl with the _______ Tattoo;

20. The Death of Mr. _______; _______ Goes to Monte Carlo; The Man Who Came to _______; The Girl _______ of a Big Man;

21. At _______ I'll Take Your Soul; Star Trek: The Motion _______; Better Living Through _______; _______, Sweet Charlotte;

ANSWERS: 15. ;!SETARIP ;RENOSIRP ;SSENIPPAH ;!POTS 16. ;SNOITCELFER ;NAMELTNEG ;NONREV ;:NAMSGNIK 17. ;ANISAMOHT ;OCIXEM ;DEKOORC ;!T'NOD 18. ;SRAEB ;SERUTNEVDA ;ESOPPUS ;GNIHCUORC 19. ;NOGARD ;!REBMUN ;ELTTIL ;SEISIAD 20. ;DNEIRF ;RENNID ;EIBREH ;UCSERAZAL 21. ;HSUH...HSUH ;YRTSIMEHC ;ERUTCIP ;THGINDIM

Puzzle 23. MINNESOTA: P_NK _ND WH_T_ L_D_SL_PP_R

	7			3		6	5	
		6						
3					1		9	
1			7		9			8
	8		3					6
			4		8	5		9
	6			7				
	2	9				8		3

Puzzle 24. MISSISSIPPI: M_GN_L__

	6		2					
	1						7	4
		4	3	1	8	5	6	
4				2	7			8
		2	6	5				
	9				1			
		7				4		2
3						7	5	

Puzzle 25. MISSOURI: H_WTH_RN

								9
					6			
				1			4	5
	8	4			5			7
	6			8				
		1				9	8	
7								2
	5		4	6		8	1	
4			3	5				

Puzzle 26. MONTANA: B_TT_RR__T

6								
7				2		3		
8				6		7	5	
							4	
	2					9		
	6		3					2
	4				3		9	7
	5		4		8		1	
			5			8		

Puzzle 27. NEBRASKA: G_LD_NR_D

	6			5				
	8	7						
		5			4	2		6
3			9					
8				3	1			
				8			7	
1			8			4	2	
	9				7	6		3

Puzzle 28. NEVADA: S_G_BR_SH

3		5		2	6	4	8	
			4	8				3
4							6	
	8			3	5			
	6			4	7			
7			1					
		2				7	5	1
				9	4	6		

Puzzle 29. NEW HAMPSHIRE: P_RPL_ L_L_C

	1				5			
					2		5	
		3		9				
			6				2	1
	9		2				3	
	6				8	5		
	3	8		1		6		
					9			2
		9	7					

Puzzle 30. NEW JERSEY: V__L_T

	1						6	4
	6		2	4	8		5	
	3		5					
	9		1				2	
2								5
1								6
5			3					7
			7		4		8	
			6	5			9	

Puzzle 31. NEW MEXICO: __CC_

	4	5			1			
	3			2				5
2		1		7			3	
	5		9					
	6	7			4			
					9		2	
	9		7		5			6
8		6	1			9		

Puzzle 32. NEW YORK: R_S_

3					7		8	
					3			4
	8				6			
6							1	8
					2	9		
2		1				5		6
		4	9					1
		2			5		7	
		6	2				9	

Puzzle 33. NORTH CAROLINA: FL_W_R_NG D_GW__D

		7					9	
	2				4			
		3				8		7
8					2	3		
1				5			8	
			7	6				5
	4			3		1	5	9
		2		1	6			

Puzzle 34. NORTH DAKOTA: W_LD PR__R__ R_S_

		7	6		4	3		
1	4		2			9	5	
	6	3			8	4		
		6						
	9		8	3		5		
			4	2				
	2		5			6		
3		9			7			

Puzzle 35. OHIO: SC_RL_T C_RN_T__N

9							2	
						7	4	3
1								
3					8			
			7		3	6		4
	1				5			9
8	4	1	5		2		9	
7	6						5	
			1					2

Puzzle 36. OKLAHOMA: M_STL_T__

	2	4				5		
					7			3
		9	8	2				1
9						7		2
	7	2		3		9		5
4	1	7	2					
	5			6				
					8		1	

Puzzle 37. OREGON: _R_G_N GR_P_

				1	9			
7				4		8	9	
4				8				
		5				1		6
		7				4		
			2		1			9
2		9						5
3			9					
			5	2	6			

Puzzle 38. PENNSYLVANIA: M__NT__N L__R_L

		5				8		9
1	3		5		8	2		
					2			1
			9			4		3
6			4			9		
7			3	1				4
5					7			
	6	2		4	5			

Puzzle 39. RHODE ISLAND: V__L_T

	4				8		5	
1								
		6	3			1		2
6								
3	5				4		1	
	8				5	9	3	
							2	
					3		9	
	9	4					8	5

Puzzle 40. SOUTH CAROLINA: __LL_W J_SS_M_N_

		5		4				
	1	3	8			2		
	7	6			3			5
				6			7	
				2	5	9		3
			7					
		8			1	5		
9							2	
		7			4		9	

Puzzle 41. SOUTH DAKOTA: P_SQ__ FL_W_R

			8	6		1	2	
	6		5			9	3	
7						8		
		1		8	9	6	7	
5							1	
2	9				6			
1			9			5		
			1	4	7			

Puzzle 42. TENNESSEE: _R_S

	8				4	9		
			7			2	1	
4	6						7	
			6		9			7
8			5					
1	5		8				2	
			2			4		6
	9		3	6				

Puzzle 43. TEXAS: T_X_S BL__B_NN_T

8	6		5	3	7			
		9			2			
	9	5	2		1			
					9		8	
		4	3					6
3					8		2	7
	7			1		6	4	

Puzzle 44. UTAH: S_G_ L_L_

			4			7		2
9	1			3	8		5	
			1					
	4			6		3		
	3							
			9				7	4
		5					2	8
7		6		9				1

Puzzle 45. VERMONT: R_D CL_V_R

	6				5			
	2			4			7	1
							5	
					2			8
2				1				6
	1		3		7	9		
			4			3		5
1			5	9				
7	8							

Puzzle 46. VIRGINIA: FL_W_R_NG D_GW__D

					3		1	
7	6		5					3
			8	7			4	
	5		2	3	9			8
			4	8			7	
3		6	7					
4		2					8	
			9		8		2	

Puzzle 47. WASHINGTON: C__ST RH_D_D_NDR_N

			5				8	
8				1				3
	4					7	2	
					5			
	7							9
			4	6	7			
	2		1			9		4
3				7		8		
7				9	4			

Puzzle 48. WEST VIRGINIA: RH_D_D_NDR_N

								6
4		2		3				
8						5		7
3	7					9		2
	1					6		
		9		2		1		
				1	6	4		
1	5		7					
					9			

Puzzle 49. WISCONSIN: V__L_T

5		4			7			2
			6			8		
					1			4
3	5		8		9			1
	4	2		7				
		9	5	2				8
					6	5	9	
				8		1		

Puzzle 50. WYOMING: _ND__N P__NTBR_SH

5					7			6
3	8		6		2	5		
					1	7		8
2	1						9	
				3				
4			1			8		3
					4			
		5	8					
		8	7	9				

Puzzle 51. US TERRITORY - PUERTO RICO: H_B_SC_S

	4	7						
		8		5		3		2
				4				
		5	9					4
			1	6		8		7
						6		
	5		8	2				3
		3			1			8
	6		5	9		7		

Puzzle 52. CANADIAN PROVINCE FLOWERS - ALBERTA: W_LD R_S_

8			3		5	9		
2				8				4
7		5	9					1
						5	2	
4					1		8	
			7	5				
		4	5			7		
		8			6			
		1		2				

Puzzle 53. BRITISH COLUMBIA: P_C_F_C D_GW__D

4	1			9		5		
	2	8				9		
7				4	3	1		
9			8	2				
			5		4			3
2			4					
1	9			5		6		
	8	3						5

Puzzle 54. MANITOBA: PR__R__ CR_C_S

4	9		2		3		7	5
					5	6		
7					6			
	6						9	4
5		8				1	6	
9	5			6				3
			3			4		1
			4	7				

FILM TRIVIA. Fill in the missing words for 4 movie titles

22. Captain _______ Mandolin; _______ Up There Likes Me; Bill & Ted's _______ Adventure; Birdman or (The _______ Virtue of Ignorance);

23. The _______ Lives of Adam and Eve; The Hobbit: An _______ Journey; Gonzo: The Life and Work of Dr. Hunter S. _______; Davy _______ King of the Wild Frontier;

24. The _______ Fastest Indian; The Lord of the Rings: The _______ of the Ring; Extremely Loud & _______ Close; The Apple _______ Gang Rides Again;

25. The _______ of a Chinese Bookie; _______ Fang 2: Myth of the _______ Wolf; The Double Life of _______; Murder on the Orient _______;

26. The Day the _______ Stood Still; The Last _______ of Noah's Ark; The Boy in the _______ Pajamas; Mary Shelley's _______;

27. The Adventures of _______ Finn; An _______ Werewolf in London; Death Wish 4: The _______; Little _______ Happy at Last;

28. The _______ of His Company; Rally _______ the Flag, Boys!; The _______ of Dorian Gray; The Night of the _______ Day;

ANSWERS: 22. ;DETCEPXENU ;TNELLECXE ;YDOBEMOS ;S'ILLEROC 23. ;:TTEKCORC ;NOSPMOHT ;DETCEPXENU ;ETAVIRP 24. ;GNILPMUD ;YLBIDERCNI ;PIHSWOLLEF ;S'DLROW 25. ;SSERPXE ;EUQINOREV ;ETIHW ;GNILLIK 26. ;NIETSNEKNARF ;DEPIRTS ;THGILF ;HTRAE 27. ;...AIROLG ;NWODKCARC ;NACIREMA ;YRREBELKCUH 28. ;GNIWOLLOF ;ERUTCIP ;DNUOR' ;ERUSAELP

Puzzle 55. NEW BRUNSWICK: P_RPL_ V__L_T

9						5	7	4
	4							
7					2		6	9
	5			1			4	
				5	3			
					6			7
	1				9			
	2	6						
					1	2	3	

Puzzle 56. NEWFOUNDLAND AND LABRADOR: P_RPL_ P_TCH_R PL_NT

9		7		4		5		
		2						1
		8					9	7
				8			6	
3			7	9		4		8
		4	1					
4								9
7				3	2			
					5			6

Puzzle 57. NORTHWEST TERRITORIES: M__NT__N _V_NS

7				6	9		8	
					1			
		3	2					
			4					3
	6	7		8				1
1				7			2	5
	8							6
						1		
	7	2				3	4	

Puzzle 58. NOVA SCOTIA: M__FL_W_R

	9			7	4	2		
							3	1
4								
1				3		7	8	2
			6		7			
				1				
3	7				5	9		
9	6						7	3
2	4							

Puzzle 59. NUNAVUT: P_RPL_ S_X_FR_G_

								3
5		3						
6		9	1		3			
8	4		7					6
			5		1			
			6					4
	2			1			3	7
		8					5	9
	5			2				1

Puzzle 60. ONTARIO: WH_T_ TR_LL__M

			4			6		
	7			8	3			1
		3	5				9	2
		6	8					
				6				7
		1			9		4	
	6					7		5
	3				2			
				3	8	1		

Puzzle 61. PRINCE EDWARD ISLAND: L_D_'S SL_PP_R

						5		
7	2							6
9	5			6	3	4		
						6	7	
6	7				8	2	3	9
			1					
	8	3	9	4	1			
			2	3	7			

Puzzle 62. QUEBEC: BL__ FL_G _R_S

6			7	4			2	
			3	6			5	
8		3					6	
				7				3
3	2	1	9					
7					9			
			6	3		5		8
				5			4	1

Puzzle 63. SASKATCHEWAN: W_ST_RN R_D L_L_

	1		2					7
		7		9		2		
							4	
							7	2
		1			3	8	9	4
	5	4						
	8	5	9			1		
		3			4			8
			6		5			

Puzzle 64. YUKON: F_R_W__D

			9	4				
	8		3				1	9
		4				8	2	
	5							
		2					6	4
						2	8	
	9	7	8		6	5		
			1	3				
		3	7					

FILM TRIVIA. Fill in the missing words for 4 movie titles

29. A _______ Night's Sex Comedy; The Chaos Class _______ the Class; Horatio _______ The Fire Ship; The Hunger Games: _______ Fire;
30. _______ Jones and the Last Crusade; _______ of a Dangerous Mind; In Search of the _______; The Private Life of _______ Holmes;
31. A _______ of Life and Death; Charlie, the _______ Cougar; The Story of Robin Hood and His _______ Men; Born on the _______ of July;
32. Pat _______ & Billy the Kid; 20,000 _______ Under the Sea; There's No _______ Like Show _______; Horatio _______ The Duel;
33. The _______ of Aimee; Master and _______ The Far Side of the World; You _______ Run Away from It; How to Make Love to a _______;
34. The Devil and Daniel _______; The _______ at the Top of the World; The Prince and the _______; The _______ of Notre Dame;
35. The _______ of Sherlock Holmes; Team _______ World Police; Where Were You When the _______ Went Out?; Eternal _______ of the Spotless Mind;

ANSWERS: 29. ;GNIHCTAC ;:REWOLBNROH ;DELIAF ;REMMUSDIM 30. ;KCOLREHS ;SYAWATSAC ;SNOISSEFNOC ;ANAIDNI 31. ;HTRUOF ;EIRREM ;EMOSENOL ;RETTAM 32. ;:REWOLBNROH ;SSENISUB ;SEUGAEL ;TTERRAG 33. ;NAMOW ;T'NAC ;:REDNAMMOC ;ECNARAEPPASID 34. ;KCABHCNUH ;LRIGWOHS ;DNALSI ;RETSBEW 35. ;ENIHSNUS ;STHGIL ;:ACIREMA ;SERUTNEVDA

PICTURE PUZZLE 9. ROCKEFELLER CENTER IN NYC WITH CHRISTMAS TREE

PICTURE PUZZLE 9. CIRCLE THE TEN DIFFERENCES

SHOPPING MATH PUZZLES

All puzzles are fun and entertaining. Sometimes we learn an unexpected appreciation for a particular area of learning when it is presented in an enjoyable manner. Most of us love to shop. So, Shopping Math Puzzles – word puzzles based upon shopping – will prove particularly enjoyable, even if word problems were not one of your favorite math assignments in school.

Each page in this book contains twenty shopping, word-problem puzzles. Some are multiple-choice, with four possible answers provided, and some require a numerical answer. The correct answers are in reverse order at the bottom of each page.

Benefits of Solving Shopping Math Puzzles

The benefits of solving Shopping Math Puzzles are many. They help teach you how to solve problems in everyday life. You began to practice and solve mathematical word puzzles in elementary school, and you continue as an adult to encounter math word"puzzles"everyday, in real-life situations.

Shopping Math Puzzles is an excellent resource to use when teachers or speech/cognitive therapists test the understanding of a new concept. The puzzles aid in not only understanding the application of math principles, but also improve reading comprehension.

Shopping Math Puzzles

Provide an Interesting and Enjoyable Activity
Shopping Math Puzzles are implicitly interesting, partly because solving them does not involve a sequence of very similar steps that are designed to practice the same skill. The novelty of the puzzles adds to their interest. Solving Shopping Math Puzzles involves detective work, which most people enjoy. We become deeply involved in the process required for solving the puzzle, and relish getting the answer after having struggled.

Create Greater Understanding of Mathematical Processes
Solving Shopping Math Puzzles requires an understanding of the mathematical process. As we struggle with a puzzle, we often immerse ourselves in obtaining the solution so much that we apply mathematical methods spontaneously. This application gives us a deep understanding of problem solving methods.

Promote Positive Attitudes

As we work through a shopping math puzzle, we become so involved we forget that the puzzle solving involves mathematics. Success when we find the answer helps us gain a positive attitude. This is especially effective when these Shopping Math Puzzles are used with students.

Introduce and Enhance Research Methods

The method used to solve Shopping Math Puzzles is similar to the Scientific Method used by a researcher. The solver moves step-by-step through the process. Hence, while solving the puzzle, you learn to apply the thinking processes of the scientific method.

Promote Flexibility and Creativity

Solving a shopping math puzzle provides an opportunity to explore ideas and to extend creativity. You need to be creative and come up with new ways of tackling problems. What works on one puzzles, may not work on the next. Flexibility in your approach is necessary.

Teach General Problem Solving Skills

The strategies and techniques used in mathematics are used to solve other types of problem. Word problems cannot be solved effectively without the four steps of problem solving:

- Understanding the problem
- Devising a plan
- Carrying out the plan
- Looking back and asking if the plan was correct and the problem solved

These steps are applicable in any problem solving situation.

Can be used to Teach Cooperative Skills

Shopping Math Puzzles are ideal to work with someone else or in a group. Research has shown that talking out loud helps learning and understanding. Sharing methods of solution can help produce original ideas and increase understanding, resulting in increased enjoyment, learning, and social skills, such as communication.

Allow for the Practice of Basic Math Skills

Shopping Math Puzzles use basic skills in an interesting situation. Frequently, more than one mathematical function is used to derive the solution. Teachers will find these Shopping Math Puzzles a creative way to not only practice basic skills, but also combine mathematical functions in a meaningful way.

Provide a Similar Approach for Mastering Other Subjects

Shopping Math Puzzles utilize a problem solving perspective that puts the math subject on a par with other subjects students encounter in school. The problem solving methods needed transfer to the mastery of other non-math school subjects.

Suggestions for Solving Word Math Puzzles

Problem solving is the process part of mathematics and it is nowhere more critical than in solving a word problem. Solving Shopping Math Puzzles involves the application of math functions in unique ways; each puzzle must be approached in an original way, considering the information given and determining what is actually being asked for in the way of a solution. Over time, you will develop a range of strategies to have at your disposal.

After reading the puzzle, you need determine what the puzzle is asking for. To do so, restate the problem in different ways, as many times as needed, until you understand what the puzzle is asking. Underline the portion of the puzzle that asks a question and, if necessary, rewrite the question in your own words.

When you approach a Shopping Math Puzzle for solution, you need to differentiate between critical and superfluous information. To do so, cross out information that is not critical for the solution. You also need to determine which arithmetic function(s) is needed to solve the puzzle.

The following steps will help you:

- Read the whole problem through to get the feel of the whole puzzle.
- Read the problem again, listing information and variables.
- Attach units of measure to the variables you identified (dollars, gallons, miles, inches, etc.).
- Define what the puzzle is asking for – the answer you need – as well as its units of measure.
- Work in an organized manner, writing neatly and clearly. This will help you think clearly.
- Draw or sketch if needed to help visualize the process.
- Label your graphs and pictures clearly.
- Work through each step of your process keeping track of variables.

Shopping Math Puzzles are designed with the objective of providing a fun mathematical activity that is both challenging and educational for everyone. The puzzles in this book will provide hours of entertainment for puzzle lovers of any age

Teachers will find the puzzles provide practice for basic math skills, teach problem solving, prepare students for real-life mathematical applications, and create an understanding of the mathematical process.

Students will find some puzzles a challenge. When the solution is found, they will experience a feeling of success which leads to a positive attitude. Flexibility and creativity are enhanced; a flexible approach is required for solution, as well as creative thinking.

Adults will enjoy the"real"world scenario of the puzzles in this book. The puzzles are not tremendously difficult, but do require some thinking. You will derive a sense of satisfaction as you complete each puzzle.

Whatever your age, your educational level, or the reason for choosing to work the puzzles in this book, you will find each puzzle provides a sense of satisfaction upon completion. Enjoy solving Shopping Math Puzzles!

SOLUTIONS SHOWN IN REVERSE AT PAGE BOTTOM.

The Benefits of Shopping Math Word Problems:

- Practical application of math in real-world situations
- Apply different math & logical concepts in one question
- Development of the brain's critical thinking skills
- Avoid confusion in real-life supermarket or department store

INTRODUCTORY FUNNY SHOPPING MATH PUZZLES

1. Popeye the Sailor Man buys 1 Can of Spinach at $23, 1 Garbage Can at $37 and 1 Pint of Extra Virgin Olive Oil for Olive at $9. How much is the difference between the most expensive item and least expensive item? [1] $29 [2] $31 [3] $24 [4] $28

2. Bullwinkle buys 1 Box of Arugula Salad at $20, Antler Polish at $25 and Fresh Mixed Nuts for Rocky the Squirrel (best buddy) at $23. How much is due if Bullwinkle has a 20% discount coupon for the Nuts?

3. Minnie Mouse buys 2 Packages of Cheese at $22, 4 Polkadot Bows at $___ and 1 Pair of Red Shorts for Mickey at $28. She pays $200 and receives the change of $36. What is the price of the Polkadot Bows?

4. Fred Flintstone buys 4 Cans of Dynasaur Delight for Dino at $28, 2 Pairs of Puncture-Proof Stone Tires at $25 and 1 Genuine Pearl-Colored Pebble Stone Necklace for Wilma at $18. How much is Fred's change if the sales tax is 7% and he pays $200? [1] $5 [2] $4 [3] $7 [4] $9

5. Homer Simpson buys 4 Bottles of Tiger-Body Hair Gel for Bart at $18, 1 Nuclear Power Science Book for Lisa at $40 and 1 Can of Royal Blue Hairspray for Marge at $20. How much is Homer's change if the sales tax is 10% and he pays $200? [1] $55 [2] $57 [3] $63 [4] $46

6. Spongebob buys 2 Pairs of Green Square Pants at $28, 1 Round Acquarium at $17 and 10 Tasty Krabby Patty Burgers at $25. How much is Spongebob's change if the sales tax is 6% and he pays $150?

7. Bugs Bunny buys 3 Organic Carrots at $28, 300 Pine Toothpicks at $16 and 1 High-Speed Treadmill with Jumping Option at $28. How much is Bunny's change if the sales tax is 6% and the rabbit pays $200?

ANSWERS: 1. ruoF 2. srallod thgiE-ytrihT derdnuH enO 3. srallod eerhT-ytnewT 4. eerhT 5. enO 6. srallod neT 7. srallod -ytrihT

1. Shopper buys 6 Dresses at $ 20, ___ Notebook/Tablets at $ 38 and 6 Home Theaters at $ 50. 16 items in the basket. How much is the missing quantity? [1] 4 [2] 3 [3] 1 [4] 6

2. Shopper buys 4 Screwdrivers at $22, 4 Jackets at $45, 1 Television at $210 and 6 Dresses at $25. How much is due if the shopper has 30% discount coupon for the Jackets?

3. Shopper buys ___ Pairs of Jeans at $ 18, 3 Pairs of Jeans at $ 24 and 4 Beds at $ 109. If the shopper has 20% discount coupon for the Pairs of Jeans then the total purchase is $580. How much is the missing quantity? [1] 6 [2] 2 [3] 3 [4] 5

4. Shopper buys 1 Handsaw at $25, 4 Pairs of Jeans at $35 and 7 Handsaws at $10. How much is due if the sales tax is 5% ?

5. Shopper buys 5 Watches at $17, 4 Dresses at $30 and 6 Pairs of Jeans at $30. How much is the difference between the most expensive item and least expensive item?

6. Shopper buys 1 Dress at $___, 6 Pairs of Jeans at $25, 4 Notebook/Tablets at $40, 5 Notebook/Tablets at $36 and 1 Blazer at $25. Difference between the most expensive item and least expensive item is $20. How much is the missing unit price?

7. Shopper buys 4 Bakeware Sets at $23, 1 Dress at $28, 4 Table Linen Sets at $___ and 2 Futons at $128. Shopper pays $500 and received the change of $68. How much is the missing unit price?

8. Shopper buys ___ Notebook/Tablets at $ 38, 3 Dresses at $ 30, 2 Watches at $ 11 and 5 Handbags at $ 54. If sales tax is 10% then the total purchase is $587. How much is the missing quantity? [1] 1 [2] 4 [3] 2 [4] 3

9. Shopper buys 6 Pairs of Wedge Shoes at $35, 7 Handbags at $54 and 3 Handsaws at $16. How much is the total purchase?

10. Shopper buys 1 Pair of Sandals at $30, 4 Pairs of Pants at $30, 6 T-Shirts at $6, 6 Containers at $20, 1 Chair at $100 and 1 Radio at $51. How much is the difference between the most expensive item and least expensive item?

11. Shopper buys 2 Pairs of Sneakers at $ 126, 2 Dresses at $ 25, ___ Pairs of Jeans at $ 36 and 7 Pairs of Shorts at $ 20. If sales tax is 10% then the total purchase is $684. How much is the missing quantity?

12. Shopper buys 6 Nut Drivers at $20, 2 Cutlery Sets at $92 and 1 Microwave Owen at $34. How much returned if the sales tax is 5% and shopper pays $400 ?

13. Shopper buys 2 Pairs of Jeans at $44, 1 Pair of Slippers at $52 and 5 Pairs of Jeans at $20. How many total items in the shopping cart?

14. Shopper buys 2 Radios at $25, 1 Futon at $129, 3 Radios at $90 and 2 Dresses at $25. How much returned if the sales tax is 7% and shopper pays $600 ? [1] $73 [2] $66 [3] $53 [4] $56

15. Shopper buys 3 Beds at $109, 5 Dresses at $23, 1 Glassware Set at $69 and 1 Hat at $56. How much change returned if shopper pays $600 ? [1] $31 [2] $28 [3] $26 [4] $33

16. Shopper buys 4 Tops at $58, 7 Notebook/Tablets at $46 and 3 Glassware Sets at $29. How much is the difference between the most expensive item and the next most expensive item? [1] $11 [2] $13 [3] $10 [4] $12

17. Shopper buys 2 Pairs of Sneakers at $104, 2 Shirtdresses at $54 and 4 Pairs of Pajamas at $56. How many total items in the shopping cart? [1] 7 [2] 6 [3] 10 [4] 8

18. Shopper buys 1 Radio at $7, 5 Hats at $14, 1 Pair of Leggings at $99, 5 Pairs of Flat Sandals at $20 and 5 Notebook/Tablets at $38. How much change returned if shopper pays $500 ? [1] $34 [2] $28 [3] $35 [4] $27

19. Shopper buys 4 Watches at $86, 2 Dinnerware Sets at $80 and 3 Pairs of Jeans at $44. How much is the difference between the most expensive item and the next most expensive item?

20. Shopper buys 5 T-Shirts at $11, 5 Pairs of Sneakers at $104 and 3 Chair Cushions at $15. How much is the total purchase?

1. enO 2. srallod ruoF-ytneveS derdnuH eviF 3. ruoF 4. srallod neveS-ytroF derdnuH owT 5. srallod neetrihT 6. srallod -ytnewT 7. srallod neetruoF 8. owT 9. srallod xiS-ytrihT derdnuH xiS 10. srallod ruoF-yteniN 11. eviF 12. srallod eviF-ytroF 13. thgiE 14. owT 15. ruoF 16. ruoF 17. ruoF 18. enO 19. srallod xiS 20. srallod ytnewT derdnuH xiS

21. Shopper buys 5 Backpacks at $14, 3 Home Theaters at $78, 3 Cameras at $49, 1 Glassware Set at $69 and 5 Pairs of Espadrilles at $20. How much is the difference between the most expensive item and the next most expensive item?

22. Shopper buys 4 Messenger Bags at $30, 4 Blazers at $___ and 7 Bakeware Sets at $34. Difference between the most expensive item and least expensive item is $10. How much is the missing unit price?

23. Shopper buys 6 Notebook/Tablets at $68, 2 T-Shirts at $11, 2 Polo Shirts at $22 and 2 Slips at $62. How many total items in the shopping cart?

24. Shopper buys 5 Cordless Tools at $108, 1 Top at $35 and 3 Mixers at $20. How much change returned if shopper pays $650 ? [1] $16 [2] $12 [3] $14 [4] $15

25. Shopper buys 4 Beds at $109, 2 Hats at $56 and 2 Pairs of Jeans at $36. How much is the difference between the most expensive item and least expensive item? [1] $73 [2] $67 [3] $61 [4] $79

26. Shopper buys 6 Watches at $40, 4 Balls at $19, 1 Chemise at $58, 5 Chair Cushions at $15 and 3 Pairs of Boots at $35. How much is the total purchase? [1] $620 [2] $637 [3] $554 [4] $531

27. Shopper buys 1 Pair of Jeans at $25, 7 Hammers at $70 and 3 Flatware Sets at $11. How much returned if the sales tax is 8% and shopper pays $600 ? [1] $6 [2] $7 [3] $8 [4] $9

28. Shopper buys 4 Pairs of Jeans at $44, 7 Nut Drivers at $31, 2 Dresses at $23, 3 Watches at $___ and 1 Nut Driver at $8. Difference between the most expensive item and the next most expensive item is $3. How much is the missing unit price?

29. Shopper buys 4 Watches at $95, 6 Radios at $32, 1 Pair of Jeans at $25 and 2 Shirts at $22. How much is due if the sales tax is 6% ?

30. Shopper buys 2 Mixers at $40, 6 Dresses at $65 and 7 Hammers at $15. How much is due if the shopper has 30% discount coupon for the Hammers?

31. Shopper buys 6 Dresses at $72, 3 Glassware Sets at $21 and 5 Pairs of Sandals at $30. How much is due if the sales tax is 7% ?

32. Shopper buys 5 Pairs of Sandals at $ 25, 7 Dresses at $ 30 and ___ Pairs of Shoes at $ 30. 18 items in the basket. How much is the missing quantity?

33. Shopper buys 6 Notebook/Tablets at $33, 7 Pairs of Flat Sandals at $20 and 7 Handsaws at $10. How much is due if the shopper has 30% discount coupon for the Notebook/Tablets?

34. Shopper buys 7 Pairs of Pantyhose at $8, 5 Radios at $___ and 1 Top at $18. Shopper pays $200 and received the change of $91. How much is the missing unit price? [1] $7 [2] $9 [3] $6 [4] $5

35. Shopper buys 1 Chair at $80, 7 Watches at $11 and 6 Radios at $___. Difference between the most expensive item and the next most expensive item is $39. How much is the missing unit price? [1] $38 [2] $44 [3] $33 [4] $41

36. Shopper buys 7 Dresses at $25, 7 Dresses at $65 and 1 Jacket at $12. How much is due if the shopper has 10% discount coupon for the Dresses? [1] $706 [2] $668 [3] $625 [4] $587

37. Shopper buys 4 Pairs of Slippers at $32, 4 Glassware Sets at $33 and 3 Headphones at $100. How much is the total purchase? [1] $560 [2] $448 [3] $453 [4] $509

38. Shopper buys 3 Cameras at $109, 2 Cutlery Sets at $92 and 1 Dress at $___. If sales tax is 7% then the total purchase is $609. How much is the missing unit price?

39. Shopper buys 6 Dresses at $65, 4 Dresses at $20 and 7 Pairs of Sandals at $24. How many total items in the shopping cart?

40. Shopper buys 6 Pairs of Stockings at $9, 3 Balls at $11 and 2 Cameras at $100. How many total items in the shopping cart?

21. srallod eniN 22. srallod ruoF-ytnewT 23. evlewT 24. ruoF 25. enO 26. eerhT 27. eerhT 28. srallod enO-ytroF 29. srallod eniN-ytneveS derdnuH xiS 30. srallod ruoF-ytroF derdnuH eviF 31. srallod yteniN derdnuH xiS 32. xiS 33. srallod eniN-ytroF derdnuH eerhT 34. enO 35. ruoF 36. eerhT 37. enO 38. srallod thgiE-ytfiF 39. neetneveS 40. nevelE

FILM TRIVIA. Fill in the missing words for 4 movie titles
36. _______ Part 2: Public Enemy #1; E.T. the _______; Bill & Ted's Bogus _______; The _______ Before Christmas;
37. _______ Blonde 2: Red, White & Blonde; Andy Hardy Gets _______ Fever; The Texas Chain Saw _______; The Rich Are _______ with Us;
38. Sky Captain and the World of _______; _______ Hardy Gives Good Sex; The Man Who Knew Too _______; The _______ Wore Tennis Shoes;
39. Pirates of the _______ Dead Man's Chest; The Lord of the _______ The Return of the King; The Black Shield of _______; Homeward Bound: The _______ Journey;
40. Alice _______ the Looking Glass; _______ Wish V: The Face of _______; What's Eating _______ Grape; Darby _______ and the Little People;
41. The Life and Death of _______ Blimp; Those Daring Young Men in Their Jaunty _______; Elite _______ The Enemy Within; The _______ Man in the World;
42. _______ Meets the Wolf Man; _______ Night or What You Will; _______ of the Valley of the Wind; Butch Cassidy and the _______ Kid;
ANSWERS: 36. ;ERAMTHGIN ;YENRUOJ ;LAIRTSERRET-ARTXE ;ENIRSEM 37. ;SYAWLA ;ERCASSAM ;GNIRPS ;YLLAGEL 38. ;RETUPMOC ;ELTTIL ;YMEREJ ;WORROMOT 39. ;ELBIDERCNI ;HTROWLAF ;:SGNIR ;:NAEBBIRAC 40. ;LLIG'O ;TREBLIG ;HTAED ;HGUORHT 41. ;TSEGNORTS ;:DAUQS ;SEIPOLAJ ;LENOLOC 42. ;ECNADNUS ;ÄACISUAN ;HTFLEWT ;NIETSNEKNARF

41. Shopper buys 1 Ball at $19, 4 Hammers at $22, 1 Chair at $200 and 5 Dresses at $25. How many total items in the shopping cart? [1] 10 [2] 12 [3] 9 [4] 11

42. Shopper buys 3 Hammers at $22, 6 Watches at $43, 6 Cameras at $12 and 5 Pairs of Espadrilles at $17. How much is due if the shopper has 30% discount coupon for the Watches? [1] $404 [2] $367 [3] $327 [4] $371

43. Shopper buys 2 Pairs of Jeans at $ 36, ___ Pairs of Jeans at $ 36, 5 Skirts at $ 40 and 5 Dresses at $ 28. $28 returned if the sales tax is 10% and shopper pays $600. How much is the missing quantity?

44. Shopper buys 3 Babydolls at $48, 3 Tops at $35, 2 Hats at $14 and 2 Pairs of Pants at $20. How much returned if the sales tax is 9% and shopper pays $350 ?

45. Shopper buys 4 Skirts at $34, 1 TV Stand at $___ and 3 Radios at $14. If the shopper has 30% discount coupon for the Radios then the total purchase is $465. How much is the missing unit price?

46. Shopper buys 3 Scanners at $50, 1 Cutlery Set at $149 and 7 Dresses at $30. How much returned if the sales tax is 8% and shopper pays $600 ? [1] $46 [2] $51 [3] $58 [4] $50

47. Shopper buys 4 Pairs of Slippers at $46, 4 Backpacks at $40 and 3 Table Linen Sets at $7. How much is the difference between the most expensive item and least expensive item? [1] $37 [2] $42 [3] $39 [4] $35

48. Shopper buys 6 Hats at $43, 7 Pairs of Sandals at $24, 6 Dresses at $25 and 1 Shirtdress at $54. How much returned if the sales tax is 8% and shopper pays $700 ? [1] $19 [2] $18 [3] $22 [4] $20

49. Shopper buys 2 Televisions at $158, 4 Pairs of Jeans at $36, 1 Chair at $100 and 2 Dresses at $30. How much is the difference between the most expensive item and the next most expensive item?

50. Shopper buys 5 Dresses at $25, 3 Nut Drivers at $___, 5 T-Shirts at $8 and 6 Handsaws at $10. Shopper pays $300 and received the change of $15. How much is the missing unit price?

51. Shopper buys 2 Televisions at $120, 4 Dresses at $23 and 7 Tops at $35. How much is the total purchase?

52. Shopper buys 3 Pairs of Jeans at $23, 7 Cameras at $___ and 7 Nut Drivers at $31. $33 returned if the sales tax is 6% and shopper pays $700. How much is the missing unit price? [1] $42 [2] $49 [3] $39 [4] $47

53. Shopper buys 1 Pair of Jeans at $___, 6 Pairs of Shorts at $20, 2 Tops at $18 and 2 Radios at $180. Difference between the most expensive item and the next most expensive item is $152. How much is the missing unit price? [1] $22 [2] $29 [3] $28 [4] $23

54. Shopper buys 1 T-Shirt at $11, 5 Jackets at $37 and 2 Mixers at $23. How much is the difference between the most expensive item and the next most expensive item?

55. Shopper buys 6 Radios at $26, 1 Pair of Sandals at $40, 6 Cutlery Sets at $46 and 1 Television at $148. How much is due if the shopper has 30% discount coupon for the Cutlery Sets? [1] $574 [2] $622 [3] $451 [4] $537

56. Shopper buys 6 Dresses at $ 30, 6 Pairs of Sandals at $ 15, ___ Radios at $ 90 and 5 Pairs of Espadrilles at $ 17. Total purchase is $535. How much is the missing quantity?

57. Shopper buys 3 Dresses at $23, 4 Jackets at $45, 4 Radios at $51 and 2 Notebook/Tablets at $68. How much is the difference between the most expensive item and the next most expensive item?

58. Shopper buys 1 Radio at $81, 3 Table Linen Sets at $14, 5 Glassware Sets at $34 and 4 Cordless Tools at $86. How many total items in the shopping cart?

59. Shopper buys 4 Radios at $13, 4 Pairs of Pants at $___, 4 Watches at $41 and 1 Television at $148. Shopper pays $500 and received the change of $36. How much is the missing unit price? [1] $22 [2] $25 [3] $28 [4] $23

60. Shopper buys 3 Camcorders at $189, 1 Dress at $20 and 3 Pairs of Jeans at $23. How much returned if the sales tax is 5% and shopper pays $700 ?

41. ruoF 42. enO 43. eerhT 44. srallod ruoF 45. srallod derdnuH eerhT 46. ruoF 47. eerhT 48. ruoF 49. srallod thgiE-ytfiF 50. srallod -ytnewT 51. srallod neveS-ytneveS derdnuH eviF 52. owT 53. eerhT 54. srallod neetruoF 55. ruoF 56. owT 57. srallod neetneveS 58. neetrihT 59. owT 60. srallod nevelE

61. Shopper buys 3 Pairs of Flat Sandals at $20, 2 Hammers at $65 and 2 Cameras at $109. How much is the difference between the most expensive item and the next most expensive item?

62. Shopper buys 2 Bakeware Sets at $ 20, 2 Pricing Guns at $ 85 and ___ Babydolls at $ 48. If the shopper has 20% discount coupon for the Pricing Guns then the total purchase is $464. How much is the missing quantity?

63. Shopper buys 2 Cutlery Sets at $115, 3 Cordless Tools at $65 and 3 Pairs of Jeans at $35. How many total items in the shopping cart?

64. Shopper buys 4 Pairs of Slippers at $48, 1 Backpack at $40 and 4 Cameras at $97. How much change returned if shopper pays $650 ? [1] $30 [2] $25 [3] $33 [4] $26

65. Shopper buys 2 Handbags at $54, 5 Watches at $40, 6 Pairs of Jeans at $24, 1 Glassware Set at $29, 3 Pairs of Pants at $17 and 3 Nut Drivers at $8. How many total items in the shopping cart?

66. Shopper buys 3 Mixers at $20, 6 Blazers at $24 and 7 Notebook/Tablets at $33. How many total items in the shopping cart? [1] 13 [2] 14 [3] 15 [4] 16

67. Shopper buys 6 Pairs of Sandals at $15, 2 Pairs of Sneakers at $113, 1 Ball at $50 and 3 Pairs of Slippers at $52. How many total items in the shopping cart? [1] 10 [2] 13 [3] 12 [4] 9

68. Shopper buys ___ Pairs of Jeans at $ 28, 5 Notebook/Tablets at $ 38 and 5 Bakeware Sets at $ 55. If the shopper has 30% discount coupon for the Notebook/Tablets then the total purchase is $464. How much is the missing quantity? [1] 5 [2] 2 [3] 4 [4] 1

69. Shopper buys 7 Watches at $11, 1 Pair of Shoes at $80 and 2 Cameras at $169. How much change returned if shopper pays $500 ? [1] $3 [2] $5 [3] $7 [4] $2

70. Shopper buys 2 Chair Cushions at $15, 6 Radios at $20 and 1 Handbag at $54. How much is the total purchase?

71. Shopper buys 1 Backpack at $45, 7 Tops at $32 and 6 Balls at $42. How much is the difference between the most expensive item and least expensive item? [1] $14 [2] $13 [3] $11 [4] $10

72. Shopper buys 7 Watches at $46, 2 Pairs of Leggings at $99 and 1 TV Stand at $100. How much returned if the sales tax is 6% and shopper pays $700 ?

73. Shopper buys 6 Pairs of Pajamas at $56, 1 Cordless Tool at $156, 2 Pairs of Espadrilles at $20 and 3 Dresses at $23. How many total items in the shopping cart?

74. Shopper buys 7 Bakeware Sets at $18, 6 Pairs of Shoes at $76 and 2 Pairs of Pants at $28. How much is the difference between the most expensive item and the next most expensive item?

75. Shopper buys 2 Polo Shirts at $10, 1 Pair of Sandals at $15, 7 Pairs of Sandals at $30, 6 Mixers at $40 and 4 Watches at $40. How much is the total purchase?

76. Shopper buys 2 Dresses at $58, 7 Handsaws at $10, 4 Pairs of Jeans at $30 and 6 Radios at $16. How much is due if the shopper has 30% discount coupon for the Dresses?

77. Shopper buys 7 Bakeware Sets at $23, 4 Containers at $20 and 7 Hammers at $15. How much is the difference between the most expensive item and least expensive item?

78. Shopper buys 4 Pairs of Shoes at $46, 1 Watch at $40, 5 Pairs of Espadrilles at $17 and 6 Dresses at $___. If sales tax is 5% then the total purchase is $576. How much is the missing unit price?

79. Shopper buys 6 Jackets at $37, 6 Skirts at $57 and 2 Glassware Sets at $34. How much is the difference between the most expensive item and least expensive item?

80. Shopper buys 1 Dress at $28, 3 Pairs of Shoes at $___ and 7 Radios at $26. $28 returned if the sales tax is 7% and shopper pays $400. How much is the missing unit price?

61. srallod ruoF-ytroF 62. xiS 63. thgiE 64. enO 65. -ytnewT 66. ruoF 67. eerhT 68. owT 69. owT 70. srallod ruoF derdnuH owT 71. owT 72. srallod eerhT-ytroF 73. evlewT 74. srallod thgiE-ytroF 75. srallod eviF-ytroF derdnuH xiS 76. srallod neveS-ytxiS derdnuH eerhT 77. srallod thgiE 78. srallod -ytroF 79. srallod eerhT-ytnewT 80. srallod xiS-ytroF

STATUE OF LIBERTY WELCOMES IMMIGRANTS IN NEW YORK HARBOR SINCE 1886

How much does it cost round-trip to take the Staten Island Ferry & sail by Lady Liberty?

ANSWER: EERF SI YRREF DNALSI NETATS EHT

81. Shopper buys 2 Hats at $43, 1 TV Stand at $100, 4 Pairs of Espadrilles at $17 and 2 Cameras at $109. How much change returned if shopper pays $500 ? [1] $31 [2] $28 [3] $24 [4] $26

82. Shopper buys 4 Skirts at $46, 6 Pairs of Shoes at $46 and 2 Jackets at $49. How much is the difference between the most expensive item and the next most expensive item? [1] $6 [2] $2 [3] $3 [4] $1

83. Shopper buys 3 Watches at $134, 1 Pair of Sandals at $___ and 3 Dresses at $25. Difference between the most expensive item and the next most expensive item is $74. How much is the missing unit price?

84. Shopper buys 7 Pairs of Jeans at $30, 1 Skirt at $17, 3 Bakeware Sets at $23 and 7 Handsaws at $6. How much is the total purchase? [1] $290 [2] $294 [3] $327 [4] $338

85. Shopper buys 3 Pairs of Shorts at $15, 1 Home Theater at $78 and 4 Mixers at $50. How much is due if the sales tax is 8% ? [1] $362 [2] $279 [3] $349 [4] $376

86. Shopper buys 2 Cameras at $ 12, ___ Cameras at $ 109 and 7 Pairs of Jeans at $ 34. 11 items in the basket. How much is the missing quantity? [1] 5 [2] 2 [3] 3 [4] 4

87. Shopper buys 3 Flatware Sets at $195, 1 Pair of Pants at $28 and 2 Jackets at $12. How much is the total purchase?

88. Shopper buys 4 Watches at $ 43, 6 Pairs of Jeans at $ 23 and ___ Pairs of Jeans at $ 36. If sales tax is 9% then the total purchase is $456. How much is the missing quantity? [1] 4 [2] 6 [3] 3 [4] 1

89. Shopper buys 5 Hats at $43, 2 Pairs of Pants at $20, 1 Jacket at $37 and 3 Dresses at $25. How much is the difference between the most expensive item and least expensive item?

90. Shopper buys 1 Backpack at $___, 1 Camera at $100 and 4 Dresses at $30. Shopper pays $250 and received the change of $13. How much is the missing unit price?

91. Shopper buys 7 Radios at $51, 6 Blazers at $24 and 4 Dresses at $___. Difference between the most expensive item and the next most expensive item is $23. How much is the missing unit price? [1] $24 [2] $28 [3] $29 [4] $26

92. Shopper buys 6 Cameras at $12, 2 Mixers at $20 and 3 Pairs of Shoes at $80. How much is the difference between the most expensive item and the next most expensive item? [1] $60 [2] $62 [3] $71 [4] $64

93. Shopper buys 2 Skirts at $40, 2 Nut Drivers at $31, 6 Handbags at $32, 1 Pair of Jeans at $23 and 1 Dress at $125. How much is the difference between the most expensive item and least expensive item?

94. Shopper buys 1 Bed at $159, 1 Dress at $28, 3 Backpacks at $40, 2 Watches at $158 and 1 Hammer at $16. How much is the total purchase? [1] $607 [2] $555 [3] $639 [4] $754

95. Shopper buys 4 Pairs of Jeans at $24, 3 Notebook/Tablets at $46 and 7 Dinnerware Sets at $34. How much is the difference between the most expensive item and least expensive item?

96. Shopper buys 5 Pairs of Jeans at $25, 4 Dresses at $30 and 1 Home Theater at $130. How much is the total purchase?

97. Shopper buys 1 Backpack at $11, 2 Watches at $134, 2 Jackets at $37, 1 Headphone at $100 and 5 Glassware Sets at $34. How many total items in the shopping cart? [1] 9 [2] 12 [3] 11 [4] 10

98. Shopper buys 3 Notebook/Tablets at $38, 7 Pairs of Shoes at $46 and 1 Dress at $30. How much is the total purchase?

99. Shopper buys 4 Televisions at $130, 1 DVD Player at $100 and 1 Radio at $14. How much is the difference between the most expensive item and the next most expensive item? [1] $24 [2] $26 [3] $31 [4] $30

100. Shopper buys 5 Tops at $58, 1 Radio at $90, 3 Skirts at $34 and 6 Dresses at $25. How much is the total purchase? [1] $669 [2] $632 [3] $537 [4] $568

81. owT 82. eerhT 83. srallod -ytxiS 84. ruoF 85. eerhT 86. owT 87. srallod neveS-ytrihT derdnuH xiS 88. eerhT 89. srallod eerhT-ytnewT 90. srallod neetneveS 91. owT 92. enO 93. srallod owT derdnuH enO 94. eerhT 95. srallod owT-ytnewT 96. srallod eviF-ytneveS derdnuH eerhT 97. eerhT 98. srallod xiS-ytxiS derdnuH ruoF 99. ruoF 100. owT

101. Shopper buys 1 Cutlery Set at $80, 7 Dresses at $65 and 1 Watch at $17. How much is the total purchase?

102. Shopper buys 5 Futons at $ 89, ___ Hammers at $ 16 and 5 Polo Shirts at $ 10. $14 returned if the sales tax is 8% and shopper pays $600. How much is the missing quantity? [1] 5 [2] 2 [3] 1 [4] 3

103. Shopper buys 1 Bed at $159, 4 Cameras at $114 and 2 Hammers at $16. How much is the difference between the most expensive item and least expensive item?

104. Shopper buys 5 Pairs of Sandals at $15, 4 Dresses at $40, 4 Bakeware Sets at $18 and 1 Radio at $220. How much is due if the shopper has 10% discount coupon for the Radio? [1] $505 [2] $449 [3] $404 [4] $419

105. Shopper buys 5 Notebook/Tablets at $38, 1 Backpack at $11 and 4 Watches at $40. How much is the difference between the most expensive item and least expensive item? [1] $24 [2] $29 [3] $25 [4] $33

106. Shopper buys 3 Pairs of Sandals at $30, 3 Glassware Sets at $28 and 5 Pricing Guns at $85. How much is due if the sales tax is 10% ?

107. Shopper buys 6 Pairs of Flat Sandals at $20, 1 Dress at $65 and 2 Cameras at $228. How much is the total purchase? [1] $641 [2] $685 [3] $583 [4] $557

108. Shopper buys 2 Radios at $90, 3 Bakeware Sets at $55, 5 Glassware Sets at $34 and 6 Pairs of Shorts at $20. How many total items in the shopping cart?

109. Shopper buys 6 Pairs of Sandals at $ 30, 5 Jackets at $ 37 and ___ Nut Drivers at $ 8. Shopper pays $500 and received the change of $87. How much is the missing quantity?

110. Shopper buys 7 Dresses at $ 28, ___ Telephones at $ 100 and 2 Messenger Bags at $ 30. 12 items in the basket. How much is the missing quantity?

111. Shopper buys ___ Polo Shirts at $ 10, 4 Glassware Sets at $ 29, 7 Radios at $ 16 and 6 Babydolls at $ 48. 20 items in the basket. How much is the missing quantity?

112. Shopper buys 2 Handsaws at $25, 6 Mobile Phones at $20 and 4 Cutlery Sets at $115. How much returned if the sales tax is 6% and shopper pays $700 ?

113. Shopper buys 4 Shirts at $22, 1 Television at $218 and 7 Watches at $46. How many total items in the shopping cart? [1] 11 [2] 14 [3] 13 [4] 12

114. Shopper buys 1 Watch at $___, 1 Pair of Sneakers at $148 and 6 Bakeware Sets at $20. Shopper pays $310 and received the change of $2. How much is the missing unit price?

115. Shopper buys 1 Headphone at $130, 4 Dinnerware Sets at $57, 2 Cutlery Sets at $92 and 2 Cameras at $12. How much is due if the sales tax is 9% ?

116. Shopper buys 4 Backpacks at $___, 1 Pair of Socks at $7, 7 Dresses at $30 and 1 Pair of Espadrilles at $20. If the shopper has 20% discount coupon for the Dresses then the total purchase is $331. How much is the missing unit price?

117. Shopper buys 2 Sweaters at $25, 6 Notebook/Tablets at $40 and 6 Dresses at $28. How much is due if the shopper has 10% discount coupon for the Dresses?

118. Shopper buys 7 Dinnerware Sets at $69, 1 Bike at $155 and 1 Backpack at $14. How much is the total purchase?

119. Shopper buys 4 Pairs of Jeans at $36, 2 Backpacks at $45 and 4 Radios at $16. How much is due if the sales tax is 5% ?

120. Shopper buys 4 Notebook/Tablets at $38, 7 Cutlery Sets at $57 and 3 Radios at $13. How much change returned if shopper pays $600 ?

101. srallod owT-ytfiF derdnuH eviF 102. ruoF 103. srallod eerhT-ytroF derdnuH enO 104. enO 105. owT 106. srallod eniN-ytfiF derdnuH xiS 107. enO 108. neetxiS 109. xiS 110. eerhT 111. eerhT 112. srallod owT-ytrihT 113. ruoF 114. srallod -ytroF 115. srallod neetneveS derdnuH xiS 116. srallod ruoF-ytrihT 117. srallod enO-ytroF derdnuH ruoF 118. srallod owT-ytfiF derdnuH xiS 119. srallod neetrihT derdnuH eerhT 120. srallod neT

121. Shopper buys 7 Dresses at $50, 3 Babydolls at $48 and 1 Jumpsuit at $25. How much is the difference between the most expensive item and least expensive item? [1] $21 [2] $22 [3] $20 [4] $25

122. Shopper buys 7 Dresses at $30, 2 Glassware Sets at $33 and 7 Jackets at $___. If sales tax is 9% then the total purchase is $583. How much is the missing unit price? [1] $37 [2] $31 [3] $38 [4] $43

123. Shopper buys 4 Bakeware Sets at $ 20, 3 Jackets at $ 57, 2 Sweaters at $ 25, 5 Bakeware Sets at $ 23, 3 Backpacks at $ 34 and ___ Pairs of Sandals at $ 22. If sales tax is 8% then the total purchase is $631. How much is the missing quantity?

124. Shopper buys 1 Pair of Sandals at $25, 2 Pairs of Shoes at $103 and 2 Headphones at $180. How much change returned if shopper pays $600 ? [1] $9 [2] $7 [3] $11 [4] $8

125. Shopper buys 1 Camera at $49, 4 Skirts at $57 and 4 Jackets at $29. How much is the difference between the most expensive item and least expensive item?

126. Shopper buys 6 Pairs of Pants at $20, 4 T-Shirts at $6, 5 Notebook/Tablets at $38, 2 Watches at $43 and 2 Jackets at $57. How much change returned if shopper pays $600 ? [1] $55 [2] $60 [3] $64 [4] $66

127. Shopper buys 5 Radios at $90, 1 Polo Shirt at $10 and 3 Blazers at $17. How many total items in the shopping cart? [1] 10 [2] 11 [3] 9 [4] 8

128. Shopper buys 4 Dresses at $23, 2 Pairs of Sandals at $22, 3 Cameras at $49 and 6 Pairs of Sandals at $15. How much is due if the sales tax is 10% ?

129. Shopper buys 7 Pairs of Jeans at $___, 1 Pair of Jeans at $30 and 2 Pairs of Shoes at $46. Difference between the most expensive item and least expensive item is $28. How much is the missing unit price? [1] $19 [2] $17 [3] $14 [4] $18

130. Shopper buys 4 Televisions at $130, 5 Blazers at $17 and 1 SD Card at $___. Difference between the most expensive item and the next most expensive item is $105. How much is the missing unit price?

131. Shopper buys 1 Watch at $41, 3 Chair Cushions at $___ and 1 Glassware Set at $34. Difference between the most expensive item and least expensive item is $8. How much is the missing unit price? [1] $26 [2] $32 [3] $33 [4] $28

132. Shopper buys 1 Mobile Phone at $20, 7 Chairs at $80 and 3 Nut Drivers at $20. How much returned if the sales tax is 5% and shopper pays $700 ? [1] $23 [2] $24 [3] $28 [4] $30

133. Shopper buys 1 Radio at $37, 3 Cordless Tools at $86, 1 Babydoll at $48, 6 Mixers at $20 and 4 Headphones at $40. How much is the total purchase? [1] $604 [2] $735 [3] $623 [4] $728

134. Shopper buys 3 Pairs of Jeans at $30, 2 Dresses at $72, 3 T-Shirts at $___, 5 Bras at $36 and 2 Mixers at $70. Difference between the most expensive item and least expensive item is $64. How much is the missing unit price? [1] $6 [2] $7 [3] $9 [4] $8

135. Shopper buys 6 Balls at $35, 7 Pairs of Sandals at $22 and 4 Handsaws at $14. How much returned if the sales tax is 9% and shopper pays $500 ?

136. Shopper buys 7 Backpacks at $11, 1 TV Stand at $250 and 1 Sofa at $299. How much change returned if shopper pays $700 ?

137. Shopper buys 1 Dress at $28, 1 Chair Cushion at $36, 4 Dresses at $40, 1 Coat at $207 and 2 Glassware Sets at $34. How much change returned if shopper pays $500 ? [1] $4 [2] $2 [3] $1 [4] $3

138. Shopper buys 2 Pairs of Jeans at $25, 4 Glassware Sets at $33 and 1 TV Stand at $300. How much is due if the sales tax is 7% ?

139. Shopper buys 6 Flatware Sets at $11, 7 Pairs of Slippers at $48 and 2 Handsaws at $___. Difference between the most expensive item and the next most expensive item is $23. How much is the missing unit price?

140. Shopper buys 5 Microwave Owens at $34, 3 Backpacks at $45, 5 Pairs of Shorts at $20 and 7 Dresses at $25. How much is due if the sales tax is 7% ?

121. ruoF 122. enO 123. eerhT 124. enO 125. srallod thgiE-ytnewT 126. ruoF 127. eerhT 128. srallod neT derdnuH ruoF 129. ruoF 130. srallod eviF-ytnewT 131. eerhT 132. eerhT 133. eerhT 134. ruoF 135. srallod owT-ytroF 136. srallod ruoF-ytneveS 137. eerhT 138. srallod neetxiS derdnuH eviF 139. srallod eviF-ytnewT 140. srallod enO-ytnewT derdnuH xiS

PICTURE PUZZLE 10. TRUMP TAJ MAHAL IN ATLANTIC CITY (HARD ROCK)

PICTURE PUZZLE 10. CIRCLE THE TEN DIFFERENCES

AIRLINE TRAVEL MATH PUZZLES

All puzzles are fun and entertaining. Sometimes we learn an unexpected appreciation for a particular area of learning when it is presented in an enjoyable manner. Most of us love to fly and enjoy geography trivia. So, Air Travel Math Puzzles – word puzzles based upon flying – will prove particularly enjoyable, even if word problems were not one of your favorite math assignments in school.

Each page in this book contains twenty flying, word-problem puzzles. Some are multiple-choice, with four possible answers provided, and some require a numerical answer. **The correct answers are in reverse order at the bottom of each page.**

The benefits of solving Air Travel Math Puzzles are many. They help teach you how to solve problems in everyday life. **They also teach you geography of major USA, Canadian, Mexican and World cities.** You began to practice and solve mathematical word puzzles in elementary school, and you continue as an adult to encounter math word"puzzles"everyday, in real-life situations.

Air Travel Math Puzzles book is an excellent resource to use when teachers or cognitive/speech therapists test the understanding of a new concept. The puzzles aid in not only understanding the application of math principles, but also improve reading comprehension.

Air Travel Math Puzzles

Provide an Interesting and Enjoyable Activity
Air Travel Math Puzzles are implicitly interesting, partly because solving them does not involve a sequence of very similar steps that are designed to practice the same skill. The novelty of the puzzles adds to their interest.

Solving Air Travel Math Puzzles involves detective work, which most people enjoy. We become deeply involved in the process required for solving the puzzle, and relish getting the answer after having struggled.

Create Greater Understanding of Mathematical Processes
Solving Air Travel Math Puzzles requires an understanding of the mathematical process. As we struggle with a puzzle, we often immerse ourselves in obtaining the solution so much that we apply mathematical methods spontaneously. This application gives us a deep understanding of problem solving methods.

SOLUTIONS SHOWN IN REVERSE AT PAGE BOTTOM.

The Benefits of Airline Travel Math Word Problems:

- **Practical application of math in real-world geography**
- **Apply different location & logical concepts in one question**
- **Development of the brain's critical thinking skills**
- **Avoid confusion in real-life travel situation**

INTRODUCTORY FUNNY TRAVEL MATH PUZZLES

1. Woody Woodpecker flies between a maple tree in London & an oak in Budapest, Hungary at a speed of 574 mph. The flight time between the trees is 4 hours. What is the distance between the trees?
[1] 2663 miles [2] 2548 miles [3] 2296 miles [4] 1836 miles

2. Frank Sinatra sings about flying to the Moon! The distance between Hoboken, NJ (Sinatra's birthplace) & the Moon (Luna) is around 1542 miles. An airplane flies between the NJ city - home to the first Blimpie sub shop - & the Moon at a speed of 514 mph. What is the flight time?

3. The Jetsons fly between London & New York City at a speed of 528 mph. The flight time between the cities is 7 hours. What is the distance between the English speaking world cities?

4. Superman: The distance between a red phonebooth in London & the Daily Planet office in Metropolis is 6864 miles. Superman's flight time between the cities is 13 hours. What is the speed of Superman?
[1] 528 miles [2] 501 miles [3] 549 miles [4] 469 miles

5. Captain Kirk: The distance between the Earth & a colony on Mars is around 2550 miles. Starship Enterprise with Captain Kirk flies between the planets at a speed of 510 mph. What is the flight time?

6. Aladdin: The distance between an oil well in Arabia & the Giza Pyramid in Egypt is around 5540 miles. Aladdin's Magical Flying Carpet flies between the landmarks at a speed of 554 mph. What is the flight time?

7. Donald Duck takes flying lessons to fly from Orlando Disney World to Paris Disneyland, a distance of 3794 miles. Donald Duck's flight time between the cities is 7 hours. What is the speed of the Duck?

ANSWERS: 1. eerhT 2. sruoh eerhT 3. selim xiS-yteniN derdnuH xiS dnasuohT eerhT 4. enO 5. sruoh eviF 6. sruoh neT 7. hpm owT-ytroF derdnuH eviF

1. An airplane flies between Chicago, IL & Mexicali, Mexico at a speed of 470 mph. The flight time between the cities is 3 hours. What is the distance between the cities?
2. The distance between Seattle, WA & Windsor, ON is around 2040 miles. An airplane flies between the cities at a speed of 510 mph. What is the flight time?
3. An airplane flies between New York, NY & Houston, TX at a speed of 510 mph. The flight time between the cities is 3 hours. What is the distance between the cities? [1] 1790 miles [2] 1530 miles [3] 1468 miles [4] 1254 miles
4. The distance between Chicago, IL & Beijing, China is 6480 miles. An airplane flight time between the cities is 12 hours. What is the speed of the airplane?
5. The distance between Denver, CO & Sydney, Australia is 8640 miles. An airplane flight time between the cities is 16 hours. What is the speed of the airplane? [1] 637 miles [2] 534 miles [3] 594 miles [4] 540 miles
6. The distance between Chicago, IL & Nassau, Bahamas is around 1380 miles. An airplane flies between the cities at a speed of 460 mph. What is the flight time? [1] 3 hours [2] 2 hours [3] 4 hours [4] 6 hours
7. The distance between London, United Kingdom & Kolkata, India is around 4950 miles. An airplane flies between the cities at a speed of 550 mph. What is the flight time? [1] 8 hours [2] 7 hours [3] 9 hours [4] 11 hours
8. The distance between New York, NY & Georgetown, Guyana is around 2700 miles. An airplane flies between the cities at a speed of 450 mph. What is the flight time?
9. The distance between London, United Kingdom & Khartoum, Sudan is around 2820 miles. An airplane flies between the cities at a speed of 470 mph. What is the flight time?
10. The distance between London, United Kingdom & Istanbul, Turkey is around 1590 miles. An airplane flies between the cities at a speed of 530 mph. What is the flight time?
11. An airplane flies between London, United Kingdom & Boston, MA at a speed of 510 mph. The flight time between the cities is 6 hours. What is the distance between the cities?
12. The distance between Dallas, TX & Concord, NH is around 1500 miles. An airplane flies between the cities at a speed of 500 mph. What is the flight time? [1] 5 hours [2] 6 hours [3] 2 hours [4] 3 hours
13. An airplane flies between Dallas, TX & Moscow, Russia at a speed of 540 mph. The flight time between the cities is 11 hours. What is the distance between the cities?
14. An airplane flies between Dallas, TX & Lisbon, Portugal at a speed of 450 mph. The flight time between the cities is 11 hours. What is the distance between the cities? [1] 4455 miles [2] 4950 miles [3] 4554 miles [4] 5742 miles
15. An airplane flies between Chicago, IL & Las Vegas, NV at a speed of 490 mph. The flight time between the cities is 3 hours. What is the distance between the cities? [1] 1411 miles [2] 1470 miles [3] 1396 miles [4] 1661 miles
16. The distance between Tegucigalpa, Honduras & Portsmouth, VA is around 1440 miles. An airplane flies between the cities at a speed of 480 mph. What is the flight time?
17. The distance between New York, NY & Budapest, Hungary is 4410 miles. An airplane flight time between the cities is 9 hours. What is the speed of the airplane? [1] 534 miles [2] 490 miles [3] 563 miles [4] 436 miles
18. The distance between New York, NY & Port of Spain, Trinidad and Tobago is 1960 miles. An airplane flight time between the cities is 4 hours. What is the speed of the airplane?
19. An airplane flies between Chicago, IL & Santo Domingo, Dominican Republic at a speed of 460 mph. The flight time between the cities is 4 hours. What is the distance between the cities? [1] 1913 miles [2] 2134 miles [3] 1527 miles [4] 1840 miles
20. The distance between Denver, CO & London, United Kingdom is around 4800 miles. An airplane flies between the cities at a speed of 480 mph. What is the flight time? [1] 8 hours [2] 9 hours [3] 10 hours [4] 11 hours

1. selim neT derdnuH ruoF dnasuohT enO 2. sruoh ruoF 3. owT 4. hpm ytroF derdnuH eviF 5. ruoF 6. enO 7. eerhT 8. sruoh xiS 9. sruoh xiS 10. sruoh eerhT 11. selim ytxiS dnasuohT eerhT 12. ruoF 13. selim ytroF derdnuH eniN dnasuohT eviF 14. owT 15. owT 16. sruoh eerhT 17. owT 18. hpm yteniN derdnuH ruoF 19. ruoF 20. eerhT

Find & Circle 2 LIONS or 2 WOLVES in Each Quadrant

21. The distance between Chihuahua, Mexico & Regina, SK is 1350 miles. An airplane flight time between the cities is 3 hours. What is the speed of the airplane?

22. The distance between Chicago, IL & Las Vegas, NV is around 1530 miles. An airplane flies between the cities at a speed of 510 mph. What is the flight time? [1] 2 hours [2] 3 hours [3] 4 hours [4] 1 hour

23. The distance between New York, NY & Sofia, Bulgaria is 4500 miles. An airplane flight time between the cities is 10 hours. What is the speed of the airplane?

24. The distance between Montreal, QC & Lincoln, NE is 1410 miles. An airplane flight time between the cities is 3 hours. What is the speed of the airplane?

25. An airplane flies between London, United Kingdom & Pristina, Kosovo at a speed of 450 mph. The flight time between the cities is 3 hours. What is the distance between the cities? [1] 1269 miles [2] 1350 miles [3] 1228 miles [4] 1390 miles

26. The distance between Chicago, IL & Panama, Panama is 2160 miles. An airplane flight time between the cities is 4 hours. What is the speed of the airplane? [1] 631 miles [2] 540 miles [3] 615 miles [4] 513 miles

27. An airplane flies between Managua, Nicaragua & Oklahoma City, OK at a speed of 480 mph. The flight time between the cities is 4 hours. What is the distance between the cities?

28. The distance between Dallas, TX & Kingston, Jamaica is 1620 miles. An airplane flight time between the cities is 3 hours. What is the speed of the airplane?

29. The distance between New York, NY & San Francisco, CA is 2550 miles. An airplane flight time between the cities is 5 hours. What is the speed of the airplane? [1] 510 miles [2] 499 miles [3] 453 miles [4] 408 miles

30. The distance between London, United Kingdom & Karachi, Pakistan is around 3710 miles. An airplane flies between the cities at a speed of 530 mph. What is the flight time?

31. An airplane flies between Chicago, IL & St. John's, NF at a speed of 540 mph. The flight time between the cities is 3 hours. What is the distance between the cities? [1] 1620 miles [2] 1798 miles [3] 1360 miles [4] 1409 miles

32. The distance between Chicago, IL & Whitehorse, YT is around 2400 miles. An airplane flies between the cities at a speed of 480 mph. What is the flight time?

33. The distance between London, United Kingdom & Lagos, Nigeria is around 3000 miles. An airplane flies between the cities at a speed of 500 mph. What is the flight time? [1] 8 hours [2] 5 hours [3] 7 hours [4] 6 hours

34. An airplane flies between London, United Kingdom & Porto Novo, Benin at a speed of 540 mph. The flight time between the cities is 6 hours. What is the distance between the cities? [1] 3434 miles [2] 3078 miles [3] 3240 miles [4] 3304 miles

35. An airplane flies between Mexico City, Mexico & Sioux Falls, SD at a speed of 460 mph. The flight time between the cities is 4 hours. What is the distance between the cities? [1] 1840 miles [2] 2152 miles [3] 1600 miles [4] 1582 miles

36. The distance between Atlanta, GA & Athens, Greece is around 5610 miles. An airplane flies between the cities at a speed of 510 mph. What is the flight time?

37. An airplane flies between New York, NY & Guatemala, Guatemala at a speed of 480 mph. The flight time between the cities is 4 hours. What is the distance between the cities? [1] 1920 miles [2] 1939 miles [3] 1785 miles [4] 1747 miles

38. The distance between Denver, CO & Hamilton, Bermuda is around 2300 miles. An airplane flies between the cities at a speed of 460 mph. What is the flight time?

39. The distance between Atlanta, GA & Bogota, Colombia is 1960 miles. An airplane flight time between the cities is 4 hours. What is the speed of the airplane?

40. The distance between London, United Kingdom & Hanoi, Vietnam is 5720 miles. An airplane flight time between the cities is 11 hours. What is the speed of the airplane? [1] 416 miles [2] 473 miles [3] 598 miles [4] 520 miles

21. hpm ytfiF derdnuH ruoF 22. owT 23. hpm ytfiF derdnuH ruoF 24. hpm ytneveS derdnuH ruoF 25. owT 26. owT 27. selim ytnewT derdnuH eniN dnasuohT enO 28. hpm ytroF derdnuH eviF 29. enO 30. sruoh neveS 31. enO 32. sruoh eviF 33. ruoF 34. eerhT 35. enO 36. sruoh nevelE 37. enO 38. sruoh eviF 39. hpm yteniN derdnuH ruoF 40. ruoF

41. An airplane flies between Denver, CO & Dublin, Ireland at a speed of 520 mph. The flight time between the cities is 9 hours. What is the distance between the cities?

42. The distance between Denver, CO & Madrid, Spain is 4950 miles. An airplane flight time between the cities is 9 hours. What is the speed of the airplane? [1] 456 miles [2] 533 miles [3] 550 miles [4] 495 miles

43. An airplane flies between Casablanca, Morocco & Oslo, Norway at a speed of 540 mph. The flight time between the cities is 4 hours. What is the distance between the cities?

44. The distance between London, United Kingdom & Philadelphia, PA is 3710 miles. An airplane flight time between the cities is 7 hours. What is the speed of the airplane? [1] 466 miles [2] 577 miles [3] 514 miles [4] 530 miles

45. An airplane flies between New York, NY & Austin, TX at a speed of 470 mph. The flight time between the cities is 3 hours. What is the distance between the cities? [1] 1649 miles [2] 1410 miles [3] 1156 miles [4] 1424 miles

46. The distance between Atlanta, GA & San Juan, Puerto Rico is 1410 miles. An airplane flight time between the cities is 3 hours. What is the speed of the airplane?

47. An airplane flies between Harrisburg, PA & Chihuahua, Mexico at a speed of 520 mph. The flight time between the cities is 4 hours. What is the distance between the cities?

48. The distance between Denver, CO & Raleigh, NC is around 1590 miles. An airplane flies between the cities at a speed of 530 mph. What is the flight time?

49. An airplane flies between New York, NY & Rapid City, SD at a speed of 540 mph. The flight time between the cities is 3 hours. What is the distance between the cities?

50. The distance between New York, NY & Oklahoma City, OK is around 1590 miles. An airplane flies between the cities at a speed of 530 mph. What is the flight time? [1] 3 hours [2] 6 hours [3] 1 hour [4] 4 hours

51. The distance between Chicago, IL & Mexico City, Mexico is around 1590 miles. An airplane flies between the cities at a speed of 530 mph. What is the flight time? [1] 3 hours [2] 1 hour [3] 4 hours [4] 6 hours

52. The distance between London, United Kingdom & Hong Kong, Hong Kong is around 5980 miles. An airplane flies between the cities at a speed of 460 mph. What is the flight time? [1] 15 hours [2] 12 hours [3] 13 hours [4] 14 hours

53. The distance between Denver, CO & Buenos Aires, Argentina is around 5850 miles. An airplane flies between the cities at a speed of 450 mph. What is the flight time? [1] 11 hours [2] 15 hours [3] 13 hours [4] 12 hours

54. An airplane flies between Dallas, TX & London, United Kingdom at a speed of 510 mph. The flight time between the cities is 9 hours. What is the distance between the cities?

55. An airplane flies between Denver, CO & Tegucigalpa, Honduras at a speed of 500 mph. The flight time between the cities is 4 hours. What is the distance between the cities? [1] 2000 miles [2] 1640 miles [3] 2160 miles [4] 1780 miles

56. An airplane flies between Dallas, TX & San Jose, CA at a speed of 540 mph. The flight time between the cities is 3 hours. What is the distance between the cities? [1] 1830 miles [2] 1328 miles [3] 1620 miles [4] 1393 miles

57. An airplane flies between Chicago, IL & Vienna, Austria at a speed of 520 mph. The flight time between the cities is 9 hours. What is the distance between the cities?

58. The distance between Denver, CO & Mexico City, Mexico is 1590 miles. An airplane flight time between the cities is 3 hours. What is the speed of the airplane?

59. The distance between Whitehorse, YT & Houston, TX is around 2820 miles. An airplane flies between the cities at a speed of 470 mph. What is the flight time?

60. An airplane flies between Dallas, TX & Dover, DE at a speed of 500 mph. The flight time between the cities is 3 hours. What is the distance between the cities? [1] 1545 miles [2] 1500 miles [3] 1245 miles [4] 1290 miles

41. selim ythgiE derdnuH xiS dnasuohT ruoF 42. eerhT 43. selim ytxiS derdnuH enO dnasuohT owT 44. ruoF 45. owT 46. hpm ytneveS derdnuH ruoF 47. selim ythgiE dnasuohT owT 48. sruoh eerhT 49. selim ytnewT derdnuH xiS dnasuohT enO 50. enO 51. enO 52. eerhT 53. eerhT 54. selim yteniN derdnuH eviF dnasuohT ruoF 55. enO 56. eerhT 57. selim ythgiE derdnuH xiS dnasuohT ruoF 58. hpm ytrihT derdnuH eviF 59. sruoh xiS 60. owT

FILM TRIVIA. Fill in the missing words for 4 movie titles

43. The _______ of Notre Dame; Back to the _______ Part II; We Need to Talk _______ Kevin; _______ the Valley of the Dolls;

44. Invasion of the Body _______; The Fall of the Roman _______; Mr. Hobbs Takes a _______; Captain _______ The First Avenger;

45. Andy Hardy's Private _______; How to Marry a _______; They Died with _______ Boots On; _______ The Life and Art of Charles Chaplin;

46. The Man Who _______ Himself; Tae Guk Gi: The _______ of War; _______ in the Garden of Good and Evil; The _______ on the River Kwai;

47. The Life and _______ of Judge Roy Bean; It _______ All Night the Day I Left; _______ Voices, Still Lives; Captain Horatio _______ R.N.;

48. Enron: The _______ Guys in the Room; A _______ Yankee in King Arthur's Court; Andy Hardy Meets _______; The Fog of War: Eleven Lessons from the Life of Robert S. _______;

49. In the Good Old _______; The _______ Gun 2½: The Smell of Fear; Buy the Ticket, Take the Ride: Hunter S. _______ on Film; The _______ of Bagger Vance;

ANSWERS: 43. ;DNOYEB ;TUOBA ;ERUTUF ;KCABHCNUH 44. ;:ACIREMA ;NOITACAV ;ERIPME ;SREHCTANS 45. ;:EILRAHC ;RIEHT ;ERIANOILLIM ;YRATERCES 46. ;EGDIRB ;THGINDIM ;DOOHREHTORB ;DETNUAH 47. ;REWOLBNROH ;TNATSID ;DENIAR ;SEMIT 48. ;ARAMANCM ;ETNATUBED ;TUCITCENNOC ;TSETRAMS 49. ;DNEGEL ;NOSPMOHT ;DEKAN ;EMITREMMUS

61. The distance between Atlanta, GA & Calgary, AB is around 1880 miles. An airplane flies between the cities at a speed of 470 mph. What is the flight time? [1] 6 hours [2] 5 hours [3] 4 hours [4] 3 hours

62. An airplane flies between New York, NY & Quito, Ecuador at a speed of 490 mph. The flight time between the cities is 6 hours. What is the distance between the cities? [1] 2499 miles [2] 2704 miles [3] 2940 miles [4] 3057 miles

63. The distance between Dallas, TX & San Jose, Costa Rica is around 1880 miles. An airplane flies between the cities at a speed of 470 mph. What is the flight time?

64. The distance between London, United Kingdom & Shanghai, China is 5610 miles. An airplane flight time between the cities is 11 hours. What is the speed of the airplane?

65. An airplane flies between Denver, CO & Sofia, Bulgaria at a speed of 460 mph. The flight time between the cities is 13 hours. What is the distance between the cities? [1] 6936 miles [2] 6996 miles [3] 5980 miles [4] 5262 miles

66. An airplane flies between London, United Kingdom & Yangon, Myanmar at a speed of 460 mph. The flight time between the cities is 12 hours. What is the distance between the cities? [1] 4802 miles [2] 5133 miles [3] 5520 miles [4] 6127 miles

67. The distance between London, United Kingdom & Khartoum, Sudan is 3120 miles. An airplane flight time between the cities is 6 hours. What is the speed of the airplane?

68. The distance between Dallas, TX & San Jose, CA is 1440 miles. An airplane flight time between the cities is 3 hours. What is the speed of the airplane? [1] 456 miles [2] 451 miles [3] 480 miles [4] 441 miles

69. The distance between New York, NY & Oslo, Norway is around 3570 miles. An airplane flies between the cities at a speed of 510 mph. What is the flight time? [1] 4 hours [2] 5 hours [3] 7 hours [4] 6 hours

70. The distance between Denver, CO & Tegucigalpa, Honduras is around 2200 miles. An airplane flies between the cities at a speed of 550 mph. What is the flight time?

71. An airplane flies between New York, NY & Las Vegas, NV at a speed of 520 mph. The flight time between the cities is 4 hours. What is the distance between the cities?

72. The distance between New York, NY & Caracas, Venezuela is 2000 miles. An airplane flight time between the cities is 4 hours. What is the speed of the airplane? [1] 595 miles [2] 560 miles [3] 570 miles [4] 500 miles

73. The distance between Atlanta, GA & Hermosillo, Mexico is 1620 miles. An airplane flight time between the cities is 3 hours. What is the speed of the airplane?

74. The distance between London, United Kingdom & Athens, Greece is around 1440 miles. An airplane flies between the cities at a speed of 480 mph. What is the flight time? [1] 1 hour [2] 3 hours [3] 2 hours [4] 6 hours

75. The distance between Chicago, IL & Edmonton, AB is around 1500 miles. An airplane flies between the cities at a speed of 500 mph. What is the flight time? [1] 2 hours [2] 3 hours [3] 5 hours [4] 4 hours

76. The distance between Denver, CO & Veracruz, Mexico is 1350 miles. An airplane flight time between the cities is 3 hours. What is the speed of the airplane?

77. The distance between London, United Kingdom & Baghdad, Iraq is around 2700 miles. An airplane flies between the cities at a speed of 540 mph. What is the flight time? [1] 5 hours [2] 3 hours [3] 1 hour [4] 2 hours

78. The distance between New York, NY & Baton Rouge, LA is 1380 miles. An airplane flight time between the cities is 3 hours. What is the speed of the airplane? [1] 483 miles [2] 460 miles [3] 386 miles [4] 533 miles

79. An airplane flies between New York, NY & Lisbon, Portugal at a speed of 450 mph. The flight time between the cities is 8 hours. What is the distance between the cities?

80. The distance between Dallas, TX & Boston, MA is around 1560 miles. An airplane flies between the cities at a speed of 520 mph. What is the flight time? [1] 2 hours [2] 3 hours [3] 5 hours [4] 4 hours

61. eerhT 62. eerhT 63. sruoh ruoF 64. hpm neT derdnuH eviF 65. eerhT 66. eerhT 67. hpm ytnewT derdnuH eviF 68. eerhT 69. eerhT 70. sruoh ruoF 71. selim ythgiE dnasuohT owT 72. ruoF 73. hpm ytroF derdnuH eviF 74. owT 75. owT 76. hpm ytfiF derdnuH ruoF 77. enO 78. owT 79. selim derdnuH xiS dnasuohT eerhT 80. owT

81. The distance between Milwaukee, WI & Las Vegas, NV is around 1500 miles. An airplane flies between the cities at a speed of 500 mph. What is the flight time?
82. The distance between New York, NY & Lima, Peru is 3780 miles. An airplane flight time between the cities is 7 hours. What is the speed of the airplane? [1] 459 miles [2] 561 miles [3] 540 miles [4] 518 miles
83. The distance between Denver, CO & Bogota, Colombia is around 2820 miles. An airplane flies between the cities at a speed of 470 mph. What is the flight time? [1] 8 hours [2] 2 hours [3] 6 hours [4] 4 hours
84. An airplane flies between Chicago, IL & Brussels, Belgium at a speed of 520 mph. The flight time between the cities is 8 hours. What is the distance between the cities? [1] 4534 miles [2] 3577 miles [3] 4160 miles [4] 4284 miles
85. An airplane flies between Chicago, IL & Whitehorse, YT at a speed of 500 mph. The flight time between the cities is 5 hours. What is the distance between the cities?
86. The distance between London, United Kingdom & Porto Novo, Benin is around 3150 miles. An airplane flies between the cities at a speed of 450 mph. What is the flight time? [1] 7 hours [2] 4 hours [3] 6 hours [4] 5 hours
87. The distance between Dallas, TX & Providence, RI is around 1380 miles. An airplane flies between the cities at a speed of 460 mph. What is the flight time? [1] 4 hours [2] 3 hours [3] 5 hours [4] 2 hours
88. An airplane flies between New York, NY & Bogota, Colombia at a speed of 450 mph. The flight time between the cities is 5 hours. What is the distance between the cities? [1] 2070 miles [2] 2025 miles [3] 2250 miles [4] 2227 miles
89. The distance between Chicago, IL & Budapest, Hungary is around 5060 miles. An airplane flies between the cities at a speed of 460 mph. What is the flight time? [1] 10 hours [2] 11 hours [3] 12 hours [4] 9 hours
90. The distance between Denver, CO & Veracruz, Mexico is 1560 miles. An airplane flight time between the cities is 3 hours. What is the speed of the airplane?
91. An airplane flies between Dallas, TX & Dover, DE at a speed of 450 mph. The flight time between the cities is 3 hours. What is the distance between the cities? [1] 1404 miles [2] 1309 miles [3] 1255 miles [4] 1350 miles
92. The distance between Chicago, IL & St. John's, NF is 1920 miles. An airplane flight time between the cities is 4 hours. What is the speed of the airplane? [1] 432 miles [2] 480 miles [3] 403 miles [4] 499 miles
93. The distance between Guatemala, Guatemala & Billings, MT is 2160 miles. An airplane flight time between the cities is 4 hours. What is the speed of the airplane?
94. The distance between Sioux Falls, SD & Virginia Beach, VA is 1380 miles. An airplane flight time between the cities is 3 hours. What is the speed of the airplane? [1] 510 miles [2] 386 miles [3] 432 miles [4] 460 miles
95. The distance between London, United Kingdom & Shanghai, China is around 5940 miles. An airplane flies between the cities at a speed of 540 mph. What is the flight time? [1] 9 hours [2] 12 hours [3] 8 hours [4] 11 hours
96. The distance between New York, NY & La Paz, Bolivia is 4160 miles. An airplane flight time between the cities is 8 hours. What is the speed of the airplane?
97. The distance between Milwaukee, WI & Las Vegas, NV is around 1410 miles. An airplane flies between the cities at a speed of 470 mph. What is the flight time?
98. The distance between Dallas, TX & Sofia, Bulgaria is 5760 miles. An airplane flight time between the cities is 12 hours. What is the speed of the airplane?
99. The distance between Tijuana, Mexico & Montgomery, AL is around 1650 miles. An airplane flies between the cities at a speed of 550 mph. What is the flight time? [1] 5 hours [2] 3 hours [3] 2 hours [4] 1 hour
100. The distance between New York, NY & Baghdad, Iraq is around 6300 miles. An airplane flies between the cities at a speed of 450 mph. What is the flight time? [1] 15 hours [2] 14 hours [3] 11 hours [4] 13 hours

81. sruoh eerhT 82. eerhT 83. eerhT 84. eerhT 85. selim derdnuH eviF dnasuohT owT 86. enO 87. owT 88. eerhT 89. owT 90. hpm ytnewT derdnuH eviF 91. ruoF 92. owT 93. hpm ytroF derdnuH eviF 94. ruoF 95. ruoF 96. hpm ytnewT derdnuH eviF 97. sruoh eerhT 98. hpm ythgiE derdnuH ruoF 99. owT 100. owT

101. An airplane flies between Chicago, IL & Hermosillo, Mexico at a speed of 450 mph. The flight time between the cities is 3 hours. What is the distance between the cities?

102. The distance between Bucharest, Romania & Louisville, KY is 5300 miles. An airplane flight time between the cities is 10 hours. What is the speed of the airplane? [1] 477 miles [2] 487 miles [3] 530 miles [4] 620 miles

103. The distance between London, United Kingdom & Yamoussoukro, Ivory Coast is around 3150 miles. An airplane flies between the cities at a speed of 450 mph. What is the flight time?

104. The distance between Ottawa, ON & Aspen, CO is 1800 miles. An airplane flight time between the cities is 4 hours. What is the speed of the airplane?

105. The distance between Dallas, TX & Philadelphia, PA is around 1590 miles. An airplane flies between the cities at a speed of 530 mph. What is the flight time?

106. An airplane flies between Atlanta, GA & Las Vegas, NV at a speed of 520 mph. The flight time between the cities is 3 hours. What is the distance between the cities?

107. The distance between Denver, CO & São Paulo, Brazil is 5500 miles. An airplane flight time between the cities is 10 hours. What is the speed of the airplane? [1] 616 miles [2] 550 miles [3] 621 miles [4] 654 miles

108. An airplane flies between London, United Kingdom & New York, NY at a speed of 520 mph. The flight time between the cities is 7 hours. What is the distance between the cities?

109. The distance between Atlanta, GA & Cairo, Egypt is 6300 miles. An airplane flight time between the cities is 14 hours. What is the speed of the airplane? [1] 432 miles [2] 450 miles [3] 499 miles [4] 454 miles

110. An airplane flies between Islamabad, Pakistan & Frankfurt, Germany at a speed of 450 mph. The flight time between the cities is 7 hours. What is the distance between the cities? [1] 2772 miles [2] 2551 miles [3] 3685 miles [4] 3150 miles

111. The distance between New York, NY & New Delhi, India is around 7280 miles. An airplane flies between the cities at a speed of 520 mph. What is the flight time? [1] 12 hours [2] 14 hours [3] 15 hours [4] 16 hours

112. The distance between New York, NY & Tokyo, Japan is 6440 miles. An airplane flight time between the cities is 14 hours. What is the speed of the airplane? [1] 441 miles [2] 460 miles [3] 515 miles [4] 450 miles

113. The distance between Salt Lake City, UT & Scranton, PA is 2120 miles. An airplane flight time between the cities is 4 hours. What is the speed of the airplane? [1] 445 miles [2] 588 miles [3] 625 miles [4] 530 miles

114. The distance between Chicago, IL & San Jose, Costa Rica is around 2000 miles. An airplane flies between the cities at a speed of 500 mph. What is the flight time? [1] 1 hour [2] 4 hours [3] 7 hours [4] 3 hours

115. The distance between Chicago, IL & Tegucigalpa, Honduras is 2080 miles. An airplane flight time between the cities is 4 hours. What is the speed of the airplane?

116. An airplane flies between London, United Kingdom & Nouakchott, Mauritania at a speed of 540 mph. The flight time between the cities is 4 hours. What is the distance between the cities? [1] 1965 miles [2] 1836 miles [3] 2332 miles [4] 2160 miles

117. The distance between San Francisco, CA & Jefferson City, MO is around 1470 miles. An airplane flies between the cities at a speed of 490 mph. What is the flight time? [1] 5 hours [2] 2 hours [3] 3 hours [4] 1 hour

118. The distance between Chicago, IL & London, United Kingdom is 3760 miles. An airplane flight time between the cities is 8 hours. What is the speed of the airplane? [1] 376 miles [2] 380 miles [3] 507 miles [4] 470 miles

119. The distance between Chicago, IL & Aguascalientes, Mexico is 1590 miles. An airplane flight time between the cities is 3 hours. What is the speed of the airplane?

120. The distance between Denver, CO & Columbia, SC is 1440 miles. An airplane flight time between the cities is 3 hours. What is the speed of the airplane? [1] 518 miles [2] 480 miles [3] 528 miles [4] 484 miles

101. selim ytfiF derdnuH eerhT dnasuohT enO 102. eerhT 103. sruoh neveS 104. hpm ytfiF derdnuH ruoF 105. sruoh eerhT 106. selim ytxiS derdnuH eviF dnasuohT enO 107. owT 108. selim ytroF derdnuH xiS dnasuohT eerhT 109. owT 110. ruoF 111. owT 112. owT 113. ruoF 114. owT 115. hpm ytnewT derdnuH eviF 116. ruoF 117. eerhT 118. ruoF 119. hpm ytrihT derdnuH eviF 120. owT

HOW MANY SQUARES ARE INSIDE A DIAGONAL WORD SQUARE PUZZLE?

Can you count all the possible squares for each puzzle type?

ANSWERS: 1. NEETRUOF 2. YTRIHT 3. EVIF-YTFIF 4. ENO-YTENIN

Puzzle Type 1.

Puzzle Type 2.

Puzzle Type 3.

Puzzle Type 4.

MINI CROSSWORD SQUARE SOLUTIONS

3x3 MINI CROSSWORD SQUARE SOLUTIONS

Answer 1.

A	C	T
G	I	G
O	L	D

Answer 2.

T	O	Y
W	E	B
O	N	E

Answer 3.

E	R	R
B	A	G
B	I	T

Answer 4.

D	A	Y
I	N	N
G	A	S

Answer 5.

A	P	T
B	I	N
E	E	L

Answer 6.

H	A	M
A	I	D
S	A	M

Answer 7.

P	I	E
E	A	T
R	A	N

Answer 8.

A	G	E
T	W	O
E	W	E

Answer 9.

E	N	D
A	G	E
R	I	G

Answer 10.

O	A	T
A	D	S
R	O	D

Answer 11.

S	E	T
P	U	B
A	X	E

Answer 12.

M	U	G
E	E	L
N	U	T

Answer 13.

O	N	E
W	W	W
L	E	E

Answer 14.

S	E	E
A	P	T
P	E	A

Answer 15.

A	N	Y
I	N	N
M	U	D

Answer 16.

D	O	G
I	V	Y
G	O	D

Answer 17.

H	E	Y
I	I	I
D	A	M

Answer 18.

V	I	C
A	I	M
T	E	A

Answer 19.

P	I	E
E	A	R
T	R	Y

Answer 20.

D	A	D
A	N	D
Y	E	S

Answer 21.

F	O	R
O	A	R
E	A	R

Answer 22.

P	A	Y
E	A	R
G	A	L

Answer 23.

C	U	T
P	E	N
U	F	O

Answer 24.

J	E	W
O	A	K
E	A	R

Answer 25.

L	E	E
E	Y	E
E	W	E

Answer 26.

H	A	S
A	I	L
M	O	P

Answer 27.

P	O	D
E	E	L
T	A	R

Answer 28.

E	A	T
A	B	C
T	A	B

Answer 29.

M	A	N
R	I	G
S	I	X

Answer 30.

H	A	G
A	U	L
M	O	M

Answer 31.

R	O	M
O	U	R
C	A	N

Answer 32.

S	E	E
O	P	T
W	R	Y

Answer 33.

D	I	P
A	I	M
M	A	N

Answer 34.

G	A	S
A	I	R
S	A	N

Answer 35.

F	E	E
A	R	T
T	W	O

Answer 36.

T	O	E
A	I	M
N	A	P

4x4 MINI CROSSWORD SQUARE SOLUTIONS

Answer 1.

B	A	B	E
O	R	A	L
W	H	A	T
S	N	U	G

Answer 2.

P	A	R	K
A	R	C	S
S	P	O	T
T	I	P	S

Answer 3.

A	G	E	S
I	R	A	Q
D	I	M	E
S	U	E	Y

Answer 4.

S	U	E	Z
E	P	I	C
A	X	I	S
S	P	O	T

Answer 5.

F	U	L	L
A	U	N	T
C	A	S	H
T	H	I	S

Answer 6.

R	A	C	Y
E	A	S	Y
N	I	G	H
T	R	E	E

Answer 7.

B	A	T	E
A	L	S	O
R	O	O	M
S	N	O	W

Answer 8.

B	I	N	D
L	E	S	T
A	C	N	E
B	I	R	D

Answer 9.

S	U	M	O
O	M	E	N
C	H	O	W
K	I	N	G

Answer 10.

S	A	N	K
P	A	R	T
I	T	C	H
T	A	S	K

Answer 11.

S	I	T	E
L	U	R	K
I	N	C	H
M	I	L	K

Answer 12.

T	H	A	W
W	I	S	E
I	N	C	A
G	A	W	K

Answer 13.

S	A	Y	S
P	L	A	Y
A	M	I	D
R	O	A	M

Answer 14.

N	I	C	E
E	A	C	H
A	I	M	S
P	I	K	E

Answer 15.

B	O	S	S
A	I	D	S
R	A	K	E
T	I	R	E

Answer 16.

S	P	A	M
A	M	O	S
N	E	O	N
G	O	N	G

Answer 17.

A	B	E	D
U	S	E	S
T	A	K	E
O	W	E	S

Answer 18.

B	A	B	E
O	I	N	K
M	A	K	E
B	A	T	E

Answer 19.

T	H	I	N
O	W	N	S
S	A	I	D
S	L	U	G

Answer 20.

S	O	O	N
C	L	A	W
O	M	A	N
W	A	V	Y

Answer 21.

H	A	L	O
O	A	T	S
L	A	N	D
E	A	T	S

Answer 22.

S	P	A	N
E	P	I	C
N	O	U	N
T	H	A	N

Answer 23.

D	I	R	K
R	E	A	R
A	R	C	S
B	U	C	K

Answer 24.

O	I	L	Y
P	A	T	H
A	U	T	O
L	E	T	S

Answer 25.

S	H	O	P
A	U	N	T
M	I	E	N
E	A	S	Y

Answer 26.

S	L	A	P
O	N	E	S
N	E	O	N
S	L	E	W

Answer 27.

C	A	F	E
O	H	I	O
D	A	I	S
E	P	I	C

Answer 28.

L	A	C	K
A	U	N	T
M	O	N	K
P	A	N	G

Answer 29.

P	E	N	S
A	L	S	O
S	C	O	W
S	L	E	D

Answer 30.

S	L	A	P
H	O	L	E
O	N	C	E
W	O	R	K

Answer 31.

P	A	P	A
L	O	S	E
O	T	T	O
T	H	U	S

Answer 32.

C	O	P	E
U	R	G	E
R	O	A	R
B	O	O	B

Answer 33.

P	L	U	S
A	R	C	S
C	L	O	G
T	H	A	W

Answer 34.

S	P	I	N
A	T	O	P
L	O	A	D
T	O	B	Y

Answer 35.

F	E	N	D
E	R	I	C
L	I	E	D
L	I	V	E

Answer 36.

W	A	V	Y
H	I	R	E
E	A	R	D
T	A	M	E

5X5 MINI CROSSWORD SQUARE SOLUTIONS

Answer 1.

S	H	E	E	T
P	U	F	F	S
A	L	L	O	Y
S	A	B	L	E
M	U	R	K	Y

Answer 2.

C	I	V	I	C
H	A	R	S	H
I	N	D	I	A
R	E	N	E	W
P	O	I	N	T

Answer 3.

S	T	U	N	T
T	H	R	E	E
A	W	A	R	E
R	E	E	F	S
S	M	E	L	T

Answer 4.

B	A	N	D	S
A	R	E	A	S
S	P	I	R	E
E	B	O	N	Y
S	P	E	C	K

Answer 5.

C	O	V	E	T
R	E	G	A	L
E	R	A	S	E
W	H	O	S	E
S	C	A	R	E

Answer 6.

B	R	E	A	K
L	O	O	P	S
A	D	O	R	E
S	U	N	N	Y
T	I	N	G	E

Answer 7.

F	O	O	D	S
E	L	E	C	T
A	B	E	L	E
S	W	E	E	P
T	O	W	N	S

Answer 8.

A	B	A	C	K
S	P	I	E	D
S	T	A	Y	S
E	M	E	R	Y
T	R	O	U	T

Answer 9.

C	H	R	I	S
L	U	M	P	S
E	E	R	I	E
A	N	G	L	E
R	E	P	L	Y

Answer 10.

C	U	B	I	C
A	L	L	A	Y
S	E	I	N	E
T	R	A	C	K
S	H	E	I	K

Answer 11.

C	A	V	E	S
R	I	P	E	N
A	R	D	O	R
F	A	D	E	D
T	A	P	E	R

Answer 12.

C	I	G	A	R
A	R	A	B	S
S	P	I	T	E
E	L	M	E	R
S	O	R	T	S

Answer 13.

S	N	A	K	E
P	L	U	M	B
I	D	E	A	S
N	Y	M	P	H
E	G	Y	P	T

Answer 14.

S	P	A	N	S
T	H	O	S	E
A	L	O	N	G
T	H	I	R	D
E	X	I	S	T

Answer 15.

F	L	I	N	T
A	L	T	A	R
C	L	U	B	S
E	R	A	S	E
S	L	U	S	H

Answer 16.

S	T	O	R	E
T	H	R	O	W
A	G	E	N	T
F	L	O	A	T
F	I	N	E	R

Answer 17.

B	R	A	I	N
L	I	N	E	S
E	A	G	L	E
A	N	N	O	Y
R	A	B	A	T

Answer 18.

W	O	R	D	S
R	A	I	S	E
A	S	K	E	W
T	H	R	E	W
H	E	R	O	N

Answer 19.

B	O	S	S	Y
E	L	V	E	S
A	B	O	U	T
R	A	D	O	N
S	H	I	E	D

Answer 20.

K	O	A	L	A
N	E	I	G	H
E	N	N	U	I
L	I	B	Y	A
T	O	N	G	A

Answer 21.

I	V	O	R	Y
S	T	I	N	T
L	L	A	M	A
E	X	A	L	T
S	U	L	K	Y

Answer 22.

T	I	R	E	S
A	R	M	E	D
S	L	I	C	E
K	N	O	B	S
S	L	I	M	E

Answer 23.

S	T	R	A	P
H	A	T	C	H
R	I	V	A	L
E	M	B	E	R
D	R	E	A	D

Answer 24.

B	L	O	C	K
I	R	O	N	S
T	R	I	E	S
S	L	A	N	T
Y	O	U	N	G

Answer 25.

C	A	M	P	S
A	R	E	N	A
M	O	U	T	H
P	R	E	S	S
S	W	I	S	H

Answer 26.

F	I	N	E	R
E	L	E	C	T
A	W	A	I	T
R	E	M	I	T
S	W	I	R	L

Answer 27.

S	P	R	A	Y
E	M	A	I	L
A	B	A	F	T
L	A	R	C	H
S	P	E	A	K

Answer 28.

P	A	T	C	H
E	L	D	E	R
S	M	A	S	H
O	P	E	N	S
S	T	O	C	K

Answer 29.

T	W	A	I	N
E	R	A	S	E
S	T	I	N	G
T	A	L	E	S
Y	A	W	N	S

Answer 30.

B	E	A	T	S
L	U	M	P	S
E	A	R	L	Y
S	U	N	N	Y
S	H	O	E	S

Answer 31.

S	C	O	T	T
P	A	T	H	S
R	U	L	E	D
A	L	L	A	Y
Y	A	W	E	D

Answer 32.

W	O	M	E	N
R	E	U	S	E
I	N	E	P	T
S	A	C	K	S
T	R	A	Y	S

Answer 33.

W	A	I	V	E
O	A	S	I	S
U	N	F	I	T
L	E	V	E	L
D	I	V	E	R

Answer 34.

D	R	O	P	S
R	O	B	I	N
E	M	C	E	E
S	T	A	K	E
S	I	D	E	S

Answer 35.

T	R	A	C	E
R	O	M	E	O
A	L	P	H	A
S	O	L	I	D
H	A	V	O	C

Answer 36.

G	A	B	O	N
R	E	B	U	S
A	I	R	E	S
S	L	I	M	Y
P	O	E	T	S

6X6 MINI CROSSWORD SQUARE SOLUTIONS

Answer 1.

B	E	M	O	A	N
A	U	R	O	R	A
L	A	Y	I	N	G
L	E	V	E	R	S
E	N	D	U	R	E
T	I	G	E	R	S

Answer 2.

S	K	O	P	J	E
M	A	S	S	E	S
I	N	D	I	E	S
L	A	N	D	E	D
E	Q	U	A	L	S
S	P	R	I	T	E

Answer 3.

P	U	R	P	L	E
A	R	O	U	S	E
S	P	E	E	D	S
S	T	A	F	F	S
E	Y	E	L	I	D
S	U	F	F	I	X

Answer 4.

M	I	N	I	N	G
A	U	S	T	I	N
N	U	T	M	E	G
A	S	S	U	M	E
G	U	I	T	A	R
E	N	A	M	E	L

Answer 5.

A	P	P	E	A	R
S	W	A	M	P	S
S	E	N	A	T	E
A	L	L	I	E	S
I	N	D	E	N	T
L	I	V	I	N	G

Answer 6.

S	L	A	C	K	S
A	P	P	L	E	S
T	R	O	W	E	L
U	N	J	U	S	T
R	E	M	I	S	S
N	E	G	A	T	E

Answer 7.

B	I	O	N	I	C
R	O	D	E	N	T
A	B	S	E	I	L
C	E	N	T	E	R
E	D	I	S	O	N
S	W	E	D	E	N

Answer 8.

S	U	R	V	E	Y
H	A	R	B	O	R
A	D	V	I	S	E
R	E	P	A	I	R
E	M	E	R	G	E
S	A	T	I	R	E

Answer 9.

P	A	L	T	R	Y
R	E	C	E	S	S
E	N	T	I	R	E
S	P	E	A	K	S
E	V	E	N	L	Y
T	O	W	E	L	S

Answer 10.

D	O	A	B	L	E
R	E	N	A	M	E
E	I	T	H	E	R
A	N	K	A	R	A
M	Y	S	T	I	C
S	C	R	E	E	N

Answer 11.

A	G	R	E	E	S
B	R	I	D	A	L
S	T	I	G	M	A
E	R	A	S	E	R
N	I	E	C	E	S
T	H	I	R	D	S

Answer 12.

T	Y	P	H	U	S
E	R	R	O	R	S
A	G	E	N	T	S
P	U	M	M	E	L
O	R	A	T	O	R
T	E	M	P	E	R

Answer 13.

P	E	T	I	T	E
E	L	E	V	E	N
N	E	A	R	L	Y
C	R	E	S	T	S
I	N	C	O	M	E
L	U	A	N	D	A

Answer 14.

A	G	E	N	T	S
C	L	O	U	D	Y
T	A	B	L	E	S
O	C	T	A	V	E
R	O	W	I	N	G
S	T	O	R	M	Y

Answer 15.

P	L	I	G	H	T
R	A	R	E	L	Y
I	O	D	I	N	E
N	E	E	D	E	D
C	O	S	T	L	Y
E	D	I	B	L	E

Answer 16.

A	C	T	I	N	G
S	T	U	P	I	D
C	I	T	I	E	S
E	X	P	E	R	T
N	O	T	I	N	G
T	I	E	R	E	D

Answer 17.

B	R	E	A	K	S
O	R	G	A	N	S
S	Q	U	A	R	E
T	H	E	I	S	M
O	B	S	E	S	S
N	U	A	N	C	E

Answer 18.

F	I	S	C	A	L
L	O	U	D	E	R
U	N	R	U	L	Y
E	X	E	M	P	T
N	I	E	C	E	S
T	U	R	B	I	D

Answer 19.

S	H	A	B	B	Y
P	A	R	D	O	N
E	T	H	N	I	C
A	T	T	A	I	N
R	O	B	E	R	T
S	I	E	S	T	A

Answer 20.

E	N	D	I	N	G
S	L	I	G	H	T
T	H	E	I	S	T
H	A	L	V	E	S
E	C	H	O	E	S
R	I	B	B	O	N

Answer 21.

T	O	W	E	R	S
A	W	N	I	N	G
S	L	E	I	G	H
T	R	A	N	C	E
E	I	G	H	T	Y
S	A	F	E	L	Y

Answer 22.

S	U	M	M	O	N
T	H	I	R	D	S
O	R	I	E	N	T
R	E	P	E	A	T
M	E	D	D	L	E
Y	A	W	N	E	D

Answer 23.

A	C	C	E	P	T
S	P	R	A	N	G
S	I	P	H	O	N
A	B	J	E	C	T
I	N	T	E	N	D
L	A	S	T	E	D

Answer 24.

B	L	A	M	E	D
L	U	X	O	R	Y
E	X	C	U	S	E
N	A	P	K	I	N
D	A	R	T	E	D
S	H	R	I	F	T

Answer 25.

T	U	R	B	A	N
H	O	U	S	E	S
E	N	W	R	A	P
S	L	E	E	V	E
I	N	S	U	R	E
S	E	L	V	E	S

Answer 26.

A	C	T	I	O	N
S	C	A	L	E	S
S	O	C	K	E	T
A	B	B	E	S	S
I	M	P	O	S	E
L	I	G	H	T	S

Answer 27.

T	H	E	I	S	T
O	U	T	P	U	T
S	A	L	I	V	A
S	A	V	I	N	G
E	U	R	O	P	E
S	T	I	C	K	S

Answer 28.

S	H	A	K	E	N
P	E	P	P	E	R
I	C	I	E	S	T
D	I	A	D	E	M
E	V	A	D	E	D
R	E	F	I	L	L

Answer 29.

S	T	R	A	I	N
T	H	I	R	T	Y
A	V	E	N	U	E
F	I	N	I	S	H
F	L	O	C	K	S
S	T	I	T	C	H

Answer 30.

S	E	C	R	E	T
C	H	I	L	L	Y
A	N	Y	W	A	Y
R	E	M	E	D	Y
C	U	R	T	S	Y
E	A	G	L	E	T

Answer 31.

P	E	T	A	L	S
E	L	I	X	I	R
T	E	E	P	E	E
E	N	T	A	I	L
R	E	S	I	S	T
S	L	U	I	C	E

Answer 32.

S	E	R	I	E	S
T	E	M	P	L	E
R	O	A	M	E	D
A	N	I	M	U	S
P	R	O	P	E	L
S	W	E	D	E	N

Answer 33.

S	O	F	T	E	R
T	H	R	O	N	G
A	B	O	U	N	D
R	E	F	U	N	D
C	O	U	N	T	Y
H	O	U	S	E	S

Answer 34.

A	S	C	E	N	T
S	C	R	O	L	L
S	C	A	L	E	S
E	L	I	C	I	T
S	C	E	N	I	C
S	T	I	G	M	A

Answer 35.

S	L	O	G	A	N
I	T	A	L	I	C
G	U	Y	A	N	A
H	A	U	L	E	D
E	T	C	H	E	D
D	R	I	L	L	S

Answer 36.

E	X	P	E	C	T
A	S	C	E	N	T
S	O	C	C	E	R
I	S	R	A	E	L
E	X	C	E	P	T
R	E	F	U	G	E

DIAGONAL WORD SQUARE PUZZLE SOLUTIONS

3x3 DIAGONAL WORD SQUARE PUZZLE SOLUTIONS

Answer 1.

A	B	C
I	T	S
D	Y	E

Answer 2.

A	N	Y
R	U	N
M	E	L

Answer 3.

T	I	E
O	I	L
T	O	N

Answer 4.

D	E	N
V	O	W
D	I	G

Answer 5.

D	E	N
A	N	Y
M	R	S

Answer 6.

C	U	B
O	A	R
W	E	B

Answer 7.

F	I	T
A	R	T
D	U	O

Answer 8.

R	A	G
O	A	K
Y	E	T

Answer 9.

E	N	D
A	B	E
T	A	B

Answer 10.

E	A	R
A	N	T
R	E	D

Answer 11.

B	O	X
O	U	R
W	O	N

Answer 12.

O	F	F
N	I	P
E	E	L

4x4 DIAGONAL WORD SQUARE PUZZLE SOLUTIONS

Answer 1.

O	I	L	Y
A	G	U	E
R	O	L	E
S	U	R	E

Answer 2.

O	X	E	N
A	N	T	S
T	I	C	K
S	H	O	E

Answer 3.

E	X	I	T
A	M	I	D
R	A	M	P
S	A	R	A

Answer 4.

S	P	R	Y
E	P	I	C
A	L	A	N
S	E	A	M

Answer 5.

F	O	L	K
A	R	C	H
C	O	O	L
T	R	A	M

Answer 6.

B	O	N	Y
L	E	S	T
A	G	E	D
B	A	R	N

Answer 7.

S	U	V	A
A	C	N	E
C	L	O	T
K	N	E	W

Answer 8.

C	E	D	E
A	R	M	Y
T	E	E	M
S	L	E	W

Answer 9.

S	A	N	D
I	T	C	H
T	H	A	N
S	L	A	B

Answer 10.

P	I	N	S
L	O	N	G
O	W	E	S
T	E	A	M

Answer 11.

B	O	N	E
O	R	E	S
L	O	A	F
D	A	V	Y

Answer 12.

O	R	A	L
A	N	N	E
T	E	C	H
S	A	L	E

5x5 DIAGONAL WORD SQUARE PUZZLE SOLUTIONS

Answer 1.

T	U	N	E	S
E	A	R	L	Y
L	I	M	I	T
L	I	K	E	D
S	C	O	L	D

Answer 2.

S	E	R	V	E
A	T	O	M	S
N	O	I	S	Y
D	R	U	N	K
S	H	A	C	K

Answer 3.

B	I	R	T	H
A	I	R	E	S
R	O	G	E	R
G	A	B	O	N
E	X	A	L	T

Answer 4.

P	O	K	E	R
A	R	M	O	R
N	I	E	C	E
E	L	M	E	R
L	O	G	I	N

Answer 5.

E	X	A	M	S
L	A	N	D	S
D	A	T	U	M
E	A	V	E	S
R	A	V	E	N

Answer 6.

F	A	R	M	S
A	L	O	F	T
L	O	O	K	S
S	P	O	U	T
E	J	E	C	T

Answer 7.

B	R	I	S	K
R	O	B	I	N
I	R	A	T	E
E	R	A	S	E
F	R	O	S	T

Answer 8.

D	A	I	S	Y
A	R	R	O	W
R	H	O	D	E
T	A	B	O	O
S	T	R	I	P

Answer 9.

C	A	M	E	L
A	L	L	E	N
S	T	Y	L	E
E	L	U	D	E
S	T	O	L	E

Answer 10.

F	L	U	S	H
R	E	A	D	Y
O	P	T	I	C
W	A	T	C	H
N	Y	M	P	H

Answer 11.

C	L	I	P	S
A	L	P	H	A
S	K	I	E	S
T	H	U	M	P
S	H	R	U	B

Answer 12.

O	W	N	E	R
A	D	U	L	T
S	T	O	N	Y
E	V	E	R	Y
S	H	O	E	S

Answer 13.

M	O	M	M	Y
A	U	D	I	T
T	A	S	K	S
C	H	R	I	S
H	A	V	O	C

Answer 14.

S	W	I	S	H
T	H	R	O	B
E	V	E	N	T
A	S	S	A	Y
M	A	N	O	R

Answer 15.

C	O	L	D	S
H	O	P	E	S
E	L	M	E	R
W	O	R	M	S
S	A	M	O	A

Answer 16.

C	H	I	L	D
A	I	S	L	E
V	I	V	I	D
E	D	D	I	E
S	T	E	A	L

Answer 17.

C	O	U	L	D
A	R	D	O	R
S	T	U	F	F
E	X	A	M	S
S	C	R	U	B

Answer 18.

S	L	A	S	H
E	Q	U	A	L
L	A	U	G	H
L	A	T	I	N
S	P	E	E	D

Answer 19.

C	H	A	R	Y
O	R	G	A	N
S	H	E	L	F
T	I	R	E	D
S	U	N	U	P

Answer 20.

G	O	L	G	I
L	A	K	E	S
A	B	B	O	T
D	O	U	B	T
E	S	S	A	Y

Answer 21.

C	D	R	O	M
R	I	N	G	S
U	R	G	E	D
M	O	L	A	R
B	R	I	E	R

Answer 22.

P	R	O	V	E
E	L	E	C	T
A	D	A	P	T
C	O	U	N	T
H	O	O	F	S

Answer 23.

C	L	A	S	S
O	D	D	L	Y
S	U	R	L	Y
T	U	M	O	R
S	A	L	E	M

Answer 24.

S	O	U	N	D
P	E	D	R	O
A	L	L	E	Y
S	C	A	L	E
M	U	L	E	S

Answer 25.

T	R	U	C	E
H	A	R	S	H
R	O	C	K	Y
E	V	O	K	E
W	A	L	K	S

Answer 26.

C	O	N	E	S
Y	A	W	N	S
R	O	B	E	S
U	S	U	A	L
S	H	A	L	L

Answer 27.

F	A	I	R	Y
E	L	L	E	N
E	R	E	C	T
D	I	N	E	R
S	M	E	L	T

Answer 28.

P	L	U	M	S
L	E	A	F	Y
E	X	A	L	T
A	W	A	R	E
D	A	R	T	S

Answer 29.

P	L	A	N	K
L	A	R	G	E
A	P	P	L	Y
N	A	M	E	D
E	I	D	E	R

Answer 30.

F	A	I	R	Y
I	R	O	N	S
R	H	I	N	O
M	E	A	L	S
S	H	E	L	L

Answer 31.

T	A	X	I	S
A	R	M	E	D
S	O	A	P	Y
K	A	T	I	E
S	L	A	I	N

Answer 32.

F	A	R	C	E
L	A	N	E	S
A	C	C	R	A
P	O	S	T	S
S	A	L	E	S

Answer 33.

D	W	E	L	L
E	R	U	P	T
A	L	I	C	E
L	A	R	V	A
S	H	A	R	E

Answer 34.

T	U	M	O	R
R	I	D	E	S
E	R	R	O	R
A	L	T	E	R
T	R	E	N	D

Answer 35.

S	L	I	C	E
O	W	I	N	G
N	I	E	C	E
A	L	T	A	R
R	U	L	E	R

Answer 36.

L	I	G	H	T
L	O	S	E	S
A	L	V	I	N
M	I	N	E	D
A	B	Y	S	S

6x6 DIAGONAL WORD SQUARE PUZZLE SOLUTIONS

Answer 1.

A	R	T	I	S	T
B	L	O	O	D	Y
O	P	T	I	N	G
R	E	C	E	S	S
T	O	W	A	R	D
S	P	E	L	L	S

Answer 2.

S	O	F	T	E	N
P	I	C	K	L	E
E	I	G	H	T	H
E	S	C	H	E	W
D	A	K	O	T	A
S	P	O	R	T	S

Answer 3.

S	I	M	I	L	E
P	U	S	H	E	D
R	A	D	I	U	S
A	L	M	O	N	D
I	N	T	A	K	E
N	A	S	S	A	U

Answer 4.

C	O	U	R	S	E
H	Y	B	R	I	D
E	X	P	E	C	T
S	P	I	R	A	L
T	H	Y	M	U	S
S	T	A	R	T	S

Answer 5.

S	N	A	T	C	H
T	H	R	A	S	H
A	B	O	D	E	S
R	O	B	U	S	T
C	A	N	A	L	S
H	E	L	P	E	D

Answer 6.

D	E	N	I	A	L
E	A	T	E	R	S
C	O	Z	I	E	R
A	M	A	Z	O	N
D	I	A	B	L	O
E	S	C	A	P	E

Answer 7.

S	H	I	N	E	S
L	E	N	G	T	H
E	D	W	A	R	D
E	S	S	A	Y	S
P	H	L	E	G	M
S	I	Z	Z	L	E

Answer 8.

P	O	U	N	D	S
A	L	T	E	R	S
S	I	E	S	T	A
S	T	U	N	T	S
E	X	I	S	T	S
S	U	N	D	A	Y

Answer 9.

A	R	C	A	N	E
S	P	E	E	C	H
T	R	O	O	P	S
H	U	N	G	E	R
M	A	R	R	E	D
A	R	O	U	S	E

Answer 10.

D	E	P	O	R	T
R	E	T	A	K	E
E	S	S	A	Y	S
A	C	T	I	N	G
M	A	N	A	G	E
S	H	A	K	E	N

Answer 11.

C	O	P	I	E	D
R	A	I	N	E	D
O	N	L	I	N	E
C	R	A	V	E	N
U	N	I	T	E	D
S	H	R	U	B	S

Answer 12.

S	A	N	D	A	L
P	A	R	K	E	R
R	E	N	D	E	R
I	M	B	I	B	E
T	W	E	N	T	Y
E	M	B	O	D	Y

7x7 DIAGONAL WORD SQUARE PUZZLE SOLUTIONS

Answer 1.

D	E	B	A	C	L	E
T	E	N	S	I	O	N
C	O	V	E	R	E	D
A	N	T	O	N	I	O
R	E	C	A	L	L	S
R	E	V	O	L	V	E
V	E	R	B	O	S	E

Answer 2.

L	O	C	K	J	A	W
D	E	F	E	N	S	E
B	U	N	N	I	E	S
S	N	A	G	G	E	D
C	O	U	N	T	R	Y
D	R	O	U	G	H	T
R	E	V	E	A	L	S

Answer 3.

B	I	Z	A	R	R	E
C	E	R	A	M	I	C
H	Y	D	R	A	N	T
E	M	P	T	I	E	D
F	O	L	D	I	N	G
S	C	R	E	A	M	S
O	B	T	R	U	D	E

Answer 4.

H	E	X	A	G	O	N
R	A	C	C	O	O	N
R	E	T	U	R	N	S
C	O	N	C	E	A	L
M	A	R	S	H	E	S
A	P	P	L	I	E	S
S	T	R	I	P	E	D

Answer 5.

S	Q	U	A	L	O	R
L	A	G	G	A	R	D
B	L	U	B	B	E	R
C	O	U	N	T	E	D
F	L	A	T	T	E	R
B	R	U	I	S	E	D
G	R	A	Z	I	E	R

Answer 6.

E	X	E	C	U	T	E
E	M	I	N	E	N	T
C	O	B	W	E	B	S
A	S	S	A	U	L	T
A	R	O	U	S	E	D
O	U	T	C	A	S	T
T	H	I	R	D	L	Y

Answer 7.

G	R	A	S	P	E	D
O	R	D	E	R	E	D
R	O	A	M	I	N	G
A	L	U	M	N	A	E
F	I	R	E	M	A	N
C	R	U	C	I	A	L
C	L	A	V	I	E	R

Answer 8.

S	U	M	M	I	N	G
S	C	O	U	R	G	E
P	R	O	C	E	E	D
A	M	A	L	G	A	M
W	O	R	L	D	L	Y
B	R	A	G	G	E	D
B	L	O	O	M	E	D

Answer 9.

U	T	I	L	I	Z	E
I	N	V	E	R	S	E
A	R	C	H	E	R	Y
T	O	B	A	C	C	O
I	S	L	A	N	D	S
H	O	L	L	A	N	D
L	O	O	S	E	L	Y

Answer 10.

K	E	T	C	H	U	P
E	N	Q	U	I	R	E
K	N	O	T	T	E	D
C	O	B	W	E	B	S
L	E	T	T	I	N	G
P	U	F	F	I	N	G
H	A	N	G	I	N	G

Answer 11.

B	U	T	C	H	E	R
P	R	E	P	A	I	D
T	O	U	C	H	E	S
B	R	U	S	Q	U	E
P	A	T	C	H	E	S
M	U	D	D	I	E	R
F	L	I	P	P	E	D

Answer 12.

M	I	C	R	O	B	E
M	I	N	I	M	A	L
I	N	D	I	A	N	A
P	E	T	T	I	N	G
B	U	N	K	E	R	S
W	I	N	N	E	R	S
A	N	T	O	N	Y	M

8x8 DIAGONAL WORD SQUARE PUZZLE SOLUTIONS

Answer 1.

S	H	I	P	M	E	N	T
S	T	R	A	P	P	E	D
E	C	O	N	O	M	I	C
S	P	A	C	I	O	U	S
C	H	E	C	K	E	R	S
S	T	R	I	K	I	N	G
C	U	S	H	I	O	N	S
C	R	U	I	S	I	N	G

Answer 2.

S	E	L	E	C	T	E	D
S	T	R	A	D	D	L	E
B	R	A	I	D	I	N	G
C	H	E	R	R	I	E	S
M	E	A	N	T	I	M	E
S	C	U	T	T	L	E	D
D	A	R	K	E	N	E	D
P	R	O	F	I	T	E	D

Answer 3.

C	H	O	P	P	I	N	G
W	O	O	D	S	H	O	P
C	O	M	P	O	U	N	D
T	E	R	M	I	N	A	L
U	N	C	T	U	O	U	S
S	O	C	I	E	T	A	L
V	E	H	I	C	L	E	S
P	O	L	L	S	T	E	R

Answer 4.

E	N	L	A	R	G	E	D
A	N	T	O	N	Y	M	S
E	N	T	I	T	L	E	D
O	P	E	R	A	T	O	R
N	E	B	R	A	S	K	A
H	A	C	I	E	N	D	A
P	R	O	P	H	E	C	Y
A	U	D	I	E	N	C	E

Answer 5.

P	R	O	D	U	C	E	S
C	O	N	T	R	A	S	T
A	P	P	E	N	D	I	X
D	I	S	S	E	I	Z	E
N	A	U	T	I	C	A	L
B	A	R	B	E	C	U	E
V	A	L	U	A	B	L	E
P	A	R	T	I	C	L	E

Answer 6.

I	N	E	D	I	B	L	E
I	N	V	I	T	I	N	G
E	T	H	I	O	P	I	A
W	A	T	E	R	W	A	Y
T	A	P	E	R	I	N	G
H	O	M	E	S	I	C	K
B	L	A	N	K	E	T	S
F	I	N	I	S	H	E	S

Answer 7.

B	R	A	W	L	I	N	G
D	I	S	C	O	L	O	R
T	H	O	U	G	H	T	S
B	R	I	G	H	T	L	Y
N	U	M	E	R	A	L	S
C	O	N	T	R	A	C	T
W	I	N	D	P	I	P	E
C	H	I	L	D	I	S	H

Answer 8.

R	E	L	E	A	S	E	D
S	E	C	U	R	I	N	G
I	N	Q	U	I	R	E	D
T	R	O	U	B	L	E	S
S	U	B	S	I	D	E	D
S	U	P	P	O	R	T	S
T	A	X	P	A	Y	E	R
R	A	N	C	H	E	R	S

Answer 9.

A	D	J	A	C	E	N	T
E	P	I	D	E	M	I	C
B	E	H	E	M	O	T	H
C	A	R	E	L	E	S	S
S	A	M	P	L	I	N	G
T	A	P	E	R	I	N	G
G	R	A	N	D	S	O	N
H	E	I	G	H	T	E	N

Answer 10.

T	H	O	U	S	A	N	D
O	R	I	G	I	N	A	L
A	B	O	R	T	I	N	G
R	E	T	U	R	N	E	D
D	O	O	M	S	D	A	Y
F	A	R	E	W	E	L	L
A	N	Y	W	H	E	R	E
P	A	I	N	L	E	S	S

Answer 11.

M	A	I	N	T	A	I	N
N	O	N	W	O	O	D	Y
K	I	N	D	N	E	S	S
A	C	Q	U	I	R	E	D
P	H	A	R	M	A	C	Y
Q	U	O	T	I	E	N	T
M	I	D	P	O	I	N	T
H	U	M	O	R	I	S	T

Answer 12.

B	E	D	C	O	V	E	R
S	E	P	A	R	A	T	E
Q	U	A	G	M	I	R	E
F	L	O	R	E	N	C	E
H	E	A	V	I	E	S	T
O	U	T	L	I	N	E	S
B	E	G	R	U	D	G	E
J	O	U	R	N	E	Y	S

9x9 DIAGONAL WORD SQUARE PUZZLE SOLUTIONS

Answer 1.

E	N	D	L	E	S	S	L	Y
E	**X**	E	R	C	I	S	E	S
C	L	**E**	R	G	Y	M	A	N
S	P	A	**C**	E	W	A	L	K
D	I	S	C	**R**	E	D	I	T
U	N	R	E	L	**A**	T	E	D
D	E	S	C	R	I	**B**	E	S
P	I	T	I	F	U	L	**L**	Y
S	T	A	I	R	C	A	S	**E**

Answer 2.

U	N	D	E	R	T	A	K	E
U	**N**	H	E	A	L	T	H	Y
D	E	**D**	U	C	T	I	V	E
B	L	U	**E**	B	E	R	R	Y
S	E	P	A	**R**	A	T	E	S
T	R	E	N	C	**H**	A	N	T
E	M	B	A	R	R	**A**	S	S
A	S	S	I	S	T	A	**N**	T
S	U	R	F	B	O	A	R	**D**

Answer 3.

D	I	S	P	E	R	S	A	L
D	**E**	F	E	N	D	I	N	G
M	I	**L**	W	A	U	K	E	E
P	O	L	**I**	T	I	C	A	L
E	X	P	A	**N**	D	I	N	G
D	I	S	P	L	**E**	A	S	E
A	S	S	A	I	L	**A**	N	T
M	E	R	C	H	A	N	**T**	S
T	I	G	H	T	R	O	P	**E**

Answer 4.

F	I	S	H	E	R	M	E	N
R	**E**	S	E	N	T	F	U	L
P	E	**R**	M	A	N	E	N	T
I	N	I	**T**	I	A	L	L	Y
O	B	E	D	**I**	E	N	C	E
B	A	C	K	S	**L**	I	D	E
D	E	T	E	C	T	**I**	V	E
E	T	I	Q	U	E	T	**T**	E
C	A	R	E	F	U	L	L	**Y**

Answer 5.

E	N	C	O	U	N	T	E	R
E	**L**	O	P	E	M	E	N	T
I	T	**I**	N	E	R	A	R	Y
A	M	A	**Z**	E	M	E	N	T
D	I	S	C	**A**	R	D	E	D
S	Y	L	L	A	**B**	L	E	S
U	N	D	E	R	W	**E**	A	R
N	O	T	O	R	I	E	**T**	Y
W	O	R	K	B	E	N	C	**H**

Answer 6.

D	E	P	L	E	T	I	O	N
D	**E**	V	I	L	M	E	N	T
I	M	**P**	R	E	S	S	E	D
S	E	D	**E**	N	T	A	R	Y
T	E	C	H	**N**	I	C	A	L
P	R	O	C	E	**D**	U	R	E
I	N	C	I	P	I	**E**	N	T
S	T	R	I	N	G	E	**N**	T
C	O	N	F	I	D	A	N	**T**

Answer 7.

D	O	U	B	T	L	E	S	S
P	**E**	N	E	T	R	A	T	E
C	E	**L**	E	S	T	I	A	L
R	E	L	**I**	G	I	O	U	S
N	A	S	H	**V**	I	L	L	E
A	F	F	L	U	**E**	N	C	E
D	O	W	N	W	A	**R**	D	S
O	R	G	A	N	I	Z	**E**	S
E	X	E	R	C	I	S	E	**D**

Answer 8.

S	U	C	C	O	T	A	S	H
S	**Y**	N	T	H	E	T	I	C
T	O	**M**	A	T	I	L	L	O
S	U	S	**P**	I	C	I	O	N
C	O	M	M	**O**	T	I	O	N
P	U	R	P	O	**S**	E	L	Y
C	L	U	T	C	H	**I**	N	G
I	N	G	E	N	U	O	**U**	S
P	E	T	R	O	L	E	U	**M**

Answer 9.

F	R	E	N	C	H	M	E	N
R	**E**	S	P	E	C	T	E	D
B	L	**A**	M	E	L	E	S	S
N	O	N	**R**	A	N	D	O	M
B	U	L	L	**F**	R	O	G	S
S	U	R	R	O	**U**	N	D	S
W	I	S	T	F	U	**L**	L	Y
S	E	R	I	O	U	S	**L**	Y
D	O	L	E	F	U	L	L	**Y**

Answer 10.

P	O	L	Y	E	S	T	E	R
P	**R**	O	D	U	C	I	N	G
P	R	**O**	B	O	S	C	I	S
D	E	A	**F**	E	N	I	N	G
C	O	N	Q	**U**	E	R	O	R
E	X	Q	U	I	**S**	I	T	E
A	U	T	H	O	R	**I**	Z	E
P	R	O	C	E	S	S	**O**	R
A	D	M	I	S	S	I	O	**N**

Answer 11.

D	I	F	F	I	C	U	L	T
S	**I**	L	L	I	N	E	S	S
P	A	**S**	S	E	N	G	E	R
F	R	A	**G**	R	A	N	C	E
S	T	A	T	**U**	T	O	R	Y
I	M	P	O	L	**I**	T	I	C
W	I	S	C	O	N	**S**	I	N
B	E	S	T	I	R	R	**E**	D
C	L	E	V	E	L	A	N	**D**

Answer 12.

C	O	N	F	I	D	E	N	T
P	**R**	O	N	O	U	N	C	E
F	R	**U**	G	A	L	I	T	Y
F	A	L	**S**	E	H	O	O	D
T	E	E	N	**A**	G	E	R	S
T	O	R	N	A	**D**	O	E	S
N	O	R	T	H	W	**E**	S	T
N	E	I	G	H	B	O	**R**	S
A	R	T	H	R	I	T	I	**S**

SUDOKU LOGIC PUZZLE SOLUTIONS

Answer 1.

6	8	1	7	4	2	3	9	5
3	5	7	6	8	9	2	4	1
4	2	9	1	5	3	6	7	8
2	1	5	8	7	6	4	3	9
9	4	3	5	2	1	7	8	6
7	6	8	9	3	4	1	5	2
5	7	2	3	6	8	9	1	4
1	3	4	2	9	5	8	6	7
8	9	6	4	1	7	5	2	3

Answer 2.

3	4	5	1	8	7	2	9	6
9	2	6	5	3	4	7	1	8
7	8	1	2	6	9	4	3	5
5	3	2	4	1	8	9	6	7
1	6	8	9	7	5	3	4	2
4	9	7	6	2	3	8	5	1
2	1	4	8	9	6	5	7	3
8	5	3	7	4	1	6	2	9
6	7	9	3	5	2	1	8	4

Answer 3.

2	1	3	5	7	6	4	9	8
4	8	7	3	9	2	6	1	5
5	6	9	1	4	8	3	7	2
7	2	6	4	3	1	8	5	9
8	5	4	7	6	9	2	3	1
9	3	1	2	8	5	7	6	4
1	7	8	9	2	3	5	4	6
6	4	5	8	1	7	9	2	3
3	9	2	6	5	4	1	8	7

Answer 4.

1	8	5	7	9	4	2	6	3
2	6	9	3	1	5	4	8	7
3	7	4	2	6	8	5	9	1
6	3	8	1	2	7	9	4	5
9	4	1	5	3	6	8	7	2
7	5	2	8	4	9	1	3	6
4	2	3	6	8	1	7	5	9
8	1	7	9	5	3	6	2	4
5	9	6	4	7	2	3	1	8

Answer 5.

6	3	9	1	2	7	8	5	4
2	1	8	5	3	4	6	9	7
4	5	7	6	9	8	1	3	2
8	9	1	3	5	2	7	4	6
3	6	4	7	8	9	2	1	5
5	7	2	4	1	6	9	8	3
1	4	6	9	7	3	5	2	8
7	8	5	2	4	1	3	6	9
9	2	3	8	6	5	4	7	1

Answer 6.

2	6	5	3	7	8	9	4	1
7	4	3	5	1	9	8	2	6
8	1	9	4	2	6	5	7	3
4	3	7	8	6	2	1	9	5
1	8	2	9	5	3	7	6	4
9	5	6	1	4	7	3	8	2
6	2	8	7	3	5	4	1	9
5	9	1	2	8	4	6	3	7
3	7	4	6	9	1	2	5	8

Answer 7.

2	8	6	1	3	4	5	7	9
5	9	4	7	2	6	1	8	3
7	1	3	5	8	9	6	4	2
4	5	1	9	7	3	2	6	8
6	2	8	4	5	1	9	3	7
3	7	9	8	6	2	4	1	5
1	4	5	3	9	7	8	2	6
9	6	7	2	1	8	3	5	4
8	3	2	6	4	5	7	9	1

Answer 8.

8	2	4	7	3	1	9	6	5
3	5	6	2	8	9	1	4	7
9	7	1	4	6	5	8	2	3
1	3	7	5	9	4	6	8	2
4	6	2	3	7	8	5	9	1
5	8	9	6	1	2	7	3	4
7	9	8	1	2	3	4	5	6
6	4	3	8	5	7	2	1	9
2	1	5	9	4	6	3	7	8

Answer 9.

4	2	9	6	1	7	8	3	5
8	5	3	2	4	9	7	1	6
6	1	7	3	5	8	4	2	9
7	8	2	4	9	5	1	6	3
3	4	5	1	7	6	9	8	2
9	6	1	8	2	3	5	4	7
1	9	6	5	3	4	2	7	8
5	3	4	7	8	2	6	9	1
2	7	8	9	6	1	3	5	4

Answer 10.

5	2	8	1	7	3	4	9	6
1	6	4	2	8	9	7	5	3
3	7	9	5	4	6	2	8	1
4	8	1	7	5	2	3	6	9
6	3	2	9	1	4	5	7	8
7	9	5	3	6	8	1	2	4
9	1	7	6	3	5	8	4	2
2	4	3	8	9	7	6	1	5
8	5	6	4	2	1	9	3	7

Answer 11.

6	9	1	2	8	4	3	5	7
4	5	3	9	6	7	2	1	8
7	8	2	3	5	1	6	9	4
1	2	5	8	3	6	7	4	9
9	7	6	4	1	5	8	3	2
3	4	8	7	9	2	1	6	5
5	6	4	1	2	8	9	7	3
2	3	7	6	4	9	5	8	1
8	1	9	5	7	3	4	2	6

Answer 12.

2	8	1	6	4	3	9	5	7
6	7	9	2	5	8	4	3	1
4	3	5	9	1	7	2	8	6
5	1	8	7	2	4	3	6	9
3	2	6	8	9	1	7	4	5
9	4	7	5	3	6	8	1	2
1	5	4	3	7	2	6	9	8
8	9	2	4	6	5	1	7	3
7	6	3	1	8	9	5	2	4

Answer 13.

9	7	5	2	3	8	6	1	4
2	1	8	7	4	6	5	9	3
6	3	4	1	5	9	2	7	8
5	8	1	3	6	4	9	2	7
7	2	6	8	9	1	4	3	5
4	9	3	5	2	7	8	6	1
3	5	7	9	8	2	1	4	6
1	4	2	6	7	5	3	8	9
8	6	9	4	1	3	7	5	2

Answer 14.

4	7	2	3	8	6	1	5	9
1	6	3	9	5	2	7	4	8
5	9	8	7	1	4	3	2	6
3	4	5	1	7	9	6	8	2
6	1	7	8	2	5	9	3	4
8	2	9	6	4	3	5	7	1
7	5	1	4	9	8	2	6	3
2	8	6	5	3	1	4	9	7
9	3	4	2	6	7	8	1	5

Answer 15.

5	9	3	4	1	8	6	7	2
2	6	7	3	5	9	1	4	8
4	8	1	7	6	2	9	3	5
8	4	9	5	3	7	2	6	1
6	1	2	8	9	4	7	5	3
7	3	5	6	2	1	8	9	4
9	7	4	1	8	5	3	2	6
3	5	8	2	7	6	4	1	9
1	2	6	9	4	3	5	8	7

Answer 16.

3	1	5	9	6	2	7	8	4
8	6	7	4	3	5	9	2	1
4	9	2	1	7	8	3	6	5
7	4	9	2	5	1	8	3	6
6	3	8	7	4	9	5	1	2
5	2	1	3	8	6	4	7	9
9	5	6	8	2	3	1	4	7
1	7	3	6	9	4	2	5	8
2	8	4	5	1	7	6	9	3

Answer 17.

6	7	5	8	3	4	9	1	2
3	4	2	9	5	1	8	7	6
8	9	1	6	7	2	5	4	3
7	2	6	5	4	9	3	8	1
1	8	3	2	6	7	4	9	5
9	5	4	3	1	8	6	2	7
4	3	8	7	2	6	1	5	9
5	1	7	4	9	3	2	6	8
2	6	9	1	8	5	7	3	4

Answer 18.

2	3	1	7	4	6	8	5	9
5	9	4	2	3	8	6	7	1
8	7	6	5	1	9	2	3	4
6	1	7	9	5	3	4	2	8
3	4	2	6	8	1	5	9	7
9	8	5	4	2	7	3	1	6
4	6	9	3	7	5	1	8	2
1	2	3	8	9	4	7	6	5
7	5	8	1	6	2	9	4	3

Answer 19.

4	9	8	1	7	6	3	2	5
3	6	7	8	2	5	1	9	4
1	2	5	4	9	3	8	6	7
5	8	2	9	3	4	7	1	6
7	4	6	2	5	1	9	3	8
9	1	3	6	8	7	5	4	2
6	3	4	7	1	8	2	5	9
2	7	1	5	6	9	4	8	3
8	5	9	3	4	2	6	7	1

Answer 20.

1	5	3	6	7	8	4	2	9
8	7	9	2	4	1	5	6	3
4	2	6	5	9	3	8	1	7
7	9	5	4	6	2	3	8	1
2	3	8	9	1	7	6	4	5
6	4	1	8	3	5	9	7	2
3	6	4	1	2	9	7	5	8
5	1	7	3	8	4	2	9	6
9	8	2	7	5	6	1	3	4

Answer 21.

1	8	5	4	7	6	2	9	3
2	3	6	9	1	5	4	8	7
7	9	4	8	3	2	6	1	5
8	6	2	1	4	3	7	5	9
4	7	3	6	5	9	8	2	1
9	5	1	7	2	8	3	4	6
5	2	9	3	8	7	1	6	4
6	4	7	2	9	1	5	3	8
3	1	8	5	6	4	9	7	2

Answer 22.

4	7	8	1	3	2	6	5	9
6	5	9	8	7	4	1	2	3
2	3	1	9	6	5	4	8	7
1	6	3	7	2	8	9	4	5
9	2	5	4	1	3	8	7	6
7	8	4	5	9	6	3	1	2
3	1	6	2	4	7	5	9	8
5	4	7	3	8	9	2	6	1
8	9	2	6	5	1	7	3	4

Answer 23.

9	7	2	8	3	4	6	5	1
5	1	6	2	9	7	3	8	4
3	4	8	6	5	1	2	9	7
6	9	4	1	8	2	7	3	5
1	5	3	7	6	9	4	2	8
2	8	7	3	4	5	9	1	6
7	3	1	4	2	8	5	6	9
8	6	5	9	7	3	1	4	2
4	2	9	5	1	6	8	7	3

Answer 24.

5	6	9	2	7	4	8	3	1
8	1	3	5	6	9	2	7	4
2	7	4	3	1	8	5	6	9
4	3	5	9	2	7	6	1	8
1	8	2	6	5	3	9	4	7
7	9	6	4	8	1	3	2	5
9	5	7	1	3	6	4	8	2
6	2	8	7	4	5	1	9	3
3	4	1	8	9	2	7	5	6

Answer 25.

6	4	2	5	3	8	1	7	9
1	9	5	7	4	6	2	3	8
8	7	3	2	1	9	6	4	5
9	8	4	1	2	5	3	6	7
3	6	7	9	8	4	5	2	1
5	2	1	6	7	3	9	8	4
7	3	6	8	9	1	4	5	2
2	5	9	4	6	7	8	1	3
4	1	8	3	5	2	7	9	6

Answer 26.

6	9	5	7	3	1	4	2	8
7	1	4	8	2	5	3	6	9
8	3	2	9	6	4	7	5	1
9	8	1	2	5	7	6	4	3
4	2	3	1	8	6	9	7	5
5	6	7	3	4	9	1	8	2
2	4	8	6	1	3	5	9	7
3	5	9	4	7	8	2	1	6
1	7	6	5	9	2	8	3	4

Answer 27.

2	6	3	1	5	8	7	4	9
4	8	7	2	6	9	1	3	5
9	1	5	3	7	4	2	8	6
3	7	1	9	4	6	8	5	2
8	5	2	7	3	1	9	6	4
6	4	9	5	8	2	3	7	1
1	3	6	8	9	5	4	2	7
7	2	4	6	1	3	5	9	8
5	9	8	4	2	7	6	1	3

Answer 28.

3	1	5	9	2	6	4	8	7
6	9	7	4	8	1	5	2	3
4	2	8	5	7	3	1	6	9
5	7	3	6	1	9	2	4	8
1	8	4	2	3	5	9	7	6
2	6	9	8	4	7	3	1	5
7	3	6	1	5	2	8	9	4
9	4	2	3	6	8	7	5	1
8	5	1	7	9	4	6	3	2

Answer 29.

8	1	4	3	7	5	2	6	9
9	7	6	1	8	2	4	5	3
5	2	3	4	9	6	7	1	8
3	8	5	6	4	7	9	2	1
4	9	7	2	5	1	8	3	6
1	6	2	9	3	8	5	7	4
2	3	8	5	1	4	6	9	7
7	5	1	8	6	9	3	4	2
6	4	9	7	2	3	1	8	5

Answer 30.

8	1	5	9	7	3	2	6	4
9	6	7	2	4	8	3	5	1
4	3	2	5	1	6	8	7	9
3	9	4	1	6	5	7	2	8
2	7	6	8	3	9	1	4	5
1	5	8	4	2	7	9	3	6
5	4	9	3	8	2	6	1	7
6	2	1	7	9	4	5	8	3
7	8	3	6	5	1	4	9	2

Answer 31.

6	4	5	8	9	1	3	7	2
7	2	9	6	5	3	8	1	4
1	3	8	4	2	7	6	9	5
2	8	1	5	7	6	4	3	9
4	5	3	9	1	8	2	6	7
9	6	7	2	3	4	5	8	1
5	1	4	3	6	9	7	2	8
3	9	2	7	8	5	1	4	6
8	7	6	1	4	2	9	5	3

Answer 32.

3	6	9	5	4	7	1	8	2
1	2	5	8	9	3	7	6	4
4	8	7	1	2	6	3	5	9
6	9	3	7	5	4	2	1	8
5	4	8	6	1	2	9	3	7
2	7	1	3	8	9	5	4	6
7	5	4	9	3	8	6	2	1
9	1	2	4	6	5	8	7	3
8	3	6	2	7	1	4	9	5

Answer 33.

5	8	7	6	2	3	4	9	1
9	2	1	8	7	4	5	6	3
4	6	3	5	9	1	8	2	7
8	9	5	1	4	2	3	7	6
1	7	6	3	5	9	2	8	4
2	3	4	7	6	8	9	1	5
7	1	9	4	8	5	6	3	2
6	4	8	2	3	7	1	5	9
3	5	2	9	1	6	7	4	8

Answer 34.

9	5	7	6	1	4	3	8	2
1	4	8	2	7	3	9	5	6
2	6	3	9	5	8	4	7	1
8	3	6	7	9	5	1	2	4
4	9	2	8	3	1	5	6	7
5	7	1	4	2	6	8	3	9
7	2	4	5	8	9	6	1	3
6	1	5	3	4	2	7	9	8
3	8	9	1	6	7	2	4	5

Answer 35.

9	7	4	8	3	6	5	2	1
6	2	8	9	5	1	7	4	3
1	5	3	2	7	4	9	8	6
3	9	6	4	1	8	2	7	5
2	8	5	7	9	3	6	1	4
4	1	7	6	2	5	8	3	9
8	4	1	5	6	2	3	9	7
7	6	2	3	4	9	1	5	8
5	3	9	1	8	7	4	6	2

Answer 36.

6	2	4	3	1	9	5	7	8
1	8	5	6	4	7	2	9	3
7	3	9	8	2	5	6	4	1
9	4	1	5	8	6	7	3	2
5	6	3	9	7	2	1	8	4
8	7	2	1	3	4	9	6	5
4	1	7	2	9	3	8	5	6
3	5	8	7	6	1	4	2	9
2	9	6	4	5	8	3	1	7

Answer 37.

5	6	8	7	1	9	3	2	4
7	3	2	6	4	5	8	9	1
4	9	1	3	8	2	5	6	7
8	2	5	4	9	7	1	3	6
9	1	7	8	6	3	4	5	2
6	4	3	2	5	1	7	8	9
2	7	9	1	3	8	6	4	5
3	5	6	9	7	4	2	1	8
1	8	4	5	2	6	9	7	3

Answer 38.

2	7	5	6	3	4	8	1	9
1	3	9	5	7	8	2	4	6
4	8	6	1	2	9	7	3	5
9	4	3	7	5	2	6	8	1
8	2	7	9	6	1	4	5	3
6	5	1	4	8	3	9	7	2
7	9	8	3	1	6	5	2	4
5	1	4	2	9	7	3	6	8
3	6	2	8	4	5	1	9	7

Answer 39.

9	4	2	1	6	8	7	5	3
1	3	5	4	7	2	8	6	9
8	7	6	3	5	9	1	4	2
6	2	9	8	3	1	5	7	4
3	5	7	6	9	4	2	1	8
4	8	1	7	2	5	9	3	6
5	6	3	9	8	7	4	2	1
2	1	8	5	4	3	6	9	7
7	9	4	2	1	6	3	8	5

Answer 40.

8	9	5	6	4	2	3	1	7
4	1	3	8	5	7	2	6	9
2	7	6	1	9	3	8	4	5
5	4	9	3	6	8	1	7	2
7	6	1	4	2	5	9	8	3
3	8	2	7	1	9	4	5	6
6	2	8	9	7	1	5	3	4
9	3	4	5	8	6	7	2	1
1	5	7	2	3	4	6	9	8

Answer 41.

9	7	5	8	6	3	1	2	4
4	6	2	5	7	1	9	3	8
8	1	3	4	9	2	7	5	6
7	2	9	6	1	5	8	4	3
3	4	1	2	8	9	6	7	5
5	8	6	7	3	4	2	1	9
2	9	7	3	5	6	4	8	1
1	3	4	9	2	8	5	6	7
6	5	8	1	4	7	3	9	2

Answer 42.

7	8	2	1	5	4	9	6	3
9	3	5	7	8	6	2	1	4
4	6	1	9	3	2	5	7	8
5	1	3	6	2	9	8	4	7
8	4	7	5	1	3	6	9	2
6	2	9	4	7	8	1	3	5
1	5	6	8	4	7	3	2	9
3	7	8	2	9	1	4	5	6
2	9	4	3	6	5	7	8	1

Answer 43.

4	3	7	1	9	6	8	5	2
8	6	2	5	3	7	4	1	9
5	1	9	8	4	2	7	6	3
6	9	5	2	8	1	3	7	4
7	2	3	4	6	9	5	8	1
1	8	4	3	7	5	2	9	6
9	5	6	7	2	4	1	3	8
3	4	1	6	5	8	9	2	7
2	7	8	9	1	3	6	4	5

Answer 44.

8	6	3	4	5	9	7	1	2
9	1	2	7	3	8	4	5	6
5	7	4	1	2	6	8	9	3
1	4	7	5	6	2	3	8	9
2	3	9	8	4	7	1	6	5
6	5	8	9	1	3	2	7	4
4	9	5	3	7	1	6	2	8
7	8	6	2	9	4	5	3	1
3	2	1	6	8	5	9	4	7

Answer 45.

9	6	1	7	8	5	4	2	3
5	2	3	6	4	9	8	7	1
4	7	8	1	2	3	6	5	9
3	4	7	9	6	2	5	1	8
2	5	9	8	1	4	7	3	6
8	1	6	3	5	7	9	4	2
6	9	2	4	7	1	3	8	5
1	3	4	5	9	8	2	6	7
7	8	5	2	3	6	1	9	4

Answer 46.

2	4	5	6	9	3	8	1	7
7	6	8	5	1	4	2	9	3
9	1	3	8	7	2	6	4	5
1	5	7	2	3	9	4	6	8
6	3	9	4	8	5	1	7	2
8	2	4	1	6	7	5	3	9
3	8	6	7	2	1	9	5	4
4	9	2	3	5	6	7	8	1
5	7	1	9	4	8	3	2	6

Answer 47.

2	3	7	5	4	9	1	8	6
8	6	5	7	1	2	4	9	3
1	4	9	6	3	8	7	2	5
4	8	3	9	2	5	6	1	7
5	7	6	3	8	1	2	4	9
9	1	2	4	6	7	5	3	8
6	2	8	1	5	3	9	7	4
3	9	4	2	7	6	8	5	1
7	5	1	8	9	4	3	6	2

Answer 48.

7	3	5	8	9	1	2	4	6
4	6	2	5	3	7	8	9	1
8	9	1	2	6	4	5	3	7
3	7	6	1	4	5	9	8	2
2	1	8	9	7	3	6	5	4
5	4	9	6	2	8	1	7	3
9	8	7	3	1	6	4	2	5
1	5	4	7	8	2	3	6	9
6	2	3	4	5	9	7	1	8

Answer 49.

5	8	4	1	9	7	6	3	2
2	6	3	4	5	8	7	1	9
9	7	1	6	3	2	8	4	5
8	9	7	2	6	1	3	5	4
3	5	6	8	4	9	2	7	1
1	4	2	3	7	5	9	8	6
7	1	9	5	2	3	4	6	8
4	2	8	7	1	6	5	9	3
6	3	5	9	8	4	1	2	7

Answer 50.

5	9	1	3	8	7	2	4	6
3	8	7	6	4	2	5	1	9
6	2	4	9	5	1	7	3	8
2	1	3	4	7	8	6	9	5
8	5	6	2	3	9	1	7	4
4	7	9	1	6	5	8	2	3
9	6	2	5	1	4	3	8	7
7	4	5	8	2	3	9	6	1
1	3	8	7	9	6	4	5	2

Answer 51.

3	4	7	2	1	9	5	8	6
9	1	8	7	5	6	3	4	2
5	2	6	3	4	8	1	7	9
6	8	5	9	3	7	2	1	4
4	3	2	1	6	5	8	9	7
1	7	9	4	8	2	6	3	5
7	5	1	8	2	4	9	6	3
2	9	3	6	7	1	4	5	8
8	6	4	5	9	3	7	2	1

Answer 52.

8	1	6	3	4	5	9	7	2
2	9	3	1	8	7	6	5	4
7	4	5	9	6	2	8	3	1
1	8	9	6	3	4	5	2	7
4	5	7	2	9	1	3	8	6
3	6	2	7	5	8	1	4	9
6	2	4	5	1	3	7	9	8
9	3	8	4	7	6	2	1	5
5	7	1	8	2	9	4	6	3

Answer 53.

4	1	6	7	9	8	5	3	2
3	2	8	1	6	5	9	7	4
7	5	9	2	4	3	1	6	8
9	3	1	8	2	7	4	5	6
5	4	7	6	3	9	8	2	1
8	6	2	5	1	4	7	9	3
2	7	5	4	8	6	3	1	9
1	9	4	3	5	2	6	8	7
6	8	3	9	7	1	2	4	5

Answer 54.

4	9	6	2	1	3	8	7	5
2	8	3	7	4	5	6	1	9
7	1	5	8	9	6	3	4	2
3	6	7	5	8	1	2	9	4
5	2	8	9	3	4	1	6	7
1	4	9	6	2	7	5	3	8
9	5	4	1	6	8	7	2	3
6	7	2	3	5	9	4	8	1
8	3	1	4	7	2	9	5	6

Answer 55.

9	3	2	1	6	8	5	7	4
6	4	1	7	9	5	8	2	3
7	8	5	3	4	2	1	6	9
3	5	8	9	1	7	6	4	2
2	6	7	4	5	3	9	1	8
1	9	4	8	2	6	3	5	7
5	1	3	2	7	9	4	8	6
8	2	6	5	3	4	7	9	1
4	7	9	6	8	1	2	3	5

Answer 56.

9	1	7	6	4	8	5	2	3
6	3	2	5	7	9	8	4	1
5	4	8	3	2	1	6	9	7
1	7	9	2	8	4	3	6	5
3	2	5	7	9	6	4	1	8
8	6	4	1	5	3	9	7	2
4	5	1	8	6	7	2	3	9
7	8	6	9	3	2	1	5	4
2	9	3	4	1	5	7	8	6

Answer 57.

7	1	5	3	6	9	2	8	4
9	2	6	8	4	1	5	3	7
8	4	3	2	5	7	6	1	9
5	9	8	4	1	2	7	6	3
2	6	7	5	8	3	4	9	1
1	3	4	9	7	6	8	2	5
3	8	1	7	2	4	9	5	6
4	5	9	6	3	8	1	7	2
6	7	2	1	9	5	3	4	8

Answer 58.

5	9	3	1	7	4	2	6	8
6	8	7	9	5	2	4	3	1
4	1	2	3	8	6	5	9	7
1	5	6	4	3	9	7	8	2
8	3	4	6	2	7	1	5	9
7	2	9	5	1	8	3	4	6
3	7	1	8	6	5	9	2	4
9	6	5	2	4	1	8	7	3
2	4	8	7	9	3	6	1	5

Answer 59.

4	8	2	9	5	7	1	6	3
5	1	3	2	6	4	7	9	8
6	7	9	1	8	3	4	2	5
8	4	5	7	9	2	3	1	6
3	6	7	5	4	1	9	8	2
2	9	1	6	3	8	5	7	4
9	2	4	8	1	5	6	3	7
1	3	8	4	7	6	2	5	9
7	5	6	3	2	9	8	4	1

Answer 60.

8	2	5	4	9	1	6	7	3
6	7	9	2	8	3	4	5	1
4	1	3	5	7	6	8	9	2
3	5	6	8	4	7	2	1	9
9	4	2	1	6	5	3	8	7
7	8	1	3	2	9	5	4	6
2	6	8	9	1	4	7	3	5
1	3	4	7	5	2	9	6	8
5	9	7	6	3	8	1	2	4

Answer 61.

1	3	6	8	2	4	5	9	7
7	2	4	5	1	9	3	8	6
9	5	8	7	6	3	4	1	2
8	4	5	3	9	2	6	7	1
6	7	1	4	5	8	2	3	9
3	9	2	1	7	6	8	5	4
4	1	7	6	8	5	9	2	3
2	8	3	9	4	1	7	6	5
5	6	9	2	3	7	1	4	8

Answer 62.

6	1	5	7	4	8	3	2	9
2	9	4	3	6	1	8	5	7
8	7	3	2	9	5	1	6	4
4	8	7	5	2	3	9	1	6
5	6	9	1	7	4	2	8	3
3	2	1	9	8	6	4	7	5
7	5	8	4	1	9	6	3	2
1	4	2	6	3	7	5	9	8
9	3	6	8	5	2	7	4	1

Answer 63.

5	1	9	2	4	6	3	8	7
8	4	7	3	9	1	2	6	5
2	3	6	7	5	8	9	4	1
3	6	8	4	1	9	5	7	2
7	2	1	5	6	3	8	9	4
9	5	4	8	7	2	6	1	3
4	8	5	9	3	7	1	2	6
6	9	3	1	2	4	7	5	8
1	7	2	6	8	5	4	3	9

Answer 64.

7	2	1	9	4	8	3	5	6
6	8	5	3	7	2	4	1	9
9	3	4	6	1	5	8	2	7
4	5	6	2	8	7	9	3	1
8	1	2	5	9	3	7	6	4
3	7	9	4	6	1	2	8	5
1	9	7	8	2	6	5	4	3
5	4	8	1	3	9	6	7	2
2	6	3	7	5	4	1	9	8

TAJ MAHAL IN AGRA, INDIA
What is it made from?

ANSWER: ELBRAM ETIHW

BALD EAGLES WAITING FOR THE SALMON RUN ON THE YUKON RIVER
Where is the largest gathering of bald eagles for a salmon run? How many eagles?

ANSWER: SELGAE DLAB DNASUOHT RUOF ;AKSALA ,REVIR TAKLIHC

PICTURE PUZZLE SOLUTIONS

PICTURE PUZZLE 1. ANSWER

PICTURE PUZZLE 2. ANSWER

PICTURE PUZZLE 3. ANSWER

PICTURE PUZZLE 4. ANSWER

PICTURE PUZZLE 5. ANSWER

PICTURE PUZZLE 6. ANSWER

PICTURE PUZZLE 7. ANSWER

PICTURE PUZZLE 8. ANSWER

PICTURE PUZZLE 9. ANSWER

PICTURE PUZZLE 10. ANSWER

Find & Circle 5 Animals in Each Quadrant: DOG, CAT, PIG, COD, FOX, OWL, HEN, APE, ANT or FLY

G	O	O	D	D	O	D	G	T	C	C	A	C	C	C	A	G	G	I	G	P	I	P	P
O	O	D	O	O	D	D	G	A	A	C	A	C	A	A	T	I	P	I	P	I	I	P	I
G	D	O	O	O	D	O	D	T	C	T	C	C	C	A	A	G	G	G	P	P	G	G	I
G	G	O	G	O	O	O	G	T	C	T	A	A	T	A	A	I	I	P	P	P	P	G	I
D	G	G	G	D	D	G	G	T	C	C	C	C	C	T	A	I	I	I	I	P	P	P	P
G	G	G	O	O	D	G	G	T	A	T	C	C	C	C	C	G	P	I	I	I	I	P	G
G	G	D	O	O	O	D	D	T	C	A	C	C	A	A	C	G	G	G	P	P	I	I	G
D	D	D	O	O	D	G	G	T	C	T	T	C	A	C	T	G	I	G	I	G	G	I	G
O	O	D	D	D	C	D	O									O	X	F	F	F	X	F	F
C	C	C	O	C	O	C	C									X	O	X	O	X	X	O	X
C	D	C	D	C	C	D	D									O	X	X	F	F	F	F	F
C	D	D	C	D	C	D	C									O	O	O	X	X	O	O	F
D	D	O	O	D	C	D	D									X	O	O	F	F	F	F	F
O	C	D	O	D	D	O	O									F	F	O	F	X	X	X	O
O	D	O	D	D	D	O	D									X	F	O	O	F	X	F	F
D	C	D	D	C	D	D	O									F	X	X	F	X	F	F	F
L	W	L	O	O	L	O	W									N	H	N	H	E	E	N	E
L	O	O	O	W	O	W	W									H	H	H	N	N	N	E	N
L	W	W	W	O	L	O	W									E	H	N	N	H	E	E	N
W	O	O	O	L	L	O	L									E	E	E	H	N	N	N	N
L	W	W	L	W	L	L	O									N	H	N	N	N	H	H	E
W	W	W	O	L	L	O	W									N	H	H	E	H	N	H	N
W	L	W	L	O	L	O	O									N	H	H	E	E	N	H	E
O	W	W	O	O	O	L	O									H	N	N	H	H	H	H	E
E	A	P	P	P	P	A	P	T	A	N	N	A	A	T	N	Y	Y	Y	Y	F	Y	Y	L
E	A	P	A	E	P	E	E	A	A	A	T	T	T	T	T	L	Y	L	Y	Y	Y	L	L
E	E	P	E	E	P	P	A	N	T	A	T	A	A	A	N	L	F	Y	F	Y	F	L	F
E	E	E	A	E	P	P	P	A	A	N	N	T	T	T	T	Y	F	F	Y	Y	L	Y	F
A	A	A	E	A	A	A	P	N	T	A	N	A	A	T	N	F	Y	Y	Y	Y	L	Y	Y
A	E	E	E	P	P	E	P	N	N	A	N	A	T	N	N	Y	F	F	Y	F	Y	L	Y
A	A	A	A	P	A	A	A	T	T	T	N	T	N	T	T	F	Y	F	L	L	Y	L	L
P	A	P	P	A	E	A	E	N	T	A	A	N	N	N	T	F	Y	F	L	L	Y	L	L

NEW YORK CITY – THE NEW WTC FREEDOM TOWER (1,776 FT (541 M))

GIANT FERRIS WHEEL(100 M (328 FT)) WITH SQUARE TREES IN PARIS, FRANCE

BURJ KHALIFA TOWER IN DUBAI - 830 M (2,722 FT), 156 FLOORS

Made in the USA
Lexington, KY
21 December 2018